A HISTORY OF THE DAVIS CUP

A History of THE DAVIS CUP

Being the Story of
The International Lawn Tennis Championship
1900–48

by

D. C. COOMBE
Captain of the 1947 New Zealand Team

HENNEL LOCKE LIMITED
49 PARK LANE, LONDON, W.1

TO

MY WIFE

who cheerfully accepted many a
dull evening and week-end while
this book was being written.

First published 1949
by HENNEL LOCKE LTD
49 Park Lane, London, W.1

Composed in Baskerville type and printed by Page & Thomas, Ltd, Chesham, Bucks
Made in Great Britain

PREFACE

by

A. K. TROWER

Wimbledon referee from 1946

Throughout the championships at Wimbledon the dressing-rooms carry a solemn admonition that knocking up before matches must not exceed three minutes. A preface being a sort of knock-up preparatory to the serious business of the subject-matter, I will obey my own injunction and be brief. The Davis Cup is always news. It is quite the best-known trophy in the world, and as such it needs no build-up.

What about the author? Perusal of the following pages will remind you—as if you didn't know—that he acquired Davis Cup status in the New Zealand team of 1937 at the age of twenty-five, and in 1947 rendered further distinguished service to his country in the capacity of non-playing Captain. Let us touch in a few more personal details. At swimming he was something of a child wonder ; at Rugby Football a five-eight of force and penetration, with a routine of converting tries from the touchline ; at soldiering a gunner who rose to command his battery, and an authentic Desert Rat. A widely travelled and much-enduring man whose all-round competence is matched only by his geniality. Encyclopedic in his knowledge of lawn tennis, and one of the best-known voices in the game. But the knock-up is over, and the court is waiting.

Coombe serving.

Play !

ACKNOWLEDGMENTS

I SHOULD like to express my thanks to the Lawn Tennis Association, for permission to peruse their records, and especially to Miss Bachelor, who supplied additional details; to Mr L. H. J. Dorey, the editor, for giving me access to the records of *Lawn Tennis and Badminton*; to the All England Lawn Tennis Club and to Messrs Slazengers, Ltd, for the loan of photographs; and to the American L.T.A., for their help with data and photographs.

D. C. C.

CONTENTS

ILLUSTRATIONS

INTRODUCTION

It is sometimes said that big things have small beginnings. This is certainly true of the International Lawn Tennis Championship, better known as the Davis Cup.

It began in the year 1900, when the cup was presented by Dwight Davis, then one of the leading American players, for competition among the tennis players of different lands. The Americans, as it originated in the United States, were naturally the first holders, and were challenged in the initial year by British Isles. They came through the first challenge round successfully. Nineteen hundred and one was a blank year: no challenge was received from any nation. Nineteen hundred and two saw British Isles trying again, to lose by a smaller margin than in their first challenge. In 1903 British Isles defeated America and the cup made the first of its many journeys. British Isles retained it till 1907, when it was won by Australasia and made its first journey to the Southern Hemisphere. Perhaps it should be made clear at this point that the nation holding the Davis Cup plays only one match, that being against the winner of the competition among all the other nations who have challenged in that particular year. In other words, the challenging nations must play off among themselves for the right to challenge the champion nation.

In 1904 we find the field widening for the first time. Belgium and France challenged, and Belgium won the right to challenge British Isles. In 1905 there were four challengers, Australasia and Austria entering the lists. The years 1906 and 1907 saw Australasia and U.S.A. disputing the right to challenge British Isles. In 1908 and 1909 U.S.A. and British Isles competed for the challenging rights against Australasia. Nineteen hundred and ten was a blank year—no challenges. In 1911 British Isles and U.S.A. again, and in 1912 British Isles and France, British Isles winning the play-off and defeating Australasia in the challenge round at Melbourne, and bringing the cup back again to England. They lost it in 1913 to U.S.A., who had come through the biggest competition thus far—no fewer than seven challengers, the new ones being Germany, Canada, and South Africa.

After ten years abroad the cup was now home again. But not for long. Australasia was the survivor of six challengers, and beat U.S.A. in the challenge round in 1914, just as the First World War commenced and shut down further play until 1919, when British Isles, coming out on top of a small field of four challengers, made a fruitless journey to Sydney to challenge Australasia. In 1920 U.S.A. made a successful challenge against the men from 'down under' at Auckland, and took the cup home again.

And there it stayed, securely held, till 1927. In these years the competition grew rapidly, with many new nations challenging each year. In 1921 and 1922 ten challenged. In 1923, after zones had been created and one or two nations had split and doubled themselves, there were sixteen challengers; in 1924 twenty-one, in 1925 twenty-two, in 1926 twenty-three, and in 1927, when France beat U.S.A. in the challenge round, there were twenty-five challengers.

France reigned as champion nation till 1933, the year Great Britain beat her after having won the biggest competition ever, for which thirty-three challenging nations entered. Great Britain ruled till 1937, when U.S.A. took the cup back to the States for two years. Then, as the Second World War commenced, Australia again wrested it from U.S.A.—a coincidence for the same countries to fight out the challenge round as war began each time—and to have the same result, a three–two win to Australia, who thus held the cup through two world wars.

They lost it to U.S.A. in 1946, the year play restarted, when twenty countries toed the mark. Nineteen hundred and forty-seven saw U.S.A. still with a firm grip on the trophy, for which twenty-two nations challenged. In 1948 twenty-nine nations challenged, but U.S.A. easily beat the surviving challenger, Australia, without losing a match.

And this, I think, is where we came in. We can examine, however, in much closer detail the foregoing lightning outline.

D. C. C.

EARLY YEARS

1900–14

1900 : U.S.A.

The first match ever played for the Davis Cup took place at Longwood, Boston, U.S.A., on August 8, 9, and 10 in the year 1900. British Isles had challenged America and sent a team of three players to oppose the home country, who also relied on three players. The American players were M. D. Whitman, D. F. Davis, the donor of the cup, and H. Ward. British Isles were represented by A. W. Gore, E. D. Black, and H. Roper Barrett.

The tie opened with Gore opposing Whitman and being somewhat summarily defeated in three straight sets. Black followed against Davis, and managed to win the first set before the American overpowered him. Next day the doubles, between Black and Roper Barrett and Davis and Ward, also went to America—in three ten-game sets. No other match was completed, though Davis and Gore did play almost two sets of a very keen nature, Davis winning the first at 9–7 and the second being halted by rain at 9–all.

As the scores show, America were much the better team, although they had some advantage in being at home. Even then they had a superiority in service and hitting power which the Englishmen could not overcome.

Detailed Results

Singles: M. D. Whitman (U.S.A.) beat A. W. Gore (B.I.) 6–1, 6–3, 6–2. D. F. Davis (U.S.A.) beat E. D. Black (B.I.) 4–6, 6–2, 6–4, 6–4.

Doubles: D. F. Davis and H. Ward (U.S.A.) beat E. D. Black and H. Roper Barrett (B.I.) 6–4, 6–4, 6–4.

1901 : NO CHALLENGE

1902 : U.S.A.

British Isles again challenged, and sent a stronger team to America. The venue was the same as two years previously, at

Longwood, and the date approximately the same. For America D. F. Davis gave way in the singles to W. A. Larned, their champion, who was able to win only one of his singles—that against J. Pim, whom he beat in three sets. In his other single he lost to R. F. Doherty after winning the first two sets. M. D. Whitman won both his singles with the loss of one set—to Pim. In the doubles R. F. Doherty and H. L. Doherty were too good for Davis and Ward in a four-set match.

The Doherty brothers were almost ready to establish dominance for the British Isles which was to last for several years.

Detailed Results

Singles: M. D. WHITMAN (U.S.A.) beat J. Pim (B.I.) 6–1, 6–1, 1–6, 6–0 ; beat R. F. Doherty (B.I.) 6–1, 7–5, 6–4. W. A. LARNED (U.S.A.) beat J. Pim (B.I.) 6–3, 6–2, 6–3 ; lost to R. F. DOHERTY (B.I.) 6–2, 6–3, 3–6, 4–6, 4–6.

Doubles: D. F. Davis and H. Ward (U.S.A.) lost to H. L. DOHERTY and R. F. DOHERTY (B.I.) 6–3, 8–10, 3–6, 4–6..

1903 : BRITISH ISLES

British Isles, again at Longwood in August and relying on a two-man team, R. F. Doherty and H. L. Doherty, won the cup from America with the loss of only one match, and that by default. H. L. Doherty led off by defeating R. D. Wrenn in three sets, and then the brothers Doherty beat the brothers Wrenn, R. D. and G. L., in a four-set doubles. The last two singles were both five-setters. H. L. Doherty beat W. A. Larned, and R. F. Doherty beat R. D. Wrenn. These matches were played simultaneously on different courts, and aroused intense excitement because of the similarity of the set scores. Both Englishmen won the first, third, and fifth sets, and each must have been very conscious all along of the progress of the other's match. One can imagine the strain of these seesaw scores, the fifth set in each match being won only by a two-game margin.

Detailed Results

Singles: R. F. Doherty (B.I.) beat R. D. Wrenn (U.S.A.) 6–4, 3–6, 6–3, 6–8, 6–4 ; defaulted to W. A. Larned (U.S.A.). H. L. Doherty (B.I.) beat R. D. Wrenn (U.S.A.) 6–0, 6–3, 6–4 ; beat W. A. Larned (U.S.A.) 6–3, 6–8, 6–0, 2–6, 7–5.

Doubles: H. L. Doherty and R. F. Doherty (B.I.) beat R. D. Wrenn and G. L. Wrenn (U.S.A.) 7–5, 9–7, 2–6, 6–3.

1904 : BRITISH ISLES

In this year the field, without America competing, widened a little, challenges coming from Belgium, France, and Austria, though the Austrians retired to the Belgians without playing the tie. This left Belgium and France to play off for the right to challenge the holders, British Isles. Belgium won by three matches to two. Even though the match between P. de Borman, Belgium, and M. Decugis, France, was defaulted by de Borman at 4–6, 3–5, the contest was a close one, for Decugis lost his other single against W. Lemaire only after a close five-set tussle, and he and P. Ayme won the doubles for France against de Borman and Lemaire also in five sets. Both countries relied on a two-man team.

Detailed Results

Singles: P. de Borman (Belg.) beat P. Ayme (Fr.) 6–1, 6–3, 2–6, 1–6, 6–3 ; lost to M. Decugis (Fr.) 4–6, 3–5 (retired). W. Lemaire (Belg.) beat P. Ayme (Fr.) 6–1, 6–0, 6–1 ; beat M. Decugis (Fr.) 5–7, 8–6, 0–6, 6–4, 6–2.

Doubles: P. de Borman and W. Lemaire (Belg.) lost to M. Decugis and P. Ayme (Fr.) 7–5, 4–6, 6–0, 4–6, 2–6.

Challenge Round

The challenge round, between Belgium and British Isles, the holders, took place at Wimbledon on July 2, 4, and 5, and in the four matches played Belgium won only one set. For British Isles H. L. Doherty and F. L. Riseley played the singles and the Doherty brothers the doubles. Belgium had the same two players who had beaten France on the same courts a week earlier. The only match in the tie which was at all close was that between F. L. Riseley and P. de Borman. The Englishman won in four sets after losing the first, but the third and fourth both went to advantage games. Riseley was much too good for Lemaire in his other single, while H. L. Doherty easily defeated de Borman. In the doubles the Belgians could win only four games in three sets against the two Dohertys. The match between H. L. Doherty and Lemaire was not played.

Detailed Results

Singles: F. L. RISELEY (B.I.) beat W. Lemaire (Belg.) 6–1, 6–4, 6–2 ; beat P. de Borman (Belg.) 4–6, 6–2, 8–6, 7–5. H. L. DOHERTY (B.I.) beat P. de Borman (Belg.) 6–4, 6–1, 6–1 ; beat W. Lemaire (Belg.) by default.

Doubles: H. L. DOHERTY and R. F. DOHERTY (B.I.) beat P. de Borman and W. Lemaire (Belg.) 6–0, 6–1, 6–3.

1905 : BRITISH ISLES

America came back again after a year's absence, and France, Belgium, Austria, and Australasia (comprising Australia and New Zealand combined) issued challenges, and played off for the right to tackle British Isles. Belgium retired, leaving the other four teams to play off. America played France, while Australasia played Austria, both matches being played at Queen's Club, London, on July 17, 18, and 19.

America had a three-man team—H. Ward and W. J. Clothier for the singles, and B. C. Wright, who partnered Ward in the doubles. France had M. Decugis and M. Germot for both singles and doubles, and in five matches won only one set, which Germot took from Clothier.

Detailed Results

Singles: H. WARD (U.S.A.) beat M. Germot (Fr.) 6–2, 6–2, 6–1 ; beat M. Decugis (Fr.) 6–2, 6–2, 6–1. W. J. CLOTHIER (U.S.A.) beat M. Germot (Fr.) 6–3, 5–7, 6–1, 6–3 ; beat M. Decugis (Fr.) 6–3, 6–4, 6–4.

Doubles: H. WARD and B. C. WRIGHT (U.S.A.) beat M. Decugis and M. Germot (Fr.) 6–2, 6–2, 6–2.

The other tie, between Australasia and Austria, saw the first appearance in the Davis Cup of a very famous pair, N. E.

Brookes, of Australia, and A. F. Wilding, of New Zealand, both of whom were destined to play many fine matches over a long period of years in both challenging and defending rôles. The third man in the Australasian team was A. W. Dunlop, who paired with Brookes in the doubles. The Austrian team of R. Kinzl and C. von Wessely was no match for this side, although both their men won a set from Wilding in the singles. This was all they could achieve, however, and Australasia thus qualified for the final round against America.

Detailed Results

Singles: N. E. BROOKES (AUSTRAL.) beat R. Kinzl (Aus.) 6–0, 6–1, 6–2 ; beat C. von Wessely (Aus.) 6–0, 6–2, 6–2. A. F. WILDING (AUSTRAL.) beat R. Kinzl (Aus.) 6–3, 4–6, 6–2, 6–4 ; beat C. von Wessely (Aus.) 4–6, 6–3, 7–5, 6–1.

Doubles: N. E. BROOKES and A. W. DUNLOP (AUSTRAL.) beat R. Kinzl and C. von Wessely (Aus.) 9–7, 6–2, 7–5.

America altered their team to play Australasia by bringing in W. A. Larned in place of Clothier for the singles and playing Wright instead of Ward as their other singles man. Their doubles team of Ward and Wright remained as against France. Australasia kept the same team as in the previous round against Austria, but they were no match for the Americans, who won comfortably by five matches to none. Norman Brookes fought a stubborn battle with Beals Wright. Two left-handed volleyers with strong services and plenty of tactical ability, they waged a really close match of sixty-six games in four sets before Wright got home. Brookes also took Larned to 14–12 in the first set before fading away, and the doubles match, between Ward and Wright and Brookes and Dunlop, was fairly close for three sets before the Americans could draw away for a 6–2 fourth set. Wilding was not yet of the calibre to worry either Wright or Larned in his singles matches, and so America passed into the challenge round against British Isles.

Detailed Results

Singles: B. C. WRIGHT (U.S.A.) beat N. E. Brookes (Austral.) 12–10, 5–7, 12–10, 6–4 ; beat A. F. Wilding (Austral.) 6–3, 6–3 (best of three sets only). W. A. LARNED (U.S.A.) beat N. E. Brookes (Austral.) 14–12, 6–0, 6–3 ; beat A. F. Wilding (Austral.) 6–3, 6–2, 6–4.

Doubles: H. WARD and B. C. WRIGHT (U.S.A.) beat N. E. Brookes and A. W. Dunlop (Austral.) 6–4, 7–5, 5–7, 6–2.

CHALLENGE ROUND

And so to the challenge round, America versus British Isles, played at Wimbledon on July 21, 22, and 24. Holcombe Ward came back as a singles player in the American team with W. A. Larned, and B. C. Wright reverted to the doubles-only rôle with Ward. H. L. Doherty and S. H. Smith played the singles for the holders, and R. F. Doherty partnered his brother in the doubles. British Isles won by five to none, but three of the five matches went the full five sets, the doubles and both Laurie Doherty's singles. Ward's volleying gave him a two-set lead against H. L. Doherty before the latter's effortless stroking gained him the ascendancy and a love set to finish with, and Larned carried the same player all the way before submitting to defeat. The doubles match was only claimed by the Doherty brothers at 8–6 in the fifth set. It was S. H. Smith who stole the honours. His powerful forehand was too much for Larned and Clothier, who substituted for Ward, and he beat them both in four sets.

Detailed Results

Singles: H. L. DOHERTY (B.I.) beat H. Ward (U.S.A.) 7–9, 4–6, 6–1, 6–2, 6–0 ; beat W. A. Larned (U.S.A.) 6–4, 2–6, 6–8, 6–4, 6–2. S. H. SMITH (B.I.) beat W. A. Larned (U.S.A.) 6–4, 6–4, 5–7, 6–4 ; beat W. J. Clothier (U.S.A.) 4–6, 6–1, 6–4, 6–3.

Doubles: H. L. DOHERTY and R. F. DOHERTY (B.I.) beat H. Ward and B. C. Wright (U.S.A.) 8–10, 6–2, 6–2, 4–6, 8–6.

1906 : BRITISH ISLES

This year there were four challengers to play off: Australasia, Austria, America, and France. Austria and France, however, retired, which left Australasia and America to play off for the right to challenge British Isles.

This tie was played at Newport, Monmouthshire, on June 7, 8, and 9, and was won by America by three matches to two.

Each nation played a two-man team. Holcombe Ward and R. D. Little represented America, and A. F. Wilding and L. O. S. Poidevin Australasia. Wilding won both his singles—against Ward in five sets, and against Little in three. Poidevin could win only one set in his single against Little and none against Ward, and he and Wilding were no match for Ward and Little in the doubles, losing in straight sets.

Detailed Results

Singles: H. WARD (U.S.A.) beat L. O. S. Poidevin (Austral.) 6–2, 6–4, 7–5 ; lost to A. F. WILDING (AUSTRAL.) 3–6, 6–3, 6–0, 4–6, 6–8. R. D. LITTLE (U.S.A.) beat L. O. S. Poidevin (Austral.) 6–2, 1–6, 7–5, 6–2 ; lost to A. F. WILDING (AUSTRAL.) 2–6, 6–8, 1–6.

Doubles: H. WARD and R. D. LITTLE (U.S.A.) beat A. F. Wilding and L. O. S. Poidevin (Austral.) 7–5, 6–2, 6-4.

CHALLENGE ROUND

The challenge round, between America and British Isles, was played at Wimbledon on June 15, 16, and 18, and the holders won by five matches to none. The British Isles team was identical with that of 1905, and again S. H. Smith proved his merit, this time winning both his singles in straight sets, losing only nine games to R. D. Little and five to H. Ward. H. L. Doherty beat Ward in three sets, but only won from Little in five, after being two sets to one down. The Doherty brothers won the doubles in four sets.

Detailed Results

Singles: S. H. SMITH (B.I.) beat H. Ward (U.S.A.) 6–1, 6–0, 6–4 ; beat R. D. Little (U.S.A.) 6–4, 6–4, 6–1. H. L. DOHERTY (B.I.) beat H. Ward (U.S.A.) 6–2, 8–6, 6–3 ; beat R. D. Little (U.S.A.) 3–6, 6–3, 6–8, 6–1, 6–3.

Doubles: H. L. DOHERTY and R. F. DOHERTY (B.I.) beat H. Ward and R. D. Little (U.S.A.) 3–6, 11–9, 9–7, 6–1.

1907 : AUSTRALASIA

This year the line-up was the same as in 1906. America and Australasia played off at Wimbledon on July 13, 15, and 16. A. F. Wilding was the only member of either team who had played in this match the previous year. N. E. Brookes had returned to the Australasian side, and the Americans relied on B. C. Wright and K. Behr. Australasia won a very narrow victory by three matches to two, but it very nearly became three–two for America. Brookes won both his singles with something to spare, but Wilding lost to Wright in four sets, and only just beat Behr in five. He was two sets to one down, and squeezed the fourth only after 5–all had been called. The doubles between these four men—as each side played a two-man team—was a long and wavering struggle, won finally by the Americans after Australasian domination at the start.

Detailed Results

Singles: N. E. BROOKES (AUSTRAL.) beat B. C. Wright (U.S.A.) 6–4, 6–4, 6–2 ; beat K. Behr (U.S.A.) 4–6, 6–4, 6–1, 6–2. A. F. WILDING (AUSTRAL.) beat K. Behr (U.S.A.) 1–6, 6–3, 3–6, 7–5, 6–3 ; lost to B. C. WRIGHT (U.S.A.) 8–6, 3–6, 3–6, 5–7.

Doubles: N. E. Brookes and A. F. Wilding (Austral.) lost to B. C. WRIGHT and K. BEHR (U.S.A.) 6–3, 10–12, 6–4, 2–6, 3–6.

CHALLENGE ROUND

The challenge round, between Australasia and the holders, British Isles, was played at Wimbledon on July 20, 22, and 23, and won by the challengers, three matches to two. The defending team was a completely altered two-man team, A. W. Gore and H. Roper Barrett playing both singles and doubles. It will be remembered that these two were members of the original British Isles team in 1900. Australasia used N. E. Brookes and A. F. Wilding, who, as against America earlier, won three of the singles and lost the doubles in five sets. Brookes was the strong man of the side, and crushed both Englishmen in straight sets. Wilding was less impressive, but won against Roper Barrett in four sets and lost to Gore in an equal number. The Englishmen gallantly won the doubles from two sets down, winning the final set at 13–11.

And so began Australasia's five-year reign as champion nation, they being the third nation to hold the trophy since it was put into competition seven years earlier.

Detailed Results

Singles: N. E. BROOKES (AUSTRAL.) beat A. W. Gore (B.I.) 7–5, 6–1, 7–5 ; beat H. Roper Barrett (B.I.) 6–2, 6–0, 6–3. A. F. WILDING (AUSTRAL.) beat H. Roper Barrett (B.I.) 1–6, 6–4, 6–3, 7–5 ; lost to A. W. GORE (B.I.) 6–3, 3–6, 5–7, 2–6.

Doubles: N. E. Brookes and A. F. Wilding (Austral.) lost to A. W. GORE and H. ROPER BARRETT (B.I.) 6–3, 6–4, 5–7, 2–6, 11–13.

1908 : AUSTRALASIA

British Isles and America were the only challenging teams this year, and their play-off took place at Boston, U.S.A., on September 17, 18, and 19. America won by four matches to one. Their team for the singles was W. A. Larned and B. C. Wright, who opposed M. J. G. Ritchie and J. C. Parke. Ritchie won British Isles' only match when he beat Beals Wright in three sets. Parke led the same player by two sets to love, but failed to win any of the next three. Larned dropped only one set in his two singles—to Ritchie. In partnership in the doubles Ritchie and Parke lost to F. B. Alexander and H. H. Hackett in four sets.

Detailed Results

Singles: W. A. LARNED (U.S.A.) beat M. J. G. Ritchie (B.I.) 4–6, 6–3, 6–2, 6–3 ; beat J. C. Parke (B.I.) 6–3, 6–3, 7–5. B. C. WRIGHT (U.S.A.) beat J. C. Parke (B.I.) 8–10, 3–6, 6–4, 6–3, 6–2 ; lost to M. J. G. RITCHIE (B.I.) 1–6, 3–6, 2–6.

Doubles: F. B. ALEXANDER and H. H. HACKETT (U.S.A.) beat M. J. G. Ritchie and J. C. Parke (B.I.) 6–3, 2–6, 7–5, 6–1.

CHALLENGE ROUND

The challenge round, between U.S.A. and Australasia, was played at Melbourne on November 27, 28, and 30, the holders winning by three matches to two. Each side used only two men—Australasia N. E. Brookes and A. F. Wilding, and America B. C. Wright and F. B. Alexander. Of these four

Wright was the hero, and his efforts almost won the cup for America. Alexander pulled his weight nobly in taking the great Brookes to five sets and also battling for five sets with Wright against Brookes and Wilding. But, hard as he tried, Alexander was on the losing end of all his three matches. Wright won both his singles, his defeat of Brookes being a particularly fine effort, as the Australian had pressed for a quick win, and looked like getting it when he won the first two sets with the loss of only three games. Beals Wright was ever a fighter, and he hung on grimly, to win 12–10 in the fifth set. His match against Wilding followed a similar course to their encounter a year earlier. Wright won in four sets after losing the first. The cool nerves of Wilding enabled him easily to defeat a highly strung and nervous Alexander in the fifth and final match, when the countries were level at two–all, Wright's magnificent win over Brookes having equalized the scores. It was too big an ordeal for Alexander to overcome, playing the vital match against an experienced campaigner and in a land far from home. He was beaten before he could get going. Wright's uphill fight against Brookes is one of the best performances ever registered in the competition when one considers the state of the match, but it was probably a greater strain on Alexander, who waited, not knowing until the last stroke had been played whether he would be required to play with all depending on him, or whether he could have a pleasant game with nothing hanging on the result!

Detailed Results

Singles: N. E. Brookes (Austral.) beat F. B. Alexander (U.S.A.) 5–7, 9–7, 6–2, 4–6, 6–3 ; lost to B. C. Wright (U.S.A.) 6–0, 6–3, 5–7, 2–6, 10–12. A. F. Wilding (Austral.) beat F. B. Alexander (U.S.A.) 6–3, 6–4, 6–1 ; lost to B. C. Wright (U.S.A.) 6–3, 5–7, 3–6, 1–6.

Doubles: N. E. Brookes and A. F. Wilding (Austral.) beat B. C. Wright and F. B. Alexander (U.S.A.) 6–4, 6–2, 5–7, 1–6, 6–4.

1909 : AUSTRALASIA

This year resulted in a repeat of the matches of 1908. British Isles and America played off at Philadelphia on September 11, 13, and 14 for the right to challenge Australasia. America won comfortably by a margin of five matches to none. Their team consisted of W. A. Larned and W. J. Clothier for the singles and H. H. Hackett and R. D. Little for the doubles, while British Isles relied on three men only—J. C. Parke and C. P. Dixon for the singles and Parke and W. C. Crawley for the doubles. The British team was unable to win a set in the singles, both Larned and Clothier being much too good for their opponents ; but Parke and Crawley took Hackett and Little to 8–6 in the fifth set of the doubles before succumbing.

Detailed Results

Singles: W. A. LARNED (U.S.A.) beat C. P. Dixon (B.I.) 6–3, 6–2, 6–0 ; beat J. C. Parke (B.I.) 6–3, 6–2, 6–3. W. J. CLOTHIER (U.S.A.) beat C. P. Dixon (B.I.) 6–3, 6–1, 6–4 ; beat J. C. Parke (B.I.) 6–4, 6–3, 8–6.

Doubles: H. H. HACKETT and R. D. LITTLE (U.S.A.) beat J. C. Parke and W. C. Crawley (B.I.) 3–6, 6–4, 6–4, 4–6, 8–6.

CHALLENGE ROUND

The challenge round was played in Sydney on November 27, 29, and 30, when the holders, represented by the trusty Brookes–Wilding team, routed the two young Americans, M. E. McLoughlin and M. H. Long, who had been called on to make the trip from the U.S.A. McLoughlin was making his first appearance in the competition in which he was later to play such a notable part, and in his single against Wilding he won the only set gained in five matches by the challengers. Long was making his only appearance in the competition. He was perhaps lucky to get the trip, as America boasted better players who were unable to go.

Detailed Results

Singles: N. E. BROOKES (AUSTRAL.) beat M. E. McLoughlin (U.S.A.) 6–2, 6–2, 6–4 ; beat M. H. Long (U.S.A.) 6–4, 7–5, 8–6. A. F. WILDING (AUSTRAL.) beat M. E. McLoughlin (U.S.A.) 3–6, 8–6, 6–2, 6–3 ; beat M. H. Long (U.S.A.) 6–2, 7–5, 6–1.

Doubles: N. E. BROOKES and A. F. WILDING (AUSTRAL.) beat M. E. McLoughlin and M. H. Long (U.S.A.) 12–10, 9–7, 6–3.

1910 : NO CHALLENGE

1911 : AUSTRALASIA

South Africa entered the lists, but did not play, and so, once more, it was left to British Isles and America to play off for the right to challenge Australasia. And again America won, this time dropping one match—the doubles. They were represented by W. A. Larned and M. E. McLoughlin in the singles and R. D. Little and T. C. Bundy in the doubles. British Isles had C. P. Dixon and A. H. Lowe for the singles and Dixon and A. E. Beamish for the doubles. The tie was played in New York on September 9, 11, and 12.

Dixon pressed Larned very close, and for a time held McLoughlin in the singles, but Lowe had to be content with winning one set in each of his matches. The British pair won the doubles in straight sets—a neat performance—but otherwise America were solid winners.

Detailed Results

Singles: W. A. LARNED (U.S.A.) beat C. P. Dixon (B.I.) 6–3, 2–6, 6–3, 3–6, 7–5; beat A. H. Lowe (B.I.) 6–3, 1–6, 7–5, 6–1. M. E. McLOUGHLIN (U.S.A.) beat C. P. Dixon (B.I.) 8–6, 3–6, 6–3, 6–3; beat A. H. Lowe (B.I.) 7–5, 6–1, 4–6, 6–3.

Doubles: R. D. Little and T. C. Bundy (U.S.A.) lost to C. P. DIXON and A. E. BEAMISH (B.I.) 3–6, 5–7, 4–6.

CHALLENGE ROUND

The challenge round this year took place at Christchurch, New Zealand, commencing on New Year's Day 1912. The holders, Australasia, proved their strength by winning without losing any of the four matches played, and without the services of A. F. Wilding.

America sent a strong team, consisting of W. A. Larned, B. C. Wright, and M. E. McLoughlin. They intended to play

Larned and Wright in the singles, but unfortunately neither Larned nor Wright was able to play on the third day, though on the first day both had been beaten in four sets, Wright by N. E. Brookes and Larned by R. W. Heath. On the second day Brookes and A. W. Dunlop beat Wright and McLoughlin in four sets, to give the holders a three-straight victory. McLoughlin substituted for Larned in the only other singles played, and fought a fine five-setter against Brookes. His thunderbolt service and generally spectacular game captured the crowd's imagination, and he became a favourite at once. Three years later " the Californian Comet," as McLoughlin was nicknamed, was to defeat Brookes in the challenge round in three sets. The beginnings of his later triumphs were already peeping through.

Detailed Results

Singles: N. E. BROOKES (AUSTRAL.) beat B. C. Wright (U.S.A.) 6–4, 2–6, 6–3, 6–3 ; beat M. E. McLoughlin (U.S.A.) 6–4, 3–6, 4–6, 6–3, 6–4. R. W. HEATH (AUSTRAL.) beat W. A. Larned (U.S.A) 2–6, 6–1, 7–5, 6–2 ; received a walk-over from B. C. Wright.

Doubles: N. E. BROOKES and A. W. DUNLOP (AUSTRAL.) beat B. C. Wright and M. E. McLoughlin (U.S.A.) 6–4, 5–7, 7–5, 6–4.

1912 : BRITISH ISLES

France re-entered the competition, and, America dropping out, France and British Isles played the pre-challenge-round tie, at Folkestone, on July 11, 12, and 13. British Isles lost one match, and one was uncompleted. Their team was C. P. Dixon and A. W. Gore for the singles and Dixon and H. Roper Barrett for the doubles, thus two of the British Isles' original team of twelve years previously coming back into competition. France's one match was won by A. H. Gobert, who beat A. W. Gore in four sets, but he lost to Dixon in an equal number. M. Decugis lost to Dixon in straight sets, and retired to Gore after losing two sets. Gobert and W. H. Laurentz snatched one set from Dixon and Roper Barrett in the doubles.

Detailed Results

Singles: C. P. DIXON (B.I.) beat M. Decugis (Fr.) 6–3, 6–2, 6–4 ; beat A. H. Gobert (Fr.) 4–6, 6–4, 6–2, 6–3. A. W. GORE (B.I.) beat M. Decugis (Fr.) 6–3, 6–0, retired ; lost to A. H. GOBERT (Fr.) 4–6, 6–4, 3–6, 3–6.

Doubles: H. ROPER BARRETT and C. P. DIXON (B.I.) beat A. H. Gobert and W. H. Laurentz (Fr.) 3–6, 6–4, 6–1, 6–1.

CHALLENGE ROUND

British Isles then sent C. P. Dixon, J. C. Parke, and A. E. Beamish on the long trip to Melbourne to challenge the holders on November 28, 29, and 30. They were successful, largely because of Parke's unexpected win over N. E. Brookes, conclusively in four sets—almost in three.

Australasia were again without A. F. Wilding, and relied on the same team for defence of the trophy as in 1911. R. W. Heath was the weak link, and, though he won one set against Dixon, he could not hold Parke at all. The holders won the doubles with Brookes and A. W. Dunlop, who beat Parke and Beamish comfortably. Brookes had no trouble with Dixon, and therefore, as already stated, the key match was between Brookes and Parke. The Irishman was full of dash and fire, and produced the passing shots to thwart the Australian's volleying attack. Parke was perhaps at his zenith in this and the following year. A fine athletic and determined player, he was capped twenty times for Ireland at Rugby football before this. He was a sparkling threequarter, with plenty of speed of foot on a Rugger field, as well as on a tennis court.

Detailed Results

Singles: J. C. PARKE (B.I.) beat N. E. Brookes (Austral.) 8–6, 6–3, 5–7, 6–2 ; beat R. W. Heath (Austral.) 6–2, 6–4, 6–4. C. P. DIXON (B.I.) beat R. W. Heath (Austral.) 5–7, 6–4, 6–4, 6–4 ; lost to N. E. BROOKES (AUSTRAL.) 2–6, 4–6, 4–6.

Doubles: J. C. Parke and A. E. Beamish (B.I.) lost to N. E. BROOKES and A. W. DUNLOP (AUSTRAL.) 4–6, 1–6, 5–7.

1913 : U.S.A.

This year the competition assumed entirely new proportions. Seven nations challenged—France, Germany, America, Australasia, Canada, South Africa, and Belgium. In the first round of the play-off France met Germany, America met Australasia, and Canada met South Africa, while Belgium drew a bye.

The France–Germany tie was played at Wiesbaden on June 3, 4, and 5, and the Germans, appearing in the competition for the first time, won comfortably by four to one—though one of their four matches admittedly was a win by default. M. Decugis scored France's only point by a five-set win against F. W. Rahe. (He did not play his other single.) France's A. H. Gobert could win only one set in both his singles—in fact, against Rahe he won only three games. The Germans also won the doubles, using H. Kleinschroth and Rahe to beat Decugis and Germot in four sets. The other German singles player was O. Kreuzer.

Detailed Results

Singles: O. KREUZER (GER.) beat A. H. Gobert (Fr.) 1–6, 6–4, 6–2, 6–3 ; beat M. Decugis (Fr.), retired. F. W. RAHE (GER.) beat A. H. Gobert (Fr.) 6–1, 6–1, 6–1 ; lost to M. DECUGIS (FR.) 6–2, 4–6, 6–2, 6–8, 5–7.

Doubles: H. KLEINSCHROTH and F. W. RAHE (GER.) beat M. Decugis and M. Germot (Fr.) 7–5, 6–4, 4–6, 9–7.

America and Australasia met at New York on June 6, 7, and 9. Both countries played a three-man team. For America M. E. McLoughlin and R. N. Williams played the singles, and McLoughlin and H. H. Hackett the doubles. Australasia were represented by S. N. Doust and H. Rice in the singles and Doust and A. B. Jones in the doubles. McLoughlin was far too good for both his opponents in the singles, winning in straight sets each time. Williams, however, almost lost to Rice in three sets before he steadied down. Once he had banked the third set at 9–7, after losing the first two, he had no more trouble. Doust won one set from him. The doubles match was won by Australasia, Jones apparently being the outstanding figure, and it was unfortunate for his team that he was not fit enough to play in the singles.

Detailed Results

Singles: M. E. McLoughlin (U.S.A.) beat H. Rice (Austral.) 6–1, 6–3, 6–3 ; beat S. N. Doust (Austral.) 6–4, 6–4, 6–2. R. N. Williams (U.S.A.) beat H. Rice 1–6, 4–6, 9–7, 6–1, 6–2 ; beat S. N. Doust (Austral.) 6–4, 6–4, 1–6, 7–5.

Doubles: M. E. McLoughlin and H. H. Hackett (U.S.A.) lost to S. N. Doust and A. B. Jones (Austral.) 6–2, 2–6, 7–5, 2–6, 7–9.

The remaining first-round tie, between Canada and South Africa, was played at Queen's Club, London, on June 19, 20, and 21, and was won by Canada four to one. Both countries played a two-man team: for Canada R. B. Powell and B. P. Schwengers, for South Africa V. R. Gauntlett and R. F. Le Sueur. Gauntlett beat Schwengers in three sets and retired to Powell. Both the other singles and also the doubles went to Canada.

Detailed Results

Singles: R. B. Powell (Can.) beat R. F. Le Sueur (S.A.) 6–3, 6–4, 3–6, 7–5 ; beat V. R. Gauntlett (S.A.), retired. B. P. Schwengers (Can.) beat R. F. Le Sueur (S.A.) 6–3, 6–3, 6–3 ; lost to V. R. Gauntlett (S.A.) 9–11, 3–6, 0–6.

Doubles: R. B. Powell and B. P. Schwengers (Can.) beat V. R. Gauntlett and R. F. Le Sueur (S.A.) 7–5, 6–3, 3–6, 6–3.

Belgium had a bye.

America and Germany met in the second round, at Nottingham, on July 10, 11, and 12. America won comfortably by five to nothing, the only really noteworthy match being that between M. E. McLoughlin and O. Froitzheim, the German gaining a two-set lead before McLoughlin came on to his game and overwhelmed him. W. F. Johnson played in place of McLoughlin for the latter's second single, and beat O. Kreuzer in four close sets. R. N. Williams dropped one set to both Kreuzer and Froitzheim, as did McLoughlin and H. H. Hackett to F. W. Rahe and H. Kleinschroth in the doubles.

Detailed Results

Singles: R. N. WILLIAMS (U.S.A.) beat O. Kreuzer (Ger.) 7–5, 6–4, 4–6, 6–1 ; beat O. Froitzheim (Ger.) 5–7, 6–1, 6–3, 6–1. M. E. McLOUGHLIN (U.S.A.) beat O. Froitzheim (Ger.) 5–7, 2–6, 6–4, 6–2, 6–2. W. F. JOHNSON (U.S.A.) beat O. Kreuzer (Ger.) 7–5, 6–4, 5–7, 6–4.

Doubles: M. E. McLOUGHLIN and H. H. HACKETT (U.S.A.) beat F. W. Rahe and H. Kleinschroth (Ger.) 6–4, 2–6, 6–3, 8–6.

Canada and Belgium played the other second-round tie, at Folkestone, on July 10 and 12, Canada winning by four matches to none. R. B. Powell played only one of his singles—against P. de Borman, whom he beat easily. B. P. Schwengers beat A. G. Watson and de Borman, and with Powell beat Watson and W. H. Duvivier. This result left Canada and America to play for the right to challenge British Isles.

Detailed Results

Singles: R. B. POWELL (CAN.) beat P. de Borman (Belg.) 6–2, 6–1, 6–1. B. P. SCHWENGERS (CAN.) beat A. G. Watson (Belg.) 6–4, 6–1, 6–0 ; beat P. de Borman (Belg.) 4–6, 6–4, 6–2, 6–2.

Doubles: B. P. SCHWENGERS and R. B. POWELL (CAN.) beat A. G. Watson and W. H. Duvivier (Belg.) 6–2, 6–2, 6–2.

The final round was played at Wimbledon on July 18 and 19, only three matches being completed, and all won by America in straight sets. R. N. Williams beat B. P. Schwengers, M. E. McLoughlin beat R. B. Powell, and McLoughlin and H. H. Hackett beat Powell and Schwengers, thus bringing America to the challenge round and the eventual winning of the trophy which they had lost ten years previously.

Detailed Results

Singles: R. N. WILLIAMS (U.S.A.) beat B. P. Schwengers (Can.) 6–4, 6–2, 6–4. M. E. McLOUGHLIN (U.S.A.) beat R. B. Powell (Can.) 10–8, 6–1, 6–4.

Doubles: H. H. HACKETT and M. E. McLOUGHLIN (U.S.A.) beat R. B. Powell and B. P. Schwengers (Can.) 6–3, 6–3, 12–10.

Challenge Round

The challenge round took place at Wimbledon on July 25, 26, and 28, and was an extremely close affair, only one match —that between C. P. Dixon and M. E. McLoughlin—being less than five sets. J. C. Parke defended magnificently for British Isles, and beat both McLoughlin and R. N. Williams in five-set matches. Dixon, the other British Isles singles player, could do little against McLoughlin, going down in three straight sets, but he almost beat Williams, finally just failing to do so at 7–5 in the fifth set. The doubles became the key match of the contest, and H. Roper Barrett and Dixon almost turned the trick. They led by two sets to one, and actually had a match ball in the fourth set. McLoughlin's fine play saved the day for America, and he and H. H. Hackett nosed out at 6–4 in the fifth set. Thus the cup returned home.

Detailed Results

Singles: M. E. McLoughlin (U.S.A.) beat C. P. Dixon (B.I.) 8–6, 6–3, 6–2 ; lost to J. C. Parke (B.I.) 10–8, 5–7, 4–6, 6–1, 5–7. R. N. Williams (U.S.A.) beat C. P. Dixon (B.I.) 8–6, 3–6, 6–2, 1–6, 7–5 ; lost to J. C. Parke (B.I.) 2–6, 7–5, 7–5, 4–6, 2–6.

Doubles: H. H. Hackett and M. E. McLoughlin (U.S.A.) beat H. Roper Barrett and C. P. Dixon (B.I.) 5–7, 6–1, 2–6, 7–5, 6–4.

1914 : AUSTRALASIA

This year, destined to be the last year of play until the First World War had finished, the challengers numbered one less than in 1913, South Africa dropping out.

British Isles played Belgium in the first round, at Folkestone, on July 7, 8, and 9, and slaughtered the visitors by five matches and fifteen sets to none. The Belgian team was the same one that had lost to Canada in 1913 at Folkestone. For British Isles J. C. Parke and T. M. Mavrogordato played the singles, and the latter partnered H. Roper Barrett for the doubles.

Detailed Results

Singles: J. C. PARKE (B.I.) beat A. G. Watson (Belg.) 6–2, 6–2, 6–3; beat P. de Borman (Belg.) 6–4, 6–3, 6–0. T. M. MAVROGORDATO (B.I.) beat P. de Borman (Belg.) 6–1, 6–3, 8–6; beat A. G. Watson (Belg.) 6–1, 6–0, 6–3.

Doubles: H. ROPER BARRETT and T. M. MAVROGORDATO (B.I.) beat A. G. Watson and W. H. Duvivier (Belg.) 6–1, 6–2, 6–2.

The other first-round match was between Australasia and Canada, and was played at Chicago on July 23, 24, and 25. Australasia fielded their best team—N. E. Brookes and A. F. Wilding—and they romped home against Canada's R. B. Powell and B. P. Schwengers without losing a set.

Detailed Results

Singles: N. E. BROOKES (AUSTRAL.) beat B. P. Schwengers (Can.) 6–2, 6–3, 6–2; beat R. B. Powell (Can.) 6–0, 6–1, 6–3. A. F. WILDING (AUSTRAL.) beat B. P. Schwengers (Can.) 7–5, 6–3, 6–1; beat R. B. Powell (Can.) 6–1, 6–2, 6–2.

Doubles: N. E. BROOKES and A. F. WILDING (AUSTRAL.) beat B. P. Schwengers and R. B. Powell (Can.) 6–4, 6–3, 6–4.

Germany and France had byes.

In the first of the two second, or semi-final, rounds British Isles played and beat France at Wimbledon on July 11, 13, and 14. J. C. Parke beat M. Decugis in five sets and M. Germot in three. T. M. Mavrogordato beat Decugis in three sets and Germot in four, but with H. Roper Barrett in the doubles he lost to the two Frenchmen in four sets.

Detailed Results

Singles: J. C. PARKE (B.I.) beat M. Decugis (Fr.) 6–2, 4–6, 3–6, 6–3, 6–3; beat M. Germot (Fr.) 7–5, 6–1, 6–3. T. M. MAVROGORDATO (B.I.) beat M. Decugis (Fr.) 6–1, 7–5, 7–5; beat M. Germot (FR.) 4–6, 7–5, 9–7, 6–2.

Doubles: H. Roper Barrett and T. M. Mavrogordato (B.I.) lost to M. DECUGIS and M. GERMOT (FR.) 3–6, 7–5, 5–7, 4–6.

Australasia and Germany played their tie at Pittsburg, U.S.A., on July 30 and 31 and August 1, on the eve of the outbreak of war. N. E. Brookes lost a set to O. Kreuzer in the singles, but all the other matches were won in three straight sets. Each country fielded only a two-man team—Brookes and A. F. Wilding and O. Froitzheim and Kreuzer.

Detailed Results

Singles: N. E. Brookes (Austral.) beat O. Froitzheim (Ger.) 10–8, 6–1, 6–2; beat O. Kreuzer (Ger.) 6–4, 6–2, 6–8, 6–2. A. F. Wilding (Austral.) beat O. Froitzheim (Ger.) 6–3, 6–4, 6–2; beat O. Kreuzer (Ger.) 6–2, 6–2, 6–4.

Doubles: N. E. Brookes and A. F. Wilding (Austral.) beat O. Froitzheim and O. Kreuzer (Ger.) 6–1, 6–1, 6–2.

Thus Australasia and British Isles had lined up for the final round, which took place at Boston on August 6 and 7, only two singles and the doubles being played, and all won by Australasia. A. H. Lowe had come back into the British Isles team, and played in the singles in place of T. M. Mavrogordato, who played the doubles only with J. C. Parke. Although Lowe lost to A. F. Wilding in three sets he had the distinction of playing in the longest set yet played in Davis Cup tennis, the third set of this match going to 16–14 before Wilding won it. N. E. Brookes and Parke waged a bitter five-set match before Brookes squeezed home at 7–5 in the fifth. The Australasians easily won the doubles in three sets, and thus became challengers to America.

Detailed Results

Singles: N. E. Brookes (Austral.) beat J. C. Parke (B.I.) 6–2, 4–6, 6–3, 1–6, 7–5. A. F. Wilding (Austral.) beat A. H. Lowe (B.I.) 6–3, 6–1, 16–14.

Doubles: N. E. Brookes and A. F. Wilding (Austral.) beat J. C. Parke and T. M. Mavrogordato (B.I.) 6–1, 6–0, 6–4.

Challenge Round

The challenge round took place at Forest Hills, New York, on August 13, 14, and 15. It was a close affair, but the Brookes-Wilding team, making their last appearance, were too evenly balanced for the younger American side, despite the brilliance of M. E. McLoughlin, who won both his singles, playing superlative tennis. On the first day he beat N. E. Brookes in a sensational encounter which hinged entirely on the first set—creating a new long-distance record of 17–15. It was a service-governed battle, with Brookes almost winning it several times, only to be prevented by the Californian's magnificent serving. With the first set in his pocket at last, McLoughlin found Brookes unable to hold him any longer, and he rode home in the next two sets, with the loss of three games in each. A. F. Wilding beat R. N. Williams in three sets, and so all was square. Brookes and Wilding beat McLoughlin and T. C. Bundy in the doubles in three sets, thus gaining a lien on the tie, because Brookes was almost certain to beat the brilliant but erratic young R. N. Williams even if Wilding could not stop McLoughlin. And just this happened on the third day. Wilding won one set from McLoughlin, and Williams one from Brookes, giving Australasia the tie and the cup by three matches to two.

Detailed Results

Singles: N. E. BROOKES (AUSTRAL.) beat R. N. Williams (U.S.A.) 6–1, 6–2, 8–10, 6–3 ; lost to M. E. MCLOUGHLIN (U.S.A.) 15–17, 3–6, 3–6. A. F. WILDING (AUSTRAL.) beat R. N. Williams (U.S.A.) 7–5, 6–2, 6–3 ; lost to M. E. MCLOUGHLIN (U.S.A.) 2–6, 3–6, 6–2, 2–6.

Doubles: N. E. BROOKES and A. F. WILDING (AUSTRAL.) beat M. E. McLoughlin and T. C. Bundy (U.S.A.) 6–3, 8–6, 9–7.

And now the First World War drew a veil over the Davis Cup competition for five years ; and Anthony Frederick Wilding, one of the most famous competitors to date, perished in the conflict.

BETWEEN THE WARS

1919–39

1919 : AUSTRALASIA

This year, when the competition recommenced, there were four challengers—France, Belgium, British Isles, and South Africa. They met in that order.

France and Belgium played at Brussels in July, and France won all the three matches played. M. Decugis turned out again for France, and beat P. de Borman, who had reappeared for Belgium, in three sets. W. H. Laurentz, France's other singles player, beat M. Lammens, Belgium, in four sets. Together the Frenchmen beat the Belgians in the doubles in three sets.

Detailed Results

Singles: M. Decugis (Fr.) beat P. de Borman (Belg.) 6–2, 6–3, 6–4. W. H. Laurentz (Fr.) beat M. Lammens (Belg.) 5–7, 6–3, 6–4, 6–2.

Doubles: M. Decugis and W. H. Laurentz (Fr.) beat P. de Borman and M. Lammens (Belg.) 6–3, 7–5, 6–2.

British Isles beat South Africa at Eastbourne on August 25, 26, and 28, by four matches to one. British Isles were represented by A. R. F. Kingscote and T. M. Mavrogordato in the singles, and H. Roper Barrett, still going after nineteen years, partnered Kingscote in the doubles. South Africa had a three-man team, consisting of L. Raymond and G. H. Dodd for the singles and Dodd and H. Aitken for the doubles. Kingscote won both his singles easily, though he dropped the first set to Raymond. Mavrogordato had a torrid time. He beat Raymond in a long, fluctuating struggle over five sets, and lost to Dodd in an equal number. " Mavro " lost the first wo sets in this latter match, pulled up to win the next two, and lost the fifth 5–7. Roper Barrett and Kingscote won the doubles in three sets.

THE ORIGINAL U.S.A. TEAM OF 1900

Left to right: M. D. Whitman, Dwight F. Davis (donor of the cup), H. Ward.

THE AUSTRALASIAN TEAM, WINNERS IN 1914

Left to right: A. F. Wilding and N. E. Brookes.

THE BRITISH ISLES TEAM OF 1903, THE FIRST SUCCESSFUL CHALLENGERS

Left to right: R. F. Doherty and H. L. Doherty.

Detailed Results

Singles: A. R. F. KINGSCOTE (B.I.) beat G. H. Dodd (S.A.) 6–3, 6–3, 6–2 ; beat L. Raymond (S.A.) 1–6, 6–0, 6–4, 6–1. T. M. MAVROGORDATO (B.I.) beat L. Raymond (S.A.) 1–6, 7–5, 2–6, 8–6, 6–1 ; lost to G. H. DODD (S.A.) 7–9, 5–7, 6–3, 6–4, 5–7.

Doubles: H. ROPER BARRETT and A. R. F. KINGSCOTE (B.I.) beat G. H. Dodd and H. Aitken (S.A.) 7–5, 9–7, 6–4.

The final round, between British Isles and France, was played at Deauville on September 25, 26, and 27. British Isles varied their team from their earlier match against South Africa. A. R. F. Kingscote was used again as one of the singles players, but Mavrogordato gave way to P. M. Davson as the other singles player, and O. G. N. Turnbull came in as Roper Barrett's partner for the doubles. France relied on two men, A. H. Gobert and W. H. Laurentz, and they very nearly won. The contest was extremely close, British Isles winning by the odd match in five, but, at the same time, scoring only the same number of sets as the French team. Kingscote beat Laurentz in five sets and Gobert in three, and was thus of very material help to his team, as Davson only succeeded in beating Laurentz after being down two sets to one, and he lost to Gobert in four sets. The French pair took the doubles in three sets by a strange score: 6–0, 6–1, 12–10.

Detailed Results

Singles: A. R. F. KINGSCOTE (B.I.) beat W. H. Laurentz (Fr.) 4–6, 6–3, 6–2, 4–6, 6–4 ; beat A. H. Gobert (Fr.) 6–4, 6–4, 7–5. P. M. DAVSON (B.I.) beat W. H. Laurentz (Fr.) 6–4, 1–6, 10–12, 6–4, 6–0 ; lost to A. H. GOBERT (FR.) 5–7, 4–6, 6–4, 4–6.

Doubles: H. Roper Barrett and O. G. N. Turnbull (B.I.) lost to A. H. GOBERT and W. H. LAURENTZ (FR.) 0–6, 1–6, 10–12.

CHALLENGE ROUND

British Isles then made the long journey to Australia for the challenge round against Australasia at Sydney on January 16, 19, and 21, 1920. The holders played two young men for the singles—G. L. Patterson, who had won the Wimbledon singles in 1919, and J. O. Anderson—while the veteran Norman Brookes partnered Patterson in the doubles. The British Isles team was A. R. F. Kingscote and A. H. Lowe for the singles and Kingscote and A. E. Beamish for the doubles. They succeeded in winning only one match—that in which Kingscote beat Anderson in three sets. Lowe almost beat the same player, just failing at 12–10 in the fifth set, after a fluctuating match. Patterson was too strong for both Englishmen, and with Brookes in the doubles he crushed Kingscote and Beamish, with the loss of only two games in three sets.

Detailed Results

Singles: G. L. PATTERSON (AUSTRAL.) beat A. H. Lowe (B.I.) 6–4, 6–3, 2–6, 6–3; beat A. R. F. Kingscote (B.I.) 6–4, 6–4, 8–6. J. O. ANDERSON (AUSTRAL.) beat A. H. Lowe (B.I.) 6–4, 5–7, 6–3, 4–6, 12–10; lost to A. R. F. KINGSCOTE (B.I.) 5–7, 2–6, 4–6.

Doubles: N. E. BROOKES and G. L. PATTERSON (AUSTRAL.) beat A. R. F. Kingscote and A. E. Beamish (B.I.) 6–0, 6–0, 6–2.

1920: U.S.A.

This year saw one new challenger appear—the Netherlands—to make the number of challengers five, the others being South Africa, France, America, and British Isles.

The Netherlands played South Africa in the first round at Arnheim, in Holland, on June 11, 12, and 13, and won by the odd match. Their team was C. J. van Lennep and A. Diemer Kool for both singles and doubles. South Africa relied on L. Raymond and C. L. Winslow. The latter won both his singles in straight sets, but Raymond, though he took van Lennep to five sets, was on the losing end three times, as he and Winslow lost the doubles also.

Detailed Results

Singles: C. J. VAN LENNEP (NETH.) beat L. Raymond (S.A.) 4–6, 6–3, 6–4, 3–6, 6–3; lost to C. L. Winslow (S.A.) 3–6, 4–6, 4–6. A. DIEMER KOOL (NETH.) beat L. Raymond (S.A.) 6–3, 6–3, 7–5; lost to C. L. WINSLOW (S.A.) 3–6, 2–6, 5–7.

Doubles: C. J. VAN LENNEP and A. DIEMER KOOL (NETH.) beat C. L. Winslow and L. Raymond (S.A.) 6–2, 7–5, 6–4.

United States of America played France at Eastbourne on July 8, 9, and 10, and won the only three matches played. This tie marked the beginning of an era—the era of " Big Bill " and " Little Bill," as W. T. Tilden and W. M. Johnston came to be known. These two men were appearing for the first time in the competition, and together for the next seven years were to dominate the Davis Cup as the backbone of perhaps the strongest Davis Cup team ever. In this tie against France Johnston beat A. H. Gobert in three sets, and Tilden beat W. H. Laurentz in four. Together the two " Bills " beat Gobert and Laurentz in three sets. An auspicious beginning for two such famous figures.

Detailed Results

Singles: W. M. JOHNSTON (U.S.A.) beat A. H. Gobert (Fr.) 6–3, 8–6, 6–3. W. T. TILDEN (U.S.A.) beat W. H. Laurentz (Fr.) 4–6, 6–2, 6–1, 6–3.

Doubles: W. M. JOHNSTON and W. T. TILDEN (U.S.A.) beat A. H. Gobert and W. H. Laurentz (Fr.) 6–2, 6–3, 6–2.

In the second round U.S.A. played British Isles at Wimbledon on July 16, 17, and 19. Both countries had a two-man team: U.S.A. " Big Bill " Tilden and " Little Bill " Johnston; British Isles A. R. F. Kingscote and J. C. Parke once more. Five–love to America, but three of the matches went to five sets. Johnston had to fight hard in both his singles, finding the Britishers very tenacious and full of fight. Kingscote even pressed him to 7–5 in the fifth set, after leading by two sets to one. Tilden, the newly crowned Wimbledon champion, was more impressive, beating Kingscote in four sets and Parke in three. The two Britishers gained a two-sets-to-one lead in the doubles, but they were forced to yield.

Detailed Results

Singles: W. M. JOHNSTON (U.S.A.) beat J. C. Parke (B.I.) 6–4, 6–4, 2–6, 3–6, 6–2; beat A. R. F. Kingscote (B.I.) 6–4, 4–6, 3–6, 6–4, 7–5. W. T. TILDEN (U.S.A.) beat A. R. F. Kingscote (B.I.) 4–6, 6–1, 6–3, 6–1; beat J. C. Parke (B.I.) 6–2, 6–3, 7–5.

Doubles: W. M. JOHNSTON and W. T. TILDEN (U.S.A.) beat J. C. Parke and A. R. F. Kingscote (B.I.) 8–6, 4–6, 4–6, 6–3, 6–2.

CHALLENGE ROUND

The United States team journeyed to Auckland for the challenge round against Australasia on December 30 and 31, 1920, and January 1, 1921. Both challengers and holders relied on two men only, though others were available. The holders played G. L. Patterson and N. E. Brookes, and U.S.A., the challengers, W. T. Tilden and W. M. Johnston. The Americans were far too strong, and regained the cup for their country by winning all five matches with something to spare, four in four sets, and one in three. The performance of Brookes, aged forty-three years, in taking both Tilden and Johnston to four sets in the singles—both matches being hard-fought struggles—and also, with Patterson, in taking the doubles into four sets, is worthy of note as one of the outstanding performances in the competition. When one remembers that Brookes was also by nature and technique a volleyer the feat becomes all the more remarkable. Patterson managed to win a set from Tilden in the singles, but was slaughtered by Johnston, who thrived on his speed.

The cup now returned home once again, this time for a seven-year period, as long as the Tilden–Johnston team remained together.

Detailed Results

Singles: W. T. TILDEN (U.S.A.) beat N. E. Brookes (Austral.) 10–8, 6–4, 1–6, 6–4; beat G. L. Patterson (Austral.) 5–7, 6–2, 6–3, 6–3. W. M. JOHNSTON (U.S.A.) beat N. E. Brookes (Austral.) 5–7, 7–5, 6–3, 6–3; beat G. L. Patterson (Austral.) 6–3, 6–1, 6–1.

Doubles: W. T. TILDEN and W. M. JOHNSTON (U.S.A.) beat N. E. Brookes and G. L. Patterson (Austral.) 4–6, 6–4, 6–0, 6–4.

1921: U.S.A.

In this year there was the greatest number of challengers so far in the competition. The newcomers were Spain,

Czechoslovakia, India, Denmark, and Japan, with British Isles, Australasia, Canada, Belgium, and France making up ten challengers. One of the newcomers, Japan, duly reached the challenge round against U.S.A. Argentina also challenged, but defaulted without playing a round, as also did the Philippines.

In the first round British Isles played Spain at Hendon on May 23, 24, and 25, with an entirely new team, consisting of F. G. Lowe and R. Lycett for the singles and Lycett and M. Woosnam—later in the year to win the Wimbledon doubles title—for the doubles. The Spanish team was a two-man one of M. Alonso and Count de Gomar. Alonso beat Lowe in three sets, and de Gomar took Lycett to five sets before losing, but otherwise the Spaniards were disposed of without too much difficulty.

Detailed Results

Singles: F. G. LOWE (B.I.) beat Count de Gomar (Sp.) 6–3, 4–6, 6–1, 6–0 ; lost to M. ALONSO (SP.) 6–8, 1–6, 6–8. R. LYCETT (B.I.) beat M. Alonso (Sp.) 6–4, 6–2, 6–4 ; beat Count de Gomar (Sp.) 6–1, 6–8, 7–9, 6–3, 6–2.

Doubles: R. LYCETT and M. WOOSNAM (B.I.) beat M. Alonso and Count de Gomar (Sp.) 2–6, 9–7, 6–2, 6–2.

In the same round Australasia played Canada at Toronto on July 23, 26, and 27. J. O. Anderson was the only member of previous Australasian teams in the side. He played in the singles, and also in the doubles with C. V. Todd. J. B. Hawkes was the other singles player, though Todd substituted for him in one match. For Canada E. H. Laframbois and P. Bennett played the singles and Bennett and G. D. Holmes the doubles. Australasia had no trouble in winning five–love, no matches being close.

Detailed Results

Singles: J. O. ANDERSON (AUSTRAL.) beat E. H. Laframbois (Can.) 4–6, 7–5, 6–0, 6–2 ; beat P. Bennett (Can.) 6–3, 6–0, 6–2. J. B. HAWKES (AUSTRAL.) beat P. Bennett (Can.) 8–6, 6–4, 6–4. C. V. TODD (AUSTRAL.) beat E. H. Laframbois (Can.) 6–2, 6–3, 6–8, 6–2.

Doubles: J. O. ANDERSON and C. V. TODD (AUSTRAL.) beat P. Bennett and G. D. Holmes (Can.) 6–2, 6–3, 6–1.

The remaining tie of this round was between Belgium and Czechoslovakia, played at Prague on June 13, 15, and 16. Belgium won by three matches to two, neither J. Washer nor M. Lammens, who played both the singles and the doubles, proving able to defeat the Czech M. Zemla, though Washer took him to five sets. Zemla, with Just as his partner, almost carried the doubles for Czechoslovakia when he and Just led two sets to love against Washer and Lammens. They only lost the third set at 8–6. K. Ardelt, the other Czech singles man, was not as good as Zemla, and both Belgians beat him in four sets.

Detailed Results

Singles: J. WASHER (BELG.) beat K. Ardelt (Czech.) 4–6, 7–5, 7–5, 6–3 ; lost to M. ZEMLA (CZECH.) 6–3, 3–6, 7–9, 6–2, 2–6. M. LAMMENS (BELG.) beat K. Ardelt (Czech.) 6–3, 6–2, 4–6, 6–1 ; lost to M. ZEMLA (CZECH.) 2–6, 4–6, 2–6.

Doubles: J. WASHER and M. LAMMENS (BELG.) beat M. Zemla and Just (Czech.) 4–6, 3–6, 8–6, 6–4, 6–0.

The next round brought Australasia and British Isles against each other, and they played off at Pittsburg, U.S.A., on August 4, 5, and 6. British Isles had M. Woosnam and F. G. Lowe for the singles and Woosnam and O. G. N. Turnbull for the doubles. Australasia were arranged as against Canada in the first round—J. O. Anderson and J. B. Hawkes for the singles and Anderson and C. V. Todd for the doubles. It became a very close conflict, turning on the doubles match, a five-set encounter which the Australasians won, from two sets to one down. Hawkes lost both his singles—to Lowe in three sets and Woosnam in five. Anderson, however, redressed the balance with wins over Lowe in four sets and Woosnam in three.

Detailed Results

Singles: J. O. ANDERSON (AUSTRAL.) beat M. Woosnam (B.I.) 6–4, 6–2, 6–4 ; beat F. G. Lowe (B.I.) 6–2, 6–3, 3–6, 6–2. J. B. Hawkes (Austral.) lost to F. G. LOWE (B.I.) 4–6, 4–6, 1–6 ; lost to M. WOOSNAM (B.I.) 3–6, 6–0, 9–7, 3–6, 3–6.

Doubles: J. O. Anderson and C. V. Todd (Austral.) beat M. Woosnam and O. G. N. Turnbull (B.I.) 4–6, 9–7, 4–6, 6–2, 6–4.

Japan had a bye ; Belgium retired.

India and France met in Paris on July 16, 17, and 18, when India gained a clear-cut win by four matches to one. The winners had as singles players M. Sleem and S. M. Jacob, with L. S. Deane and A. A. Fyzee playing the doubles. France played W. H. Laurentz and J. Samazeuilh in the singles and Laurentz and J. Brugnon in the doubles. Sleem won both his singles comfortably, but Jacob lost to Samazeuilh in three sets. The other singles was played between Deane and Brugnon, the former winning in five sets. The doubles went to India also in five sets. A noteworthy feature of this tie was that it was Jacques Brugnon's first appearance in the Davis Cup competition. He was the first of the famous " Four Musketeers " who were to make France's Davis Cup team a household word only a few years later.

Detailed Results

Singles: M. Sleem (Ind.) beat W. H. Laurentz (Fr.) 4–6, 6–2, 3–6, 6–2, 6–0 ; beat J. Samazeuilh (Fr.) 6–1, 6–3, 6–3. S. M. Jacob (Ind.) lost to J. Samazeuilh (Fr.) 3–6, 6–8, 5–7. L. S. Deane (Ind.) beat J. Brugnon (Fr.) 6–3, 4–6, 7–5, 4–6, 8–6.

Doubles: L. S. Deane and A. A. Fyzee (Ind.) beat W. H. Laurentz and J. Brugnon (Fr.) 6–1, 2–6, 5–7, 6–2, 6–4.

Australasia and Denmark met in the third round at Cleveland, Ohio, on August 19, 20, and 21. The Danes were making their first appearance, having had a bye in the first round and a default from Argentina in the second round. They played V. Ingersley and E. Tegner in the singles, and the latter partnered P. Henriksen in the doubles. J. O. Anderson and N. Peach played for Australasia in the singles and Anderson and C. V. Todd in the doubles. Only one match went beyond three sets—that between Peach and Ingersley, which the Australian won in five sets. Australasia's five–love win was never in doubt.

Detailed Results

Singles: J. O. ANDERSON (AUSTRAL.) beat V. Ingersley (Den.) 6–0, 6–1, 7–5 ; beat E. Tegner (Den.) 6–0, 6–2, 6–1. N. PEACH (AUSTRAL.) beat E. Tegner (Den.) 7–5, 6–2, 6–4 ; beat V. Ingersley (Den.) 3–6, 6–2, 6–0, 3–6, 6–2.

Doubles: J. O. ANDERSON and C. V. TODD (AUSTRAL.) beat E. Tegner and P. Henriksen (Den.) 6–3, 6–3, 6–2.

Japan, having received walk-overs from the Philippines and Belgium in the previous rounds, played their first match, against India, at Chicago on August 18, 19, and 20, and their two-man team of Z. Shimizu and I. Kumagae celebrated with a five–love win. M. Sleem and A. H. Fyzee played the singles for India, and Fyzee and L. S. Deane the doubles. The Japanese were not extended, and though Deane and Fyzee carried the doubles to five sets, they lost the fifth to love.

Detailed Results

Singles: Z. SHIMIZU (JAP.) beat M. Sleem (Ind.) 7–5, 2–6, 6–0, 6–2 ; beat A. H. Fyzee (Ind.) 6–2, 6–1, 9–7. I. KUMAGAE (JAP.) beat M. Sleem (Ind.) 9–7, 6–1, 6–1 ; beat A. H. Fyzee (Ind.) 3–6, 6–3, 6–3, 9–7.

Doubles: Z. SHIMIZU and I. KUMAGAE (JAP.) beat A. H. Fyzee and L. S. Deane (Ind.) 6–1, 6–1, 2–6, 2–6, 6–0.

Japan and Australasia met in the final round at Newport, U.S.A., on August 22, 26, and 27. J. B. Hawkes and J. O. Anderson played the singles for Australasia, and Anderson and C. V. Todd the doubles. Japan again relied on two men, Z. Shimizu and I. Kumagae. It was a very close tie, although Japan won by the seemingly wide margin of four to one. Shimizu won his two singles with something over, beating Anderson in three sets and Hawkes in four, but Kumagae won both his against the same two players only with the greatest difficulty. Anderson led him by two sets to one, and lost the fourth at 7–5 only, while Hawkes was even nearer defeating him when leading two sets to love and carrying the third set to 8–6. Australasia won only the doubles—in four sets—but they almost won two of the four singles also. This result put Japan into the challenge round for the first and only time.

Detailed Results

Singles: Z. SHIMIZU (JAP.) beat J. O. Anderson (Austral.) 6–4, 7–5, 6–4 ; beat J. B. Hawkes (Austral.) 4–6, 6–2, 6–3, 6–2. I. KUMAGAE (JAP.) beat J. O. Anderson (Austral.) 3–6, 6–4, 2–6, 7–5, 6–2 ; beat J. B. Hawkes (Austral.) 3–6, 2–6, 8–6, 6–2, 6–3.

Doubles: Z. Shimizu and I. Kumagae (Jap.) lost to J. O. ANDERSON and C. V. TODD (AUSTRAL.) 6–4, 4–6, 6–8, 0–6.

CHALLENGE ROUND

Although U.S.A. beat Japan in the challenge round by five matches to love the tie provided a goodly measure of excitement. It was played at New York on September 2, 3, and 5.

Zenzo Shimizu, the Japanese Number One, covered himself with distinction in his memorable match against W. T. Tilden. He won the first two sets, and took the third to 5–all before fading out of the picture—a remarkable effort when one compares his stroke equipment with Tilden's. The little Japanese also won a set from W. M. Johnston, the other American singles player, and Johnston was generally harder to take a set from than Tilden all through his career. The other Japanese, I. Kumagae, was not quite of the same calibre as Shimizu, and he could not win a set against either Tilden or Johnston. In partnership Shimizu and Kumagae took one set from R. N. Williams and W. M. Washburn, the American doubles pair.

Detailed Results

Singles: W. T. TILDEN (U.S.A.) beat Z. Shimizu (Jap.) 5–7, 4–6, 7–5, 6–2, 6–1 ; beat I. Kumagae (Jap.) 9–7, 6–4, 6–1. W. M. JOHNSTON (U.S.A.) beat Z. Shimizu (Jap.) 6–3, 5–7, 6–2, 6–4 ; beat I. Kumagae (Jap.) 6–2, 6–4, 6–2.

Doubles: R. N. WILLIAMS and W. M. WASHBURN (U.S.A.) beat Z. Shimizu and I. Kumagae (Jap.) 6–2, 7–5, 4–6, 7–5.

1922 : U.S.A.

In this year there was the same number of actual challengers as in the previous year—namely, ten. Canada, Hawaii, the Philippines, and Japan retired without playing a tie. The countries who actually toed the mark were Australasia, Belgium, India, Rumania, France, Denmark, Czechoslovakia, Spain, Italy, and British Isles, the last-named country retiring after beating Italy in the second round, having had a bye in the first.

Australasia and Belgium played their first-round match at Scarborough on June 22, 23, and 24. Four matches only were played, all won by Australasia, who fielded a strong team, consisting of G. L. Patterson and J. O. Anderson for the singles and Anderson and P. O'Hara Wood for the doubles. Belgium relied on J. Washer and A. G. Watson for both singles and doubles. Washer could not win a set against either Patterson or Anderson in the singles. Watson, who played Anderson only, did no better. In partnership in the doubles, however, the Belgians took Anderson and O'Hara Wood to five sets after losing the first two.

Detailed Results

Singles: J. O. ANDERSON (AUSTRAL.) beat J. Washer (Belg.) 6–4, 6–3, 6–2 ; beat A. G. Watson (Belg.) 6–2, 6–1, 6–2. G. L. PATTERSON (AUSTRAL.) beat J. Washer (Belg.) 6–3, 6–4, 6–4.

Doubles: J. O. ANDERSON and P. O'HARA WOOD (AUSTRAL.) beat J. Washer and A. G. Watson (Belg.) 6–1, 6–2, 4–6, 7–9, 7–5.

The only other first-round tie was between India and Rumania, the latter challenging for the first time. The tie was played at Beckenham, near London, on June 19 and 20, and India swept the board, winning all five matches. Rumania had a two-man team, N. Mishu and M. Stern. India used A. A. and A. H. Fyzee for the singles and A. H. Fyzee and C. Ramaswami for the doubles. The only close match was between Mishu and A. A. Fyzee, in which the Rumanian led by two sets to love, before losing at 6–0 in the fifth set.

Detailed Results

Singles: A. A. FYZEE (IND.) beat N. Mishu (Rum.) 3–6, 5–7, 6–4, 6–4, 6–0 ; beat M. Stern (Rum.) 6–2, 6–2, 6–1. A. H. FYZEE (IND.) beat N. Mishu (Rum.) 4–6, 6–1, 6–1, 7-5 ; beat M. Stern (Rum.) 6–0, 6–1, 6–1.

Doubles: A. H. Fyzee and C. Ramaswami (Ind.) beat N. Mishu and M. Stern (Rum.) 6–2, 6–4, 6–0.

In the second round France and Denmark met in Copenhagen on June 17, 18, and 19. France scored a four–one victory. E. Tegner and V. Ingersley again represented Denmark in the singles, and E. Worm came in to partner Tegner in the doubles. The French team was notable for the first appearance of two more of the shortly to be famous "Four Musketeers," Jean Borotra and Henri Cochet. Borotra played both in the singles and, with Cochet as partner, in the doubles. Cochet substituted for J. Couitéas in one single. Two of Borotra's three matches went to five sets—his single against Tegner and the doubles, which the Danes nearly won in four sets. Couitéas lost his single to Ingersley in three sets, but the latter could not win a set from Borotra. Cochet's singles début was a good three-straight win over Tegner.

Detailed Results

Singles: J. Borotra (Fr.) beat E. Tegner (Den.) 6–0, 3–6, 6–4, 1–6, 6–4 ; beat V. Ingersley (Den.) 6–3, 6–2, 6–4. J. Couitéas (Fr.) lost to V. Ingersley (Den.) 6–8, 3–6, 1–6. H. Cochet (Fr.) beat E. Tegner (Den.) 7–5, 6–2, 9–7.

Doubles: H. Cochet and J. Borotra (Fr.) beat E. Tegner and E. Worm (Den.) 3–6, 6–2, 2–6, 10–8, 6–2.

Australasia played Czechoslovakia at Roehampton, London, in this round, on July 14 and 15, and won easily five–none. G. L. Patterson and J. O. Anderson again played the singles for the winners, and this time Patterson and R. C. Wertheim formed the doubles team. The Czechs had a two-man team of F. von Röhrer and K. Ardelt. Both won a set from Patterson in the singles, and von Röhrer also won one against Anderson. But that was the extent of their success.

Detailed Results

Singles: G. L. Patterson (Austral.) beat F. von Röhrer (Czech.) 6–1, 6–3, 3–6, 6–2 ; beat K. Ardelt (Czech.) 6–3, 6–2, 2–6, 6–2. J. O. Anderson (Austral.) beat K. Ardelt (Czech.) 7–5, 6–4, 6–4 ; beat F. von Röhrer (Czech.) 4–6, 6–4, 6–3, 6–0.

Doubles: G. L. PATTERSON and R. C. WERTHEIM (AUSTRAL.) beat K. Ardelt and F. von Röhrer (Czech.) 9–7, 6–0, 6–3.

Another second-round match played in England was that between Spain and India, played at Bristol on June 13, 14, and 15. India's team was identical with the one used in the tie against Rumania in the previous round. For the singles Spain had M. Alonso and Count de Gomar, and E. Flaquer partnered Count de Gomar in the doubles. The Indians won only one match, the doubles, after a long, bitter struggle of five sets, three of which went to advantage games. It took Count de Gomar five sets to dispose of A. H. Fyzee, but otherwise Spain were in calm waters.

Detailed Results

Singles: M. ALONSO (SP.) beat A. H. Fyzee (Ind.) 6–1, 6–2, 6–2; beat A. A. Fyzee (Ind.) 6–3, 6–4, 0–6, 6–4.
COUNT DE GOMAR (SP.) beat A. H. Fyzee (Ind.) 1–6, 6–2, 6–3, 3–6, 6–1; beat A. A. Fyzee (Ind.) 6–1, 6–3, 3–6, 6–3.

Doubles: Count de Gomar and E. Flaquer (Sp.) lost to A. H. FYZEE and C. RAMASWAMI (IND.) 6–3, 5–7, 9–11, 10–8, 4–6.

British Isles played their only match of this year at Roehampton, London, on June 19, 20, and 21, against Italy, whom they defeated by four matches to love, one match being unplayed. British Isles were represented by A. R. F. Kingscote and F. G. Lowe in the singles and Kingscote and F. L. Riseley in the doubles. Italy used Count Balbi di Robecco and C. Colombo for both singles and doubles. They were unable to win a set in any match; the one between Kingscote and Count Balbi di Robecco was not played.

Detailed Results

Singles: A. R. F. KINGSCOTE (B.I.) beat C. Colombo (It.) 7–5, 6–4, 6–1; retired to COUNT BALBI DI ROBECCO (IT.)
F. G. LOWE (B.I.) beat Count Balbi di Robecco (It.) 6–1, 6–3, 6–1; beat C. Colombo (It.) 6–1, 6–2, 6–0.

Doubles: A. R. F. KINGSCOTE and F. L. RISELEY (B.I.) beat Count Balbi di Robecco and C. Colombo (It.) 6–1, 6–4, 6–0.

In the third round British Isles retired to Spain, thus putting the latter country into the final round. The other third-round tie was played at Boston, U.S.A., on August 10, 11, and 14, between Australasia and France. Both used a two-man team —Australasia G. L. Patterson and P. O'Hara Wood, France A. H. Gobert and H. Cochet. The tie was closer than the four–one score to Australasia would suggest at first glance. Patterson was down two sets to love against Gobert before finally winning, and he and O'Hara Wood were behind two sets to one in the doubles, and only home at 10–8 in the fifth. Cochet lost to Patterson in four sets, but beat O'Hara Wood in five. Gobert lost to O'Hara Wood in four sets.

Detailed Results

Singles: G. L. PATTERSON (AUSTRAL.) beat A. H. Gobert (Fr.) 4–6, 3–6, 6–3, 6–4, 6–3 ; beat H. Cochet (Fr.) 6–2, 2–6, 6–4, 6–2. P. O'HARA WOOD (AUSTRAL.) beat A. H. Gobert (Fr.) 2–6, 6–2, 6–1, 6–4 ; lost to H. COCHET (FR.) 4–6, 6–3, 0–6, 9–7, 4–6.

Doubles: G. L. PATTERSON and P. O'HARA WOOD (AUSTRAL.) beat A. H. Gobert and H. Cochet (Fr.) 6–0, 6–8, 4–6, 6–3, 10–8.

The final, or pre-challenge, round between Australasia and Spain took place at Philadelphia on August 17, 18, and 19. Australasia scored another four–one win, a little more easily than against France. Australasia again used G. L. Patterson and P. O'Hara Wood, while Spain relied on two players also, M. Alonso and Count de Gomar. Patterson was in good form, and beat both the Spaniards in straight sets, and with O'Hara Wood won the doubles in three sets also. O'Hara Wood was less happy. He beat Count de Gomar after being two sets down, and lost to Alonso after being two sets up—a rather unusual reversal.

Detailed Results

Singles: G. L. PATTERSON (AUSTRAL.) beat Count de Gomar (Sp.) 6–3, 8–6, 6–4 ; beat M. Alonso (Sp.) 8–6, 6–2, 6–2. P. O'HARA WOOD (AUSTRAL.) beat Count de Gomar (Sp.) 6–8, 3–6, 6–0, 6–4, 6–1 ; lost to M. ALONSO (SP.) 6–2, 6–3, 2–6, 6–8, 1–6.

Doubles: G. L. PATTERSON and P. O'HARA WOOD (AUSTRAL.) beat M. Alonso and Count de Gomar (Sp.) 6–3, 6–3, 6–4.

CHALLENGE ROUND

The challenge round, producing yet another meeting between Australasia and U.S.A., was played at Forest Hills, New York, on September 1, 2, and 5. The holders won comfortably by four matches to one. The issue was never in doubt.

The challengers brought in J. O. Anderson again for the singles with G. L. Patterson. P. O'Hara Wood partnered Patterson in the doubles. U.S.A. chose W. T. Tilden and W. M. Johnston for the singles and Tilden and V. Richards for the doubles. Johnston thrashed both the Australasians in the singles, losing only six games to Anderson in three sets, and only five in three sets to Patterson. Tilden beat Patterson in straight sets, the first two of which went to advantage and the third to love. Anderson gave the American champion a good fight, at one stage leading his famous opponent by two sets to one. The Patterson–O'Hara Wood team shocked the Americans Tilden and Richards by defeating them in three sets with the loss of only seven games, thus scoring the challengers' only win.

Detailed Results

Singles: W. T. TILDEN (U.S.A.) beat G. L. Patterson (Austral.) 7–5, 10–8, 6–0; beat J. O. Anderson (Austral.) 6–4, 5–7, 3–6, 6–4, 6–2. W. M. JOHNSTON (U.S.A.) beat J. O. Anderson (Austral.) 6–1, 6–2, 6–3; beat G. L. Patterson (Austral.) 6–2, 6–2, 6–1.

Doubles: W. T. Tilden and V. Richards (U.S.A.) lost to G. L. PATTERSON and P. O'HARA WOOD (AUSTRAL.) 4–6, 0–6, 3–6.

1923: U.S.A.

This year the International Lawn Tennis Championship expanded a great deal. Zoning was introduced—an American Zone and a European Zone. Four countries challenged in the former zone and twelve in the latter. Ireland became a separate challenger instead of combining with England, and

New Zealand separated from Australia, the latter challenging on their own. The total number of challengers was the greatest so far: sixteen nations in all played off to challenge U.S.A.

European Zone

Czechoslovakia met Switzerland at Territet on May 31 and June 1 and 2. The Swiss won a narrow victory by three matches to two. They used a four-man team. C. F. Aeschliman and C. Martin played the singles and G. A. Sautter and M. Ferrier the doubles. The Czechs used only two men—M. Zemla and F. von Röhrer. The latter fought two five-set singles, but lost them both. Zemla beat Martin in four sets, but lost to Aeschliman in the same number. The Czechs took the doubles in four sets, losing the first.

Detailed Results

Singles: C. F. Aeschliman (Switz.) beat M. Zemla (Czech.) 7–5, 6–2, 8–10, 6–3 ; beat F. von Röhrer (Czech.) 4–6, 7–5, 13–11, 3–6, 6–0. C. Martin (Switz.) beat F. von Röhrer (Czech.) 2–6, 6–3, 6–3, 6–8, 6–2 ; lost to M. Zemla (Czech.) 4–6, 6–3, 3–6, 4–6.

Doubles: G. A. Sautter and M. Ferrier (Switz.) lost to M. Zemla and F. von Röhrer (Czech.) 6–4, 4–6, 5–7, 6–8.

Ireland in their first independent challenge beat India in Dublin on June 1, 2, and 4 by three matches to two. They played a four-man team of the Hon. C. Campbell and E. D. McCrea for the singles and S. F. Scroope and L. A. Meldon for the doubles. India played S. M. Jacob and A. H. Fyzee in the singles, and Fyzee partnered L. S. Deane for the doubles. McCrea won both his singles, and Campbell beat Fyzee, to give Ireland their three matches and the tie. The doubles went to five sets and to India, for whom Jacob won his single against Campbell.

Detailed Results

Singles: Hon. C. Campbell (Ire.) beat A. H. Fyzee (Ind.) 6–4, 7–5, 6–2 ; lost to S. M. Jacob (Ind.) 2–6, 2–6, 3–6. E. D. McCrea (Ire.) beat A. H. Fyzee (Ind.) 7–5, 9–7, 2–6, 6–3 ; beat S. M. Jacob (Ind.) 6–4, 6–2, 6–4.

Doubles: S. F. Scroope and L. A. Meldon (Ire.) lost to L. S. DEANE and A. H. FYZEE (IND.) 6–0, 3–6, 6–8, 6–4, 6–8.

France played Denmark at Bordeaux on May 15, 16, and 17, and won by four matches to one. They used a three-man team, H. Cochet and R. Lacoste for the singles and Cochet and J. Samazeuilh for the doubles. René Lacoste was the fourth and last of the "Four Musketeers" to appear in the competition. His first match was against the Dane H. Larsen, and he lost at 8–6 in the fifth set after losing the first two sets and winning the next two. Cochet beat E. Tegner in five sets and E. Worm in three. Samazeuilh beat Tegner in five sets also. France won the doubles against Worm and Tegner in three sets.

Detailed Results

Singles: H. COCHET (FR.) beat E. Tegner (Den.) 6–1, 6–4, 1–6, 5–7, 6–4; beat E. Worm (Den.) 6–3, 8–6, 6–1. R. Lacoste (Fr.) lost to H. LARSEN (DEN.) 4–6, 4–6, 6–2, 8–6, 6–8. J. SAMAZEUILH (FR.) beat E. Tegner (Den.) 5–7, 6–1, 1–6, 8–6, 6–4.

Doubles: H. COCHET and J. SAMAZEUILH (FR.) beat E. Tegner and E. Worm (Den.) 6–1, 7–5, 6–3.

Great Britain beat Belgium by three matches to two at Brussels on May 30 and 31 and June 1. Belgium's two-man team of A. G. Watson and J. Washer was not evenly balanced enough to beat the British team of R. Lycett and J. B. Gilbert in the singles and Lycett and L. A. Godfree in the doubles. Washer won both his singles with the loss of one set only—to Gilbert—but Watson was not now of the same calibre, and could not win a set in any of his matches—even the doubles with Washer.

Detailed Results

Singles: R. LYCETT (G.B.) beat A. G. Watson (Belg.) 6–2, 8–6, 6–2; lost to J. WASHER (BELG.) 1–6, 3–6, 4–6. J. B. GILBERT (G.B.) beat A. G. Watson (Belg.) 6–4, 6–2, 6–2; lost to J. WASHER (BELG.) 2–6, 6–4, 2–6, 3–6.

Doubles: R. LYCETT and L. A. GODFREE (G.B.) beat J. Washer and A. G. Watson (Belg.) 6–1, 6–4, 6–1.

THE CHALLENGE-ROUND DOUBLES MATCH AT FOREST HILLS, NEW YORK, 1923

Left to right: W. T. Tilden and R. N. Williams (U.S.A.); J. O. Anderson and J. B. Hawkes (Australia).

THE U.S.A. TEAM OF 1925

Left to right: W. T. Tilden, R. N. Williams, V. Richards, W. M. Johnston.

THE AMERICANS OF 1947

Left to right: J. A. Kramer and F. R. Schroeder.

Spain defeated Great Britain at Manchester at the beginning of June by the odd match in five. Great Britain's team was altered from the previous, J. D. P. Wheatley taking the place of J. B. Gilbert in the singles, but R. Lycett and L. A. Godfree remained the doubles team, with Lycett also as the other singles player. Spain relied on two men only—Count de Gomar and E. Flaquer. The latter lost both his singles, but only at 11–9 in the fifth set to Wheatley, after leading two sets to love. He won only two games against Lycett. Count de Gomar redressed the balance nicely for Spain, however, by winning both his singles and, with Flaquer, the doubles also.

Detailed Results

Singles: E. Flaquer (Sp.) lost to R. LYCETT (G.B.) 0–6, 1–6, 1–6 ; lost to J. D. P. WHEATLEY (G.B.) 6–0, 6–4, 3–6, 1–6, 9–11. COUNT DE GOMAR (SP.) beat R. Lycett (G.B.) 6–4, 6–1, 7–5 ; beat J. D. P. Wheatley (G.B.) 4–6, 10–8, 6–1, 6–2.

Doubles: E. FLAQUER and COUNT DE GOMAR (SP.) beat R. Lycett and L. A. Godfree (G.B.) 6–2, 6–3, 4–6, 6–3.

The Netherlands and Italy played off the remaining match of this round at Noordwijk, Holland, on June 1, 2, and 3, and the home country gained a sweeping victory by five matches to none. Each country relied on two men only : for the Netherlands C. J. van Lennep and A. Diemer Kool, and for Italy H. L. de Morpurgo and C. Colombo. The only close match was the single between de Morpurgo and Diemer Kool, in which the Italian led by two sets to one before finally going down in the fifth set.

Detailed Results

Singles: C. J. VAN LENNEP (NETH.) beat H. L. de Morpurgo (It.) 6–1, 0–6, 6–3, 6–2 ; beat C. Colombo (It.) 6–2, 3–6, 6–2, 6–3. A. DIEMER KOOL (NETH.) beat H. L. de Morpurgo (It.) 7–5, 5–7, 3–6, 6–4, 6–4 ; beat C. Colombo (It.) 6–2, 6–1, 5–7, 6–4.

Doubles: C. J. VAN LENNEP and A. DIEMER KOOL (NETH.) beat H. L. de Morpurgo and C. Colombo (It.) 6–4, 6–4, 6–3.

In the semi-final round of the European Zone France and Switzerland had a close match at Lyons on July 13, 14, and 15, France getting home by three to two. Switzerland used C. F. Aeschliman and C. Martin for the singles and G. A. Sautter and Aeschliman in the doubles. France had only one of the " Musketeers " in action, H. Cochet, who played singles only. P. Blanchy was the other singles player, and he also partnered J. Samazeuilh in the doubles. This player won both his singles, but the doubles went to Switzerland after France had led two sets to love. Cochet lost to Martin in five sets, and just beat Aeschliman in the same number.

Detailed Results

Singles: P. BLANCHY (FR.) beat C. F. Aeschliman (Switz.) 6–4, 6–2, 6–4 ; beat C. Martin (Switz.) 7–5, 6–3, 6–2. H. COCHET (FR.) beat C. F. Aeschliman (Switz.) 1–6, 6–3, 6–3, 5–7, 6–4 ; lost to C. MARTIN (SWITZ.) 6–4, 4–6, 6–3, 1–6, 3–6.

Doubles: P. Blanchy and J. Samazeuilh (Fr.) lost to C. F. AESCHLIMAN and G. A. SAUTTER (SWITZ.) 10–8, 6–3, 2–6, 4–6, 4–6.

The other semi-finalists, Spain and the Netherlands, met at Eastbourne on July 9, 10, and 11, and Spain were easy five–love winners. Their two-man team of Count de Gomar and E. Flaquer was far too strong for the Dutchmen, who were without A. Diemer Kool. C. J. van Lennep and van der Feen played the singles and H. Timmer and C. A. Bryan the doubles. The last three were all newcomers, in their first Davis Cup match. No match went the full distance.

Detailed Results

Singles: COUNT DE GOMAR (SP.) beat C. J. van Lennep (Neth.) 6–4, 6–3, 6–3 ; beat van der Feen (Neth.) 6–3, 6–0, 7–5. E. FLAQUER (SP.) beat C. J. van Lennep (Neth.) 5–7, 6–3, 8–6, 6–1 ; beat van der Feen (Neth.) 4–6, 6–2, 6–3, 6–0.

Doubles: COUNT DE GOMAR and E. FLAQUER (SP.) beat H. Timmer and C. A. Bryan (Neth.) 6–4, 6–3, 6–2.

Thus France and Spain qualified for the final round, and it was played at Deauville on July 28, 29, and 30. France, with three of her "Musketeers" and P. Blanchy, won by three matches to two. R. Lacoste and Blanchy played the singles and H. Cochet and J. Brugnon the doubles. Spain, as in earlier rounds, had only Count de Gomar and E. Flaquer. The former again nobly did all he could to win the tie by beating Blanchy and, with Flaquer, beating Cochet and Brugnon in the doubles in a long, five-set match. He could not, however, beat young René Lacoste, who overcame him in four sets. Flaquer was nowhere near beating either of the Frenchmen in his two singles, and so France became the first winners of the new European Zone.

Detailed Results

Singles: R. LACOSTE (FR.) beat Count de Gomar (Sp.) 6–3, 6–4, 5–7, 6–4; beat E. Flaquer (Sp.) 6–1, 6–3, 6–2. P. BLANCHY (FR.) beat E. Flaquer (Sp.) 6–1, 6–2, 3–6, 6–1; lost to COUNT DE GOMAR (SP.) 3–6, 6–2, 2–6, 2–6.

Doubles: H. Cochet and J. Brugnon (Fr.) lost to COUNT DE GOMAR and E. FLAQUER (SP.) 4–6, 6–8, 13–11, 6–1, 4–6.

AMERICAN ZONE

This was a much smaller competition, with only four challenging nations—Japan, Canada, Australia, and Hawaii.

Japan played and defeated Canada by five to none at Montreal on July 26, 27, and 28. Each country employed a three-man team. W. Crocker and W. Le Roy Rennie played the singles for Canada, and J. Wright partnered Crocker in the doubles. The Japanese team was Z. Shimizu and M. Fukuda for the singles and Shimizu and S. Kashio for the doubles. Crocker put up a fight against Shimizu, winning the first set and pushing the second and fourth sets to advantage. The other four matches were all won by Japan in straight sets.

Detailed Results

Singles: Z. SHIMIZU (JAP.) beat W. Crocker (Can.) 3–6, 9–7, 6–1, 8–6; beat W. Le Roy Rennie (Can.) 6–2, 6–3, 6–0. M. FUKUDA (JAP.) beat W. Le Roy Rennie (Can.) 6–2, 6–1, 6–0; beat W. Crocker (Can.) 6–2, 6–3, 6–2.

Doubles: Z. SHIMIZU and S. KASHIO (JAP.) beat W. Crocker and J. Wright (Can.) 6–1, 6–2, 6–2.

Australia and Hawaii played their tie at Orange, New Jersey, on July 26, 27, and 28. As was to be expected, Australia were too strong for the Hawaiian team. They played J. O. Anderson and J. B. Hawkes in the singles and also the doubles. These two did not drop a set to the two-man team of their opponents, B. Detrick and W. N. Ecklund. The latter, however, scored a fairish win over R. E. Schlesinger, who substituted for Anderson on the third day ; and so the score to Australia was four to one.

Detailed Results

Singles: J. O. ANDERSON (AUSTRAL.) beat B. Detrick (Hawa.) 6–1, 6–3, 6–3. J. B. HAWKES (AUSTRAL.) beat B. Detrick (Hawa.) 6–3, 6–1, 6–1 ; beat W. N. Ecklund (Hawa.) 6–2, 6–1, 6–4. R. E. Schlesinger (Austral.) lost to W. N. ECKLUND (HAWA.) 4–6, 6–4, 1–6, 4–6.

Doubles: J. O. ANDERSON and J. B. HAWKES (AUSTRAL.) beat W. N. Ecklund and B. Detrick (Hawa.) 6–0, 8–6, 7–5.

The final match of this zone, between Australia and Japan, took place on August 9, 11, and 12 at Chicago, and was won by Australia's two-man team of J. O. Anderson and J. B. Hawkes by four matches to one. Japan used the same side that had beaten Canada in the previous round, but they were not nearly strong enough to worry the Australians, who almost made a clean sweep, as Hawkes led Z. Shimizu by two sets to one in the only match Australia lost. Anderson crushed Shimizu with the loss of only six games in three sets. He dropped a set to M. Fukuda, who was beaten by Hawkes setless. The Japanese took only five games in three sets in the doubles match.

Detailed Results

Singles: J. O. ANDERSON (AUSTRAL.) beat Z. Shimizu (Jap.) 6–0, 6–3, 6–3 ; beat M. Fukuda (Jap.) 6–1, 3–6, 6–2, 6–1. J. B. HAWKES (AUSTRAL.) beat M. Fukuda (Jap.) 6–3, 6–4, 6–3 ; lost to Z. SHIMIZU (JAP.) 4–6, 6–3, 6–2, 1–6, 4–6.

Doubles: J. O. ANDERSON and J. B. HAWKES (AUSTRAL.) beat Z. Shimizu and S. Kashio (Jap.) 6–1, 6–2, 6–2.

INTER-ZONE ROUND

The winners of the two zones, Australia and France, played off for the final right to challenge U.S.A. They met at Boston, U.S.A., on August 16, 17, and 18. Australia, with their J. O. Anderson–J. B. Hawkes team, had another four-to-one win, their third in succession, and, as against Hawaii, the match lost was lost by a substitute, I. McInnes, deputizing for Hawkes against R. Lacoste on the third day. Anderson beat both Lacoste and P. Hirsch, who deputized for J. Brugnon, in three sets. Hawkes beat Brugnon in three sets also, and the fourth single, between Lacoste and McInnes, was also a three-setter only, though this time going to France. The doubles match, between Anderson and Hawkes and Lacoste and Brugnon, was in absolute contrast to the rather one-sided singles. It was a tremendous five-set battle, won by the Australians in the sixteenth game of the fifth set. Thus Australia became challengers for 1923.

Detailed Results

Singles: J. O. ANDERSON (AUSTRAL.) beat R. Lacoste (Fr.) 7–5, 6–3, 6–4 ; beat P. Hirsch (Fr.) 7–5, 6–2, 6–0. J. B. HAWKES (AUSTRAL.) beat J. Brugnon (Fr.) 6–2, 6–1, 7–5. I. McInnes (Austral.) lost to R. LACOSTE (FR.) 2–6, 1–6, 2–6.

Doubles: J. O. ANDERSON and J. B. HAWKES (AUSTRAL.) beat J. Brugnon and R. Lacoste (Fr.) 6–8, 6–3, 6–3, 6–8, 9–7.

CHALLENGE ROUND

The challenge round, Australia versus U.S.A., was played at Forest Hills, New York, on August 31 and September 1 and 3. The holders retained the trophy by four matches to one. They played W. T. Tilden and W. M. Johnston in the singles and Tilden and R. N. Williams in the doubles. The challengers played J. O. Anderson and J. B. Hawkes for the singles and the doubles. Anderson was in great form, and lowered " Little Bill " Johnston's colours in five sets. This was

Johnston's first Davis Cup loss. (He had only three in the eight years he so worthily represented his country.) Anderson also won a set from Tilden, and carried the fourth set in their match to 7–5. The doubles was an enormous match: the first two sets, which were divided, totalled no less than fifty-six games. A further three sets—comprising only a meagre twenty-five games—were played before Tilden and Williams emerged as victors. Eighty-one games! This was the longest match so far in the competition. Hawkes, always a good man in doubles, was not strong enough as Australia's Number Two singles man to worry either Tilden or Johnston. He scored seven games against the former in three sets, and only three against Johnston, who was always ruthless in crushing opponents when he could, which was practically every time. It can be seen that the U.S.A. had a very firm grip on the cup with a very strong team.

Detailed Results

Singles: W. T. Tilden (U.S.A.) beat J. B. Hawkes (Austral.) 6–4, 6–2, 6–1; beat J. O. Anderson (Austral.) 6–2, 6–3, 1–6, 7–5. W. M. Johnston (U.S.A.) beat J. B. Hawkes (Austral.) 6–0, 6–2, 6–1; lost to J. O. Anderson (Austral.) 6–4, 2–6, 6–2, 5–7, 2–6.

Doubles: W. T. Tilden and R. N. Williams (U.S.A.) beat J. O. Anderson and J. B. Hawkes (Austral.) 17–15, 11–13, 2–6, 6–3, 6–2.

1924: U.S.A.

The number of challengers had now grown to twenty-one, fifteen of them in the European and the remaining six in the American Zone.

European Zone

Great Britain and Belgium led off by playing each other at Torquay on May 12, 13, and 14. Great Britain won a three–two victory. The tie was a replica of the meeting between these two countries the previous year in Brussels. The Belgian team was the same—J. Washer and A. G. Watson. For Great Britain A. R. F. Kingscote played the singles instead of R. Lycett, and L. A. Godfree had a new partner for the doubles in M. Woosnam. The other British singles man was J. B. Gilbert, who went one better than he had done against Washer a year earlier. This time he lost in five sets after a very close match, in which he had a lead of two sets to one. Washer had no difficulty with Kingscote in his other single, winning in three sets. Watson was again not able to win a set for Belgium in any of his three matches—not even the doubles, with Washer to help him.

Detailed Results

Singles: A. R. F. KINGSCOTE (G.B.) beat A. G. Watson (Belg.) 7–5, 6–2, 6–3 ; lost to J. WASHER (BELG.) 3–6, 3–6, 2–6. J. B. GILBERT (G.B.) beat A. G. Watson (Belg.) 6–4, 6–3, 6–1 ; lost to J. WASHER (BELG.) 3–6, 9–7, 6–2, 4–6, 6–8.

Doubles: M. WOOSNAM and L. A. GODFREE (G.B.) beat J. Washer and A. G. Watson (Belg.) 6–4, 8–6, 6–4.

In the second round France journeyed to Dublin, to play Ireland on May 31 and June 2 and 3, and won by five to nil, with J. Couitéas and R. Lacoste playing the singles and Lacoste and J. Brugnon the doubles. Ireland played E. D. McCrea and H. V. S. Dillon in the singles and Dillon and L. A. Meldon in the doubles. Both Irishmen took Couitéas to five sets, Dillon even leading him by two sets to love. Lacoste was a horse of another colour, however, and won all his matches, including the doubles, in three straight sets.

Detailed Results

Singles: J. COUITÉAS (FR.) beat E. D. McCrea (Ire.) 6–3, 8–6, 3–6, 4–6, 7–5 ; beat H. V. S. Dillon (Ire.) 4–6, 1–6, 6–2, 11–9, 6–2. R. LACOSTE (FR.) beat H. V. S. Dillon (Ire.) 6–1, 6–2, 6–2 ; beat E. D. McCrea (Ire.) 6–1, 6–3, 6–1.

Doubles: J. BRUGNON and R. LACOSTE (FR.) beat L. A. Meldon and H. V. S. Dillon (Ire.) 8–6, 6–1, 6–2.

India and the Netherlands met at Arnheim, in Holland, on May 30 and 31 and June 1, and the visitors scored a good win by four to one. S. M. Jacob and M. Sleem played the singles for India, and S. M. Hadi partnered Jacob in the doubles. C. J. van Lennep and H. Timmer were the Netherlands' two-man team. India won all the singles, Sleem being successful in three sets in both of his, but Jacob could only win in five sets each time. Van Lennep won the first set against him to love, and the second to three, and seemed assured of victory, but Jacob, a great sticker, got home at 9–7 in the fifth set. All his matches went the full distance, as he and Hadi lost the doubles after five sets.

Detailed Results

Singles: S. M. Jacob (Ind.) beat C. J. van Lennep (Neth.) 0–6, 3–6, 6–2, 7–5, 9–7 ; beat H. Timmer (Neth.) 3–6, 8–6, 6–3, 2–6, 6–1. M. Sleem (Ind.) beat H. Timmer (Neth.) 6–0, 6–2, 6–2 ; beat C. J. van Lennep (Neth.) 6–3, 6–3, 7–5.

Doubles: S. M. Hadi and S. M. Jacob (Ind.) lost to C. J. van Lennep and H. Timmer (Neth.) 4–6, 6–4, 6–3, 2–6, 4–6.

Great Britain played Spain in this round at Birmingham on May 31 and June 2 and 3, and reversed the result of their 1923 encounter at Manchester, winning by the same margin by which they had lost then—three to two. In the Spanish team M. Alonso was in place of Count de Gomar, while the other man was E. Flaquer, as a year earlier. The British were J. D. P. Wheatley and J. B. Gilbert for the singles and M. Woosnam and L. A. Godfree for the doubles. Alonso won both his singles—in five sets over Gilbert and four over Wheatley. Flaquer was again Spain's weak link: he could not win a match. J. M. Alonso substituted for him in his second singles, but was no more successful, winning only four games against Gilbert, all in the second set. Woosnam and Godfree beat M. Alonso and Flaquer in four sets.

Detailed Results

Singles: J. D. P. Wheatley (G.B.) beat E. Flaquer (Sp.) 6–3, 1–6, 8–6, 6–1 ; lost to M. Alonso (Sp.) 3–6, 7–9, 6–2, 4–6. J. B. Gilbert (G.B.) beat J. M. Alonso (Sp.) 6–0, 6–4, 6–0 ; lost to M. Alonso (Sp.) 2–6, 7–9, 6–3, 6–4, 4–6.

Doubles: M. Woosnam and L. A. Godfree (G.B.) beat M. Alonso and E. Flaquer (Sp.) 6–1, 6–4, 6–8, 6–2.

Denmark won a close tie against Hungary at Copenhagen on May 16, 17, and 18 by three to two, the result largely hinging on the doubles, an exciting struggle won by Denmark after five sets, four of which went to advantage games. Each country played a three-man team—for Denmark A. Petersen and E. Ulrich in the singles and Ulrich and Thalbitzer in the doubles, and for Hungary B. von Kehrling and I. de Takacs in the singles and von Kehrling and Peteri in the doubles. Von Kehrling was Hungary's strong man, and won both his singles in three sets. De Takacs was the opposite, however, and won only one set in his two matches.

Detailed Results

Singles: A. PETERSEN (DEN.) beat I. de Takacs (Hun.) 6–2, 6–3, 6–3 ; lost to B. VON KEHRLING (HUN.) 2–6, 4–6, 3–6. E. ULRICH (DEN.) beat I. de Takacs (Hun.) 6–0, 4–6, 6–2, 6–3 ; lost to B. VON KEHRLING (HUN.) 8–10, 0–6, 4–6.

Doubles: E. ULRICH and THALBITZER (DEN.) beat B. von Kehrling and Peteri (Hun.) 7–5, 7–5, 2–6, 5–7, 7–5.

Switzerland comfortably defeated Austria at Vienna on May 17, 18, and 19 by four to one. For the winners C. F. Aeschliman and C. Martin played the singles and Aeschliman and G. A. Sautter the doubles, a sound, experienced team. For Austria Count L. Salm and P. Brick played the singles and Counts L. and O. Salm the doubles. Aeschliman won both his singles in three sets, but Martin only just beat Brick in five sets, and lost to Count L. Salm in three sets. The Salms lost the doubles in four sets, after winning the first set.

Detailed Results

Singles: C. F. AESCHLIMAN (SWITZ.) beat P. Brick (Aus.) 6–2, 6–3, 6–3 ; beat Count L. Salm (Aus.) 7–5, 8–6, 7–5. C. MARTIN (SWITZ.) beat P. Brick (Aus.) 6–2, 3–6, 6–8, 7–5, 6–2 ; lost to COUNT L. SALM (AUS.) 6–8, 4–6, 2–6.

Doubles: C. F. AESCHLIMAN and G. A. SAUTTER (SWITZ.) beat Count L. Salm and Count O. Salm (Aus.) 2–6, 6–3, 6–4, 6–4.

Czechoslovakia were at home, in Prague, on May 23, 24, and 25, to New Zealand, challenging for the first time as a separate entity, with a veteran two-man team of F. M. B. Fisher and J. C. Peacock. The Czechs opposed them with F. von Röhrer and M. Zemla in the singles and Zemla and

J. Kozeluh in the doubles. Only four matches were played, and all won by the Czechs. Fisher performed well for New Zealand, taking von Röhrer to five sets in the only single he played, and with Peacock taking the doubles to the same number. Peacock was not so effective, and could not win a set in either of his singles.

Detailed Results

Singles: F. VON RÖHRER (CZECH.) beat F. M. B. Fisher (N.Z.) 3–6, 6–0, 6–4, 0–6, 6–4; beat J. C. Peacock (N.Z.) 6–2, 7–5, 6–3. M. ZEMLA (CZECH.) beat J. C. Peacock (N.Z.) 7–5, 6–4, 7–5.

Doubles: M. ZEMLA and J. KOZELUH (CZECH.) beat J. C. Peacock and F. M. B. Fisher (N.Z.) 4–6, 6–3, 6–8, 6–2, 7–5.

This brings us to the third round of the European Zone. Italy and South Africa have got through to it on defaults by Rumania and Argentina respectively.

France and India met in Paris on June 17 and 18, and France won the four matches played. Their team was R. Lacoste and H. Cochet for the singles and Cochet and J. Brugnon for the doubles. The French team was now settling down towards the formidable combination it was soon to become. India relied on M. Sleem and S. M. Jacob for the singles and A. H. Fyzee and S. M. Hadi for the doubles. Sleem fought gallantly against his young French opponents, taking Cochet to five sets and also winning a set from Lacoste. Jacob won a set from Cochet, but did not play Lacoste. The doubles went to France in three sets.

Detailed Results

Singles: R. LACOSTE (FR.) beat M. Sleem (Ind.) 4–6, 6–4, 6–2, 6–4. H. COCHET (FR.) beat S. M. Jacob (Ind.) 6–4, 4–6, 6–4, 6–2; beat M. Sleem (Ind.) 6–4, 0–6, 6–4, 2–6, 6–0.

Doubles: H. COCHET and J. BRUGNON (FR.) beat A. H. Fyzee and S. M. Hadi (Ind.) 6–1, 6–4, 7–5.

Great Britain and South Africa played at Scarborough on June 9, 10, and 11, and the home country won by four matches to one, the losers having to be content with winning the doubles only. In this match P. D. B. Spence and L. Raymond beat M. Woosnam and L. A. Godfree in three close sets. J. D. P. Wheatley beat Spence and I. Richardson, substitute for Raymond, in the singles without dropping a set. J. B. Gilbert, the other British singles string, had harder work. He only beat Raymond at 8–6 in the fifth set, and dropped the opening set in his match with Spence.

Detailed Results

Singles: J. D. P. WHEATLEY (G.B.) beat P. D. B. Spence (S.A.) 6–4, 6–3, 6–3 ; beat I. Richardson (S.A.) 6–3, 6–4, 6–4. J. B. GILBERT (G.B.) beat L. Raymond (S.A.) 6–1, 4–6, 6–2, 3–6, 8–6 ; beat P. D. B. Spence (S.A.) 4–6, 6–1, 6–1, 6–1.

Doubles: M. Woosnam and L. A. Godfree (G.B.) lost to P. D. B. SPENCE and L. RAYMOND (S.A.) 9–11, 5–7, 4–6.

Denmark and Italy met at Copenhagen on June 14, 15, and 16, and Denmark won by three to two. The Danes used three men—E. Tegner and A. Petersen for the singles and Tegner and E. Ulrich for the doubles. Italy used only two men—H. L. de Morpurgo and C. Colombo. The former, a most formidable player, just beginning his career, beat both Danes in the singles in straight sets, but Colombo offset this by losing both his singles. The Danes won the key match, the doubles, in four sets.

Detailed Results

Singles: E. TEGNER (DEN.) beat C. Colombo (It.) 6–0, 8–6, 3–6, 6–4 ; lost to H. L. DE MORPURGO (IT.) 3–6, 1–6, 3–6. A. PETERSEN (DEN.) beat C. Colombo (It.) 6–2, 6–3, 6–4 ; lost to H. L. DE MORPURGO (IT.) 5–7, 2–6, 2–6.

Doubles: E. TEGNER and E. ULRICH (DEN.) beat H. L. de Morpurgo and C. Colombo (It.) 7–5, 7–5, 4–6, 6–0.

Czechoslovakia played Switzerland in Prague on June 4, 5, and 6, and were too strong for the Swiss by four to one. Both countries played the same teams they had used in the second round. C. F. Aeschliman did his very best. He beat M. Zemla in five sets, and led F. von Röhrer two sets to love before succumbing in five sets. C. Martin was not able to hold either Czech in his singles, and the home team won the doubles against Aeschliman and G. A. Sautter easily in three sets.

Detailed Results

Singles: F. VON RÖHRER (CZECH.) beat C. Martin (Switz.) 2–6, 6–2, 6–3, 8–6 ; beat C. F. Aeschliman (Switz.) 2–6, 4–6, 7–5, 6–2, 6–4. M. ZEMLA (CZECH.) beat C. Martin (Switz.) 6–2, 6–2, 6–2; lost to C. F. AESCHLIMAN (SWITZ.) 3–6, 6–8, 6–4, 6–1, 1–6.

Doubles: M. ZEMLA and J. KOZELUH (CZECH.) beat C. F. Aeschliman and G. A. Sautter (Switz.) 6–2, 6–3, 6–2.

In the fourth, or semi-final, round of the European Zone France and Great Britain met at Eastbourne on July 26 and 29. France won with some difficulty by four to one. Great Britain brought A. R. F. Kingscote back into the team for the singles with J. B. Gilbert, and M. Woosnam and L. A. Godfree again played the doubles. France fielded the " Four Musketeers "—R. Lacoste and H. Cochet for the singles and J. Borotra and J. Brugnon for the doubles. This team in this order was to win the cup from U.S.A. three years later. Cochet had a lot of difficulty in his singles, losing to Gilbert in five sets, and only beating Kingscote in the same number. Lacoste beat Gilbert in three sets, but required five to dispose of Kingscote. Borotra and Brugnon won the doubles in four sets. The first two were divided, but then the Frenchmen drew away to win comfortably.

Detailed Results

Singles: H. COCHET (FR.) beat A. R. F. Kingscote (G.B.) 3–6, 6–4, 4–6, 6–3, 6–3 ; lost to J. B. GILBERT (G.B.) 7–5, 6–1, 7–9, 6–8, 2–6. R. LACOSTE (FR.) beat J. B. Gilbert (G.B.) 6–4, 7–5, 6–3 ; beat A. R. F. Kingscote (G.B.) 8–6, 3–6, 3–6, 6–2, 6–4.

Doubles: J. BOROTRA and J. BRUGNON (FR.) beat M. Woosnam and L. A. Godfree (G.B.) 6–4, 4–6, 6–3, 6–1.

The other semi-final tie, between Czechoslovakia and Denmark, was played at Copenhagen on July 25, 26, and 27, and Czechoslovakia won by three matches to two. The Czechs played M. Zemla and F. von Röhrer in the singles and Zemla and J. Kozeluh in the doubles. For Denmark A. Petersen and E. Worm played the singles, and the latter partnered E. Ulrich in the doubles. Each country won two singles. Zemla beat Petersen in three sets, but lost to Worm in four. Von Röhrer beat Worm in five sets and lost to Petersen in four. An unusual situation, as each of the four singles players won and lost a match. The Czechs won the doubles match easily.

Detailed Results

Singles: M. ZEMLA (CZECH.) beat A. Petersen (Den.) 6–2, 7–5, 7–5 ; lost to E. WORM (DEN.) 2–6, 6–3, 4–6, 8–10. F. VON RÖHRER (CZECH.) beat E. Worm (Den.) 6–4, 3–6, 3–6, 6–3, 10–8 ; lost to A. PETERSEN (DEN.) 6–3, 3–6, 5–7, 0–6.

Doubles: M. ZEMLA and J. KOZELUH (CZECH.) beat E. Worm and E. Ulrich (Den.) 6–1, 6–3, 6–1.

France and Czechoslovakia met in the European Zone final round on August 3, 4, and 5 at Evian-les-Bains. The home country played R. Lacoste and H. Cochet in the singles and Cochet and J. Brugnon in the doubles. P. Macenauer replaced F. von Röhrer in the Czech team. Otherwise it was as against Denmark. The Frenchmen were much too strong. Lacoste beat both M. Zemla and Macenauer in straight sets. Cochet beat Zemla easily enough, but was carried to five sets by Macenauer. He and Brugnon won the doubles in four sets, giving France a five–nil victory.

Detailed Results

Singles: R. LACOSTE (FR.) beat P. Macenauer (Czech.) 6–2, 10–8, 6–4 ; beat M. Zemla (Czech.) 6–3, 6–2, 6–2. H. COCHET (FR.) beat M. Zemla (Czech.) 6–1, 8–6, 6–4 ; beat P. Macenauer (Czech.) 6–4, 3–6, 7–5, 3–6, 6–2.

Doubles: H. COCHET and J. BRUGNON (FR.) beat M. Zemla and J. Kozeluh (Czech.) 7–5, 3–6, 6–4, 6–4.

AMERICAN ZONE

In the first round Canada opposed Cuba at Ottawa on July 24, 25, and 26. The Canadian team of J. Wright and

W. Crocker won by the odd match in five. The Cubans used four men—R. Paris and I. Zagas for the singles and V. Banet and Vellaba for the doubles. Banet substituted for Zagas in the second round of singles. Crocker won both his singles in three sets, while Wright lost both his in five sets. Canada took the doubles in three sets.

Detailed Results

Singles: J. Wright (Can.) lost to R. PARIS (CUBA) 8–10, 6–3, 6–2, 0–6, 3–6 ; lost to V. BANET (CUBA) 6–4, 4–6, 3–6, 6–3, 4–6. W. CROCKER (CAN.) beat I. Zagas (Cuba) 6–1, 6–2, 6–2 ; beat R. Paris (Cuba) 6–3, 7–5, 6–3.

Doubles: J. WRIGHT and W. CROCKER (CAN.) beat Vellaba and V. Banet (Cuba) 7–5, 7–5, 6–2.

The other first-round tie was between Australia and China, played in New York on August 1, 2, and 3. The Australians, a two-man team, consisting of G. L. Patterson and P. O'Hara Wood, scored the biggest win ever recorded in the Davis Cup competition. In five matches the Chinese took only fifteen games, an average of one per set. China were represented by P. Kong and W. Lock Wei in the singles and Lock Wei and C. K. Huang in the doubles.

Detailed Results

Singles: G. L. PATTERSON (AUSTRAL.) beat W. Lock Wei (Chin.) 6–1, 6–2, 6–2 ; beat P. Kong (Chin.) 6–0, 6–0, 6–2. P. O'HARA WOOD (AUSTRAL.) beat P. Kong (Chin.) 6–0, 6–1, 6–2 ; beat W. Lock Wei (Chin.) 6–0, 6–0, 6–2.

Doubles: G. L. PATTERSON and P. O'HARA WOOD (AUSTRAL.) beat W. Lock Wei and C. K. Huang (Chin.) 6–1, 6–2, 6–0.

Canada and Japan met in the second round at Montreal on August 7, 8, and 9, and Japan won the tie by four to one, winning all the singles and losing the doubles. For the winners Z. Shimizu and S. Okamoto played the singles, and T. Harada partnered Okamoto in the doubles. Canada relied on J. Wright and W. Crocker, as against Cuba. Crocker extended Shimizu to five sets, but this was the only match that went the full distance. As has been mentioned, Wright and Crocker won the doubles in three sets.

Detailed Results

Singles: S. Okamoto (Jap.) beat J. Wright (Can.) 8–6, 6–4, 7–5 ; beat W. Crocker (Can.) 6–2, 9–7, 4–6, 6–2. Z. Shimizu (Jap.) beat W. Crocker (Can.) 4–6, 7–5, 6–4, 0–6, 6–1 ; beat J. Wright (Can.) 4–6, 6–3, 6–4, 6–0.

Doubles: S. Okamoto and T. Harada (Jap.) lost to W. Crocker and J. Wright (Can.) 5–7, 4–6, 3–6.

Australia met Mexico at Baltimore on August 7, 8, and 9, and again G. L. Patterson and P. O'Hara Wood won five matches without losing a set. The Mexican team was M. Llano and I. de la Borbolla for the singles and de la Borbolla and F. Gerdes for the doubles, the latter substituting for Llano in the singles on the third day.

Detailed Results

Singles: G. L. Patterson (Austral.) beat M. Llano (Mex.) 6–0, 6–1, 6–2 ; beat I. de la Borbolla (Mex.) 6–2, 6–1, 6–1. P. O'Hara Wood (Austral.) beat I. de la Borbolla (Mex.) 6–3, 6–0, 9–7 ; beat F. Gerdes (Mex.) 6–1, 6–2, 6–1.

Doubles: G. L. Patterson and P. O'Hara Wood (Austral.) beat I. de la Borbolla and F. Gerdes (Mex.) 6–4, 6–4, 6–0.

These matches brought Australia and Japan to the zone final round, which was played at Providence, Rhode Island, on August 14, 15, and 16, when Australia won easily by five matches to love, only one match going beyond three sets. Japan used the same team as against Canada, but neither Z. Shimizu nor S. Okamoto was able to get a set from G. L. Patterson. Shimizu could not win one from O'Hara Wood either, but Okamoto did take the Australian to five sets. Patterson and O'Hara Wood won the doubles from Okamoto and T. Harada in three sets. Australia thus played three ties and won the American Zone with the loss of only two sets in fifteen matches. Certainly they could be called decisive winners, having won forty-five sets of the forty-seven they had played.

Detailed Results

Singles: G. L. PATTERSON (AUSTRAL.) beat Z. Shimizu (Jap.) 7–5, 11–9, 6–4 ; beat S. Okamoto (Jap.) 7–5, 6–1, 6–4. P. O'HARA WOOD (AUSTRAL.) beat S. Okamoto (Jap.) 6–4, 2–6, 6–4, 2–6, 6–1 ; beat Z. Shimizu (Jap.) 6–4, 6–4, 6–2.

Doubles: G. L. PATTERSON and P. O'HARA WOOD (AUSTRAL.) beat S. Okamoto and T. Harada (Jap.) 7–5, 6–2, 6–4.

INTER-ZONE ROUND

The inter-zone final, between Australia and France, was played at Boston on September 4, 5, and 6, and was a very close affair. France played R. Lacoste and J. Borotra in the singles and Lacoste and J. Brugnon in the doubles, and almost gained a vital two–love lead on the first day against the Patterson–O'Hara Wood Australian team. Lacoste led off by beating Patterson in three sets, and Borotra at one stage seemed certain of beating O'Hara Wood, when he won the first and third sets with the loss of only one game in each. O'Hara Wood rose to the occasion, however, and his resolute driving wore Borotra's net attack down, so that O'Hara Wood was able to take the fifth set at 6–2. Australia won the doubles in three sets, with something to spare, to lead two to one. On the third day Patterson, in devastating form, beat Borotra in three quick sets. In the last match Lacoste notched another win for France by quietly defeating O'Hara Wood in four sets.

Detailed Results

Singles: G. L. PATTERSON (AUSTRAL.) beat J. Borotra (Fr.) 6–3, 6–1, 6–3 ; lost to R. LACOSTE (FR.) 3–6, 2–6, 8–10. P. O'HARA WOOD (AUSTRAL.) beat J. Borotra (Fr.) 1–6, 6–4, 1–6, 6–4, 6–2 ; lost to R. LACOSTE (FR.) 10–8, 1–6, 1–6, 5–7.

Doubles: G. L. PATTERSON and P. O'HARA WOOD (AUSTRAL.) beat R. Lacoste and J. Brugnon (Fr.) 6–4, 6–4, 6–2.

CHALLENGE ROUND

The challenge round, between Australia and U.S.A., was played at Philadelphia on September 11, 12, and 13, and the holders' strength was emphasized by a five–nil win, with the loss of only one set. This year the defenders, for the only time during this long reign, varied their singles players by replacing W. M. Johnston with V. Richards. W. T. Tilden played in the singles and partnered Johnston in the doubles. The matches call for little comment: neither G. L. Patterson nor P. O'Hara Wood was able to extend Tilden or Richards, and all four singles went to U.S.A. in three sets. Patterson and O'Hara Wood won the first set of the doubles against Tilden and Johnston, but then fizzled out. U.S.A. had never won a challenge round with more decision, nor were they to again.

Detailed Results

Singles: W. T. Tilden (U.S.A.) beat G. L. Patterson (Austral.) 6–4, 6–2, 6–2; beat P. O'Hara Wood (Austral.) 6–2, 6–1, 6–1. V. Richards (U.S.A.) beat P. O'Hara Wood (Austral.) 6–3, 6–2, 6–4; beat G. L. Patterson (Austral.) 6–3, 7–5, 6–4.

Doubles: W. T. Tilden and W. M. Johnston (U.S.A.) beat G. L. Patterson and P. O'Hara Wood (Austral.) 5–7, 6–3, 6–4, 6–1.

1925: U.S.A.

This year the number of challengers increased by one in the European Zone, the American Zone remaining at six challengers.

European Zone

In the first round the Netherlands met Czechoslovakia at Noordwijk, Holland, on May 15, 16, and 18, and the Dutch won by three matches to two. The winners' team comprised H. Timmer and A. Diemer Kool for the singles and C. J. van Lennep and Diemer Kool for the doubles. The Czechs played P. Macenauer and J. Kozeluh in the singles and Kozeluh and M. Zemla in the doubles. Diemer Kool lost both his singles, but Timmer won both his, and the Dutch pair won the doubles, as often, the key match.

Detailed Results

Singles: A. Diemer Kool (Neth.) lost to P. MACENAUER (CZECH.) 6–3, 3–6, 2–6, 1–6 ; lost to J. KOZELUH (CZECH.) 6–3, 3–6, 6–3, 1–6, 1–6. H. TIMMER (NETH.) beat J. Kozeluh (Czech.) 6–3, 6–4, 6–2 ; beat P. Macenauer (Czech.) 6–1, 6–2, 6–2.

Doubles: C. J. VAN LENNEP and A. DIEMER KOOL (NETH.) beat M. Zemla and J. Kozeluh (Czech.) 6–3, 6–1, 8–6.

Sweden journeyed to Berne to play Switzerland on May 16, 17, and 18, and to gain a victory by three to two. Both countries relied on only two men—for Sweden S. Malmstrom and M. Wallenberg, and for Switzerland C. F. Aeschliman and C. Martin. Both the Swedes beat Martin easily, and Malmstrom also beat Aeschliman, who, however, beat Wallenberg and with Martin won the doubles match.

Detailed Results

Singles: S. MALMSTROM (Sw.) beat C. F. Aeschliman (Switz.) 6–3, 6–3, 7–9, 6–3 ; beat C. Martin (Switz.) 6–1, 6–2, 6–1. M. WALLENBERG (Sw.) beat C. Martin (Switz.) 6–1, 6–3, 6–3 ; lost to C. F. AESCHLIMAN (SWITZ.) 3–6, 3–6, 7–5, 4–6.

Doubles: M. Wallenberg and S. Malmstrom (Sw.) lost to C. F. AESCHLIMAN and C. MARTIN (SWITZ.) 6–3, 5–7, 5–7, 5–7.

India and Belgium met at Brussels on May 16, 17, and 18, when India scored a narrow three–two victory. For India S. M. Jacob and E. B. Andreae played the singles, while S. M. Hadi and Jagat Mohan Lal played the doubles. The Belgian side was the familiar J. Washer–A. G. Watson team for both the singles and the doubles. Watson was again not on the winning side in his singles, but he and Washer pulled off the doubles in five sets after being two down. Washer beat Andreae in three sets, but was beaten by Jacob in five, this being the vital match of the tie.

Detailed Results

Singles: S. M. JACOB (IND.) beat J. Washer (Belg.) 6–4, 4–6, 6–3, 5–7, 6–4 ; beat A. G. Watson (Belg.) 6–3, 6–1, 6–3. E. B. ANDREAE (IND.) beat A. G. Watson (Belg.) 6–0, 6–3, 6–0 ; lost to J. WASHER (BELG.) 5–7, 1–6, 1–6.

Doubles: S. M. Hadi and Jagat Mohan Lal (Ind.) lost to J. WASHER and A. G. WATSON (BELG.) 6–4, 6–2, 4–6, 5–7, 3–6.

Ireland journeyed to Vienna to play Austria on May 15, 16, and 17, and, although they lost the tie by the apparently conclusive margin of four to one, it was in fact a much closer affair, which could have been easily reversed. Austria relied on two men only—Count L. Salm and P. Brick. Ireland played L. A. Meldon and C. F. Scroope in the singles and C. F. and S. F. Scroope in the doubles. Salm performed the unusual and remarkable feat of winning both his singles after being down two sets. Brick beat Meldon, but received a walk-over from C. F. Scroope, who led him by two sets to love, and retired at the end of the third set, which Brick won at 7–5. The Scroopes won the doubles for Ireland's only success.

Detailed Results

Singles: COUNT L. SALM (AUS.) beat C. F. Scroope (Ire.) 0–6, 2–6, 6–3, 6–2, 6–3 ; beat L. A. Meldon (Ire.) 8–10, 4–6, 7–5, 8–6, 6–1. P. BRICK (AUS.) beat L. A. Meldon (Ire.) 6–4, 6–2, 6–4 ; beat C. F. Scroope (Ire.) 5–7, 1–6, 7–5, retired.

Doubles: Count L. Salm and P. Brick (Aus.) lost to S. F. SCROOPE and C. F. SCROOPE (IRE.) 1–6, 4–6, 6–0, 5–7.

France and Hungary played their tie at Budapest on May 8, 9, and 10, when the French team scored a four–one win. They played R. Lacoste and J. Borotra in both the singles and the doubles. B. von Kehrling and I. de Takacs played the singles for Hungary and von Kehrling and Kelemen the doubles. The Frenchmen had no difficulty in winning, despite von Kehrling's defeat of Borotra in four sets. P. Feret substituted in the singles for Lacoste on the third day, and easily beat de Takacs.

Detailed Results

Singles: J. BOROTRA (FR.) beat I. de Takacs (Hun.) 6–2, 6–2, 6–1 ; lost to B. VON KEHRLING (HUN.) 8–6, 1–6, 4–6, 2–6. R. LACOSTE (FR.) beat B. von Kehrling (Hun.) 6–3, 6–3, 6–3. P. FERET (FR.) beat I. de Takacs (Hun.) 6–1, 6–0, 6–2.

Doubles: J. Borotra and R. Lacoste (Fr.) beat B. von Kehrling and Kelemen (Hun.) 6–4, 6–2, 8–10, 6–3.

Italy beat Portugal at Lisbon on May 8, 9, and 10 by four to one. Their team was H. L. de Morpurgo and C. Serventi for the singles and de Morpurgo and P. Gaslini for the doubles. Portugal, entering for the first time, had as a team J. de Verda and A. Casanovas as the singles players, and F. de Vasconcellos to partner Casanovas in the doubles. De Morpurgo dominated the three matches in which he took part, and won them all with something to spare. Serventi, on the other hand, was unable to beat Casanovas, and received a default from de Verda when the score had reached two sets all in their match.

Detailed Results

Singles: C. Serventi (It.) beat J. de Verda (Port.) 5–7, 6–1, 8–6, 4–6, retired ; lost to A. Casanovas (Port.) 6–4, 4–6, 6–2, 4–6, 6–8. H. L. de Morpurgo (It.) beat A. Casanovas (Port.) 6–0, 6–1, 6–2 ; beat J. de Verda (Port.) 6–2, 6–1, 6–8, 6–2.

Doubles: H. L. de Morpurgo and P. Gaslini (It.) beat F. de Vasconcellos and A. Casanovas (Port.) 6–3, 6–1, 3–6, 9–7.

Denmark and Rumania met at Roehampton, London, on May 12, 13, and 14, and Denmark won quite easily by four to one. Their team was E. Worm and E. Ulrich for the singles and Ulrich and P. Henriksen for the doubles. For Rumania N. Mishu and Dr Luppu played the singles and the doubles. Mishu contrived to beat Worm in four sets, but all the other matches were won by the Danes in three sets.

Detailed Results

Singles: E. Worm (Den.) beat Dr Luppu (Rum.) 6–2, 6–2, 6–4 ; lost to N. Mishu (Rum.) 3–6, 3–6, 7–5, 3–6. E. Ulrich (Den.) beat N. Mishu (Rum.) 7–5, 6–1, 6–2 ; beat Dr Luppu (Rum.) 6–1, 6–2, 8–6.

Doubles: E. Ulrich and P. Henriksen (Den.) beat N. Mishu and Dr Luppu (Rum.) 7–5, 6–0, 6–1.

Great Britain visited Poland and played the tie at Warsaw on May 15, 16, and 17, winning a very hollow victory, with the loss of only sixteen games in five matches. The British singles players were F. G. Lowe and J. D. P. Wheatley, with C. H. Kingsley and L. A. Godfree as the doubles pair. Poland's team was M. Sjwede and M. Soerster for the singles and M. Kuchar and J. Steinart for the doubles. Lowe lost only two games in the six sets of his singles, and Wheatley only six.

Detailed Results

Singles: F. G. Lowe (G.B.) beat M. Sjwede (Pol.) 6–0, 6–0, 6–1; beat M. Soerster (Pol.) 6–0, 6–0, 6–1. J. D. P. Wheatley (G.B.) beat M. Sjwede (Pol.) 6–2, 6–0, 6–0; beat M. Soerster (Pol.) 6–1, 6–2, 6–1.

Doubles: C. H. Kingsley and L. A. Godfree (G.B.) beat M. Kuchar and J. Steinart (Pol.) 6–4, 6–2, 6–2.

Round two saw the Netherlands and Sweden playing at Noordwijk, Holland, on June 12, 13, and 14, when the home team won by five to nil. The Netherlands' team was the same as in the first round against Czechoslovakia. The Swedes relied on M. Wallenberg and C. E. von Braun only, but they were no match for the Dutchmen.

Detailed Results

Singles: H. Timmer (Neth.) beat C. E. von Braun (Sw.) 7–5, 6–1, 6–0; beat M. Wallenberg (Sw.) 6–1, 6–4, 6–2. A. Diemer Kool (Neth.) beat M. Wallenberg (Sw.) 6–2, 4–6, 6–3, 6–0; beat C. E. von Braun (Sw.) 8–6, 6–1, 6–2.

Doubles: C. J. van Lennep and A. Diemer Kool (Neth.) beat M. Wallenberg and C. E. von Braun (Sw.) 3–6, 6–1, 6–4, 9–7.

India played Austria at Vienna on June 12, 13, and 14, and won all four matches played in straight sets. India's team was S. M. Jacob and E. B. Andreae in the singles and Jagat Mohan Lal and A. H. Fyzee in the doubles. Austria were represented by Count L. Salm and P. Brick in the singles and by Salm and M. Relly in the doubles.

Detailed Results

Singles: S. M. Jacob (Ind.) beat P. Brick (Aus.) 8–6, 6–1, 6–1; beat Count L. Salm (Aus.) 6–4, 6–4, 7–5. E. B. Andreae (Ind.) beat Count L. Salm (Aus.) 6–4, 6–2, 8–6.

Doubles: JAGAT MOHAN LAL and A. H. FYZEE (IND.) beat Count L. Salm and M. Relly (Aus.) 6–0, 6–3, 6–1.

France were at home to Italy in Paris on June 12, 13, and 14, and beat the Italians by five to nil. The French team was R. Lacoste and J. Borotra in the singles and Lacoste and J. Brugnon in the doubles. For Italy there were H. L. de Morpurgo and C. Colombo only. P. Feret substituted for Lacoste on the last day, and won the only five-set match of the tie—against Colombo.

Detailed Results

Singles: R. LACOSTE (FR.) beat H. L. de Morpurgo (It.) 6–0, 6–2, 2–6, 6–2. J. BOROTRA (FR.) beat C. Colombo (It.) 6–4, 6–1, 6–1 ; beat H. L. de Morpurgo (It.) 6–1, 2–6, 12–10, 6–1. P. FERET (FR.) beat C. Colombo (It.) 8–6, 3–6, 1–6, 6–2, 6–3.

Doubles: R. LACOSTE and J. BRUGNON (FR.) beat H. L. de Morpurgo and C. Colombo (It.) 6–1, 6–1, 6–1.

Great Britain met Denmark in Copenhagen on May 27 and 28, and won all three matches played. The British team was J. B. Gilbert and J. D. P. Wheatley for the singles and C. H. Kingsley and L. A. Godfree for the doubles. The Danish singles men were A. Petersen and E. Ulrich, and the latter with E. Worm played the doubles. Both singles went to five sets, and in both the Danes led two sets to one. The doubles went to Great Britain in three sets.

Detailed Results

Singles: J. D. P. WHEATLEY (G.B.) beat A. Petersen (Den.) 4–6, 6–4, 1–6, 6–2, 6–2. J. B. GILBERT (G.B.) beat E. Ulrich (Den.) 6–1, 9–11, 3–6, 6–4, 6–2.

Doubles: C. H. KINGSLEY and L. A. GODFREE (G.B.) beat E. Ulrich and E. Worm (Den.) 7–5, 7–5, 6–2.

In the third, or semi-final, round the Netherlands played India at Noordwijk, Holland, on July 10, 11, and 12, the Dutchmen winning four to one. Their team was only a two-man one of C. J. van Lennep and A. Diemer Kool, H. Timmer having dropped out. India this time played Jagat Mohan Lal and A. H. Fyzee in the singles with S. M. Hadi to partner the latter in the doubles. Fyzee beat van Lennep in a long and fluctuating match, but this was India's only success.

Detailed Results

Singles: A. Diemer Kool (Neth.) beat Jagat Mohan Lal (Ind.) 3–6, 6–3, 6–4, 6–1 ; beat A. H. Fyzee (Ind.) 7–5, 6–1, 6–4. C. J. van Lennep (Neth.) beat Jagat Mohan Lal (Ind.) 6–2, 6–4, 7–5 ; lost to A. H. Fyzee (Ind.) 1–6, 4–6, 11–9, 6–3, 4–6.

Doubles: A. Diemer Kool and C. J. van Lennep (Neth.) beat A. H. Fyzee and S. M. Hadi (Ind.) 6–4, 6–2, 6–3.

In the other semi-final France played Great Britain at Eastbourne on July 11, 13, and 14, France winning all four matches played, with R. Lacoste and J. Borotra playing the singles and Lacoste and J. Brugnon the doubles. Great Britain fielded an altered team, with O. G. N. Turnbull and G. R. O. Crole-Rees as singles players and L. A. Godfree and J. D. P. Wheatley as doubles players. Turnbull won a set from Lacoste, and Crole-Rees one from Borotra, but that was all for Britain.

Detailed Results

Singles: R. Lacoste (Fr.) beat O. G. N. Turnbull (G.B.) 3–6, 6–1, 7–5, 6–2 ; beat G. R. O. Crole-Rees (G.B.) 6–2, 6–4, 6–2. J. Borotra (Fr.) beat G. R. O. Crole-Rees (G.B.) 6–4, 10–8, 4–6, 6–0.

Doubles: R. Lacoste and J. Brugnon (Fr.) beat L. A. Godfree and J. D. P. Wheatley (G.B.) 6–4, 6–4, 6–3.

France and the Netherlands were thus the finalists of the European Zone, and they played this final round at Noordwijk, Holland, on July 18, 19, and 20. Again only four matches were played, and all were won by France, whose team was the same as in the semi-final against Great Britain. H. Timmer returned to the Netherlands team, and C. J. van Lennep reverted to his rôle of doubles only. The other Netherlands singles man was, of course, A. Diemer Kool. Timmer won a set from R. Lacoste, and Diemer Kool and van Lennep won a set in the doubles from Lacoste and J. Brugnon. But France, later in this year to become the challenging nation for the first time, were never threatened. The only match they had lost in this zone was Borotra's single against von Kehrling in the first-round tie with Hungary. They were now a very strong team.

Detailed Results

Singles: R. LACOSTE (FR.) beat H. Timmer (Neth.) 5–7, 7–5, 6–2, 6–2 ; beat A. Diemer Kool (Neth.) 6–4, 6–4, 6–1. J. BOROTRA (FR.) beat A. Diemer Kool (Neth.) 6–2, 6–4, 10–8.

Doubles: R. LACOSTE and J. BRUGNON (FR.) beat A. Diemer Kool and C. J. van Lennep (Neth.) 6–2, 6–3, 6–8, 6–4.

AMERICAN ZONE

In the first round of this zone Spain opposed Cuba at Havana on July 4, 5, and 6. The older country won by five matches to nil. The Spanish team was M. Alonso and E. Flaquer for the singles and M. Alonso and J. M. Alonso for the doubles. The Cuban team was V. Banet and R. Paris in the singles and Paris and R. Chacon in the doubles. The Spaniards lost no sets, though two of the three in the doubles went to advantage games.

Detailed Results

Singles : M. ALONSO (SP.) beat V. Banet (Cu.) 6–4, 6–1, 6–1 ; beat R. Paris (Cu.) 6–1, 6–0, 6–3. E. FLAQUER (SP.) beat R. Paris (Cu.) 6–3, 6–3, 6–2 ; beat V. Banet (Cu.) 6–1, 6–0, 6–0.

Doubles: M. ALONSO and J. M. ALONSO (SP.) beat R. Paris and R. Chacon (Cu.) 8–6, 6–4, 8–6.

Spain played Mexico in the second round, at Mexico City, on July 17, 18, and 19, and again won by five matches to none. Their team was the same as against Cuba. The Mexican team was a two-man one, of C. Butlin and I. de la Borbolla. Butlin won a long first set against E. Flaquer, but all the other matches went to Spain in three sets only.

Detailed Results

Singles: M. ALONSO (SP.) beat C. Butlin (Mex.) 6–2, 6–1, 6–2 ; beat I. de la Borbolla (Mex.) 6–4, 6–4, 6–2. E. Flaquer (SP.) beat I. de la Borbolla (Mex.) 6–2, 6–4, 6–2 ; beat C. Butlin (Mex.) 10–12, 6–4, 6–1, 7–5.

Doubles: M. Alonso and J. M. Alonso (Sp.) beat I. de la Borbolla and C. Butlin (Mex.) 6–4, 6–2, 7–5.

In the third round Spain met Japan, who had received a walk-over from China, at Baltimore, on August 13, 14, and 15. Japan were just too good, winning an exciting encounter by the odd match. The winners had only two men, T. Harada and Z. Shimizu, while the Spanish team was as before. Harada won both his singles, and Shimizu lost both his. Together they managed to pull off the doubles against the brothers Alonso after five sets, in which the Spaniards squared the match after being two sets down.

Detailed Results

Singles: T. Harada (Jap.) beat E. Flaquer (Sp.) 6–2, 6–4, 6–0; beat M. Alonso (Sp.) 2–6, 6–4, 6–3, 6–4. Z. Shimizu (Jap.) lost to E. Flaquer (Sp.) 6–3, 0–6, 3–6, 4–6; lost to M. Alonso (Sp.) 5–7, 0–6, 6–3, 3–6.

Doubles: T. Harada and Z. Shimizu (Jap.) beat M. Alonso and J. M. Alonso (Sp.) 6–2, 6–3, 2–6, 8–10, 6–3.

Australia and Canada, having received second-round walk-overs from Hawaii and New Zealand respectively, met at Montreal on August 13, 14, and 15. Australia's team of G. L. Patterson and J. O. Anderson for the singles and Patterson and J. B. Hawkes for the doubles won this tie five to none. Canada used two men only—W. Crocker and J. Wright. Neither could do anything against Anderson, nor could they together against Patterson and Hawkes in the doubles, but Wright succeeded in winning the first two sets in his single against Patterson before going down to defeat. Crocker also pressed Patterson for three close sets.

Detailed Results

Singles: J. O. Anderson (Austral.) beat W. Crocker (Can.) 6–1, 6–3, 6–2; beat J. Wright (Can.) 6–2, 6–4, 6–1. G. L. Patterson (Austral.) beat J. Wright (Can.) 5–7, 3–6, 6–3, 6–1, 6–3; beat W. Crocker (Can.) 6–4, 11–9, 6–4.

Doubles: G. L. Patterson and J. B. Hawkes (Austral.) beat W. Crocker and J. Wright (Can.) 6–0, 6–2, 6–4.

Thus the American Zone finalists were Australia and Japan, who met in their play-off at Boston, U.S.A., on August 20, 21, and 22, when Australia proved the better team by four matches to one. Both countries fielded the same teams that they had used previously. G. L. Patterson easily beat Z. Shimizu, but could not hold T. Harada, who beat him in four sets. J. O. Anderson beat Harada in four sets, and Australia took the doubles in three sets. J. B. Hawkes, substituting for Anderson, beat M. Fukuda, substituting for Shimizu, in three quick sets.

Detailed Results

Singles: G. L. PATTERSON (AUSTRAL.) beat Z. Shimizu (Jap.) 6–1, 6–4, 6–2 ; lost to T. HARADA (JAP.) 2–6, 6–3, 1–6, 5–7. J. O. ANDERSON (AUSTRAL.) beat T. Harada (Jap.) 6–4, 3–6, 6–3, 6–1. J. B. HAWKES (AUSTRAL.) beat M. Fukuda (Jap.) 6–1, 6–3, 6–0.

Doubles: G. L. PATTERSON and J. B. HAWKES (AUSTRAL.) beat Z. Shimizu and T. Harada (Jap.) 6–1, 6–2, 9–7.

INTER-ZONE ROUND

France and Australia met in the inter-zone round at Forest Hills, New York, on September 4, 5, and 7. France won by three to one. They used only two men—R. Lacoste and J. Borotra—against Australia's three-man team which had beaten Canada and Japan. G. L. Patterson crushed Lacoste in the opening match, but Borotra squared the tie by beating J. O. Anderson also in straight sets. The doubles match was a long seesaw affair, which finally went to France in the eighteenth game of the final set. Borotra's defeat of Patterson in four sets on the third day sealed the tie, and the Anderson–Lacoste match was not played. France were thus challengers for the first time.

Detailed Results

Singles: R. Lacoste (Fr.) lost to G. L. PATTERSON (AUSTRAL.) 3–6, 4–6, 2–6. J. BOROTRA (FR.) beat J. O. Anderson (Austral.) 6–4, 6–3, 8–6 ; beat G. L. Patterson (Austral.) 4–6, 6–4, 6–1, 6–3.

Doubles: R. Lacoste and J. Borotra (Fr.) beat G. L. Patterson and J. B. Hawkes (Austral.) 6–4, 3–6, 6–4, 1–6, 10–8.

Challenge Round

The challenge round, between France and U.S.A., the holders, took place at Philadelphia on September 10, 11, and 12. The American team—W. T. Tilden and W. M. Johnston for the singles, with V. Richards and R. N. Williams for the doubles—was one of the strongest teams, if not *the* strongest team, ever to appear in the competition. France opposed this redoubtable side with R. Lacoste and J. Borotra only, and, although they did not win a match, these two young men both showed that they very soon would. Tilden had a very strenuous match with each. First of all, Borotra led him by two sets to one, and almost took the fourth set as well ; and then Lacoste, on the third day, held a lead against him of two sets and had match points in the third set. Johnston did not permit such liberties in his singles against these two. Lacoste snatched a set from him, but Borotra could score only five games in three sets against the great " Little Bill." Richards and Williams were good enough all the time to prevent Lacoste and Borotra winning a set in the doubles.

Detailed Results

Singles: W. T. Tilden (U.S.A.) beat J. Borotra (Fr.) 4–6, 6–0, 2–6, 9–7, 6–4 ; beat R. Lacoste (Fr.) 3–6, 10–12, 8–6, 7–5, 6–2. W. M. Johnston (U.S.A.) beat R. Lacoste (Fr.) 6–1, 6–1, 6–8, 6–3 ; beat J. Borotra (Fr.) 6–1, 6–4, 6–0.

Doubles: V. Richards and R. N. Williams (U.S.A.) beat R. Lacoste and J. Borotra (Fr.) 6–4, 6–4, 6–3.

1926 : U.S.A.

In this year there were twenty-three challengers, eighteen in the European Zone and five in the American Zone.

European Zone

Italy and Rumania were the first countries in action, and they played their tie in Bucharest on April 27, 28, and 29.

The Italians had an easy victory without losing a match. H. L. de Morpurgo and C. Serventi represented the winners and N. Mishu and A. San Galli represented Rumania. Italy won four matches in three sets, and the match between Mishu and Serventi was defaulted by the former in the fourth set, with the Italian ahead by two sets to one.

Detailed Results

Singles: H. L. de Morpurgo (It.) beat N. Mishu (Rum.) 6–2, 6–1, 6–3 ; beat A. San Galli (Rum.) 6–1, 6–1, 6–2. C. Serventi (It.) beat A. San Galli (Rum.) 6–2, 6–2, 6–1 ; beat N. Mishu (Rum.) 2–6, 6–3, 6–1, 0–1, retired.

Doubles: H. L. de Morpurgo and C. Serventi (It.) beat N. Mishu and A. San Galli (Rum.) 6–3, 6–3, 7–5.

The tie between South Africa and Portugal was the next to be played—at Sutton, near London, on April 30 and May 1 and 3. South Africa were represented by P. D. B. Spence and J. J. Lezard, and had a clear-cut four–one win. Portugal fielded three men—J. de Verda and A. Casanovas for the singles and F. de Vasconcellos as Verda's partner for the doubles. De Verda beat Lezard and won a set from Spence, but otherwise the South Africans were much superior.

Detailed Results

Singles: P. D. B. Spence (S.A.) beat A. Casanovas (Port.) 6–1, 6–1, 6–4 ; beat J. de Verda (Port.) 6–1, 2–6, 6–2, 6–2. J. J. Lezard (S.A.) beat A. Casanovas (Port.) 6–4, 6–1, 6–2 ; lost to J. de Verda (Port.) 3–6, 2–6, 1–6.

Doubles: P. D. B. Spence and J. J. Lezard (S.A.) beat J. de Verda and F. de Vasconcellos (Port.) 6–1, 6–4, 6–2.

The remaining first-round match was between the Netherlands and Belgium at Noordwijk, Holland, on May 7, 8, and 9, the Netherlands winning by three matches to two. The Dutch team of C. J. van Lennep and H. Timmer for the singles and van Lennep and A. Diemer Kool for the doubles was a better-balanced one than Belgium's—J. Washer and A. Laloux for the singles and Washer and G. François for the doubles. Washer won both his singles, and almost the doubles as well, which would have been a great single-handed triumph. Laloux was not the class of either Timmer or Lennep. The Belgian pair led two sets to none in the doubles, but the Netherlands pair hung on, and finally triumphed at 7–5 in the fifth set in this—as so often—key match.

Detailed Results

Singles: C. J. VAN LENNEP (NETH.) beat A. Laloux (Belg.) 6–0, 6–0, 6–2 ; lost to J. WASHER (BELG.) 6–4, 3–6, 6–8, 6–3, 2–6. H. TIMMER (NETH.) beat A. Laloux (Belg.) 6–1, 6–0, 6–1 ; lost to J. WASHER (BELG.) 1–6, 3–6, 5–7.

Doubles: C. J. VAN LENNEP and A. DIEMER KOOL (NETH.) beat J. Washer and G. François (Belg.) 0–6, 8–10, 6–3, 6–2, 7–5.

Argentina and Hungary met at Barcelona on May 16, 17, and 18. In this second-round tie Argentina won a victory which again emphasized how good one man must be if he is to win a tie on his own. Each country played a two-man team, B. von Kehrling and I. de Takacs for Hungary and W. Robson and E. M. Obarrio for Argentina. Von Kehrling won both his singles, but de Takacs lost his, and with von Kehrling also lost the doubles in three sets.

Detailed Results

Singles: W. ROBSON (ARGENT.) beat I. de Takacs (Hun.) 6–4, 6–1, 6–1 ; lost to B. VON KEHRLING (HUN.) 3–6, 6–3, 3–6, 2–6. E. M. OBARRIO (ARGENT.) beat I. de Takacs (Hun.) 6–0, 6–4, 6–0 ; lost to B. VON KEHRLING (HUN.) 3–6, 5–7, 4–6.

Doubles: E. M. OBARRIO and W. ROBSON (ARGENT.) beat B. von Kehrling and I. de Takacs (Hun.) 6–2, 6–4, 6–3.

Spain and Ireland met at Dublin on May 20, 21, and 22, and the visitors won a narrow victory by three matches to two. Ireland's team was E. A. McGuire and L. A. Meldon for the singles and Meldon and B. Haughton for the doubles. Spain had only two men—N. F. Sindreu and A. Juanico. The Irishmen won the doubles and Meldon's single against Juanico, and Spain the rest.

Detailed Results

Singles: N. F. SINDREU (SP.) beat E. A. McGuire (Ire.) 6–3, 6–2, 6–3 ; beat L. A. Meldon (Ire.) 6–1, 6–1, 6–2. A. JUANICO (SP.) beat E. A. McGuire (Ire.) 6–4, 7–5, 2–6, 6–4 ; lost to L. A. MELDON (IRE.) 1–6, 4–6, 4–6.

Doubles: N. F. Sindreu and A. Juanico (Sp.) lost to L. A. MELDON and B. HAUGHTON (IRE.) 4–6, 6–8, 3–6.

Great Britain and Poland played their tie at Harrogate on May 8, 10, and 11. The home team won easily by five to none and without losing a set. O. G. N. Turnbull and J. D. P. Wheatley played the singles for Great Britain and G. R. O. Crole-Rees and C. H. Kingsley the doubles. Poland's team was S. Czetwertynski and R. Kleinadel for the singles and the latter and J. Steinart for the doubles.

Detailed Results

Singles: O. G. N. TURNBULL (G.B.) beat R. Kleinadel (Pol.) 6–1, 7–5, 6–0 ; beat S. Czetwertynski (Pol.) 6–0, 6–2, 7–5. J. D. P. WHEATLEY (G.B.) beat S. Czetwertynski (Pol.) 6–4, 6–3, 6–4 ; beat R. Kleinadel (Pol.) 6–2, 6–4, 6–1.

Doubles: G. R. O. CROLE-REES and C. H. KINGSLEY (G.B.) beat J. Steinart and R. Kleinadel (Pol.) 7–5, 6–4, 6–3.

Italy and the Netherlands played at Rome on May 16, 17, and 18, and the home team won by the odd match. H. L. de Morpurgo and C. Serventi made up Italy's team, and for the Netherlands H. Timmer and C. J. van Lennep played the singles, and C. A. Bryan partnered Timmer in the doubles. De Morpurgo was strong enough to win all three matches in which he took part without dropping a set. But Serventi could only win with de Morpurgo's aid in the doubles, and he lost both his singles.

Detailed Results

Singles: H. L. DE MORPURGO (IT.) beat C. J. van Lennep (Neth.) 6–3, 6–3, 6–4 ; beat H. Timmer (Neth.) 6–4, 6–2, 6–3. C. Serventi (It.) lost to C. J. VAN LENNEP (NETH.) 3–6, 6–3, 1–6, 4–6 ; lost to H. TIMMER (NETH.) 4–6, 2–6, 4–6.

Doubles: H. L. DE MORPURGO and C. SERVENTI (IT.) beat C. A. Bryan and H. Timmer (Neth.) 6–3, 6–4, 6–3.

Sweden and Switzerland met at Malmö, Sweden, on May 11, 12, and 13. The Swedes, on their own court, were strong enough to win by three to two, both the matches they lost being five-setters. Both countries were represented by only two men—for Sweden M. Wallenberg and S. Malmstrom (as in this same match in Berne a year earlier) and for Switzerland C. F. Aeschliman and J. Wuarin, the latter in place of C. Martin. The story was much the same as in 1925. The Swiss won the doubles, and Aeschliman won one single, this time beating Malmstrom and losing to Wallenberg, thus reversing his previous year's effort.

Detailed Results

Singles: M. WALLENBERG (Sw.) beat C. F. Aeschliman (Switz.) 6–4, 4–6, 6–2, 6–1 ; beat J. Wuarin (Switz.) 4–6, 6–1, 6–1, 6–1. S. MALMSTROM (Sw.) beat J. Wuarin (Switz.) 6–4, 6–1, 6–2 ; lost to C. F. AESCHLIMAN (SWITZ.) 6–1, 2–6, 2–6, 6–4, 3–6.

Doubles: M. Wallenberg and S. Malmstrom (Sw.) lost to C. F. AESCHLIMAN and J. WUARIN (SWITZ.) 6–4, 2–6, 4–6, 6–4, 4–6.

France and Denmark played each other at Copenhagen on May 14, 15, and 16. The French team was naturally too strong, with three of the " Musketeers " playing, but the Danes, although they did not win a match, pushed three of them to five sets. R. Lacoste and H. Cochet were the French singles players and Cochet and J. Brugnon the doubles players. Brugnon substituted for Lacoste in the latter's second single. The Danish team was A. Petersen and E. Ulrich for the singles and Ulrich and P. Henriksen for the doubles. Petersen took Cochet to five sets, and Ulrich took Brugnon to the same number. The Danes also pressed the doubles to the full distance, leading two sets to one after three sets.

Detailed Results

Singles: R. LACOSTE (FR.) beat A. Petersen (Den.) 6–4, 7–5, 6–1. J. BRUGNON (FR.) beat E. Ulrich (Den.) 6–1, 6–2, 6–8, 3–6, 6–1. H. COCHET (FR.) beat A. Petersen (Den.) 3–6, 6–2, 3–6, 7–5, 6–4 ; beat E. Ulrich (Den.) 6–2, 6–3, 2–6, 6–2.

Doubles: H. COCHET and J. BRUGNON (FR.) beat E. Ulrich and P. Henriksen (Den.) 4–6, 6–3, 4–6, 7–5, 6–0.

The Czechoslovakia-versus-India match at Prague on May 14, 15, and 16 completed this round. The Czechs won with the loss of one match only. Their team was P. Macenauer and J. Kozeluh for the singles, and M. Zemla partnered the latter in the doubles. For India A. A. and A. H. Fyzee played the singles and A. H. Fyzee and S. W. Bobb the doubles. The lone Indian success was A. A. Fyzee's win over Macenauer in four sets.

Detailed Results

Singles: P. MACENAUER (CZECH.) beat A. H. Fyzee (Ind.) 6–2, 7–5, 5–7, 6–0 ; lost to A. A. FYZEE (IND.) 4–6, 6–4, 7–9, 0–6. J. KOZELUH (CZECH.) beat A. A. Fyzee (Ind.) 6–3, 6–2, 7–5 ; beat A. H. Fyzee (Ind.) 6–1, 6–3, 6–1.

Doubles: J. KOZELUH and M. ZEMLA (CZECH.) beat A. H. Fyzee and S. W. Bobb (Ind.) 6–2, 6–3, 6–1.

Spain and Argentina met in the third round, at Barcelona, on May 29, 30, and 31. Spain won three of the four matches played, but only just got home in two of them. E. Flaquer and N. F. Sindreu were Spain's singles players, and Flaquer and J. Morales their doubles pair. Argentina had their two-man team of W. Robson and E. M. Obarrio. Only three of the four singles were played, and all went to five sets. Obarrio lost both his, but Robson beat Sindreu. Spain claimed the doubles in three sets.

Detailed Results

Singles: E. FLAQUER (SP.) beat E. M. Obarrio (Argent.) 4–6, 5–7, 6–0, 6–0, 6–2. N. F. SINDREU (SP.) beat E. M. Obarrio (Argent.) 5–7, 6–1, 7–5, 4–6, 6–3 ; lost to W. ROBSON (ARGENT.) 6–4, 5–7, 7–5, 4–6, 2–6.

Doubles: E. FLAQUER and J. MORALES (SP.) beat E. M. Obarrio and W. Robson (Argent.) 6–4, 9–7, 6–3.

Great Britain played Italy at Rome on May 27, 28, and 29, and won a victory by three to two. Italy's two-man team of H. L. de Morpurgo and C. Serventi was too lop-sided to beat the better-balanced British team of four men—

O. G. N. Turnbull and J. D. P. Wheatley for the singles and G. R. O. Crole-Rees and C. H. Kingsley for the doubles. Great Britain's margin might have been wider, as Wheatley defaulted to de Morpurgo when leading in the third set with two sets up. Turnbull took de Morpurgo to five sets, and both Englishmen beat Serventi. Great Britain won the doubles in five sets from two sets down.

Detailed Results

Singles: J. D. P. Wheatley (G.B.) beat C. Serventi (It.) 5–7, 6–4, 6–1, 6–3 ; lost to H. L. de Morpurgo (It.) 6–2, 6–3, 3–2 (retired). O. G. N. Turnbull (G.B.) beat C. Serventi (It.) 3–6, 6–1, 6–1, 6–2 ; lost to H. L. de Morpurgo (It.) 6–4, 2–6, 6–4, 4–6, 2–6.

Doubles: G. R. O. Crole-Rees and C. H. Kingsley (G.B.) beat H. L. de Morpurgo and C. Serventi (It.) 3–6, 6–8, 6–4, 6–3, 6–3.

Sweden and South Africa played their tie at Kensington, London, on May 31 and June 1 and 3, and the South Africans were defeated by four to one. The Swedish team was S. Malmstrom and O. Garell for the singles and the doubles. South Africa had P. D. B. Spence and G. R. Sherwell for the singles and Spence and J. J. Lezard for the doubles. Spence's win over Garell was their only success, the Swedes winning all the other matches in straight sets.

Detailed Results

Singles: O. Garell (Sw.) beat G. R. Sherwell (S.A.) 6–4, 6–4, 6–1 ; lost to P. D. B. Spence (S.A.) 4–6, 4–6, 6–8. S. Malmstrom (Sw.) beat G. R. Sherwell (S.A.) 8–6, 6–3, 6–4 ; beat P. D. B. Spence (S.A.) 8–6, 6–3, 6–1.

Doubles: S. Malmstrom and O. Garell (Sw.) beat P. D. B. Spence and J. J. Lezard (S.A.) 6–2, 8–6, 8–6.

France and Czechoslovakia met at Prague on May 24 and 25. Only three matches were played, and all won by France. Their team was R. Lacoste and H. Cochet for the singles and Lacoste and J. Brugnon for the doubles. The Czechs had their usual team of J. Kozeluh and P. Macenauer for the singles and Kozeluh and M. Zemla for the doubles. Kozeluh extended Lacoste to five sets, but Macenauer went down to

Cochet in three. The doubles was a long, wavering battle, finally going to France at 7–5 in the fifth set.

Detailed Results

Singles: R. Lacoste (Fr.) beat J. Kozeluh (Czech.) 7–5, 5–7, 6–3, 6–8, 6–3. H. Cochet (Fr.) beat P. Macenauer (Czech.) 6–3, 6–4, 6–3.

Doubles: R. Lacoste and J. Brugnon (Fr.) beat J. Kozeluh and M. Zemla (Czech.) 6–2, 3–6, 6–8, 6–2, 7–5.

In the fourth, or semi-final, round Great Britain and Spain met at Barcelona on July 9, 10, and 11, and Great Britain won easily by four to one. The British team was J. C. Gregory and C. H. Kingsley for the singles and Kingsley and G. R. O. Crole-Rees for the doubles. Spain played E. Flaquer and N. F. Sindreu in the singles and Flaquer and J. Morales in the doubles. Kingsley had a long match with Sindreu before winning in the fifth set. H. K. Lester substituted for him on the third day against Morales, who substituted for Flaquer. Lester lost in three sets, giving Spain their only match.

Detailed Results

Singles: J. C. Gregory (G.B.) beat E. Flaquer (Sp.) 6–3, 6–0, 6–2 ; beat N. F. Sindreu (Sp.) 2–6, 6–4, 6–2, 6–3. C. H. Kingsley (G.B.) beat N. F. Sindreu (Sp.) 7–5, 2–6, 7–5, 3–6, 6–3. H. K. Lester (G.B.) lost to J. Morales (Sp.) 3–6, 2–6, 2–6.

Doubles: G. R. O. Crole-Rees and C. H. Kingsley (G.B.) beat E. Flaquer and J. Morales (Sp.) 11–9, 6–4, 6–2.

The French team journeyed to Stockholm to play Sweden on July 14, 15, and 16, and they won a clear-cut five–nil victory. J. Borotra had come into the team in place of R. Lacoste. He played in the singles and the doubles with J. Brugnon. H. Cochet was the other singles player. Sweden relied on their two-man team of S. Malmstrom and M. Wallenberg. Malmstrom played very well, and almost beat Borotra. He led the Frenchman two sets to love, and pushed him to advantage games in the third set, before going down. He also played a five-setter with Cochet. Wallenberg could win only one set in his singles—from Borotra. France took the doubles in three sets.

Detailed Results

Singles: H. Cochet (Fr.) beat M. Wallenberg (Sw.) 6–3, 6–3, 6–3; beat S. Malmstrom (Sw.) 6–3, 5–7, 6–4, 4–6, 6–3. J. Borotra (Fr.) beat S. Malmstrom (Sw.) 3–6, 2–6, 8–6, 6–3, 6–3; beat M. Wallenberg (Sw.) 6–8, 6–4, 6–2, 6–1.

Doubles: J. Borotra and J. Brugnon (Fr.) beat M. Wallenberg and S. Malmstrom (Sw.) 6–4, 6–1, 6–1.

Great Britain and France met in the European Zone final at Cabourg, in France, on July 24, 25, and 26. France again won without loss of a match, though only four matches were played. Their team was at full strength, with R. Lacoste and H. Cochet for the singles and J. Borotra and J. Brugnon for the doubles. Great Britain used J. C. Gregory and O. G. N. Turnbull for the singles and G. R. O. Crole-Rees and C. H. Kingsley for the doubles. Lacoste beat Turnbull in three sets, but Cochet had to go to five to dispose of Gregory, who led him two sets to one. In the only other single played Brugnon, substituting for Cochet, beat Turnbull after losing the first two sets. France romped away with the doubles in three sets. They thus won the European Zone without losing a single match.

Detailed Results

Singles: R. Lacoste (Fr.) beat O. G. N. Turnbull (G.B.) 6–4, 6–4, 6–4. H. Cochet (Fr.) beat J. C. Gregory (G.B.) 7–5, 4–6, 7–9, 7–5, 6–0. J. Brugnon (Fr.) beat O. G. N. Turnbull (G.B.) 4-6, 1–6, 6–2, 6–4, 6–0.

Doubles: J. Borotra and J. Brugnon (Fr.) beat C. H. Kingsley and G. R. O. Crole-Rees (G.B.) 6–1, 6–0, 6–3.

American Zone

There was only one match in the first round, between Japan and Mexico, played at Mexico City on June 11, 12, and 13, and won by Japan by four to one with their three-man team of T. Harada and T. Toba for the singles and Harada and T. Tawara for the doubles. Mexico played A. Unda and M. Llano in the singles and Llano and C. Butlin in the doubles. On the third day Tawara substituted for Harada, and Butlin and Lozano substituted for Unda and Llano respectively. Butlin won Mexico's only match when he beat Toba in three sets.

Detailed Results

Singles: T. Harada (Jap.) beat A. Unda (Mex.) 6–2, 6–4, 6–2 ; T. Toba (Jap.) beat M. Llano (Mex.) 6–1, 3–6, 7–5, 6–2 ; lost to C. Butlin (Mex.) 2–6, 3–6, 1–6. T. Tawara (Jap.) beat Lozano (Mex.) 6–1, 6–3, 6–4.

Doubles: T. Harada and T. Tawara (Jap.) beat C. Butlin and M. Llano (Mex.) 6–0, 9–7, 6–4.

Japan's next match was against Philippine Islands at San Francisco on June 25, 26, and 27. F. and G. Aragon made up the Philippine team, and T. Harada and T. Tawara did all the work for Japan, and won all the matches in the tie. F. Aragon took Tawara to five sets, and with G. Aragon took the Japanese to five sets also in the doubles.

Detailed Results

Singles: T. Harada (Jap.) beat F. Aragon (Phil.) 6–0, 6–4, 6–3 ; beat G. Aragon (Phil.) 6–2, 6–3, 7–5. T. Tawara (Jap.) beat G. Aragon (Phil.) 8–6, 6–1, 8–6 ; beat F. Aragon (Phil.) 6–2, 8–6, 4–6, 1–6, 7–5.

Doubles: T. Harada and T. Tawara (Jap.) beat G. Aragon and F. Aragon (Phil.) 6–3, 1–6, 5–7, 6–2, 6–2.

The other match in this round was between Cuba and Canada and played at Havana, Cuba, on July 16, 17, and 18. Cuba won a narrow victory by three matches to two. Their team was V. Banet and R. Paris in the singles and Paris and R. Chacon in the doubles. Canada played J. Wright and W. Crocker in both singles and doubles. Paris was the hero of the match for Cuba. He beat Crocker in three sets and Wright in five, being two sets to one down to the latter. In the doubles Paris and Chacon squeezed home in another five-set match after being down two to one. They only won the fourth set at 8–6. Banet was unable to win a set for Cuba in his singles against either Canadian, so it was undoubtedly Paris's tie.

Detailed Results

Singles: V. Banet (Cu.) lost to J. Wright (Can.) 4–6, 5–7, 2–6 ; lost to W. Crocker (Can.) 4–6, 4–6, 1–6. R. Paris (Cu.) beat W. Crocker (Can.) 6–4, 6–2, 6–4 ; beat J. Wright (Can.) 2–6, 6–4, 2–6, 6–3, 6–4.

Doubles: R. Paris and R. Chacon (Cu.) beat J. Wright and W. Crocker (Can.) 8–6, 3–6, 6–8, 8–6, 6–2.

Japan and Cuba met in the American Zone final round at Montreal on August 19, 20, and 21. Japan's two men, T. Harada and T. Tawara, beat the Cuban team, the same one which had beaten Canada, by five matches to none, without loss of a set.

Detailed Results

Singles: T. HARADA (JAP.) beat R. Paris (Cu.) 7–5, 6–0, 6–3; beat V. Banet (Cu.) 6–2, 6–2, 6–3. T. TAWARA (JAP.) beat V. Banet (Cu.) 9–7, 6–1, 6–2; beat R. Paris (Cu.) 6–2, 6–0, 6–2.

Doubles: T. HARADA and T. TAWARA (JAP.) beat R. Paris and R. Chacon (Cu.) 6–4, 6–3, 6–2.

INTER-ZONE ROUND

France, European Zone winners, met Japan, American Zone winners, at Forest Hills, New York, on August 26, 27, and 28. France won by three to two, but almost let the tie slip through their fingers. They were in danger of being two down on the first day, when T. Harada beat R. Lacoste and T. Tawara led H. Cochet by two sets to love. The latter saved the third set at 7–5, and went on to win the next two sets in comparative comfort. He and J. Brugnon beat Harada and Tawara in the doubles with the loss of only two games. Lacoste beat Tawara easily on the third day, but Harada won his second single against Cochet in four sets, showing fine form. This put France into the challenge round for the second time.

Detailed Results

Singles: R. LACOSTE (FR.) beat T. Tawara (Jap.) 6–1, 6–3, 6–2; lost to T. HARADA (JAP.) 4–6, 6–4, 3–6, 7–9. H. COCHET (FR.) beat T. Tawara (Jap.) 1–6, 4–6, 7–5, 6–3, 6–2; lost to T. HARADA (JAP.) 1–6, 3–6, 6–0, 4–6.

Doubles: H. COCHET and J. BRUGNON (FR.) beat T. Harada and T. Tawara (Jap.) 6–0, 6–0, 6–2.

CHALLENGE ROUND

This final tie, between France, challengers, and the holders, U.S.A., was played at Philadelphia on September 9, 10, and 11. France went one better than in 1925 and lost only by four matches to one. U.S.A. played the same defending team as in the previous year—W. T. Tilden and W. M. Johnston for the singles and R. N. Williams and V. Richards for the doubles. The challenging team was R. Lacoste and J. Borotra for the singles and H. Cochet and J. Brugnon for the doubles. Johnston overpowered both Frenchmen, with the loss of one set—to Lacoste. Tilden beat Borotra easily, but was forced to bow to Lacoste in four sets—a great triumph for the young Frenchman, who had come so near to beating the great " Big Bill " a year earlier. Richards and Williams made short work of the doubles for U.S.A. Few people, after this result, would have expected that France would win the following year. Their team, however, was an improving one in every respect. The American team was just the opposite: they had reached, or even passed, their peak. These two factors were enough in the year to come to give France her first possession of the cup, the beginning of an illustrious six-year reign.

Detailed Results

Singles: W. M. JOHNSTON (U.S.A.) beat R. Lacoste (Fr.) 6–0, 6–4, 0–6, 6–0; beat J. Borotra (Fr.) 8–6, 6–4, 9–7. W. T. TILDEN (U.S.A.) beat J. Borotra (Fr.) 6–2, 6–3, 6–3; lost to R. LACOSTE (FR.) 6–4, 4–6, 6–8, 6–8.

Doubles: R. N. WILLIAMS and V. RICHARDS (U.S.A.) beat H. Cochet and J. Brugnon (Fr.) 6–4, 6–4, 6–2.

1927: FRANCE

The competition grew still larger in this year, there being twenty-five actual challengers, twenty-one in the European Zone and four in the American Zone.

EUROPEAN ZONE

India and Spain met in the first round, at Barcelona, on May 7, 8, and 9, when India won by the odd match in five. For India K. Prasada and A. H. Fyzee played all matches, and for Spain E. Flaquer and A. Juanico played the singles and Flaquer and J. Morales the doubles. Fyzee lost his two singles, but Prasada was too strong for both the Spaniards, and he and Fyzee also won the doubles.

Detailed Results

Singles: K. PRASADA (IND.) beat E. Flaquer (Sp.) 6–2, 6–2, 6–3 ; beat A. Juanico (Sp.) 11–9, 6–4, 6–3. A. H. Fyzee (Ind.) lost to E. FLAQUER (SP.) 5–7, 0–6, 2–6 ; lost to A. JUANICO (SP.) 6–3, 3–6, 6–3, 4–6, 1–6.

Doubles: K. PRASADA and A. H. FYZEE (IND.) beat E. Flaquer and J. Morales (Sp.) 0–6, 6–3, 6–3, 6–3.

Great Britain played Sweden at Birmingham on May 6, 7, and 9, and the home team won by four matches to one. Their team was E. Higgs and C. H. Kingsley for the singles and L. A. Godfree and J. C. Gregory for the doubles. The Swedes were O. Garell and S. Malmstrom for the singles and Malmstrom and H. Müller for the doubles. Malmstrom scored Sweden's only success when he beat Kingsley in three sets. Higgs beat him in five.

Detailed Results

Singles: C. H. KINGSLEY (G.B.) beat O. Garell (Sw.) 6–2, 6–1, 7–5 ; lost to S. MALMSTROM (SW.) 4–6, 2–6, 3–6. E. HIGGS (G.B.) beat S. Malmstrom (Sw.) 3–6, 6–3, 6–0, 3–6, 6–2 ; beat O. Garell (Sw.) 8–6, 8–6, 3–6, 9–7.

Doubles: L. A. GODFREE and J. C. GREGORY (G.B.) beat S. Malmstrom and H. Müller (Sw.) 4–6, 6–3, 6–1, 6–1.

Denmark and the Netherlands played their tie at Harrogate on May 19, 20, and 21. Denmark won by four to one. Their team was E. Ulrich and A. Petersen for the singles and Ulrich and P. Henriksen for the doubles. The Netherlands were represented by H. Timmer and C. A. Bryan in the singles and Timmer and C. J. van Lennep for the doubles. Timmer scored the Netherlands' only win by beating Petersen in four sets. Bryan took the same player to five sets before losing.

Detailed Results

Singles: E. ULRICH (DEN.) beat H. Timmer (Neth.) 6–0, 1–6, 6–4, 7–5 ; beat C. A. Bryan (Neth.) 6–1, 6–3, 6–0. A. PETERSEN (DEN.) beat C. A. Bryan (Neth.) 6–2, 6–1, 1–6, 3–6, 6–1 ; lost to H. TIMMER (NETH.) 3–6, 4–6, 6–4, 6–8.

Doubles: P. HENRIKSEN and E. ULRICH (DEN.) beat H. Timmer and C. J. van Lennep (Neth.) 6–1, 3–6, 6–3, 6–4.

Switzerland and Austria met at Bâle on April 29 and 30 and May 1. The home team won by three to two. The Swiss team of C. F. Aeschliman and J. Wuarin for the singles and Aeschliman and M. Ferrier for the doubles was too strong for the Austrian three-man team of F. Matejka and H. W. Artens for the singles and Artens and Count L. Salm for the doubles, and won the first three matches. The Austrians won both singles on the third day, when the Swiss eased the pressure.

Detailed Results

Singles: C. F. AESCHLIMAN (SWITZ.) beat F. Matejka (Aus.) 4–6, 6–1, 6–1, 6–3; lost to H. W. ARTENS (AUS.) 5–7, 1–6, 2–6. J. WUARIN (SWITZ.) beat H. W. Artens (Aus.) 6–1, 6–0, 6–4; lost to F. MATEJKA (AUS.) 3–6, 2–6, 4–6.

Doubles: C. F. AESCHLIMAN and M. FERRIER (SWITZ.) beat Count L. Salm and H. W. Artens (Aus.) 10–8, 6–4, 7–9, 6–2.

The remaining first-round match, between Ireland and South Africa, was played at Dublin on May 6, 7, and 9, when South Africa swept the board for a five–nothing win. For the winners P. D. B. Spence and J. Condon played the singles, and L. Raymond partnered Condon for the doubles. For Ireland the Hon. C. Campbell and A. St J. Mahony were the singles players and Mahony and L. A. Meldon the doubles pair. Campbell won the first two sets against Condon, and Meldon, substituting for Campbell on the third day, won the third and fourth sets against Spence. South Africa took all the other matches in three straight sets.

Detailed Results

Singles: J. CONDON (S.A.) beat Hon. C. Campbell (Ire.) 3–6, 2–6, 6–3, 6–3, 6–4; beat A. St J. Mahony (Ire.) 6–0, 8–6, 6–1. P. D. B. SPENCE (S.A.) beat A. St J. Mahony (Ire.) 6–2, 6–3, 8–6; beat L. A. Meldon (Ire.) 6–3, 6–1, 4–6, 3–6, 6–4.

Doubles: L. RAYMOND and J. CONDON (S.A.) beat L. A. Meldon and A. St J. Mahony (Ire.) 6–3, 6–2, 7–5.

Czechoslovakia and Greece met in the second round, at Prague, on May 6, 7, and 8. The result was four to one for the Czechs. Their team was J. Kozeluh and M. Gottlieb in the singles and Kozeluh and M. Zemla for the doubles. F. Soyka substituted for Gottlieb on the third day. Greece relied on two men—A. J. Zerlendi and M. Zachos. The former beat Gottlieb in five sets, but the Czechs lost no sets in the other four matches.

Detailed Results

Singles: J. KOZELUH (CZECH.) beat M. Zachos (Gr.) 6–0, 6–1, 6–1 ; beat A. J. Zerlendi (Gr.) 6–2, 6–2, 6–2. M. Gottlieb (Czech.) lost to A. J. ZERLENDI (GR.) 5–7, 7–5, 6–4, 7–9, 2–6. F. SOYKA (CZECH.) beat M. Zachos (Gr.) 6–4, 6–3, 6–2.

Doubles: J. KOZELUH and M. ZEMLA (CZECH.) beat A. J. Zerlendi and M. Zachos (Gr.) 6–2, 6–3, 6–4.

Belgium and Poland played each other at Brussels on May 20, 21, and 22, when Belgium won easily by five to none. Their team was J. Washer and H. W. Botsford for both singles and doubles. The Polish singles players were R. Kleinadel and S. Czetwertynski, with M. Stolarow partnering Kleinadel in the doubles. It was almost a hollow victory for Belgium.

Detailed Results

Singles: J. WASHER (BELG.) beat S. Czetwertynski (Pol.) 6–2, 6–2, 6–2 ; beat R. Kleinadel (Pol.) 6–0, 6–0, 6–1. H. W. BOTSFORD (BELG.) beat R. Kleinadel (Pol.) 6–3, 9–7, 6–2 ; beat S. Czetwertynski (Pol.) 6–2, 7–5, 4–6, 6–2.

Doubles: J. WASHER and H. W. BOTSFORD (BELG.) beat R. Kleinadel and M. Stolarow (Pol.) 8–6, 9–7, 6–1.

India visited Zagreb to play Yugoslavia on May 20, 21, and 22, and won in straight sets the only three matches played. Each side used but two players—India K. Prasada and A. H. Fyzee, and Yugoslavia D. Balas and G. Dungyersky.

Detailed Results

Singles: K. PRASADA (IND.) beat G. Dungyersky (Yugo.) 6–2, 7–5, 6–2. A. H. FYZEE (IND.) beat D. Balas (Yugo.) 6–4, 6–2, 6–1.

Doubles: K. PRASADA and A. H. FYZEE (IND.) beat G. Dungyersky and D. Balas (Yugo.) 6–1, 6–2, 6–4.

Denmark played Great Britain at Harrogate on May 19, 20, and 21, and scored a narrow three–two win. For Great Britain J. C. Gregory and E. Higgs played the singles and Gregory and L. A. Godfree the doubles. The Danes used two men only—E. Ulrich and E. Worm. Ulrich was the Danish hero. He won both his singles in five sets—the one against Higgs from two sets down, against Gregory from two sets up—and he and Worm won the doubles in four sets.

Detailed Results

Singles: E. ULRICH (DEN.) beat J. C. Gregory (G.B.) 6–0, 6–3, 3–6, 3–6, 6–2 ; beat E. Higgs (G.B.) 1–6, 3–6, 6–2, 6–2, 6–4. E. Worm (Den.) lost to J. C. GREGORY (G.B.) 8–6, 4–6, 8–10, 4–6 ; lost to E. HIGGS (G.B.) 3–6, 4–6, 10–8, 8–10.

Doubles: E. ULRICH and E. WORM (DEN.) beat L. A. Godfree and J. C. Gregory (G.B.) 6–4, 1–6, 6–2, 7–5.

South Africa were too strong for Switzerland at Montreux on May 20, 21, and 22 by a five–nothing margin. The winners' team was J. Condon and P. D. B. Spence in the singles and Spence and L. Raymond in the doubles. Switzerland relied on C. F. Aeschliman and J. Wuarin in the singles and Aeschliman and M. Ferrier in the doubles. Wuarin won Switzerland's only set—against Condon on the first day.

Detailed Results

Singles: J. CONDON (S.A.) beat J. Wuarin (Switz.) 6–0, 6–2, 2–6, 9–7 ; beat C. F. Aeschliman (Switz.) 6–4, 6–4, 6–2. P. D. B. SPENCE (S.A.) beat C. F. Aeschliman (Switz.) 6–4, 6–4, 9–7 ; beat J. Wuarin (Switz.) 6–1, 8–6, 6–2.

Doubles: P. D. B. SPENCE and L. RAYMOND (S.A.) beat M. Ferrier and C. F. Aeschliman (Switz.) 6–2, 9–7, 6–4.

Germany went to Lisbon to play Portugal on May 13, 14, and 15, and won a comfortable victory by five to none. The German team consisted of G. Demasius and H. Moldenhauer for both singles and doubles, while J. de Verda and A. Casanovas were the only two Portuguese players. F. W. Rahe substituted for Demasius on the third day. De Verda took Moldenhauer to five sets in the only long match.

Detailed Results

Singles: G. Demasius (Ger.) beat J. de Verda (Port.) 4–6, 6–0, 6–3, 6–3 ; F. W. Rahe (Ger.) beat A. Casanovas (Port.) 6–4, 6–4, 1–6, 6–3. H. Moldenhauer (Ger.) beat J. de Verda (Port.) 6–8, 6–3, 5–7, 6–2, 6–1 ; beat A. Casanovas (Port.) 6–2, 6–2, 6–4.

Doubles: G. Demasius and H. Moldenhauer (Ger.) beat J. de Verda and A. Casanovas (Port.) 6–4, 4–6, 6–1, 6–2.

Italy played Hungary at Budapest on May 13, 14, and 15, and squeezed home by the odd match with their two-man team of H. L. de Morpurgo and G. de Stefani. Hungary played B. von Kehrling and I. de Takacs in the singles, von Kehrling and Dr Peteri in the doubles. De Morpurgo won both his singles, though he had difficulty in subduing von Kehrling. De Stefani lost both his, even though he led de Takacs two sets to love. The Italians won the doubles.

Detailed Results

Singles: H. L. de Morpurgo (It.) beat B. von Kehrling (Hun.) 5–7, 6–4, 6–4, 5–7, 6–1 ; beat I. de Takacs (Hun.) 6–2, 6–1, 7–5. G. de Stefani (It.) lost to I. de Takacs (Hun.) 6–2, 6–1, 4–6, 3–6, 4–6 ; lost to B. von Kehrling (Hun.) 2–6, 1–6, 4–6.

Doubles: H. L. de Morpurgo and G. de Stefani (It.) beat B. von Kehrling and Dr Peteri (Hun.) 6–3, 7–5, 8–6.

France beat Rumania in Paris on May 13, 14, and 15, with the loss of one set in five matches. The French team was J. Borotra and R. Lacoste for the singles and Borotra and J. Brugnon for the doubles. Brugnon substituted for Lacoste in the singles on the last day. Rumania used two men only—N. Mishu and G. Poulieff—but they were not in the class.

Detailed Results

Singles: J. Borotra (Fr.) beat G. Poulieff (Rum.) 6–1, 6–2, 6–2 ; beat N. Mishu (Rum.) 6–4, 2–6, 6–4, 7–5. R. Lacoste (Fr.) beat N. Mishu (Rum.) 6–3, 6–2, 6–2. J. Brugnon (Fr.) beat G. Poulieff (Rum.) 6–1, 6–1, 6–0.

Doubles: J. Borotra and J. Brugnon (Fr.) beat N. Mishu and G. Poulieff (Rum.) 6–4, 6–1, 8–6.

In the third round South Africa met Germany in Berlin on June 10, 11, and 12, The South Africans won by four to one. They used L. Raymond and P. D. B. Spence for both singles and doubles, though J. Condon substituted for Raymond on the third day. The Germans were H. Landmann and O. Froitzheim for the singles and Landmann and H. Kleinschroth for the doubles, with H. Moldenhauer substituting for Froitzheim on the third day, and winning Germany's only point by beating Condon in five sets. Spence had to go to five sets in both his singles, just beating the veteran Froitzheim on the post.

Detailed Results

Singles: L. RAYMOND (S.A.) beat H. Landmann (Ger.) 7–5, 8–6, 6–2. J. Condon (S.A.) lost to H. MOLDENHAUER (GER.) 6–4, 3–6, 3–6, 6–3, 4–6. P. D. B. SPENCE (S.A.) beat O. Froitzheim (Ger.) 2–6, 6–4, 6–3, 4–6, 7–5 ; beat H. Landmann (Ger.) 6–3, 6–8, 6–4, 1–6, 6–2.

Doubles: L. RAYMOND and P. D. B. SPENCE (S.A.) beat H. Landmann and H. Kleinschroth (Ger.) 7–5, 6–4, 9–11, 6–3.

Denmark beat India at Copenhagen on June 9, 10, and 11, with plenty in hand, by a margin of five–love. The Danish team was A. Petersen and E. Ulrich for the singles and Ulrich and P. Henriksen for the doubles. K. Prasada and A. H. Fyzee were India's only players. The latter won a set from Ulrich and fought hard for two others.

Detailed Results

Singles: A. PETERSEN (DEN.) beat K. Prasada (Ind.) 6–4, 6–4, 6–3 ; beat A. H. Fyzee (Ind.) 6–0, 6–2, 6–4. E. ULRICH (DEN.) beat A. H. Fyzee (Ind.) 1–6, 6–3, 9–7, 11–9 ; beat K. Prasada (Ind.) 6–4, 7–5, 6–4.

Doubles: P. HENRIKSEN and E. ULRICH (DEN.) beat K. Prasada and A. H. Fyzee (Ind.) 6–2, 6–2, 6–3.

Czechoslovakia were at home in Prague to Belgium on June 10, 11, and 12, and won a good victory over the latter by four matches to one. The Czech team was J. Kozeluh and F. von Röhrer for the singles and Kozeluh and M. Zemla for the doubles. Belgium's team was J. Washer and H. W. Botsford for both singles and doubles. Washer beat von Röhrer in three sets, but went down to Kozeluh after leading by two sets to love. Kozeluh won the third and fourth sets in advantage games, and found Washer spent enough to take the fifth set to love.

Detailed Results

Singles: J. KOZELUH (CZECH.) beat J. Washer (Belg.) 2–6, 3–6, 7–5, 8–6, 6–0 ; beat H. W. Botsford (Belg.) 6–3, 6–2, 6–4. F. VON RÖHRER (CZECH.) beat H. W. Botsford (Belg.) 6–2, 6–3, 4–6, 6–4 ; lost to J. WASHER (BELG.) 4–6, 5–7, 3–6.

Doubles: J. KOZELUH and M. ZEMLA (CZECH.) beat J. Washer and H. W. Botsford (Belg.) 8–6, 10–8, 6–4.

France played and beat Italy by three to two at Rome on June 11, 12, and 13. The French team was H. Cochet and R. Lacoste for the singles and Cochet and J. Brugnon for the doubles. The Italian team for both singles and doubles was H. L. de Morpurgo and G. de Stefani. De Morpurgo again proved his ability by defeating Cochet and extending Lacoste to five sets. He and de Stefani beat Cochet and Brugnon in the doubles in three sets. All sterling performances.

Detailed Results

Singles: H. COCHET (FR.) beat G. de Stefani (It.) 6–1, 6–3, 6–3 ; lost to H. L. DE MORPURGO (IT.) 5–7, 7–5, 1–6, 5–7. R. LACOSTE (FR.) beat H. L. de Morpurgo (It.) 2–6, 6–0, 6–2, 0–6, 6–1 ; beat G. de Stefani (It.) 6–3, 6–8, 6–1, 6–3.

Doubles: H. Cochet and J. Brugnon (Fr.) lost to H. L. DE MORPURGO and G. DE STEFANI (IT.) 4–6, 4–6, 4–6.

In the fourth, or semi-final, round Denmark went to Czechoslovakia, to Prague, to defeat their hosts by three matches to two, on July 8, 9, and 10. The Danish team was a two-man team of A. Petersen and E. Ulrich. The Czech team was J. Kozeluh and F. von Röhrer for the singles and Kozeluh and M. Zemla for the doubles, as usual. Kozeluh won both his singles, Ulrich only taking a set from him. Von Röhrer could not beat either Dane, though he battled hard and took Petersen to five sets after being two sets down. The doubles was the key to the contest, and was gallantly won by the Danes from two sets down, each of the last three sets going to advantage games.

Detailed Results

Singles: A. PETERSEN (DEN.) beat F. von Röhrer (Czech.) 7–5, 6–1, 4–6, 8–10, 6–3 ; lost to J. KOZELUH (CZECH.) 4–6, 10–12, 3–6. E. ULRICH (DEN.) beat F. von Röhrer (Czech.) 6–4, 6–4, 10–8 ; lost to J. KOZELUH (CZECH.) 6–0, 1–6, 5–7, 4–6.

Doubles: A. PETERSEN and E. ULRICH (DEN.) beat M. Zemla and J. Kozeluh (Czech.) 3–6, 4–6, 8–6, 7–5, 9–7.

The other semi-final tie of this zone, between France and South Africa, was played at Eastbourne on July 8, 9, and 11. France won by five matches to none. Their team was H. Cochet and R. Lacoste for the singles and J. Borotra and J. Brugnon for the doubles, the team which was to win the cup from America a couple of months later. South Africa relied on J. Condon and L. Raymond for both singles and doubles. Lacoste won both his singles in three sets, but Cochet dropped a long twenty-game set to Condon. The other single was played between two substitutes, Brugnon and P. D. B. Spence, and won by Brugnon in three sets. Borotra and Brugnon also took the doubles in three.

Detailed Results

Singles: H. COCHET (FR.) beat J. Condon (S.A.) 6–0, 9–11, 6–2, 7–5. J. BRUGNON (FR.) beat P. D. B. Spence (S.A.) 6–2, 6–3, 6–4. R. LACOSTE (FR.) beat L. Raymond (S.A.) 6–2, 6–2, 6–1 ; beat J. Condon (S.A.) 7–5, 6–3, 6–1.

Doubles: J. BOROTRA and J. BRUGNON (FR.) beat L. Raymond and J. Condon (S.A.) 7–5, 6–4, 8–6.

The European Zone final round, between France and Denmark, took place at Copenhagen on July 21 and 22. Only three matches were played, and all won by France, whose singles players were H. Cochet and J. Borotra, with J. Brugnon partnering the latter in the doubles. E. Ulrich and A. Petersen played both singles and doubles for Denmark, and both fought well against superior forces. The result, however, was rather a foregone conclusion.

Detailed Results

Singles: H. COCHET (FR.) beat E. Ulrich (Den.) 9–7, 9–7, 6–4. J. BOROTRA (FR.) beat A. Petersen (Den.) 6–8, 6–2, 6–1, 6–0.

Doubles: J. BOROTRA and J. BRUGNON (FR.) beat E. Ulrich and A. Petersen (Den.) 6–4, 6–0, 6–3.

AMERICAN ZONE

Japan and Mexico met at St Louis on July 29, 30, and 31, when Japan won with the loss of one match in five. Their team was Y. Ohta and T. Harada for the singles and Harada and Z. Shimizu for the doubles. Mexico were represented by R. Kinsey and A. Unda in the singles and Kinsey and C. Butlin in the doubles. Japan won all the singles, despite Kinsey's efforts, particularly against Ohta, whom Kinsey led by two sets to love. Mexico took the doubles in five sets.

Detailed Results

Singles: Y. OHTA (JAP.) beat R. Kinsey (Mex.) 2–6, 1–6, 6–4, 6–1, 6–2; beat A. Unda (Mex.) 6–1, 4–6, 6–3, 6–4. T. HARADA (JAP.) beat A. Unda (Mex.) 6–2, 6–3, 6–3; beat R. Kinsey (Mex.) 9–7, 6–0, 0–6, 6–1.

Doubles: Z. Shimizu and T. Harada (Jap.) lost to R. KINSEY and C. BUTLIN (MEX.) 5–7, 2–6, 6–2, 6–3, 3–6.

Canada and Cuba met at Toronto on July 18, 19, and 20, when Canada won the tie by three to two. The Canadians played J. Wright and W. Crocker for both singles and doubles. Cuba used R. Paris and V. Banet for the singles and Paris and R. Chacon for the doubles. Paris beat Wright after losing the first two sets, but could not hold Crocker. Wright beat Banet in five sets. G. Nunns substituted for Crocker in the other singles, and went down to Banet in four sets. The Canadians won the doubles very easily.

Detailed Results

Singles: J. WRIGHT (CAN.) beat V. Banet (Cu.) 2–6, 6–2, 6–4, 4–6, 6–4; lost to R. PARIS (CU.) 6–1, 6–2, 5–7, 5–7, 4–6. W. CROCKER (CAN.) beat R. Paris (Cu.) 6–4, 8–6, 6–4. G. Nunns (Can.) lost to V. BANET (CU.) 3–6, 2–6, 7–5, 3–6.

Doubles: J. WRIGHT and W. CROCKER (CAN.) beat R. Paris and R. Chacon (Cu.) 6–0, 6–3, 6–0.

Japan played Canada at Montreal on August 18, 19, and 20, in the American Zone final, and won the narrowest of victories, Canada actually equalling their set score. The Japanese team was T. Harada and Y. Ohta for the singles and T. Toba and Harada for the doubles. Canada relied again on J. Wright and W. Crocker. Wright was in excellent form, and won both his singles in three sets. Crocker lost to both Japanese in his singles. The doubles match, once again the key, was a long, seesawing struggle, the Japanese pair leading off with the opening set, and just getting home at 10–8 in the final set.

Detailed Results

Singles: T. HARADA (JAP.) beat W. Crocker (Can.) 7–5, 6–0, 6–4 ; lost to J. WRIGHT (CAN.) 3–6, 3–6, 6–8. Y. OHTA (JAP.) beat W. Crocker (Can.) 6–4, 3–6, 10–8, 6–3 ; lost to J. WRIGHT (CAN.) 3–6, 4–6, 4–6.

Doubles: T. HARADA and T. TOBA (JAP.) beat J. Wright and W. Crocker (Can.) 6–3, 4–6, 7–5, 3–6, 10–8.

INTER-ZONE ROUND

This tie between France, winners of the European Zone, and Japan, winners of the American Zone, took place at Boston on August 25, 26, and 27. Only three matches were played, and all were won by France, with ease in three sets. The French team was R. Lacoste and H. Cochet in the singles and Cochet and J. Brugnon in the doubles. Japan played T. Harada and Y. Ohta in both singles and doubles. The Frenchmen were superior in all respects, and majestically qualified as challengers to U.S.A., for the third successive year.

Detailed Results

Singles: R. LACOSTE (FR.) beat T. Harada (Jap.) 6–1, 6–1, 6–2. H. COCHET (FR.) beat Y. Ohta (Jap.) 6–0, 6–3, 6–2.

Doubles: H. COCHET and J. BRUGNON (FR.) beat T. Harada and Y. Ohta (Jap.) 9–7, 6–1, 6–2.

N. E. Brookes (Australasia)

R. Lacoste (France)

W. T. Tilden (U.S.A.)

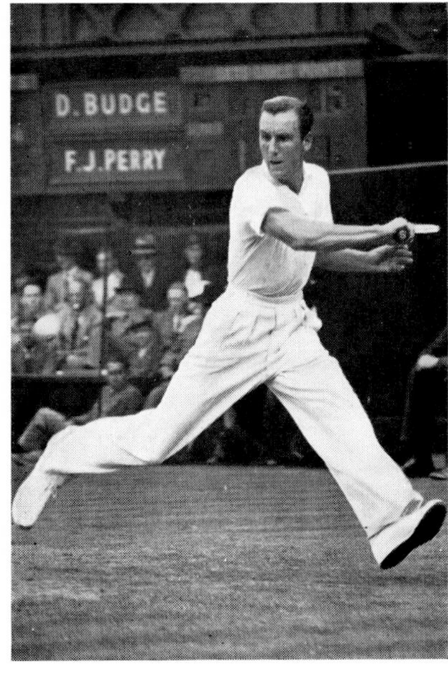

F. J. Perry (Great Britain)

J. Borotra struck by a Ball and knocked out at Forest Hills, New York, 1925

Left to right: J. B. Hawkes, G. L. Patterson (Australia) ; Borotra (on ground) and R. Lacoste (France).

Challenge Round

This eventful contest between France and the holders, U.S.A., as a result of which the cup changed hands, took place at Philadelphia on September 8, 9, and 10. France won by three matches to two. The defending country again relied on W. T. Tilden and W. M. Johnston for the singles, but played a different doubles team in Tilden and F. T. Hunter. France had, of course, her " Four Musketeers," but played them in a different order from the previous year. R. Lacoste and H. Cochet were the singles players and J. Borotra and J. Brugnon the doubles pair. Lacoste and Johnston opened the proceedings, and the Frenchman's three-set win marked the end of Johnston's long run of Davis Cup victories. The heyday of the great " Little Bill " was past. Tilden beat Cochet in the second match in four sets, but had to work very hard to do so. The doubles match, on the second day, was won by U.S.A. in five sets, a further drain on Tilden's stamina, with both the French singles players resting. On the third day the Frenchmen were required to win both singles against the hitherto well-nigh invincible " Bills," Tilden and Johnston. That Lacoste and Cochet were able to do this with the loss of only one set each proved their maturity as Davis Cup giants, and also the end of a famous seven-year domination by the Americans. France became the first, and so far the only, European Continental holders of the Davis Cup.

Detailed Results

Singles: R. Lacoste (Fr.) beat W. M. Johnston (U.S.A.) 6–3, 6–2, 6–2 ; beat W. T. Tilden (U.S.A.) 6–4, 4–6, 6–3, 6–3. H. Cochet (Fr.) beat W. M. Johnston (U.S.A.) 6–4, 4–6, 6–2, 6–4 ; lost to W. T. Tilden (U.S.A.) 4–6, 6–2, 2–6, 6–8.

Doubles: J. Borotra and J. Brugnon (Fr.) lost to W. T. Tilden and F. T. Hunter (U.S.A.) 6–3, 3–6, 3–6, 6–4, 0–6.

1928: FRANCE

This year the number of challengers again increased, to reach the new high total of thirty-two, twenty-six in the European Zone and six in the American Zone.

European Zone

In the first round Italy played Australia at Genoa on May 4, 5, and 6. Italy won by four to one, with their team of H. L. de Morpurgo and G. de Stefani for the singles and de Morpurgo and P. Gaslini for the doubles. The Australian team was G. L. Patterson and J. H. Crawford for the singles and Patterson and H. C. Hopman for the doubles. De Morpurgo won both his singles, beating Patterson in five sets and Crawford in three. Patterson beat de Stefani in three quick sets, but Hopman, substituting for Crawford, lost to this Italian in three advantage sets. The doubles went to Italy in five sets.

Detailed Results

Singles: H. L. de Morpurgo (It.) beat J. H. Crawford (Austral.) 7–5, 6–3, 6–2 ; beat G. L. Patterson (Austral.) 1–6, 6–4, 6–3, 2–6, 6–1. G. de Stefani (It.) beat H. C. Hopman (Austral.) 7–5, 8–6, 10–8 ; lost to G. L. Patterson (Austral.) 1–6, 3–6, 3–6.

Doubles: H. L. de Morpurgo and P. Gaslini (It.) beat G. L. Patterson and H. C. Hopman (Austral.) 6–3, 6–4, 1–6, 1–6, 6–2.

Rumania were at home to Belgium at Bucharest on May 4, 5, and 6, and won a fine victory by five to none. Their team was N. Mishu and G. Luppu for the singles, with L. Dorner partnering Mishu in the doubles. The Belgian side was A. Ewbank and M. Iweins d'Eeckhoutte for the singles and Ewbank and A. Lacroix for the doubles. Luppu did well to win both his singles in five sets, especially the game against Iweins d'Eeckhoutte from two sets down.

Detailed Results

Singles: N. Mishu (Rum.) beat M. Iweins d'Eeckhoutte (Belg.) 6–3, 8–6, 3–6, 6–3 ; beat A. Ewbank (Belg.) 6–4, 6–1, 6–4. G. Luppu (Rum.) beat A. Ewbank (Belg.) 6–3, 7–9, 7–5, 7–9, 6–3 ; beat M. Iweins d'Eeckhoutte (Belg.) 3–6, 4–6, 6–4, 6–4, 6–0.

Doubles: N. Mishu and L. Dorner (Rum.) beat A. Ewbank and A. Lacroix (Belg.) 6–4, 4–6, 6–2, 7–5.

Germany played Greece at Munich on May 4, 5, and 6, and won by four to one, Greece's one being a default. For Germany the veteran O. Froitzheim and Dr Buss played the singles and H. Kleinschroth and C. Bergmann the doubles. The Greek team consisted of A. J. Zerlendi and M. Balli. The single between Froitzheim and Zerlendi was defaulted by the German.

Detailed Results

Singles: O. FROITZHEIM (GER.) beat M. Balli (Gr.) 3–6, 6–3, 6–1, 9–7 ; retired to A. J. ZERLENDI (GR.). DR BUSS (GER.) beat A. J. Zerlendi (Gr.) 7–5, 6–4, 4–6, 6–2 ; beat M. Balli (Gr.) 6–1, 6–4, 6–4.

Doubles: H. KLEINSCHROTH and C. BERGMANN (GER.) beat M. Balli and A. J. Zerlendi (Gr.) 6–1, 6–3, 6–4.

Spain and Chile met at Barcelona on April 7, 8, and 9. Spain won by the odd match in five. The Spanish team was N. F Sindreu and A. Juanico for the singles and E. Flaquer and J. Morales for the doubles. Chile were represented by D. I. and L. Torralva. L. Torralva beat Juanico in the singles, and together the Torralvas won the doubles in five sets. Spain won the other three matches, though D. I. Torralva took Juanico to five sets.

Detailed Results

Singles: N. F. SINDREU (SP.) beat D. I. Torralva (Chil.) 6–3, 6–2, 3–6, 6–3 ; beat L. Torralva (Chil.) 6–4, 7–5, 6–4. A. JUANICO (SP.) beat D. I. Torralva (Chil.) 6–4, 4–6, 6–3, 3–6, 6–1 ; lost to L. TORRALVA (CHIL.) 4–6, 2–6, 2–6.

Doubles: E. Flaquer and J. Morales (Sp.) lost to D. I. TORRALVA and L. TORRALVA (CHIL.) 6–4, 2–6, 3–6, 9–7, 2–6.

Finland journeyed to Zagreb to defeat Yugoslavia on May 4, 5, and 6 by four to one. Both countries relied on a two-man team—for Finland A. Grahn and B. Grotenfelt, and for Yugoslavia A. Popovic and F. Schaffers. The latter scored Yugoslavia's only success when he beat Grotenfelt in four sets.

Detailed Results

Singles: A. Grahn (Fin.) beat A. Popovic (Yugo.) 6–2, 6–2, 6–2; beat F. Schaffers (Yugo.) 6–2, 6–0, 6–1. B. Grotenfelt (Fin.) beat A. Popovic (Yugo.) 6–4, 1–6, 6–3, 7–5; lost to F. Schaffers (Yugo.) 3–6, 6–2, 7–9, 5–7.

Doubles: A. Grahn and B. Grotenfelt (Fin.) beat A. Popovic and F. Schaffers (Yugo.) 6–2, 6–2, 8–6.

Great Britain played Argentina at Torquay on May 3, 4, and 5, and won by a margin of four to one. Great Britain's team was J. C. Gregory and E. Higgs in the singles and G. R. O. Crole-Rees and C. G. Eames in the doubles. Argentina had only two men—W. Robson and R. Boyd. Boyd beat Higgs, and in partnership the Argentinians put up a grand fight in the doubles, only losing at 7–5 in the final set, after being two sets down. Robson fought a protracted match with Gregory of sixty-nine games in four sets.

Detailed Results

Singles: J. C. Gregory (G.B.) beat W. Robson (Argent.) 10–12, 13–11, 6–3, 8–6; beat R. Boyd (Argent.) 6–4, 11–9, 6–2. E. Higgs (G.B.) beat W. Robson (Argent.) 7–5, 6–2, 2–6, 7–5; lost to R. Boyd (Argent.) 3–6, 6–4, 3–6, 3–6.

Doubles: G. R. O. Crole-Rees and C. G. Eames (G.B.) beat W. Robson and R. Boyd (Argent.) 6–4, 6–1, 9–11, 1–6, 7–5.

Hungary beat Norway at Christiana at the beginning of May by five to none. The Hungarian team was B. von Kehrling and I. de Takacs for the singles and von Kehrling and Dr Peteri for the doubles. Norway were represented by R. Christoffersen and T. Torkildsen. The latter won one set from von Kehrling and two sets from de Takacs.

Detailed Results

Singles: B. von Kehrling (Hun.) beat R. Christoffersen (Norw.) 6–1, 6–3, 6–1; beat T. Torkildsen (Norw.) 7–5, 3–6, 6–3, 6–1. I. de Takacs (Hun.) beat T. Torkildsen (Norw.) 7–5, 7–9, 6–4, 1–6, 6–2; beat R. Christoffersen (Norw.) 6–1, 6–1, 6–2.

Doubles: B. von Kehrling and Dr Peteri (Hun.) beat T. Torkildsen and R. Christoffersen (Norw.) 6–2, 6–2, 4–6, 6–0.

The Netherlands and Ireland met at Dublin on May 10, 11, and 12, when the Netherlands won comfortably enough by five to none. Theirs was a two-man team, of H. Timmer and A. Diemer Kool. Ireland also used only two men—C. F. Scroope and C. H. D. O'Callaghan. Scroope took Diemer Kool to five sets, but that was the only match to go the full distance.

Detailed Results

Singles: H. Timmer (Neth.) beat C. F. Scroope (Ire.) 6–2, 6–2, 6–2; beat C. H. D. O'Callaghan (Ire.) 6–1, 6–2, 6–0. A. Diemer Kool (Neth.) beat C. H. D. O'Callaghan (Ire.) 6–2, 5–7, 6–1, 6–2; beat C. F. Scroope (Ire.) 3–6, 6–3, 5–7, 6–1, 6–1.

Doubles: H. Timmer and A. Diemer Kool (Neth.) beat C. H. D. O'Callaghan and C. F. Scroope (Ire.) 6–4, 8–6, 8–6.

Denmark beat Poland at Warsaw by five to none on May 4, 5, and 6. The Danish team was E. Ulrich and A. Petersen. The Polish team was G. Stolarow and P. Warminski for the singles and G. and M. Stolarow for the doubles. The Poles could collect only two sets in five matches against the sound, experienced play of the Danes.

Detailed Results

Singles: E. Ulrich (Den.) beat G. Stolarow (Pol.) 3–6, 6–4, 6–0, 6–4; beat P. Warminski (Pol.) 6–4, 6–4, 8–6. A. Petersen (Den.) beat P. Warminski (Pol.) 6–2, 3–6, 6–4, 6–2; beat G. Stolarow (Pol.) 6–1, 6–0, 6–2.

Doubles: E. Ulrich and A. Petersen (Den.) beat G. Stolarow and M. Stolarow (Pol.) 6–1, 6–3, 6–4.

Austria had an easy passage against the Philippines at Vienna on May 4 and 5, winning the three matches played. Austria's team was H. W. Artens and F. Matejka for the singles and Artens and Count L. Salm for the doubles. The Philippines were represented by Arragon and Ingayo in both singles and doubles.

Detailed Results

Singles: H. W. ARTENS (AUS.) beat Arragon (Phil.) 6–3, 6–3, 6–3. F. MATEJKA (AUS.) beat Ingayo (Phil.) 6–2, 6–2, 6–4.

Doubles: COUNT L. SALM and H. W. ARTENS (AUS.) beat Arragon and Ingayo (Phil.) 6–2, 11–13, 6–0, 6–3.

India and Switzerland met in the second round at Zürich on May 12, 13, and 14, and India won by three to two. Their players were M. Sleem and E. V. Bobb for the singles and A. M. D. Pitt and H. L. Soni for the doubles. The Swiss team was C. F. Aeschliman and J. Wuarin for the singles and Aeschliman and M. Ferrier for the doubles. Switzerland won one single, when Aeschliman beat Bobb, and the doubles in five sets from two sets down.

Detailed Results

Singles: M. SLEEM (IND.) beat C. F. Aeschliman (Switz.) 6–3, 9–7, 6–2 ; beat J. Wuarin (Switz.) 6–1, 6–1, 6–4. E. V. BOBB (IND.) beat J. Wuarin (Switz.) 6–3, 6–1, 7–9, 6–3 ; lost to C. F. AESCHLIMAN (SWITZ.) 4–6, 6–1, 4–6, 2–6.

Doubles: A. M. D. Pitt and H. L. Soni (Ind.) lost to C. F. AESCHLIMAN and M. FERRIER (SWITZ.) 6–4, 10–8, 3–6, 4–6, 1–6.

Italy beat Rumania at Rome on May 17, 18, and 19 by four to none. Italy played their strong team of H. L. de Morpurgo and G. de Stefani in the singles and de Morpurgo and P. Gaslini in the doubles. The Rumanian team was Dr Luppu and L. Dorner for both singles and doubles. Dr Luppu did well to take de Stefani to five sets, and the Rumanians also took the doubles to the full distance.

Detailed Results

Singles: H. L. DE MORPURGO (IT.) beat Dr Luppu (Rum.) 6–2, 6–2, 6–2 ; a bye (L. Dorner retired). G. DE STEFANI (IT.) beat L. Dorner (Rum.) 6–3, 6–2, 6–2 ; beat Dr Luppu (Rum.) 3–6, 6–4, 6–4, 5–7, 9–7.

Doubles: H. L. DE MORPURGO and P. GASLINI (IT.) beat Dr Luppu and L. Dorner (Rum.) 6–2, 6–4, 4–6, 3–6, 6–4.

Germany and Spain had a close contest at Berlin on May 17, 18, and 19, which Germany won by three to two. Their singles men were H. Moldenhauer and D. Prenn, with K. Bergmann and H. Kleinschroth for the doubles. The Spanish team was E. Flaquer and N. F. Sindreu for the singles and Flaquer and R. Morales for the doubles. Prenn beat both Spaniards—Sindreu in five sets and Flaquer in four. Moldenhauer lost to Sindreu in five sets. He beat Flaquer in four. The Spaniards won the doubles in five sets.

Detailed Results

Singles: H. MOLDENHAUER (GER.) beat E. Flaquer (Sp.) 6–4, 3–6, 7–5, 6–3 ; lost to N. F. SINDREU (SP.) 4–6, 1–6, 7–5, 6–1, 3–6. D. PRENN (GER.) beat N. F. Sindreu (Sp.) 5–7, 6–2, 2–6, 6–3, 6–4 ; beat E. Flaquer (Sp.) 4–6, 6–3, 6–2, 6–4.

Doubles: K. Bergmann and H. Kleinschroth (Ger.) lost to E. FLAQUER and R. MORALES (SP.) 5–7, 3–6, 6–2, 9–7, 1–6.

Great Britain beat Finland at Helsingfors by five to none on May 18, 19, and 20. The British team was J. C. Gregory and E. Higgs for the singles, with G. R. O. Crole-Rees and C. G. Eames for the doubles. The Finnish team was A. Grahn and B. Grotenfelt in both singles and doubles. R. Granholm substituted for Grotenfelt on the third day against Gregory. No match went to five sets.

Detailed Results

Singles: J. C. GREGORY (G.B.) beat A. Grahn (Fin.) 6–0, 1–6, 6–1, 6–1 ; beat R. Granholm (Fin.) 6–2, 6–1, 6–2. E. HIGGS (G.B.) beat B. Grotenfelt (Fin.) 6–2, 6–1, 2–6, 6–0 ; beat A. Grahn (Fin.) 4–6, 6–1, 6–4, 6–4.

Doubles: G. R. O. CROLE-REES and C. G. EAMES (G.B.) beat A. Grahn and B. Grotenfelt (Fin.) 6–3, 6–2, 6–2.

The Netherlands and Hungary met at Noordwijk, Holland, on May 18, 19, and 20, and the Netherlands won by three to two. The Dutch singles men were H. Timmer and A. Diemer Kool, with O. Koopman substituting for the latter on the third day. Timmer and Koopman played the doubles. The Hungarian team was B. von Kehrling and I. de Takacs for the singles and von Kehrling and Dr Peteri for the doubles. Timmer won the tie for the Netherlands by beating both Hungarians in three sets and, with Koopman, winning the doubles in four sets. Diemer Kool was forced to retire against von Kehrling at 1–1 in the fifth set of their match. Koopman lost to de Takacs.

Detailed Results

Singles: H. TIMMER (NETH.) beat I. de Takacs (Hun.) 6–2, 6–0, 6–1 ; beat B. von Kehrling (Hun.) 6–3, 6–4, 6–3. A. Diemer Kool (Neth.) lost to B. VON KEHRLING (HUN.) 5–7, 6–4, 6–2, 1–6, 1–1 (retired). O. Koopman (Neth.) lost to I. DE TAKACS (HUN.) 4–6, 2–6, 5–7.

Doubles: H. TIMMER and O. KOOPMAN (NETH.) beat B. von Kehrling and Dr Peteri (Hun.) 1–6, 6–4, 6–2, 7–5.

Austria and Denmark met at Copenhagen on May 23, 24, and 25. The visitors won by four to one. Their team was H. W. Artens and F. Matejka for the singles, with Artens and Count L. Salm for the doubles. The Danish team was A. Petersen and E. Ulrich for the singles and Ulrich and P. Henriksen for the doubles. All the singles were won by Austria, but Denmark claimed the doubles. Petersen took Matejka to five sets in the closest single, and Ulrich fought hard against Artens for four sets.

Detailed Results

Singles: H. W. ARTENS (AUS.) beat A. Petersen (Den.) 6–4, 6–2, 7–5 ; beat E. Ulrich (Den.) 6–4, 6–4, 3–6, 9–7. F. MATEJKA (AUS.) beat E. Ulrich (Den.) 6–1, 6–2, 6–2 ; beat A. Petersen (Den.) 8–6, 6–2, 5–7, 2–6, 6–3.

Doubles: Count L. Salm and H. W. Artens (Aus.) lost to E. ULRICH and P. HENRIKSEN (DEN.) 6–8, 0–6, 9–11.

Czechoslovakia and Sweden met at Stockholm on May 17, 18, and 19, when the Czechs won quite handily by four to one. The Czech team was J. Kozeluh and R. Menzel in the singles and Kozeluh and P. Macenauer in the doubles. The Swedish team was S. Malmstrom and O. Garell in the singles and Malmstrom and Wennergren in the doubles. Macenauer substituted for Kozeluh against Malmstrom, and was the only Czech loser.

Detailed Results

Singles: J. KOZELUH (CZECH.) beat O. Garell (Sw.) 8–6, 6–0, 6–1. P. Macenauer (Czech.) lost to S. MALMSTROM (Sw.) 8–10, 6–1, 5–7, 3–6. R. MENZEL (CZECH.) beat S. Malmstrom (Sw.) 6–3, 6–3, 3–6, 7–5 ; beat O. Garell (Sw.) 6–2, 6–0, 5–7, 8–6.

Doubles: J. KOZELUH and P. MACENAUER (CZECH.) beat S. Malmstrom and Wennergren (Sw.) 6–0, 6–2, 6–4.

New Zealand played Portugal at Lisbon on May 11, 12, and 13, and beat the home country by four to one. New Zealand's was a two-man team, of E. D. Andrews and R. R. T. Young. Portugal's team was J. de Verda and A. Pinto Coelho for the singles and de Verda and F. de Vasconcellos for the doubles. Young lost to de Verda, but beat Pinto Coelho. Andrews was much too strong for both his opponents, and he and Young won the doubles also.

Detailed Results

Singles: E. D. ANDREWS (N.Z.) beat A. Pinto Coelho (Port.) 6–3, 6–4, 6–0 ; beat J. de Verda (Port.) 6–4, 6–3, 6–1. R. R. T. YOUNG (N.Z.) beat A. Pinto Coelho (Port.) 4–6, 6–1, 6–3, 6–0 ; lost to J. DE VERDA (PORT.) 2–6, 2–6, 3–6.

Doubles: E. D. ANDREWS and R. R. T. YOUNG (N.Z.) beat J. de Verda and F. de Vasconcellos (Port.) 5–7, 6–4, 6–2, 6–2.

In the third round Italy played India at Turin on June 9, 10, and 11, and scored a clear-cut four-one win. Their team was H. L. de Morpurgo and G. de Stefani for both singles and doubles. The Indian singles players were M. Sleem and E. V. Bobb, who also played the doubles. India's only point was Sleem's win over de Stefani in four sets.

Detailed Results

Singles: H. L. DE MORPURGO (IT.) beat M. Sleem (Ind.) 6–3, 6–3, 6–1 ; beat E. V. Bobb (Ind.) 6–2, 6–4, 6–4. G. DE STEFANI (IT.) beat E. V. Bobb (Ind.) 6–4, 6–1, 6–3 ; lost to M. SLEEM (IND.) 4–6, 6–8, 6–4, 3–6.

Doubles: H. L. DE MORPURGO and G. DE STEFANI (IT.) beat M. Sleem and E. V. Bobb (Ind.) 6–3, 6–3, 3–6, 6–3.

Great Britain and Germany met at Edgbaston, Birmingham, on June 7, 8, and 9, the home team winning by four to one. The British team was the same as in rounds one and two—E. Higgs and J. C. Gregory for the singles and G. R. O. Crole-Rees and C. G. Eames for the doubles. Germany's team was H. Moldenhauer and O. Froitzheim for the singles and D. Prenn and H. Kleinschroth for the doubles. Higgs beat Moldenhauer in five sets, but lost to Prenn, substitute for Froitzheim, in the same number. Froitzheim retired to Gregory when the Englishman led by two sets to one. Moldenhauer took Gregory to five sets, and the British pair won the doubles in three.

Detailed Results

Singles: E. Higgs (G.B.) beat H. Moldenhauer (Ger.) 6–4, 4–6, 6–2, 0–6, 6–4 ; lost to D. Prenn (Ger.) 6–3, 1–6, 5–7, 6–2, 3–6. J. C. Gregory (G.B.) beat O. Froitzheim (Ger.) 6–4, 4–6, 6–0 (retired) ; beat H. Moldenhauer (Ger.) 2–6, 6–4, 3–6, 6–1, 6–2.

Doubles: G. R. O. Crole-Rees and C. G. Eames (G.B.) beat H. Kleinschroth and D. Prenn (Ger.) 7–5, 6–2, 6–4.

The Netherlands and Austria played their tie at The Hague on June 7, 8, and 9, and the home team won the only three matches played. Both countries used only two men—the Netherlands H. Timmer and A. Diemer Kool and Austria F. Matejka and H. W. Artens. Timmer beat Matejka in five sets from two sets down, and Diemer Kool beat Artens in the same number. The Dutchmen won the doubles in three sets quite easily.

Detailed Results

Singles: H. Timmer (Neth.) beat F. Matejka (Aus.) 2–6, 5–7, 6–0, 6–3, 6–4. A. Diemer Kool (Neth.) beat H. W. Artens (Aus.) 6–3, 4–6, 6–3, 3–6, 6–0.

Doubles: H. Timmer and A. Diemer Kool (Neth.) beat F. Matejka and H. W. Artens (Aus.) 6–2, 6–3, 6–0.

New Zealand defaulted to Czechoslovakia in the remaining match of this round.

In the fourth, or semi-final, round Italy played and defeated Great Britain at Felixstowe on June 20, 21, and 22 by four matches to one. The winners played H. L. de Morpurgo and G. de Stefani in the singles and de Morpurgo and P. Gaslini in the doubles. The British team was, as before—E. Higgs and J. C. Gregory for the singles and G. R. O. Crole-Rees and C. G. Eames for the doubles. De Morpurgo beat both Englishmen in three sets. De Stefani beat Gregory in four sets, but lost to Higgs in five. The Italians scraped home in the doubles in five sets after a very close fight.

Detailed Results

Singles: H. L. DE MORPURGO (IT.) beat E. Higgs (G.B.) 7–5, 6–4, 7–5 ; beat J. C. Gregory (G.B.) 6–0, 6–1, 6–2. G. DE STEFANI (IT.) beat J. C. Gregory (G.B.) 3–6, 6–3, 6–3, 6–2 ; lost to E. HIGGS (G.B.) 1–6, 6–3, 3–6, 7–5, 2–6.

Doubles: H. L. DE MORPURGO and P. GASLINI (IT.) beat G. R. O. Crole-Rees and C. G. Eames (G.B.) 6–4, 3–6, 4–6, 9–7, 7–5.

The other match in this round, between the Netherlands and Czechoslovakia, took place in Prague on June 22, 23, and 24, and was won by the Czechs by three to two. Their team was J. Kozeluh and P. Macenauer in the singles and Kozeluh and R. Menzel in the doubles. H. Timmer and C. J. van Lennep comprised the Dutch team in both singles and doubles. Van Lennep could not win a set in either of his singles, but Timmer beat Kozeluh in four sets, though he lost to Macenauer in an equal number. The Dutchmen claimed the doubles also in four sets.

Detailed Results

Singles: J. KOZELUH (CZECH.) beat C. J. van Lennep (Neth.) 6–2, 6–0, 6–2 ; lost to H. TIMMER (NETH.) 3–6, 6–1, 1–6, 4–6. P. MACENAUER (CZECH.) beat H. Timmer (Neth.) 6–2, 0–6, 6–0, 6–4 ; beat C. J. van Lennep (Neth.) 6–2, 6–2, 6–2.

Doubles: J. Kozeluh and R. Menzel (Czech.) lost to H. TIMMER and C. J. VAN LENNEP (NETH.) 3–6, 6–3, 2–6, 4–6.

The two remaining countries, Italy and Czechoslovakia, played off the final of the European Zone at Milan on July 13, 14, and 15. Italy won by the odd match in five. G. de

Stefani had dropped out of their team, leaving H. L. de Morpurgo and P. Gaslini to play both singles and doubles. The Czechs relied on J. Kozeluh and P. Macenauer for the singles and for the doubles too. De Morpurgo was Italy's strong man, and again won both his singles in straight sets. Gaslini lost to Kozeluh in four sets, but beat Macenauer in the same number. The Czechs won the doubles with the loss of one set.

Detailed Results

Singles: H. L. DE MORPURGO (IT.) beat P. Macenauer (Czech.) 6–3, 6–3, 6–4 ; beat J. Kozeluh (Czech.) 6–1, 6–2, 6–0. P. GASLINI (IT.) beat P. Macenauer (Czech.) 0–6, 6–4, 6–4, 6–3 ; lost to J. KOZELUH (CZECH.) 1–6, 7–9, 6–3, 4–6.

Doubles: H. L. de Morpurgo and P. Gaslini (It.) lost to J. KOZELUH and P. MACENAUER (CZECH.) 6–8, 6–4, 4–6, 4–6.

AMERICAN ZONE

Japan and Cuba met in the first round at Havana on April 30 and May 1. Japan won by three to none. The Cuban side consisted of only two men—R. Paris and V. Banet. For Japan Y. Ohta and T. Toba played the singles and Toba and T. Abe the doubles. The Japanese dropped one set only—in the doubles.

Detailed Results

Singles: Y. OHTA (JAP.) beat R. Paris (Cu.) 6–1, 6–1, 6–3. T. TOBA (JAP.) beat V. Banet (Cu.) 6–1, 6–2, 6–1.

Doubles: T. TOBA and T. ABE (JAP.) beat R. Paris and V. Banet (Cu.) 6–3, 6–3, 4–6, 9–7.

U.S.A., in the rôle of challengers again for the first time since 1920, beat Mexico at Mexico City on April 7 and 8 by three to none. J. F. Hennessey and W. T. Tilden played the singles for America, and Tilden and A. Jones the doubles. R. G. Kinsey and R. Tapia were Mexico's singles players, with A. Unda partnering Kinsey in the doubles. Mexico won a set in the four-handed game, but that was all they could do.

Detailed Results

Singles: W. T. TILDEN (U.S.A.) beat R. G. Kinsey (Mex.) 6–1, 6–2, 6–4. J. F. HENNESSEY (U.S.A.) beat R. Tapia (Mex.) 6–2, 9–7, 6–1.

Doubles: W. T. TILDEN and A. JONES (U.S.A.) beat R. G. Kinsey and A. Unda (Mex.) 6–2, 4–6, 6–3, 6–3.

Japan and Canada met in the second round at Montreal on May 25, 26, and 28, when Japan won a very close contest by three to one. The Canadian team was J. Wright and W. Crocker for the singles and Wright and A. Ham for the doubles. Japan's team was T. Toba and Y. Ohta for the singles and Toba and T. Abe for the doubles, as against Cuba in the previous round. Crocker, in his only single, beat Toba in four sets. Wright lost both his singles in five sets, after leading Toba two sets to love and Ohta two sets to one. Wright and Ham were also two sets up in the doubles before finally losing in the eighteenth game of the final set. The result could well have been reversed.

Detailed Results

Singles: T. TOBA (JAP.) beat J. Wright (Can.) 7–9, 3–6, 6–3, 6–0, 6–4 ; lost to W. CROCKER (CAN.) 0–6, 2–6, 6–4, 3–6. Y. OHTA (JAP.) beat J. Wright (Can.) 4–6, 6–4, 1–6, 6–4, 6–1.

Doubles: T. TOBA and T. ABE (JAP.) beat J. Wright and A. Ham (Can.) 5–7, 2–6, 6–3, 6–4, 10–8.

U.S.A. won an easy victory against China at Kansas City on May 25, 26, and 27 by a margin of five to none, without losing a set. The American singles players were G. M. Lott and J. F. Hennessey, while W. T. Tilden and W. F. Coen played the doubles. P. Kong and G. Lum played both singles and doubles for China. The match was remarkable only for two things : Lott set up a Davis Cup record when he beat Kong without losing a game, and W. F. Coen became the youngest player to take part in the competition—at the age of sixteen.

Detailed Results

Singles: G. M. LOTT (U.S.A.) beat P. Kong (Chin.) 6–0, 6–0, 6–0 ; beat G. Lum (Chin.) 6–3, 6–2, 6–0. J. F. HENNESSEY (U.S.A.) beat G. Lum (Chin.) 6–3, 6–4, 6–0 ; beat P. Kong (Chin.) 6–1, 6–0, 6–1.

Doubles: W. T. TILDEN and W. F. COEN (U.S.A.) beat P. Kong and G. Lum (Chin.) 6–2, 6–1, 6–3.

In the American Zone final round U.S.A. beat Japan at Chicago on June 1, 2, and 3 by five to none. For the winners W. T. Tilden and J. F. Hennessey played the singles and Tilden and G. M. Lott the doubles. Japan relied on Y. Ohta and T. Abe for the singles and Abe and T. Toba for the doubles. Tilden dropped the opening set in his single against Ohta, and W. F. Coen, substituting for Hennessey on the third day, did likewise against Abe. U.S.A. won the doubles in three sets, only the second one being close.

Detailed Results

Singles: W. T. TILDEN (U.S.A.) beat Y. Ohta (Jap.) 6–8, 6–3, 6–1, 6–0; beat T. Abe (Jap.) 6–2, 6–3, 6–0. J. F. HENNESSEY (U.S.A.) beat Y. Ohta (Jap.) 8–6, 6–3, 6–3. W. F. COEN (U.S.A.) beat T. Abe (Jap.) 7–9, 6–2, 6–4, 7–5.

Doubles: W. T. TILDEN and G. M. LOTT (U.S.A.) beat T. Abe and T. Toba (Jap.) 6–1, 10–8, 6–2.

INTER-ZONE ROUND

U.S.A. and Italy met for the right to challenge France at Paris on July 20, 21, and 22. U.S.A. won by four to one. This time their team was F. T. Hunter and J. F. Hennessey for the singles, with Hennessey and G. M. Lott for the doubles. Italy used only two players—H. L. de Morpurgo and P. Gaslini, and their only success was de Morpurgo's win over Hunter in five sets. They could not win a set in any other match.

Detailed Results

Singles: F. T. HUNTER (U.S.A.) beat P. Gaslini (It.) 6–1, 6–1, 6–0; lost to H. L. DE MORPURGO (IT.) 4–6, 8–6, 3–6, 6–3, 3–6. J. F. HENNESSEY (U.S.A.) beat H. L. de Morpurgo (It.) 6–4, 7–5, 6–2; beat P. Gaslini (It.) 7–5, 6–3, 6–4.

Doubles: J. F. HENNESSEY and G. M. LOTT (U.S.A.) beat H. L. de Morpurgo and P. Gaslini (It.) 6–2, 6–3, 6–1.

Challenge Round

This final tie for 1928 took place at Paris on July 27, 28, and 29. France, the holders, chose R. Lacoste and H. Cochet as their singles players, with Cochet and J. Borotra as the doubles team. U.S.A., the challengers, chose W. T. Tilden and J. F. Hennessey as their singles players, with Tilden and F. T. Hunter as their doubles pair. France were too strong for them, and won by four matches to one. The match which went to the U.S.A. was, on previous form, probably the one least likely to do so. In it Tilden turned the tables on Lacoste and beat the young Frenchman in five sets, no mean feat even for Tilden. Hennessey performed well enough to win the first set against each of his formidable opponents. Tilden just could not quite get one against Cochet. The doubles was a five-set affair which ended on the French side of the ledger.

Detailed Results

Singles: R. Lacoste (Fr.) beat J. F. Hennessey (U.S.A.) 4–6, 6–1, 7–5, 6–3 ; lost to W. T. Tilden (U.S.A.) 6–1, 4–6, 4–6, 6–2, 3–6. H. Cochet (Fr.) beat J. F. Hennessey (U.S.A.) 5–7, 9–7, 6–3, 6–0 ; beat W. T. Tilden (U.S.A.) 9–7, 8–6, 6–4.

Doubles: H. Cochet and J. Borotra (Fr.) beat W. T. Tilden and F. T. Hunter (U.S.A.) 6–4, 6–8, 7–5, 4–6, 6–2.

1929 : FRANCE

This year twenty-nine countries challenged, twenty-four in the European Zone and five in the American Zone, but one of the European challengers, Portugal, withdrew without playing a match.

European Zone

Czechoslovakia and Austria met at Vienna on April 26, 27, and 28. Czechoslovakia won by three to two. Their team was J. Kozeluh and R. Menzel in the singles and Kozeluh and P. Macenauer in the doubles. Austria relied on F. Matejka and H. W. Artens. Matejka won both his singles, but the other matches were all won by Czechoslovakia.

Detailed Results

Singles: J. KOZELUH (CZECH.) beat H. W. Artens (Aus.) 6–4, 6–3, 8–10, 6–4 ; lost to F. MATEJKA (AUS.) 3–6, 5–7, 1–6. R. MENZEL (CZECH.) beat H. W. Artens (Aus.) 6–3, 6–4, 6–2 ; lost to F. MATEJKA (AUS.) 8–10, 3–6, 1–6.

Doubles: J. KOZELUH and P. MACENAUER (CZECH.) beat F. Matejka and H. W. Artens (Aus.) 6–4, 7–5, 6–2.

Belgium and Rumania met at Brussels on May 4, 5, and 6. These countries had been opponents a year earlier in Bucharest, but a change of venue meant a change of result, and this time Belgium won by four to one. They used only two players for both singles and doubles—A. Ewbank and A. Lacroix. The Rumanian team was N. Mishu and Dr Luppu for the singles, and L. Dorner partnered Luppu in the doubles. Mishu scored the only Rumanian success when he beat Ewbank in four sets.

Detailed Results

Singles: A. LACROIX (BELG.) beat N. Mishu (Rum.) 6–2, 6–4, 3–6, 6–3 ; beat Dr Luppu (Rum.) 8–6, 6–4, 6–3. A. EWBANK (BELG.) beat Dr Luppu (Rum.) 6–2, 4–6, 6–2, 6–4 ; lost to N. MISHU (RUM.) 2–6, 4–6, 8–6, 3–6.

Doubles: A. LACROIX and A. EWBANK (BELG.) beat Dr Luppu and L. Dorner (Rum.) 7–5, 6–2, 6–1.

Denmark beat Chile at Copenhagen on May 4, 5, and 6, with the loss of one match in five. The Danish team was E. Ulrich and P. Henriksen for singles and doubles, and for Chile L. and D. I. Torralva played both. L. Torralva beat Ulrich, to gain Chile's only win.

Detailed Results

Singles: P. HENRIKSEN (DEN.) beat L. Torralva (Chil.) 8–6, 7–5, 7–5 ; beat D. I. Torralva (Chil.) 5–7, 7–5, 6–4, 6–4. E. ULRICH (DEN.) beat D. I. Torralva (Chil.) 6–2, 6–4, 7–5 ; lost to L. TORRALVA (CHIL.) 5–7, 4–6, 6–8.

Doubles: E. ULRICH and P. HENRIKSEN (DEN.) beat L. Torralva and D. I. Torralva (Chil.) 6–2, 6–3, 6–4.

THE FAMOUS "FOUR MUSKETEERS" OF FRANCE, WINNERS IN 1927

Left to right: J. Brugnon, H. Cochet, R. Lacoste, J. Borotra,

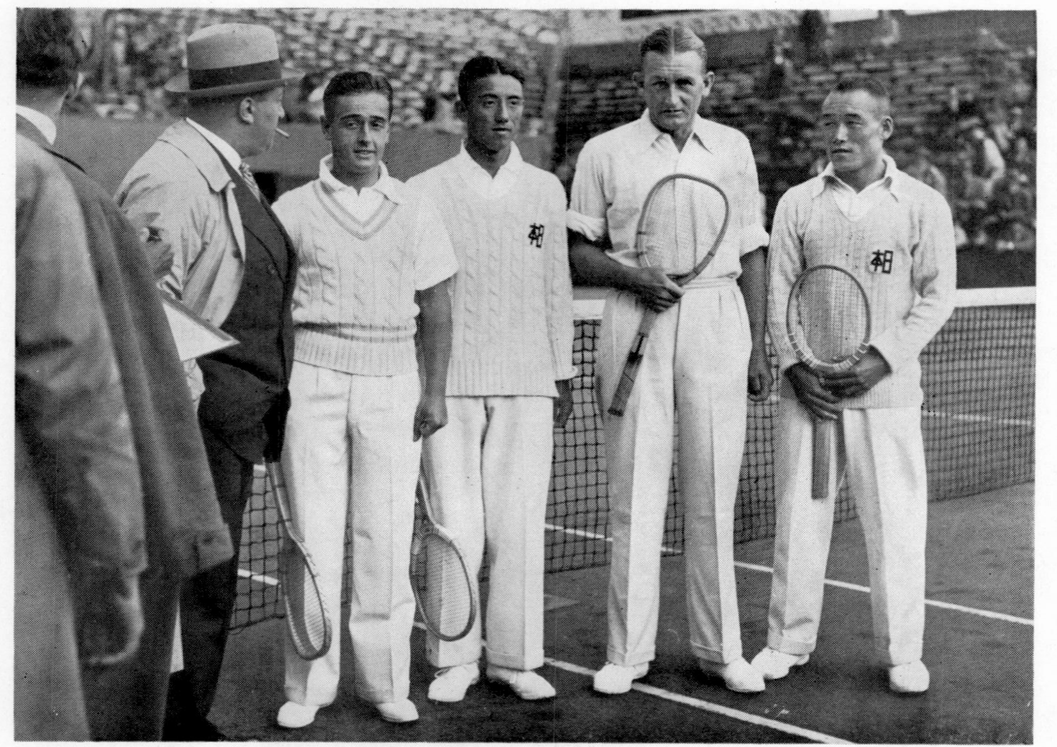

Australia versus Japan in Paris, 1933

Left to right: A. K. Quist (Australia), R. Nunoi (Japan), J. H. Crawford (Australia), J. Satoh (Japan).

Greece and Yugoslavia met at Athens on May 4, 5, and 6. Greece won by four to one. Their team was A. J. Zerlendi and C. Efstratiades in the singles and Zerlendi and K. Georgiades in the doubles. Yugoslavia's team was Sefer and K. Friedrich in both singles and doubles, and their only success was Friedrich's win over Efstratiades.

Detailed Results

Singles: A. J. ZERLENDI (GR.) beat K. Friedrich (Yugo.) 6–3, 6–0, 6–2; beat Sefer (Yugo.) 6–4, 7–5, 6–4. C. EFSTRATIADES (GR.) beat Sefer (Yugo.) 6–2, 7–5, 3–6, 6–3; lost to K. FRIEDRICH (YUGO.) 1–6, 3–6, 4–6.

Doubles: A. J. ZERLENDI and K. GEORGIADES (GR.) beat Sefer and K. Friedrich (Yugo.) 6–3, 6–3, 6–3.

Hungary and Norway met again, this time at Oslo, on May 10, 11, and 12, when Hungary won by four to one, with exactly the same team as in 1928—B. von Kehrling and I. de Takacs for the singles and von Kehrling and Dr Peteri for the doubles. For Norway J. Neilsen and T. Torkildsen played the singles and the doubles. The latter beat I. de Takacs in four sets.

Detailed Results

Singles: B. VON KEHRLING (HUN.) beat J. Neilsen (Norw.) 11–9, 1–6, 6–2, 6–2; beat T. Torkildsen (Norw.) 6–1, 6–2, 6–1. I. DE TAKACS (HUN.) beat J. Neilsen (Norw.) 6–1, 6–1, 7–5; lost to T. TORKILDSEN (NORW.) 6–1, 1–6, 1–6, 2–6.

Doubles: B. VON KEHRLING and DR PETERI (HUN.) beat J. Neilsen and T. Torkildsen (Norw.) 6–4, 6–4, 6–1.

Monaco, a newcomer, beat Switzerland at Monte Carlo on March 29, 30, and 31 in a thrilling encounter by three to two. The Swiss team was C. F. Aeschliman and J. Wuarin, and for Monaco R. Gallèpe and V. Landau played all matches. Both these players beat Wuarin in four sets, and Gallèpe almost beat Aeschliman as well, only losing at 7–5 in the final set. Monaco won the doubles at 8–6 in the fifth set after an exciting match.

Detailed Results

Singles: R. Gallèpe (Mon.) beat J. Wuarin (Switz.) 6–3, 6–8, 6–4, 6–4 ; lost to C. F. Aeschliman (Switz.) 7–5, 3–6, 5–7, 6–3, 5–7. V. Landau (Mon.) beat J. Wuarin (Switz.) 4–6, 6–3, 6–2, 6–2 ; lost to C. F. Aeschliman (Switz.) 2–6, 1–6, 2–6.

Doubles: R. Gallèpe and V. Landau (Mon.) beat C. F. Aeschliman and J. Wuarin (Switz.) 4–6, 6–4, 6–4, 3–6, 8–6.

Egypt beat Finland at Helsingfors on May 4, 5, and 7 by four to one. Their team was J. Grandguillot and L. Wahid for the singles, and N. Zahar partnered the former in the doubles. A. Grahn and R. Granholm were the Finnish singles men, and Grahn and B. Grotenfelt the doubles. Granholm's win over Wahid was Finland's only victory.

Detailed Results

Singles: J. Grandguillot (Egy.) beat A. Grahn (Fin.) 1–6, 6–4, 6–2, 5–7, 6–4 ; beat R. Granholm (Fin.) 2–6, 3–6, 6–3, 7–5, 6–2. L. Wahid (Egy.) beat A. Grahn (Fin.) 3–6, 6–0, 6–2, 6–3 ; lost to R. Granholm (Fin.) 4–6, 4–6, 3–6.

Doubles: J. Grandguillot and N. Zahar (Egy.) beat A. Grahn and B. Grotenfelt (Fin.) 7–5, 6–2, 6–3.

Germany beat Spain at Barcelona on May 17, 18, and 19 by four to one, only four matches being completed, and all won by Germany, whose team was H. Moldenhauer and D. Prenn for both singles and doubles. Spain's team was E. Maier and N. F. Sindreu for the singles and Maier and Tejada for the doubles. Tejada substituted for Sindreu on the third day. Moldenhauer won his singles easily, and also the doubles with Prenn. Sindreu chased Prenn for five sets, but finally lost. Kleinschroth, substituting for Prenn, retired when two sets down to Maier.

Detailed Results

Singles: H. Moldenhauer (Ger.) beat E. Maier (Sp.) 6–1, 6–2, 6–3 ; beat Tejada (Sp.) 6–0, 6–2, 6–3. D. Prenn (Ger.) beat N. F. Sindreu (Sp.) 6–3, 5–7, 6–4, 4–6, 6–4. H. Kleinschroth (Ger.) lost to E. Maier (Sp.) 5–7, 3–6, retired.

Doubles: H. MOLDENHAUER and D. PRENN (GER.) beat E. Maier and Tejada (Sp.) 6–3, 1–6, 7–5, 6–1.

Italy beat Ireland in Dublin on May 16, 17, and 18 by five to none. The Italian team was H. L. de Morpurgo and G. de Stefani in the singles and de Morpurgo and A. del Bono in the doubles. The Irish team was G. L. Rogers and E. A. McGuire in the singles and Rogers and N. G. Holmes in the doubles. De Stefani beat McGuire at 8–6 in the fifth set in the only five-setter. Italy took the other three singles in four sets and the doubles in three.

Detailed Results

Singles: H. L. DE MORPURGO (IT.) beat G. L. Rogers (Ire.) 8–6, 6–1, 5–7, 6–2; beat E. A. McGuire (Ire.) 6–0, 5–7, 6–4, 6–2. G. DE STEFANI (IT.) beat E. A. McGuire (Ire.) 6–4, 4–6, 8–6, 4–6, 8–6; beat G. L. Rogers (Ire.) 4–6, 7–5, 6–2, 7–5.

Doubles: H. L. DE MORPURGO and A. DEL BONO (IT.) beat G. L. Rogers and N. G. Holmes (Ire.) 6–4, 7–5, 7–5.

Czechoslovakia beat Belgium at Prague on May 10, 11, and 12 by four to one, but only three matches were completed, all won by the Czechs, whose team was R. Menzel and J. Kozeluh for the singles and Kozeluh and P. Macenauer for the doubles. The Belgian team was A. Lacroix and A. Ewbank for all matches. Ewbank retired to Menzel, and Malecek, substituting for Kozeluh, retired to Lacroix in the third set, the first two having been divided.

Detailed Results

Singles: R. MENZEL (CZECH.) beat A. Lacroix (Belg.) 6–3, 6–1, 6–1; beat A. Ewbank (Belg.), retired. J. KOZELUH (CZECH.) beat A. Ewbank (Belg.) 7–5, 12–10, 6–4. J. Malecek (Czech.) lost to A. LACROIX (BELG.) 3–6, 6–3, 0–1 (retired).

Doubles: J. KOZELUH and P. MACENAUER (CZECH.) beat A. Lacroix and A. Ewbank (Belg.) 6–2, 6–3, 6–4.

Greece visited Copenhagen to play Denmark on May 17, 18, and 19, but they won only one match of the five. E. Ulrich and P. Henriksen represented Denmark, and A. J. Zerlendi and G. Zafiropoulo represented Greece. Zerlendi beat Ulrich in four sets, the fourth being of thirty-two games, but Denmark won all the other matches in straight sets.

Detailed Results

Singles: P. HENRIKSEN (DEN.) beat A. J. Zerlendi (Gr.) 6–0, 7–5, 6–4 ; beat G. Zafiropoulo (Gr.) 6–4, 6–4, 6–1. E. ULRICH (DEN.) beat G. Zafiropoulo (Gr.) 6–3, 6–4, 6–2 ; lost to A. J. ZERLENDI (GR.) 6–3, 6–8, 5–7, 15–17.

Doubles: P. HENRIKSEN and E. ULRICH (DEN.) beat A. J. Zerlendi and G. Zafiropoulo (Gr.) 6–2, 6–4, 6–3.

Hungary beat Monaco at Budapest on May 14, 15, and 16 by the odd match in five. The Hungarian team was B. von Kehrling and I. de Takacs in the singles and von Kehrling and Dr Peteri in the doubles. Monaco again relied on R. Gallèpe and V. Landau. Their successes were Landau's defeat of de Takacs in three sets and a four-set win in the doubles. Gallèpe could not quite hold de Takacs, and neither he nor Landau was capable of extending von Kehrling.

Detailed Results

Singles: I. DE TAKACS (HUN.) beat R. Gallèpe (Mon.) 6–3, 1–6, 9–7, 8–6 ; lost to V. LANDAU (MON.) 3–6, 2–6, 3–6. B. VON KEHRLING (HUN.) beat V. Landau (Mon.) 6–4, 6–4, 6–2 ; beat R. Gallèpe (Mon.) 6–0, 6–3, 6–1.

Doubles: B. von Kehrling and Dr Peteri (Hun.) lost to R. GALLÈPE and V. LANDAU (MON.) 4–6, 6–3, 2–6, 8–10.

Egypt were beaten by the Netherlands at The Hague on May 17, 18, and 19 by four to one. The Netherlands relied on H. Timmer and A. Diemer Kool only, but Egypt played J. Grandguillot and L. Wahid in the singles and N. Zahar and R. Danon in the doubles. Their only win was achieved by Grandguillot, who beat Diemer Kool in five sets.

Detailed Results

Singles: A. DIEMER KOOL (NETH.) beat N. Zahar (Egy.) 2–6, 8–6, 6–2, 6–1 ; lost to J. GRANDGUILLOT (EGY.) 2–6, 6–1, 10–8, 4–6, 1–6. H. TIMMER (NETH.) beat L. Wahid (Egy.) 3–6, 6–2, 6–1, 6–2 ; beat J. Grandguillot (Egy.) 7–5, 6–0, 3–6, 6–2.

Doubles: A. DIEMER KOOL and H. TIMMER (NETH.) beat N. Zahar and R. Danon (Egy.) 9–7, 6–8, 6–4, 6–1.

South Africa accounted for Sweden at Saltsjöbaden, Sweden, on May 17, 18, and 19, by five to none. Their singles players were L. Raymond and C. J. J. Robbins, with Raymond and N. G. Farquharson for the doubles. Swéden were represented by S. Malmstrom and K. Ostberg in the singles and Ostberg and H. Müller in the doubles. Malmstrom put up a four-set fight against Robbins, but otherwise South Africa were much too strong.

Detailed Results

Singles: L. RAYMOND (S.A.) beat S. Malmstrom (Sw.) 6–2, 6–3, 6–2 ; beat K. Ostberg(Sw.) 7–5, 6–0, 6–0. C. J. J. ROBBINS (S.A.) beat K. Ostberg (Sw.) 6–2, 6–1, 6–1 ; beat S. Malmstrom (Sw.) 6–8, 10–8, 9–7, 6–4.

Doubles: L. RAYMOND and N. G. FARQUHARSON (S.A.) beat K. Ostberg and H. Müller (Sw.) 8–6, 6–2, 6–2.

Great Britain eliminated Poland at Warsaw on May 10, 11, and 12 by five to none, without loss of a set. The British singles players were H. W. Austin and G. P. Hughes, with G. R. O. Crole-Rees and C. G. Eames for the doubles. The Polish singles men were A. Tarnowski and M. Stolarow, the latter playing in the doubles with J. Loth.

Detailed Results

Singles: H. W. AUSTIN (G.B.) beat A. Tarnowski (Pol.) 6–1, 6–1, 6–1 ; beat M. Stolarow (Pol.) 6–1, 11–9, 7–5. G. P. HUGHES (G.B.) beat A. Tarnowski (Pol.) 6–1, 6–0, 7–5 ; beat M. Stolarow (Pol.) 7–5, 6–1, 6–2.

Doubles: G. R. O. CROLE-REES and C. G. EAMES (G.B.) beat J. Loth and M. Stolarow (Pol.) 6–1, 6–4, 6–3.

Germany beat Italy in the third round, at Hamburg, on June 7, 8, and 9 by a narrow margin—three to two. The winners' team was H. Landmann and H. Moldenhauer in the singles, with Moldenhauer and D. Prenn as the doubles pair. Italy's team was, as against Ireland in round two, H. L. de Morpurgo and G. de Stefani in the singles and de Morpurgo and A. del Bono in the doubles. De Stefani lost both his singles in five sets. De Morpurgo beat Landmann, but went down to Moldenhauer in five sets. Italy took the doubles in three sets. The closeness of the tie may be gauged from the fact that all Germany's three wins were in five sets, while Italy's two were in three sets.

Detailed Results

Singles: H. LANDMANN (GER.) beat G. de Stefani (It.) 3–6, 6–4, 6–3, 3–6, 6–3 ; lost to H. L. DE MORPURGO (IT.) 4–6, 0–6, 5–7. H. MOLDENHAUER (GER.) beat H. L. de Morpurgo (It.) 5–7, 6–3, 6–3, 3–6, 6–2 ; beat G. de Stefani (It.) 6–3, 3–6, 5–7, 6–4, 6–3.

Doubles: H. Moldenhauer and D. Prenn (Ger.) lost to H. L. DE MORPURGO and A. DEL BONO (IT.) 6–8, 3–6, 3–6.

Czechoslovakia beat Denmark at Copenhagen on June 5, 6, and 7 quite comfortably by four to one. The Czech team was J. Kozeluh and R. Menzel in the singles and Kozeluh and P. Macenauer in the doubles. E. Ulrich and P. Henriksen were Denmark's only players. The former beat Kozeluh from two sets down, to win Denmark's only victory.

Detailed Results

Singles: J. KOZELUH (CZECH.) beat P. Henriksen (Den.) 5–7, 6–2, 6–2, 6–4 ; lost to E. ULRICH (DEN.) 6–4, 7–5, 1–6, 2–6, 2–6. R. MENZEL (CZECH.) beat P. Henriksen (Den.) 9–7, 6–2, 6–3 ; beat E. Ulrich (Den.) 7–5, 7–5, 6–2.

Doubles: J. KOZELUH and P. MACENAUER (CZECH.) beat P. Henriksen and E. Ulrich (Den.) 6–1, 4–6, 6–4, 6–2.

Hungary just beat the Netherlands at Budapest on June 7, 8, and 9 by three to two. For Hungary B. von Kehrling and I. de Takacs played the singles, as usual, and also the doubles. H. Timmer and A. Diemer Kool made up the Dutch team. Von Kehrling beat both Dutchmen, and de Takacs beat Timmer in a long five-set struggle, to give Hungary the necessary three wins. Diemer Kool beat de Takacs, and with Timmer won the doubles in five sets.

Detailed Results

Singles: B. VON KEHRLING (HUN.) beat H. Timmer (Neth.) 8–6, 6–3, 3–6, 6–3 ; beat A. Diemer Kool (Neth.) 6–2, 6–1, 6–2. I. DE TAKACS (HUN.) beat H. Timmer (Neth.) 5–7, 7–5, 6–8, 6–1, 6–4 ; lost to A. DIEMER KOOL (NETH.) 2–6, 2–6, 4–6.

Doubles: B. von Kehrling and I. de Takacs (Hun.) lost to H. TIMMER and A. DIEMER KOOL (NETH.) 6–1, 2–6, 6–4, 3–6, 2–6.

Great Britain beat South Africa easily at Bournemouth on June 6, 7, and 8 by five to none in the remaining match of this round. The British singles players were H. W. Austin and J. C. Gregory, the latter pairing with I. G. Collins for the doubles. South Africa's team was L. Raymond and C. J. J. Robbins for the singles, with Raymond and N. G. Farquharson for the doubles. The British players were not threatened, and lost only two sets in the whole tie. Austin dropped one against Raymond, and the South Africans won another in the doubles.

Detailed Results

Singles: H. W. AUSTIN (G.B.) beat L. Raymond (S.A.) 8–6, 6–1, 2–6, 6–3 ; beat C. J. J. Robbins (S.A.) 6–0, 6–4, 6–1. J. C. GREGORY (G.B.) beat L. Raymond (S.A.) 6–4, 6–1, 6–2 ; beat C. J. J. Robbins (S.A.) 6–1, 6–1, 6–4.

Doubles: J. C. GREGORY and I. G. COLLINS (G.B.) beat L. Raymond and N. G. Farquharson (S.A.) 2–6, 6–3, 6–2, 6–1.

At Bucharest on June 14, 15, and 16 Great Britain beat Hungary by three to two in the fourth, or semi-final, round of the European Zone. The British team was again H. W. Austin and J. C. Gregory for the singles and Gregory and I. G. Collins for the doubles. Hungary's team was B. von Kehrling and I. de Takacs for the singles and von Kehrling and K. Aschner for the doubles. Von Kehrling scored his country's two wins by beating Gregory in five sets and Austin in four, but de Takacs could not win a set from either. The doubles, once more the key, went to Great Britain in four sets.

Detailed Results

Singles: J. C. GREGORY (G.B.) beat I. de Takacs (Hun.) 6–1, 6–0, 6–3 ; lost to B. VON KEHRLING (HUN.) 7–5, 5–7, 7–5, 2–6, 3–6. H. W. AUSTIN (G.B.) beat I. de Takacs (Hun.) 6–4, 6–2, 6–2 ; lost to B. VON KEHRLING (HUN.) 6–3, 4–6, 2–6, 2–6.

Doubles: J. C. GREGORY and I. G. COLLINS (G.B.) beat B. von Kehrling and K. Aschner (Hun.) 6–2, 4–6, 6–2, 6–3.

In the other semi-final Germany beat Czechoslovakia at Prague by three to one on June 19, 20, and 21. Their team was H. Moldenhauer and H. Landmann for the singles, with D. Prenn partnering Moldenhauer in the doubles. The Czech team was P. Macenauer and R. Menzel for the singles and Macenauer and J. Kozeluh in the doubles. Moldenhauer won all his matches, including the doubles, in straight sets. Landmann played only one of his singles, against Menzel, who beat him in five sets.

Detailed Results

Singles: H. MOLDENHAUER (GER.) beat P. Macenauer (Czech.) 6–3, 6–4, 8–6; beat R. Menzel (Czech.) 6–4, 8–6, 6–4. H. Landmann (Ger.) lost to R. MENZEL (CZECH.) 3–6, 3–6, 6–3, 6–0, 4–6.

Doubles: H. MOLDENHAUER and D. PRENN (GER.) beat J. Kozeluh and P. Macenauer (Czech.) 6–2, 6–2, 6–3.

The European Zone final, between Great Britain and Germany, took place at Berlin on July 12, 13, and 14, and was won by Germany in an unfortunate manner, as the last match was unfinished, and lost by Great Britain owing to Austin's retirement with cramp. The British team was H. W. Austin and J. C. Gregory for the singles, with Gregory and I. G. Collins for the doubles. Germany played H. Moldenhauer and D. Prenn in the singles and H. Kleinschroth and H. Landmann in the doubles. The Germans gained a two–love lead on the first day, when Prenn and Moldenhauer beat Gregory and Austin respectively in straight sets. Great Britain, however, squared the tie by winning the doubles and Gregory's single against Moldenhauer, both in three sets. This left all depending on the Austin–Prenn single, a fluctuating five-setter in which Austin was forced to give up with cramp at 1–5 down in the final set, to give Germany victory.

Detailed Results

Singles: D. PRENN (GER.) beat J. C. Gregory (G.B.) 6–3, 6–3, 6–2; beat H. W. Austin (G.B.) 4–6, 6–2, 6–4, 4–6, 5–1 (retired). H. MOLDENHAUER (GER.) beat H. W. Austin (G.B.) 6–4, 6–2, 6–3; lost to J. C. GREGORY (G.B.) 0–6, 2–6, 3–6.

Doubles: H. Kleinschroth and H. Landmann (Ger.) lost to J. C. GREGORY and I. G. COLLINS (G.B.) 4–6, 2–6, 0–6.

AMERICAN ZONE

In the first round of this zone U.S.A. beat Canada by five to none at Montreal on May 16, 17, and 18. The American team was J. van Ryn and J. F. Hennessey for singles and doubles. Canada played J. Wright and W. Crocker in the singles, with A. Ham partnering Wright in the doubles. W. L. Allison substituted for Hennessey against Crocker, whom he beat in five sets in the only full-distance match in the tie.

Detailed Results

Singles: J. VAN RYN (U.S.A.) beat W. Crocker (Can.) 9–7, 6–2, 6–3; beat J. Wright (Can.) 6–1, 6–0, 6–1. J. F. HENNESSEY (U.S.A.) beat J. Wright (Can.) 6–3, 4–6, 6–1, 7–5. W. L. ALLISON (U.S.A.) beat W. Crocker (Can.) 2–6, 6–4, 9–7, 4–6, 6–2.

Doubles: J. VAN RYN and J. F. HENNESSEY (U.S.A.) beat J. Wright and A. Ham (Can.) 6–1, 6–1, 1–6, 6–2.

In the second round, at Washington, U.S.A. beat Japan on May 23, 24, and 25 by four to one. America again relied on J. van Ryn and J. F. Hennessey only. Japan also used only two men, Y. Ohta and T. Abe. Ohta scored a good win against van Ryn in five sets, coming from behind to do so.

Detailed Results

Singles: J. VAN RYN (U.S.A.) beat T. Abe (Jap.) 6–2, 4–6, 6–3, 6–2; lost to Y. OHTA (JAP.) 4–6, 7–5, 6–2, 4–6, 5–7. J. F. HENNESSEY (U.S.A.) beat T. Abe (Jap.) 8–6, 6–1, 3–6, 6–1; beat Y. Ohta (Jap.) 6–2, 6–2, 6–3.

Doubles: J. VAN RYN and J. F. HENNESSEY (U.S.A.) beat Y. Ohta and T. Abe (Jap.) 6–3, 6–4, 6–2.

In the other second-round tie Cuba beat Mexico at Havana on May 17, 18, and 20 by three to one. The Cuban team was V. Banet and G. Vollmer in the singles and R. Morales and G. Upmann in the doubles. The Mexican team was I. de la Borbolla and R. Tapia in the singles and R. Kinsey and A. Unda in the doubles. Mexico won the doubles, but could not win a set in the singles.

Detailed Results

Singles: V. Banet (Cu.) beat I. de la Borbolla (Mex.) 6–2, 6–3, 8–6 ; G. Vollmer (Cu.) beat I. de la Borbolla (Mex.) 6–3, 6–3, 8–6 ; beat R. Tapia (Mex.) 6–2, 6–3, 6–1.

Doubles: R. Morales and G. Upmann (Cu.) lost to R. Kinsey and A. Unda (Mex.) 2–6, 12–10, 4–6, 3–6.

The zone final round, between U.S.A. and Cuba, was played at Detroit on May 30 and 31 and June 1, when the Americans won a sweeping five–nil victory. J. F. Hennessey and J. van Ryn were again America's singles players, with van Ryn and W. L. Allison for the doubles. Allison and G. M. Lott played the third-day singles as substitutes ; thus the winners played four different men in the singles, a unique happening. The Cuban team was R. Morales and G. Vollmer in the singles and Morales and G. Upmann for the doubles. Upmann also came into the singles on the third day as a substitute for Morales. The Cubans could not win a set in any match.

Detailed Results

Singles: J. F. Hennessey (U.S.A.) beat R. Morales (Cu.) 6–0, 6–3, 6–4. J. van Ryn (U.S.A.) beat G. Vollmer (Cu.) 6–0, 6–1, 6–1. W. L. Allison (U.S.A.) beat G. Vollmer (Cu.) 6–3, 6–2, 7–5. G. M. Lott (U.S.A.) beat G. Upmann (Cu.) 6–4, 6–3, 6–3.

Doubles: J. van Ryn and W. L. Allison (U.S.A.) beat R. Morales and G. Upmann (Cu.) 6–2, 6–0, 6–1.

Inter-zone Round

U.S.A., winners of the American Zone, and Germany, winners of the European Zone, met at Berlin on July 19, 20, and 21, for the right to challenge France. U.S.A. won easily by five to none. The American team was W. T. Tilden and F. T. Hunter in the singles and W. L. Allison and J. van Ryn in the doubles. Germany relied on two men, H. Moldenhauer and D. Prenn. Tilden did not lose a set to either German, but Hunter dropped one to Prenn and two to Moldenhauer. Allison and van Ryn lost the first set in the doubles, but polished off the next three. This tie turned out to be Moldenhauer's last match in the Davis Cup competition, as he died as the result of an accident before play began next year. U.S.A. were thus again challengers to France.

Detailed Results

Singles: W. T. Tilden (U.S.A.) beat H. Moldenhauer (Ger.) 6–2, 6–4, 6–4 ; beat D. Prenn (Ger.) 6–1, 6–4, 6–1. F. T. Hunter (U.S.A.) beat H. Moldenhauer (Ger.) 6–3, 1–6, 6–4, 4–6, 6–1 ; beat D. Prenn (Ger.) 3–6, 6–3, 6–4, 6–3.

Doubles: W. L. Allison and J. van Ryn (U.S.A.) beat H. Moldenhauer and D. Prenn (Ger.) 9–11, 6–2, 6–4, 6–3.

Challenge Round

This final tie took place in Paris on July 26, 27, and 28, when France, the holders, beat the challengers, U.S.A., by three matches to two. France relied on two players only, H. Cochet and J. Borotra, R. Lacoste being out of commission through illness. Actually he was never to play again in the competition in which he proved himself such an invaluable member of his country's team. U.S.A. chose W. T. Tilden and G. M. Lott to play the singles, with W. L. Allison and J. van Ryn as the doubles pair. Cochet, at the height of his career, beat Tilden with the loss of only six games in three sets, and Lott by three sets to one, with plenty to spare. Borotra was less happy and less efficient. Tilden beat him, as he always did out of doors, in four sets, but Lott was not quite experienced enough to overcome such a seasoned campaigner, and Borotra beat him in four sets. Allison and van Ryn did very well to beat Cochet and Borotra in three sets, more especially as U.S.A. were two matches down when the doubles took place. It had to be won for the Americans to keep the tie alive. This was achieved by a young, virile pair full of dash and enterprise and fight. France's strength, however, was clearly displayed when only two of the " Four Musketeers " were required to hold the fort, and then could do it with something over.

Detailed Results

Singles: H. Cochet (Fr.) beat W. T. Tilden (U.S.A.) 6–3, 6–1, 6–2 ; beat G. M. Lott (U.S.A.) 6–1, 3–6, 6–0, 6–3. J. Borotra (Fr.) beat G. M. Lott (U.S.A.) 6–1, 3–6, 6–4, 7–5 ; lost to W. T. Tilden (U.S.A.) 6–4, 1–6, 4–6, 5–7.

Doubles: J. Borotra and H. Cochet (Fr.) lost to J. van Ryn and W. L. Allison (U.S.A.) 1–6, 6–8, 4–6.

1930: FRANCE

This year twenty-eight countries challenged—twenty-four in the European Zone and four in the American Zone.

European Zone

India beat Greece at Athens on April 19, 20, and 22 by three to two. India's players were J. Charanjiva and H. L. Soni, while A. J. Zerlendi and O. Garangiotis played the singles for Greece, with Garangiotis and M. Balli as the doubles pair. Zerlendi won two four-set victories in his singles, but India won all the other matches—in four sets too.

Detailed Results

Singles: J. Charanjiva (Ind.) beat O. Garangiotis (Gr.) 7–5, 1–6, 6–2, 6–4 ; lost to A. J. Zerlendi (Gr.) 4–6, 2–6, 6–3, 4–6. H. L. Soni (Ind.) beat O. Garangiotis (Gr.) 11–9, 6–4, 5–7, 6–4 ; lost to A. J. Zerlendi (Gr.) 3–6, 6–4, 5–7, 1–6.

Doubles: J. Charanjiva and H. L. Soni (Ind.) beat M. Balli and O. Garangiotis (Gr.) 6–2, 3–6, 6–1, 9–7.

Japan beat Hungary at Budapest on May 2, 3, and 4 by four to none, one match being unfinished. Hungary's team was B. von Kehrling and I. de Takacs in the singles, with K. Aschner partnering von Kehrling in the doubles. Japan's team was Y. Ohta and T. Harada in the singles, with Harada and T. Abe for the doubles. H. Satoh substituted for Harada on the third day against de Takacs. The match between von Kehrling and Ohta was unfinished, play stopping when von Kehrling led by two sets to one and 6–all in the fourth set. Except in this match Japan were much too strong.

Detailed Results

Singles: Y. Ohta (Jap.) beat I. de Takacs (Hun.) 6–1, 6–4, 6–0 ; versus B. von Kehrling (Hun.) 6–4, 4–6, 5–7, 6–6 (unfinished). T. Harada (Jap.) beat B. von Kehrling (Hun.) 2–6, 6–3, 8–6, 6–2. H. Satoh (Jap.) beat I. de Takacs (Hun.) 6–4, 6–3, 6–3.

Doubles: T. HARADA and T. ABE (JAP.) beat B. von Kehrling and K. Aschner (Hun.) 6–2, 6–2, 3–6, 6–4.

Yugoslavia beat Sweden at Belgrade on May 2 and 3 by three to none. The Yugoslav team was K. Friedrich and F. Schaffers for the singles, I. Radovic partnering Schaffers in the doubles. Sweden were represented by J. Soederstrom and H. Ramberg. The latter took Friedrich to five sets, but Soederstrom lost to Schaffers in four, and the Swedes also lost the doubles in four sets.

Detailed Results

Singles: K. FRIEDRICH (YUGO.) beat H. Ramberg (Sw.) 6–3, 1–6, 6–4, 5–7, 6–4. F. SCHAFFERS (YUGO.) beat J. Soederstrom (Sw.) 4–6, 6–3, 6–1, 6–0 ; beat H. Ramberg (Sw.) 6–0, 3–1 (retired).

Doubles: F. SCHAFFERS and I. RADOVIC (YUGO.) beat H. Ramberg and J. Soederstrom (Sw.) 6–3, 6–1, 5–7, 6–2.

Spain beat Belgium at Antwerp by four to one on May 2, 3, and 4. The Spanish team was E. Maier and A. Juanico in the singles and Maier and Saprissa in the doubles. Belgium's team was A. Lacroix and A. Ewbank in the singles and Ewbank and L. de Borman in the doubles. Maier beat Lacroix in five sets and Ewbank in three. Juanico beat Lacroix in three sets and lost to Ewbank in five. Spain took the doubles in five sets.

Detailed Results

Singles: E. MAIER (SP.) beat A. Lacroix (Belg.) 3–6, 6–1, 2–6, 6–2, 6–3 ; beat A. Ewbank (Belg.) 6–2, 6–1, 6–1. A. JUANICO (SP.) beat A. Lacroix (Belg.) 6–3, 6–3, 7–5 ; lost to A. EWBANK (BELG.) 3–6, 5–7, 6–2, 6–2, 1–6.

Doubles: E. MAIER and SAPRISSA (SP.) beat A. Ewbank and L. de Borman (Belg.) 6–1, 4–6, 1–6, 8–6, 6–3.

Australia beat Switzerland at Zürich on May 2, 3, and 4 by five to none, without strain. Australia's team was E. F. Moon and J. H. Crawford in the singles, with H. C. Hopman and J. Willard for the doubles. The Swiss team was C. F. Aeschliman and H. Chiesa in the singles, with Aeschliman and J. Wuarin for the doubles. Moon, a slow starter, dropped the opening set in each of his singles. The Swiss pair also took the first set in the doubles.

Detailed Results

Singles: J. H. CRAWFORD (AUSTRAL.) beat C. F. Aeschliman (Switz.) 6–0, 6–3, 6–1 ; beat H. Chiesa (Switz.) 6–4, 10–8, 6–3. E. F. MOON (AUSTRAL.) beat H. Chiesa (Switz.) 3–6, 6–2, 6–1, 6–1 ; beat C. F. Aeschliman (Switz.) 3–6, 6–1, 6–4, 6–3.

Doubles: J. WILLARD and H. C. HOPMAN (AUSTRAL.) beat J. Wuarin and C. F. Aeschliman (Switz.) 2–6, 6–4, 6–2, 6–3.

Ireland beat Monaco at Dublin by four to one on May 3, 5, and 6. The Irish team was G. L. Rogers and E. A. McGuire for the singles, with V. Allman Smith partnering Rogers in the doubles. Monaco relied on V. Landau and R. Gallèpe. McGuire had to work very hard to beat Landau in five sets, and lost to Gallèpe in three. Rogers's single against Landau and the doubles were plain sailing for Ireland.

Detailed Results

Singles: G. L. ROGERS (IRE.) beat V. Landau (Mon.) 6–1, 6–4, 6–2 ; beat R. Gallèpe (Mon.) 2–6, 8–6, 6–2, 11–9. E. A. MCGUIRE (IRE.) beat V. Landau (Mon.) 13–11, 0–6, 2–6, 6–4, 6–1 ; lost to R. GALLÈPE (MON.) 2–6, 5–7, 5–7.

Doubles: G. L. ROGERS and V. ALLMAN SMITH (IRE.) beat R. Gallèpe and V. Landau (Mon.) 6–1, 6–1, 6–4.

Poland beat Rumania at Warsaw on May 2, 3, 4, and 5 by three to two. Rumania's was a two-man team of N. Mishu and G. Poulieff. Poland played I. Tloczynski and M. Stolarow in the singles and M. Stolarow and G. Stolarow in the doubles. Rumania won the doubles, and Mishu beat Stolarow, who, however, beat Poulieff in five sets. Tloczynski won both his singles despite his youth.

Detailed Results

Singles: M. STOLAROW (POL.) beat G. Poulieff (Rum.) 3–6, 6–1, 6–2, 7–9, 6–3 ; lost to N. MISHU (RUM.) 3–6, 6–4, 4–6, 1–6. I. TLOCZYNSKI (POL.) beat G. Poulieff (Rum.) 6–3, 7–5, 6–4 ; beat N. Mishu (Rum.) 6-3, 7–9, 7–5, 4–6, 6–0.

Doubles: M. Stolarow and G. Stolarow (Pol.) lost to N. MISHU and G. POULIEFF (RUM.) 6–1, 2–6, 3–6, 5–7.

Great Britain beat Germany in London on April 24, 25, and 26 by three to two. It was a close struggle, with Great Britain two down after the first day's play. The British team was H. W. Austin and H. G. N. Lee for the singles with J. C. Gregory and I. G. Collins for the doubles. Germany's team was D. Prenn and H. Landmann in the singles and H. Kleinschroth and W. Dessart in the doubles. On the first day Landmann beat Austin in five sets, Austin's bogey, cramp, worrying him at the end. Austin did well to overcome Prenn on the third day in three sets. Lee lost to Prenn on the first day, but beat Landmann safely enough in the critical final match. The Englishmen won the doubles comfortably.

Detailed Results

Singles: H. W. AUSTIN (G.B.) beat D. Prenn (Ger.) 6–3, 6–4, 7–5 ; lost to H. LANDMANN (GER.) 3–6, 6–8, 7–5, 6–4, 4–6. H. G. N. LEE (G.B.) beat H. Landmann (Ger.) 5–7, 6–3, 6–2, 6–3 ; lost to D. PRENN (GER.) 4–6, 9–7, 3–6, 2–6.

Doubles: J. C. GREGORY and I. G. COLLINS (G.B.) beat H. Kleinschroth and W. Dessart (Ger.) 6–2, 6–4, 6–3.

In the second round Czechoslovakia beat Denmark at Prague on May 16, 17, and 18 by three to two. The Danes relied on two men only, E. Ulrich and E. Worm. J. Kozeluh and R. Menzel were the Czech singles men, with Menzel and F. von Röhrer for the doubles. Ulrich beat Kozeluh in five sets, and the Danes just won the doubles, also in five sets.

Detailed Results

Singles: J. KOZELUH (CZECH.) beat E. Worm (Den.) 7–5, 6–2, 10–8 ; lost to E. ULRICH (DEN.) 6–0, 2–6, 5–7, 6–3, 5–7. R. MENZEL (CZECH.) beat E. Worm (Den.) 6–2, 6–2, 4–6, 6–2 ; beat E. Ulrich (Den.) 6–2, 6–2, 6–1.

Doubles: R. Menzel and F. von Röhrer (Czech.) lost to E. ULRICH and E. WORM (DEN.) 3–6, 6–1, 4–6, 6–4, 7–9.

The Netherlands beat Finland at Amsterdam on May 16, 17, and 18 by four to one. The Netherlands' team was

H. Timmer and A. Diemer Kool for singles and doubles. Finland played A. Grahn and B. Grotenfelt in the singles and Grahn and R. Granholm in the doubles. Their only success was Grahn's win over Diemer Kool. The Netherlands won all the other matches in three sets.

Detailed Results

Singles: H. TIMMER (NETH.) beat R. Grotenfelt (Fin.) 6–1, 6–1, 6–0 ; beat A. Grahn (Fin.) 6–1, 6–3, 6–2. A. DIEMER KOOL (NETH.) beat B. Grotenfelt (Fin.) 6–2, 6–0, 6–0 ; lost to A. GRAHN (FIN.) 6–8, 6–8, 4–6.

Doubles: H. TIMMER and A. DIEMER KOOL (NETH.) beat A. Grahn and R. Granholm (Fin.) 6–4, 6–1, 6–2.

Japan beat India in London on June 7, 8, and 9 by five to none. India's team was J. Charanjiva and A. Madan Mohan in the singles, with H. L. Soni partnering the former in the doubles. T. Harada and Y. Ohta played the singles for Japan, with T. Abe partnering Harada in the doubles. Japan took all the singles in three sets—even the substitute ones—but India led two sets to love in the doubles before going down in five sets.

Detailed Results

Singles: T. HARADA (JAP.) beat J. Charanjiva (Ind.) 6–3, 6–3, 6–1. Y. OHTA (JAP.) beat A. Madan Mohan (Ind.) 6–2, 7–5, 6–4 ; beat H. L. Soni (Ind.) 6–1, 6–4, 6–0. H. SATOH (JAP.) beat A. Madan Mohan (Ind.) 10–8, 6–1, 6–2.

Doubles: T. HARADA and T. ABE (JAP.) beat J. Charanjiva and H. L. Soni (Ind.) 5–7, 4–6, 6–2, 6–2, 6–2.

Spain beat Yugoslavia at Zagreb on May 17, 18, and 20 by three to none. Both countries relied on two men only—Spain on E. Maier and A. Juanico, and Yugoslavia on K. Friedrich and F. Schaffers. The Spaniards did not lose a set.

Detailed Results

Singles: E. MAIER (SP.) beat F. Schaffers (Yugo.) 6–3, 6–4, 6–3. A. JUANICO (SP.) beat K. Friedrich (Yugo.) 6–0, 6–1, 6–3.

Doubles: E. MAIER and A. JUANICO (SP.) beat K. Friedrich and F. Schaffers (Yugo.) 6–0, 6–1, 6–3.

Australia beat Ireland at Dublin by four to one on May 15, 16, and 17. Their team was E. F. Moon and J. H. Crawford in the singles, with H. C. Hopman and J. Willard in the doubles. Ireland's team was G. L. Rogers and E. A. McGuire for the singles, with Rogers and V. Allman Smith for the doubles. Rogers played very well, beating Crawford in five sets and reaching match point against Moon. McGuire could not hold either Australian, nor could Ireland add to their match total in the doubles.

Detailed Results

Singles: J. H. CRAWFORD (AUSTRAL.) beat E. A. McGuire (Ire.) 6–1, 6–2, 6–4 ; lost to G. L. ROGERS (IRE.) 3–6, 6–3, 5–7, 6–2, 3–6. E. F. MOON (AUSTRAL.) beat G. L. Rogers (Ire.) 4–6, 2–6, 6–3, 6–2, 12–10 ; beat E. A. McGuire (Ire.) 6–2, 7–5, 3–6, 8–6.

Doubles: J. WILLARD and H. C. HOPMAN (AUSTRAL.) beat G. L. Rogers and V. Allman Smith (Ire.) 6–4, 6–2, 6–2.

Great Britain beat Poland at Torquay on May 10, 12, and 13 very easily by five to none. The British singles players were N. Sharpe and H. G. N. Lee, with J. C. Gregory and I. G. Collins in the doubles. Poland's players were I. Tloczynski and M. Stolarow in the singles, with Tloczynski and P. Warminski in the doubles. The Poles could not win a set in any match. In fact, in the doubles they could not even win a game.

Detailed Results

Singles: H. G. N. LEE (G.B.) beat I. Tloczynski (Pol.) 6–1, 6–4, 6–2 ; beat M. Stolarow (Pol.) 6–4, 6–2, 8–6. N. SHARPE (G.B.) beat M. Stolarow (Pol.) 6–3, 6–4, 6–1 ; beat I. Tloczynski (Pol.) 6–2, 6–1, 6–1.

Doubles: J. C. GREGORY and I. G. COLLINS (G.B.) beat I. Tloczynski and P. Warminski (Pol.) 6–0, 6–0, 6–0.

Austria beat Norway at Oslo on May 16, 17, and 18 by four to none. The Austrian players were H. W. Artens and F. Matejka. Norway's singles men were T. Torkildsen and J. Nielsen, and with Nielsen in the doubles was R. Christoffersen. Nielsen won a set from Artens, but otherwise Norway went down in three sets each time.

Detailed Results

Singles: H. W. ARTENS (AUS.) beat T. Torkildsen (Norw.) 6–4, 6–3, 6–4 ; beat J. Nielsen (Norw.) 0–6, 6–1, 6–1, 7–5. F. MATEJKA (AUS.) beat J. Nielsen (Norw.) 6–2, 6–1, 6–0.

Doubles: H. W. ARTENS and F. MATEJKA (AUS.) beat J. Nielsen and R. Christoffersen (Norw.) 6–2, 6–4, 6–3.

Italy beat Egypt at Rome on May 9, 10, and 11 by five to none. The Italian team was H. L. de Morpurgo and G. de Stefani for the singles and de Morpurgo and P. Gaslini for the doubles. Egypt were represented by L. Wahid and J. Grandguillot in the singles and N. Zahar and Riches in the doubles. Riches also substituted for Wahid in the singles on the third day. The Egyptians carried the doubles to five sets, but could not win a set in the singles.

Detailed Results

Singles: H. L. DE MORPURGO (IT.) beat L. Wahid (Egy.) 6–1, 6–4, 6–2 ; beat J. Grandguillot (Egy.) 6–4, 6–1, 6–2. G. DE STEFANI (IT.) beat J. Grandguillot (Egy.) 6–2, 6–1, 6–2 ; beat Riches (Egy.) 6–0, 6–2, 6–0.

Doubles: H. L. DE MORPURGO and P. GASLINI (IT.) beat N. Zahar and Riches (Egy.) 5–7, 8–6, 6–1, 3–6, 7–5.

In the third round Czechoslovakia beat the Netherlands at Scheveningen, Holland, on May 30 and 31 and June 1 by a narrow margin—three to two. The Dutch team of H. Timmer and A. Diemer Kool put up a grand fight. J. Kozeluh and R. Menzel were the Czech team. Timmer won both his singles, and with Diemer Kool almost the doubles as well.

Detailed Results

Singles: J. KOZELUH (CZECH.) beat A. Diemer Kool (Neth.) 6–4, 4–6, 6–3, 6–3 ; lost to H. TIMMER (NETH.) 1–6, 3–6, 1–6. R. MENZEL (CZECH.) beat A. Diemer Kool (Neth.) 6–3, 6–3, 6–2 ; lost to H. TIMMER (NETH.) 6–8, 0–6, 6–4, 5–7.

Doubles: J. KOZELUH and R. MENZEL (CZECH.) beat H. Timmer and A. Diemer Kool (Neth.) 7–9, 6–2, 6-1, 3–6, 6–4.

Japan and Spain met at Barcelona on June 7, 8, and 9, when Japan won by four to one. Their team was Y. Ohta and T. Harada in the singles, with Harada and T. Abe in the doubles. The Spanish team was E. Maier and A. Juanico in the singles and Maier and N. F. Sindreu in the doubles. Japan won all the singles comfortably, but were outplayed by the Spaniards in the doubles.

Detailed Results

Singles: Y. OHTA (JAP.) beat A. Juanico (Sp.) 6–1, 3–6, 6–2, 6–2; beat E. Maier (Sp.) 6–1, 6–1, 6–1. T. HARADA (JAP.) beat A. Juanico (Sp.) 6–0, 6–3, 6–3; beat E. Maier (Sp.) 3–6, 6–2, 6–0, 6–4.

Doubles: T. Harada and T. Abe (Jap.) lost to E. MAIER and N. F. SINDREU (SP.) 6–2, 4–6, 4–6, 4–6.

Australia beat Great Britain at Eastbourne on June 6, 7, and 9 by four to one. The Australian team was J. H. Crawford and H. C. Hopman in singles and doubles. The British team was J. C. Gregory and H. G. N. Lee in the singles and Gregory and I. G. Collins in the doubles. Lee fought two five-set singles, but lost both after leading two sets to one in each. Gregory lost to Crawford in four sets and to Hopman in three. Great Britain took the doubles in straight sets.

Detailed Results

Singles: J. H. CRAWFORD (AUSTRAL.) beat H. G. N. Lee (G.B.) 3–6, 6–2, 4–6, 6–2, 6–2; beat J. C. Gregory (G.B.) 6–2, 7–5, 6–8, 6–3. H. C. HOPMAN (AUSTRAL.) beat J. C. Gregory (G.B.) 8–6, 6–4, 9–7; beat H. G. N. Lee (G.B.) 6–3, 4–6, 7–9, 6–2, 6–4.

Doubles: J. H. Crawford and H. C. Hopman (Austral.) lost to J. C. GREGORY and I. G. COLLINS (G.B.) 6–8, 8–10, 2–6.

Italy survived a close tie against Austria at Vienna on June 6, 7, and 8 by three to two. Italy were without the services of de Stefani, and played H. L. de Morpurgo and P. Gaslini in singles and doubles. Austria relied on H. W. Artens and F. Matejka for all matches. De Morpurgo won both his singles in three sets, but this was offset by Gaslini's losing both his in three sets also. The doubles was therefore the key, and in this the Italians scraped home in the tenth game of the fifth set.

Detailed Results

Singles: H. L. DE MORPURGO (IT.) beat F. Matejka (Aus.) 6–2, 6–2, 6–3 ; beat H. W. Artens (Aus.) 6–2, 6–2, 6–2. P. Gaslini (It.) lost to H. W. ARTENS (AUS.) 6–8, 2–6, 2–6 ; lost to F. MATEJKA (AUS.) 3–6, 4–6, 5–7.

Doubles: H. L. DE MORPURGO and P. GASLINI (IT.) beat H. W. Artens and F. Matejka (Aus.) 9–11, 8–6, 6–1, 1–6, 6–4.

In the fourth, or semi-final, round Japan beat Czechoslovakia at Prague on June 14, 15, and 16 by three to two. The Japanese team, as usual, was T. Harada and Y. Ohta in the singles, with Harada and T. Abe in the doubles. The Czech team was R. Menzel and J. Kozeluh only. Menzel was in good form, and won both his singles, but Japan won the other three matches.

Detailed Results

Singles: T. HARADA (JAP.) beat J. Kozeluh (Czech.) 6–2, 6–3, 6–3 ; lost to R. MENZEL (CZECH.) 11–9, 3–6, 5–7, 1–6. Y. OHTA (JAP.) beat J. Kozeluh (Czech.) 6–4, 4–6, 6–4, 7–5 ; lost to R. MENZEL (CZECH.) 2–6, 6–4, 3–6, 3–6.

Doubles: T. HARADA and T. ABE (JAP.) beat J. Kozeluh and R. Menzel (Czech.) 1–6, 7–5, 8–6, 9–7.

Italy beat Australia at Milan on June 14, 15, and 16 by three to two. The Italian team was H. L. de Morpurgo and G. de Stefani for the singles, with de Morpurgo and P. Gaslini for the doubles. The Australian side was J. H. Crawford and H. C. Hopman for the singles and Hopman and J. Willard in the doubles. Both Australians forced de Morpurgo to five sets, but neither could beat him. De Stefani beat Hopman in four sets, but lost to Crawford in three. The Australians won the doubles in four sets.

Detailed Results

Singles: H. L. DE MORPURGO (IT.) beat J. H. Crawford (Austral.) 5–7, 6–2, 6–4, 3–6, 6–4 ; beat H. C. Hopman (Austral.) 8–6, 2–6, 6–4, 1–6, 6–1. G. DE STEFANI (IT.) beat H. C. Hopman (Austral.) 6–3, 3–6, 7–5, 6–2 ; lost to J. H. CRAWFORD (AUSTRAL.) 4–6, 3–6, 2–6.

Doubles: H. L. de Morpurgo and P. Gaslini (It.) lost to H. C. HOPMAN and J. WILLARD (AUSTRAL.) 7–9, 7–9, 6–4, 4–6.

In the final round of this zone Italy played Japan at Genoa on July 11, 12, and 13. In a very close struggle Italy prevailed by three to two. The Italian team was H. L. de Morpurgo and G. de Stefani only, while Japan relied on Y. Ohta and T. Harada for the singles and Harada and T. Abe for the doubles. Harada beat both Italians in straight sets, and with Abe carried the doubles into five sets from two sets down before losing. Ohta lost to de Stefani in four sets, and could win only three games against de Morpurgo.

Detailed Results

Singles: H. L. DE MORPURGO (IT.) beat Y. Ohta (Jap.) 6–0, 6–2, 6–1 ; lost to T. HARADA (JAP.) 4–6, 3–6, 5–7. G. DE STEFANI (IT.) beat Y. Ohta (Jap.) 6–3, 6–4, 4–6, 6–4 ; lost to T. HARADA (JAP.) 2–6, 5–7, 5–7.

Doubles: H. L. DE MORPURGO and G. DE STEFANI (IT.) beat T. Harada and T. Abe (Jap.) 8–6, 9–7, 6–8, 2–6, 6–1.

AMERICAN ZONE

In the only first-round match of this zone U.S.A. easily beat Canada at Philadelphia on May 15, 16, and 17. The American team was J. van Ryn and G. M. Lott in the singles, with van Ryn and W. L Allison in the doubles. Allison and J. H. Doeg played the singles on the third day as substitutes. Canada's team was J. Wright and M. Rainville in the singles and Wright and W. Crocker in the doubles. Wright won Canada's only set—against van Ryn.

Detailed Results

Singles: J. VAN RYN (U.S.A.) beat J. Wright (Can.) 6–2, 6–2, 3–6, 6–2. G. M. LOTT (U.S.A.) beat M. Rainville (Can.) 6–2, 6–2, 8–6. J. H. DOEG (U.S.A.) beat J. Wright (Can.) 6–2, 6–3, 6–2. W. L. ALLISON (U.S.A.) beat M. Rainville (Can.) 6–2, 6–2, 7–5.

Doubles: J. VAN RYN and W. L. ALLISON (U.S.A.) beat J. Wright and W. Crocker (Can.) 6–0, 6–4, 6–2.

Cuba having retired to Mexico, the latter country opposed U.S.A. in the American Zone final round at Washington on May 22, 23, and 24, but failed to win a match. The American team was W. L. Allison and G. M. Lott for the singles, with Allison and J. van Ryn in the doubles. Van Ryn and J. H. Doeg substituted for Allison and Lott as singles men on the third day. The Mexican team was R. Tapia and I. de la Borbolla in the singles, with M. Llano and A. Unda in the doubles. F. Sendel substituted for de la Borbolla on the third day. Tapia extended Allison to 7–5 in the fifth set, but de la Borbolla could not win a single game against Lott. This was the latter's second 18–0 Davis Cup victory.

Detailed Results

Singles: W. L. Allison (U.S.A.) beat R. Tapia (Mex.) 6–3, 3–6, 6–8, 6–2, 7–5. G. M. Lott (U.S.A.) beat I. de la Borbolla (Mex.) 6–0, 6–0, 6–0. J. H. Doeg (U.S.A.) beat F. Sendel (Mex.) 6–1, 6–0, 6–2. J. van Ryn (U.S.A.) beat R. Tapia (Mex.) 6–2, 6–3, 6–1.

Doubles: J. van Ryn and W. L. Allison (U.S.A.) beat M. Llano and A. Unda (Mex.) 6–0, 6–1, 6–3.

Inter-zone Round

This tie, between U.S.A. and the European Zone winners, Italy, was played at Paris on July 18, 19, and 20, and won by U.S.A. by four to one. Italy's team was H. L. de Morpurgo and G. de Stefani for the singles and de Morpurgo and P. Gaslini for the doubles. U.S.A. played W. L. Allison and G. M. Lott in the singles and Allison and J. van Ryn in the doubles. De Stefani almost beat Allison in the first match, winning the first two sets and having long leads in the fourth and fifth sets. Allison, though not in form, hung on with great determination, and finally got home at 10–8 in the fifth set. De Morpurgo fought hard against Lott, but could win only the first set. U.S.A. took the doubles in five sets, and on the third day Lott easily beat de Stefani, but Allison went down to de Morpurgo in four sets. U.S.A. thus once again qualified for the challenge round against the holders, France.

Detailed Results

Singles: W. L. ALLISON (U.S.A.) beat G. de Stefani (It.) 4–6, 7–9, 6–4, 8–6, 10–8 ; lost to H. L. DE MORPURGO (IT.) 5–7, 2–6, 7–5, 4–6. G. M. LOTT (U.S.A.) beat G. de Stefani (It.) 6–3, 6–1, 6–3 ; beat H. L. de Morpurgo (It.) 3–6, 9–7, 10–8, 6–3.

Doubles: W. L. ALLISON and J. VAN RYN (U.S.A.) beat H. L. de Morpurgo and P. Gaslini (It.) 5–7, 6–2, 6–4, 1–6, 6–3.

CHALLENGE ROUND

This tie took place at Paris on July 25, 26, and 27, and France retained the trophy by four matches to one. The defending team was H. Cochet and J. Borotra in the singles, with Cochet and J. Brugnon as doubles pair. The challenging U.S.A. team was W. T. Tilden, playing his eleventh successive and final challenge round, and G. M. Lott for the singles, with W. L. Allison and J. van Ryn for the doubles. Tilden, according to his custom on outdoor courts, beat Borotra in the opening match in four sets after losing the first set. Cochet completely outplayed Lott in three sets, to make the tie one–all. Cochet and Brugnon beat Allison and van Ryn in four sets, to put France two to one up. Lott put up a wonderful fight against Borotra, just going down at 8–6 in the fifth set. In the last match Cochet beat Tilden in four sets. It might be mentioned here that the honour of having beaten W. T. Tilden in Davis Cup singles is confined to two men—both Frenchmen—R. Lacoste, who achieved it twice, and H. Cochet, who did it three times. In Davis Cup doubles the great " Big Bill " was beaten only twice—with V. Richards by G. L. Patterson and P. O'Hara Wood, and with F. T. Hunter by H. Cochet and J. Borotra. Some record ! He played thirty-nine Davis Cup matches in all, twenty-seven of them in challenge rounds. Of these latter he won twenty, never losing in a pre-challenge round. Yes, sir ! Some record !

Detailed Results

Singles: J. BOROTRA (FR.) beat G. M. Lott (U.S.A.) 5–7, 6–3, 2–6, 6–2, 8–6 ; lost to W. T. TILDEN (U.S.A.) 6–2, 5–7, 4–6, 5–7. H. COCHET (FR.) beat W. T. Tilden (U.S.A.) 4–6, 6–3, 6–1, 7–5 ; beat G. M. Lott (U.S.A.) 6–4, 6–2, 6–2.

Doubles: H. Cochet and J. Brugnon (Fr.) beat W. Allison and J. van Ryn (U.S.A.) 6–3, 7–5, 1–6, 6–2.

1931: FRANCE

This year there were thirty challenging countries, twenty-two in the European Zone, three in the North American Zone, and five in the new South American Zone, introduced for the first time, the American Zone being thus divided into two parts.

European Zone

Great Britain beat Monaco at Plymouth in the first round on April 23, 24, and 25 by five to none, without loss of a set. Great Britain's team, later to contest the challenge round, was H. W. Austin and F. J. Perry for the singles, with G. P. Hughes and C. H. Kingsley for the doubles. Monaco relied on R. Gallèpe and V. Landau.

Detailed Results

Singles: H. W. Austin (G.B.) beat V. Landau (Mon.) 6–0, 6–0, 6–1 ; beat R. Gallèpe (Mon.) 6–0, 6–1, 6–2. F. J. Perry (G.B.) beat R. Gallèpe (Mon.) 6–3, 6–2, 7–5. C. H. Kingsley (G.B.) beat V. Landau (Mon.) 6–0, 6–1, 6–4.

Doubles: C. H. Kingsley and G. P. Hughes (G.B.) beat R. Gallèpe and V. Landau (Mon.) 6–0, 6–2, 6–0.

South Africa and Germany met at Düsseldorf on May 1, 2, and 3, when South Africa won comfortably by five to none. Their team was V. G. Kirby and L. Raymond in the singles, with Kirby and N. G. Farquharson in the doubles. The German team was Dr Buss and E. Nourney in the singles, the latter also playing the doubles with W. Dessart. Nourney extended Raymond to five sets in the only close match.

Detailed Results

Singles: V. G. Kirby (S.A.) beat Dr Buss (Ger.) 1–6, 6–1, 6–2, 6–3 ; beat E. Nourney (Ger.) 4–6, 6–3, 6–4, 6–3. L. Raymond (S.A.) beat E. Nourney (Ger.) 3–6, 6–3, 4–6, 6–4, 7–5 ; beat Dr Buss (Ger.) 4–6, 6–3, 7–5, 8–6.

Doubles: V. G. Kirby and N. G. Farquharson (S.A.) beat E. Nourney and W. Dessart (Ger.) 6–2, 6–3, 6–3.

Ireland beat Switzerland at Montreux on May 2, 4, and 5 by five to none. The Irish team was G. L. Rogers and E. A. McGuire in the singles, with Rogers and C. F. Scroope for the doubles. The Swiss team was made up of C. F. Aeschliman and H. C. Fisher only. The only five-setter was between McGuire and Aeschliman, which the Irishman won after being a set down at the interval. The third set of the doubles went to twenty-four games and to Ireland, whose pair won the match in four sets.

Detailed Results

Singles: G. L. ROGERS (IRE.) beat C. F. Aeschliman (Switz.) 6–2, 7–5, 6–2; beat H. C. Fisher (Switz.) 6–1, 2–6, 6–2, 8–6. E. A. MCGUIRE (IRE.) beat H. C. Fisher (Switz.) 6–4, 7–5, 7–5; beat C. F. Aeschliman (Switz.) 5–7, 7–5, 2–6, 8–6, 6–2.

Doubles: G. L. ROGERS and C. F. SCROOPE (IRE.) beat C. F. Aeschliman and H. C. Fisher (Switz.) 6–3, 5–7, 13–11, 6–2.

Greece beat Austria at Athens on April 16, 17, and 18 by a narrow three–two margin. The Greek team was A. J. Zerlendi and O. Garangiotis in the singles and M. Balli and K. Georgiades in the doubles. The Austrian team was H. W. Artens and F. Matejka in the singles, with Artens and M. Haberl in the doubles. Garangiotis won both his singles in five sets, and Zerlendi beat Artens in five sets also. Matejka beat Zerlendi in four sets, and Austria won the doubles in the same number.

Detailed Results

Singles: A. J. ZERLENDI (GR.) beat H. W. Artens (Aus.) 1–6, 6–3, 1–6, 6–2, 8–6; lost to F. MATEJKA (AUS.) 3–6, 2–6, 8–6, 3–6. O. GARANGIOTIS (GR.) beat F. Matejka (Aus.) 8–6, 3–6, 7–5, 1–6, 6–4; beat H. W. Artens (Aus.) 6–1, 2–6, 6–4, 6–8, 6–2.

Doubles: M. Balli and K. Georgiades (Gr.) lost to H. W. ARTENS and M. HABERL (AUS.) 7–5, 3–6, 4–6, 4–6.

Czechoslovakia beat Spain at Prague on May 1, 2, and 3 by three to two. The Czech team was R. Menzel and L.

Hecht for the singles, with Menzel and F. von Röhrer for the doubles. Spain relied on two men, E. G. Maier and M. Alonso. Maier beat Hecht, and the Spaniards won the doubles. Alonso lost to Hecht in five sets. Menzel was too good for both the Spaniards, beating Maier in three sets and Alonso in four.

Detailed Results

Singles: R. MENZEL (CZECH.) beat E. G. Maier (Sp.) 6–3, 6–2, 6–3 ; beat M. Alonso (Sp.) 6–8, 6–2, 6–1, 6–3. L. HECHT (CZECH.) beat M. Alonso (Sp.) 6–3, 4–6, 7–5, 0–6, 6–1 ; lost to E. G. MAIER (SP.) 6–4, 3–6, 4–6, 4–6.

Doubles: R. Menzel and F. von Röhrer (Czech.) lost to M. ALONSO and E. G. MAIER (SP.) 1–6, 7–9, 1–6.

Italy beat Hungary at Budapest on May 1, 2, and 3 by four to one. The Italian team was H. L. de Morpurgo and G. de Stefani in the singles and de Morpurgo and A. del Bono in the doubles. Hungary's team was B. von Kehrling and I. de Takacs in the singles, with E. Gabrowitz partnering von Kehrling in the doubles. De Morpurgo unexpectedly lost to von Kehrling in straight sets, but Italy took all the other matches, de Stefani beating von Kehrling in five sets.

Detailed Results

Singles: H. L. DE MORPURGO (IT.) beat I. de Takacs (Hun.) 6–3, 8–6, 6–1 ; lost to B. VON KEHRLING (HUN.) 3–6, 3–6, 4–6. G. DE STEFANI (IT.) beat I. de Takacs (Hun.) 6–3, 6–3, 6–3 ; beat B. von Kehrling (Hun.) 6–2, 4–6, 6–2, 4–6, 6–2.

Doubles: H. L. DE MORPURGO and A. DEL BONO (IT.) beat B. von Kehrling and E. Gabrowitz (Hun.) 8–6, 3–6, 7–5, 7–5.

In the second round Japan beat Yugoslavia at Zagreb on May 8, 9, and 10 by five to none. Their team was J. and H. Satoh in the singles, with J. Satoh and M. Kawachi in the doubles. Yugoslavia relied on F. Kukuljevic and F. Schaffers. The former took H. Satoh to five sets, and the Yugoslav pair pushed the doubles into four.

Detailed Results

Singles: J. SATOH (JAP.) beat F. Kukuljevic (Yugo.) 6–3, 6–3, 6–2; beat F. Schaffers (Yugo.) 7–5, 6–3, 6–0. H. SATOH (JAP.) beat F. Schaffers (Yugo.) 6–3, 6–4, 7–5; beat F. Kukuljevic (Yugo.) 6–3, 6–2, 3–6, 5–7, 6–2.

Doubles: J. SATOH and M. KAWACHI (JAP.) beat F. Schaffers and F. Kukuljevic (Yugo.) 9–7, 3–6, 9–7, 6–3.

Egypt beat Finland at Helsinki on May 8, 9, and 10 by four to one. The home team was A. Grahn and B. Grotenfelt. The Egyptian team was J. Grandguillot and L. Wahid in the singles, with Grandguillot and A. Shukri for the doubles. Grahn beat Wahid in four sets, to notch Finland's only win. The doubles was a long, seesawing five-setter which finally went to Egypt.

Detailed Results

Singles: J. GRANDGUILLOT (EGY.) beat A. Grahn (Fin.) 3–6, 7–5, 7–5, 6–2; beat B. Grotenfelt (Fin.) 3–6, 6–1, 6–4, 6–2. L. WAHID (EGY.) beat B. Grotenfelt (Fin.) 6–3, 2–6, 6–4, 6–4; lost to A. GRAHN (FIN.) 6–8, 3–6, 8–6, 3–6.

Doubles: J. GRANDGUILLOT and A. SHUKRI (EGY.) beat A. Grahn and B. Grotenfelt (Fin.) 6–4, 2–6, 6–4, 3–6, 7–5.

Great Britain easily beat Belgium at Brussels on May 9, 10, and 11 by the widest margin of five to none—again without loss of a set. The British team was H. W. Austin and F. J. Perry in the singles and Perry and G. P. Hughes in the doubles. A. Lacroix and L. de Borman played both singles and doubles for Belgium.

Detailed Results

Singles: H. W. AUSTIN (G.B.) beat A. Lacroix (Belg.) 6–4, 6–4, 6–4; beat L. de Borman (Belg.) 6–0, 6–1, 6–0. F. J. PERRY (G.B.) beat L. de Borman (Belg.) 6–2, 6–0, 6–2; beat A. Lacroix (Belg.) 8–6, 6–4, 7–5.

Doubles: G. P. HUGHES and F. J. PERRY (G.B.) beat L. de Borman and A. Lacroix (Belg.) 6–1, 6–4, 6–2.

South Africa beat Ireland at Dublin on May 14, 15, and 16 by four to one. The Irish team was G. L. Rogers and

E. A. McGuire in the singles, with Rogers and C. F. Scroope in the doubles, the same team as had beaten Switzerland in the previous round. The South African team was P. D. B. Spence and V. G. Kirby in the singles and Spence and N. G. Farquharson in the doubles. Rogers beat Spence in five sets, and with Scroope carried the doubles to five sets. Kirby won both his singles, and Spence was too good for McGuire.

Detailed Results

Singles: P. D. B. SPENCE (S.A.) beat E. A. McGuire (Ire.) 6–3, 6–4, 6–2 ; lost to G. L. ROGERS (IRE.) 4–6, 2–6, 6–4, 6–4, 4–6. V. G. KIRBY (S.A.) beat E. A. McGuire (Ire.) 4–6, 6–3, 7–5, 7–5 ; beat G. L. Rogers (Ire.) 3–6, 7–5, 10–8, 6–2.

Doubles: P. D. B. SPENCE and N. G. FARQUHARSON (S.A.) beat G. L. Rogers and C. F. Scroope (Ire.) 1–6, 6–1, 7–5, 2–6, 6–3.

Czechoslovakia beat Greece at Athens on May 15, 16, and 17 by four to one. The winners' team was R. Menzel and L. Hecht in the singles, with Menzel and F. Marsalek in the doubles. The Greek team was A. J. Zerlendi and O. Garangiotis in the singles, with M. Balli and G. Nicholaides in the doubles. Greece's only success was the win of Garangiotis over Hecht.

Detailed Results

Singles: R. MENZEL (CZECH.) beat A. J. Zerlendi (Gr.) 6–2, 6–2, 6–1 ; beat O. Garangiotis (Gr.) 6–1, 6–3, 6–1. L. HECHT (CZECH.) beat A. J. Zerlendi (Gr.) 6–2, 6–4, 3–6, 6–4 ; lost to O. GARANGIOTIS (GR.) 6–1, 6–8, 2–6, 9–11.

Doubles: R. MENZEL and F. MARSALEK (CZECH.) beat M. Balli and G. Nicholaides (Gr.) 6–2, 6–2, 6–4.

Italy beat the Netherlands at Turin on May 15, 16, and 17 by three to none. The Italian team was H. L. de Morpurgo and G. de Stefani in the singles and de Morpurgo and A. del Bono in the doubles. The Dutch team was Knappert and I. van der Heide, who were no match for such experienced and competent opponents.

Detailed Results

Singles: H. L. de Morpurgo (It.) beat Knappert (Neth.) 6–3, 6–1, 6–1. G. de Stefani (It.) beat I. van der Heide (Neth.) 6–3, 6–3, 6–3.

Doubles: H. L. de Morpurgo and A. del Bono (It.) beat I. van der Heide and Knappert (Neth.) 2–6, 6–2, 6–4, 6–1.

Denmark beat Rumania at Copenhagen on May 13, 14, and 15 by five to none. There were two players only on each side—for Denmark E. Ulrich and P. Henriksen, and for Rumania N. Mishu and C. Bunea. The former pushed Henriksen to five sets, but Denmark won all the other matches in three sets.

Detailed Results

Singles: E. Ulrich (Den.) beat N. Mishu (Rum.) 6–4, 6–4, 9–7; beat C. Bunea (Rum.) 6–1, 6–1, 6–0. P. Henriksen (Den.) beat C. Bunea (Rum.) 6–0, 6–2, 6–3; beat N. Mishu (Rum.) 4–6, 6–1, 6–4, 4–6, 6–1.

Doubles: E. Ulrich and P. Henriksen (Den.) beat N. Mishu and C. Bunea (Rum.) 6–4, 6–2, 6–3.

Poland beat Norway at Oslo on May 13, 14, and 15 by three to none. Their team was J. Hebda and I. Tloczynski in the singles, with M. Stolarow partnering the latter in the doubles. The Norwegian singles players were J. Nielsen and T. Torkildsen, with R. Christoffersen and O. Fagerstroem as the doubles pair, who won Norway's only set.

Detailed Results

Singles: J. Hebda (Pol.) beat J. Nielsen (Norw.) 6–1, 6–1, 6–2. I. Tloczynski (Pol.) beat T. Torkildsen (Norw.) 6–2, 6–1, 7–5.

Doubles: M. Stolarow and I. Tloczynski (Pol.) beat R. Christoffersen and O. Fagerstroem (Norw.) 6–2, 6–2, 5–7, 6–2.

In the third round Japan beat Egypt at Paris on June 2, 3, and 4 by five to none. The winners' team was J. and H. Satoh in the singles, with J. Satoh and M. Kawachi in the doubles. The Egyptian team was P. Grandguillot and L. Wahid in the singles, with Wahid and A. Shukri in the doubles. Wahid took both his singles into five sets ; the second one was against Kawachi, who substituted for J. Satoh on the third day. Japan took all the other matches in three sets.

Detailed Results

Singles: J. SATOH (JAP.) beat P. Grandguillot (Egy.) 6–0, 6–1, 6–0. H. SATOH (JAP.) beat L. Wahid (Egy.) 6–4, 2–6, 6–1, 6–8, 6–1 ; beat A. Shukri (Egy.) 6–0, 6–1, 6–2. M. KAWACHI (JAP.) beat L. Wahid (Egy.) 6–3, 4–6, 8–6, 3–6, 6–2.

Doubles: J. SATOH and M. KAWACHI (JAP.) beat L. Wahid and A. Shukri (Egy.) 6–2, 6–2, 6–1.

Great Britain beat South Africa at Eastbourne on June 4, 5, and 6 by five to none. The British team was H. W. Austin and F. J. Perry in the singles and G. P. Hughes and Perry in the doubles. South Africa's team was V. G. Kirby and N. G. Farquharson in the singles, the latter partnering P. D. B. Spence in the doubles. South Africa did not win a match, but Kirby came very near to doing so against Austin, having several match points in the fourth set. Farquharson won a set from Austin, but could not get one from Perry, though Kirby did. Great Britain took the doubles in three sets.

Detailed Results

Singles: H. W. AUSTIN (G.B.) beat V. G. Kirby (S.A.) 6–2, 6–8, 2–6, 10–8, 6–3 ; beat N. G. Farquharson (S.A.) 6–2, 5–7, 6–2, 6–3. F. J. PERRY (G.B.) beat N. G. Farquharson (S.A.) 6–2, 6–3, 6–3 ; beat V. G. Kirby (S.A.) 3–6, 6–4, 6–1, 6–4.

Doubles: F. J. PERRY and G. P. HUGHES (G.B.) beat N. G. Farquharson and P. D. B. Spence (S.A.) 8–6, 6–4, 6–3.

Czechoslovakia beat Italy at Prague on June 4, 5, and 6 by three to none. Italy's team was H. L. de Morpurgo and G. de Stefani in the singles and de Morpurgo and A. del Bono in the doubles. The Czech team was R. Menzel and L. Hecht in the singles, with Menzel and F. Marsalek in the doubles. Menzel beat de Morpurgo in four sets, as did Hecht Stefani, and the Czechs took the doubles in three sets.

Detailed Results

Singles: R. MENZEL (CZECH.) beat H. L. de Morpurgo (It.) 6–3, 6–3, 4–6, 6–2. L. HECHT (CZECH.) beat G. de Stefani (It.) 6–4, 7–5, 3–6, 8–6.

Doubles: R. MENZEL and F. MARSALEK (CZECH.) beat H. L. de Morpurgo and A. del Bono (It.) 6–3, 6–4, 6–1.

Denmark only just beat Poland at Copenhagen on May 20, 21, and 22 by three to two. The winners relied on their two-man team of E. Ulrich and P. Henriksen. The Polish team was I. Tloczynski and J. Hebda in the singles, with M. Stolarow partnering the former in the doubles. Tloczynski won both his singles, and very nearly the doubles as well, he and Stolarow holding a two-sets-to-one lead, and only yielding to the Danes at 6–4 in the fifth set. Hebda could not win a set in either of his singles.

Detailed Results

Singles: E. ULRICH (DEN.) beat J. Hebda (Pol.) 6–2, 6–4, 6–3 ; lost to I. TLOCZYNSKI (POL.) 6–8, 1–6, 6–3, 8–6, 2–6. P. HENRIKSEN (DEN.) beat J. Hebda (Pol.) 6–3, 6–1, 6–2 ; lost to I. TLOCZYNSKI (POL.) 2–6, 6–4, 3–6, 2–6.

Doubles: E. ULRICH and P. HENRIKSEN (DEN.) beat M. Stolarow and I. Tloczynski (Pol.) 6–4, 7–9, 3–6, 6–3, 6–4.

In the fourth, or semi-final, round Great Britain beat Japan at Eastbourne on June 12, 13, and 15 by five to none. As usual, the British team was H. W. Austin and F. J. Perry in the singles and Perry and G. P. Hughes in the doubles. Japan's team was J. and H. Satoh in the singles and J. Satoh and M. Kawachi in the doubles. Kawachi substituted for J. Satoh on the third day in the singles. Great Britain won all the singles in four sets and the doubles in three.

Detailed Results

Singles: H. W. AUSTIN (G.B.) beat H. Satoh (Jap.) 0–6, 6–2, 6–4, 6–1 ; beat M. Kawachi (Jap.) 6–1, 0–6, 8–6, 6–2. F. J. PERRY (G.B.) beat J. Satoh (Jap.) 6–1, 4–6, 7–5, 7–5 ; beat H. Satoh (Jap.) 6–2, 6–3, 4–6, 6–2.

Doubles: F. J. PERRY and G. P. HUGHES (G.B.) beat J. Satoh and M. Kawachi (Jap.) 6–4, 6–4, 8–6.

In the other semi-final match Czechoslovakia beat Denmark at Copenhagen on June 16, 17, and 18 by five to none. The Czech team was again R. Menzel and L. Hecht in the singles and Menzel and F. Marsalek in the doubles. The Danish team was E. Ulrich and P. Henriksen in the singles and Ulrich and E. Worm in the doubles. Ulrich could not win a set in either of his singles, but Henriksen pushed Hecht to a twenty-game fifth set before losing. Worm played in place of Henriksen against Menzel, and won a set, the opening one.

Detailed Results

Singles: R. MENZEL (CZECH.) beat E. Ulrich (Den.) 6–3, 6–2, 7–5; beat E. Worm (Den.) 3–6, 6–2, 6–4, 6–1. L. HECHT (CZECH.) beat E. Ulrich (Den.) 6–3, 6–2, 6–2; beat P. Henriksen (Den.) 6–8, 6–0, 3–6, 6–2, 11–9.

Doubles: R. MENZEL and F. MARSALEK (CZECH.) beat E. Ulrich and E. Worm (Den.) 9–7, 1–6, 6–3, 6–0.

The final of the European Zone, between Great Britain and Czechoslovakia, took place at Prague on July 9, 10, and 11, and was won by Great Britain by four matches to one. Great Britain's team was again H. W. Austin and F. J. Perry in the singles and Perry and G. P. Hughes in the doubles. The Czech team was their usual one of R. Menzel and L. Hecht in the singles, with Menzel and F. Marsalek as the doubles pair. Perry beat both Czechs in three sets, a good performance on their home court. Austin beat Menzel in five sets, but lost to Hecht in three, this being Great Britain's only lost match in winning the zone, as Perry and Hughes took the doubles in four sets.

Detailed Results

Singles: H. W. AUSTIN (G.B.) beat R. Menzel (Czech.) 3–6, 6–2, 6–8, 6–3, 6–3; lost to L. HECHT (CZECH.) 2–6, 5–7, 4–6. F. J. PERRY (G.B.) beat L. Hecht (Czech.) 6–1, 8–6, 6–3; beat R. Menzel (Czech.) 7–5, 6–3, 7–5.

Doubles: F. J. PERRY and G. P. HUGHES (G.B.) beat R. Menzel and F. Marsalek (Czech.) 6–4, 4–6, 6–4, 6–2.

NORTH AMERICAN ZONE

This zone comprised three challengers—U.S.A., Mexico, and Canada. In the first round U.S.A. beat Mexico at Mexico

City on May 1, 2, and 3 by five to none. The American team was W. L. Allison and F. X. Shields in the singles, with Shields and S. B. Wood in the doubles. Mexico's team was R. Tapia and A. Unda in the singles and Tapia and M. Llano in the doubles, with J. Acosta as substitute for Unda in the singles on the third day. U.S.A. did not lose a set.

Detailed Results

Singles: W. L. ALLISON (U.S.A.) beat A. Unda (Mex.) 6–3, 6–1, 6–3 ; beat R. Tapia (Mex.) 6–4, 6–3, 6–2. F. X. Shields (U.S.A.) beat R. Tapia (Mex.) 6–4, 6–4, 6–2 ; beat J. Acosta (Mex.) 6–3, 6–0, 6–3.

Doubles: F. X. SHIELDS and S. B. WOOD (U.S.A.) beat R. Tapia and M. Llano (Mex.) 6–3, 6–3, 6–4.

U.S.A. beat Canada in the zone final round, at Montreal, on May 21, 22, and 23 by four to one. The American team was a two-man one of F. X. Shields and S. B. Wood. J. Wright and M. Rainville were Canada's two-man team. Shields was in good form, and beat both Canadians in three sets, but Wood lost to Rainville in five sets. He beat Wright in three, and with Shields won the doubles in three sets also.

Detailed Results

Singles: F. X. SHIELDS (U.S.A.) beat J. Wright (Can.) 8–6, 6–2, 6–2 ; beat M. Rainville (Can.) 6–1, 6–4, 6–1. S. B. WOOD (U.S.A.) beat J. Wright (Can.) 8–6, 6–3, 6–4 ; lost to M. RAINVILLE (CAN.) 6–4, 4–6, 3–6, 6–2, 4–6.

Doubles: F. X. SHIELDS and S. B. WOOD (U.S.A.) beat J. Wright and M. Rainville (Can.) 8–6, 6–4, 6–2.

SOUTH AMERICAN ZONE

In this new zone there were five original entrants, but, as Brazil withdrew after the draw had been made, the effect was for Argentina to play each of the remaining three countries.

In the first round Argentina beat Paraguay at Asuncion on March 26, 27, and 28 by five to none, with great ease. Argentina's team was L. del Castillo and A. Zappa in the singles and W. Robson and A. R. Sissener in the doubles. Paraguay's team was A. Cusmanich and A. Portaluppi in the singles, with

Cusmanich and L. Sosa in the doubles. H. R. Walters and I. Ubaldi played the singles as substitutes on the third day.

Detailed Results

Singles: L. del Castillo (Argent.) beat A. Cusmanich (Para.) 6–3, 6–0, 6–2; beat H. R. Walters (Para.) 6–0, 6–0, 6–1. A. Zappa (Argent.) beat A. Portaluppi (Para.) 6–1, 6–1, 6–1; beat I. Ubaldi (Para.) 6–2, 6–0, 6–1.

Doubles: W. Robson and A. R. Sissener (Argent.) beat A. Cusmanich and L. Sosa (Para.) 6–0, 6–3, 6–0.

In the second round Argentina beat Uruguay at Buenos Aires on April 2, 3, and 4 by five to none. Argentina were represented by L. del Castillo and R. Boyd in the singles and W. Robson and A. Zappa in the doubles. Uruguay's team was J. C. da Silva and E. Stanham in singles and doubles. On the third day C. E. Gainza and E. Hernandez substituted for da Silva and Stanham. Argentina again did not lose a set.

Detailed Results

Singles: L. del Castillo (Argent.) beat J. C. da Silva (Uru.) 6–1, 6–2, 6–0; beat C. E. Gainza (Uru.) 6–0, 6–0, 6–1. R. Boyd (Argent.) beat E. Stanham (Uru.) 6–2, 6–1, 6–3; beat E. Hernandez (Uru.) 6–0, 6–0, 6–1.

Doubles: W. Robson and A. Zappa (Argent.) beat J. C. da Silva and E. Stanham (Uru.) 6–1, 6–2, 6–1.

In the final round of this zone Argentina beat Chile at Santiago on April 11, 12, and 13 by three to none. The winners' team was A. Zappa and W. Robson in the singles and Zappa and L. del Castillo in the doubles. Chile's team was E. Schronherr and L. Page in the singles and R. Conrads and H. Müller in the doubles. Schronherr took the only set against Argentina in this zone—from Zappa.

Detailed Results

Singles: A. Zappa (Argent.) beat E. Schronherr (Chil.) 2–6, 6–2, 6–0, 6–0. W. Robson (Argent.) beat L. Page (Chil.) 6–2, 6–2, 6–4.

Doubles: A. Zappa and L. del Castillo (Argent.) beat R. Conrads and H. Müller (Chil.) 6–1, 6–0, 6–0.

American Inter-zone Round

U.S.A. beat Argentina at Washington on May 28, 29, and 30 by five to none. America's team was again F. X. Shields and S. B. Wood for singles and doubles, with C. S. Sutter playing the singles in place of Wood on the third day. Argentina's team was W. Robson and R. Boyd in the singles and A. Zappa and L. del Castillo in the doubles. Robson won a set from Shields and also one from Sutter, but Boyd lost to both Shields and Wood in straight sets. Zappa and Castillo fought well in the doubles, and won a set against Shields and Wood.

Detailed Results

Singles: F. X. Shields (U.S.A.) beat W. Robson (Argent.) 3–6, 6–2, 6–2, 6–2 ; beat R. Boyd (Argent.) 6–2, 6–2, 6–2. S. B. Wood (U.S.A.) beat R. Boyd (Argent.) 6–4, 6–1, 6–2. C. S. Sutter (U.S.A.) beat W. Robson (Argent.) 3–6, 6–4, 6–3, 6–3.

Doubles: F. X. Shields and S. B. Wood (U.S.A.) beat A. Zappa and L. del Castillo (Argent.) 6–4, 8–6, 2–6, 6–2.

Inter-zone Round

This tie, between Great Britain and U.S.A., was played in Paris on July 17, 18, and 19. Great Britain won by three matches to two, an excellent performance, illustrating the returning strength of Great Britain as a power in the tennis world. Their team was once again H. W. Austin and F. J. Perry in the singles, with Perry and G. P. Hughes in the doubles. U.S.A. were represented by F. X. Shields and S. B. Wood in the singles and G. M. Lott and J. van Ryn in the doubles. Austin opened by beating Wood in four sets, losing the first set, but Shields squared the issue by beating Perry in three sets. Lott and van Ryn put U.S.A. ahead by winning the doubles in four sets, and at the end of the second day Great Britain's cause did not appear rosy. Austin played very well to beat Shields in three sets and square the tie. Perry beat Wood in four sets in the final match, and Great Britain had reached the challenge round again after a lapse of twelve years. This team had played six matches in the Davis Cup this year, with the seventh, a final match, to come.

Detailed Results

Singles: H. W. AUSTIN (G.B.) beat S. B. Wood (U.S.A.) 2–6, 6–0, 8–6, 7–5 ; beat F. X. Shields (U.S.A.) 8–6, 6–3, 7–5. F. J. PERRY (G.B.) beat S. B. Wood (U.S.A.) 6–3, 8–10, 6–3, 6–3 ; lost to F. X. SHIELDS (U.S.A.) 8–10, 4–6, 2–6.

Doubles: G. P. Hughes and F. J. Perry (G.B.) lost to G. M. LOTT and J. VAN RYN (U.S.A.) 1–6, 3–6, 6–4, 3–6.

CHALLENGE ROUND

This final tie between Great Britain, the challengers, and the defending country, France, took place in Paris on July 24, 25, and 26, when the holders retained the trophy by three matches to two. France's team was H. Cochet and J. Borotra in the singles and Cochet and J. Brugnon in the doubles, Great Britain played H. W. Austin and F. J. Perry in the singles and C. H. Kingsley and G. P. Hughes in the doubles, Kingsley not having played since the first-round tie against Monaco. Cochet was the man who saved France. He was the dominating figure of the whole encounter. He beat Austin in four sets, only just saving the second set after losing the first ; with Brugnon he won the doubles on the second day in four sets, and, with the countries two–all on the third day, he beat Perry in four sets in the deciding match. Borotra, the other French singles man, lost a long five-set match to Perry on the first day, the young Englishman's stamina being a little too much for his older opponent, and on the third day he lost to Austin in four sets, the fluency of the Englishman's ground shots thwarting his volleying attack.

Detailed Results

Singles: H. COCHET (FR.) beat H. W. Austin (G.B.) 3–6, 11–9, 6–2, 6–4 ; beat F. J. Perry (G.B.) 6–4, 1–6, 9–7, 6–3. J. Borotra (Fr.) lost to H. W. AUSTIN (G.B.) 5–7, 3–6, 6–3, 5–7 ; lost to F. J. PERRY (G.B.) 6–4, 8–10, 0–6, 6–4, 4–6.

Doubles: H. COCHET and J. BRUGNON (FR.) beat G. P. Hughes and C. H. Kingsley (G.B.) 6–1, 5–7, 6–3, 8–6.

1932: FRANCE

In this year there were thirty challengers altogether—twenty-two in the European Zone, five in the North American Zone, and three in the South American Zone.

European Zone

In the first round Hungary beat Finland at Budapest on May 3, 4, and 5 by five to none. B. von Kehrling and E. Gabrowitz were the Hungarian team, while A. Biaudet and B. Grotenfelt represented Finland, but they were unable to win a set in five matches.

Detailed Results

Singles: B. von Kehrling (Hun.) beat A. Biaudet (Fin.) 6–1, 6–2, 6–2; beat B. Grotenfelt (Fin.) 6–0, 6–3, 6–4. E. Gabrowitz (Hun.) beat B. Grotenfelt (Fin.) 6–0, 6–2, 6–1; beat A. Biaudet (Fin.) 6–1, 6–1, 6–1.

Doubles: B. von Kehrling and E. Gabrowitz (Hun.) beat A. Biaudet and B. Grotenfelt (Fin.) 6–4, 6–3, 6–3.

Germany beat India at Berlin on May 6, 7, and 8 by five to none. The German team was D. Prenn and G. von Cramm in the singles, with W. Dessart and E. Nourney as the doubles pair. The Indian team was A. Madan Mohan and J. Charanjiva in the singles, with K. Prasada partnering the latter in the doubles. The Germans won all four singles in straight sets, but the Indians pushed the doubles to five sets.

Detailed Results

Singles: D. Prenn (Ger.) beat A. Madan Mohan (Ind.) 6–2, 7–5, 6–1; beat J. Charanjiva (Ind.) 6–3, 6–1, 6–2. G. von Cramm (Ger.) beat J. Charanjiva (Ind.) 6–2, 6–0, 6–1; beat A. Madan Mohan (Ind.) 6–3, 8–6, 6–3.

Doubles: W. Dessart and E. Nourney (Ger.) beat J. Charanjiva and K. Prasada (Ind.) 6–4, 2–6, 3–6, 6–2, 6–3.

Austria beat Czechoslovakia at Prague on May 6, 7, and 8 by three to two. The Austrian team was H. W. Artens and F. Matejka in the singles and Artens and H. Kinzel in the doubles. The Czech team was R. Menzel and L. Hecht in the singles and Menzel and F. Marsalek in the doubles. Matejka played very well in beating Menzel in five sets and Hecht in three. Although Artens lost to Menzel, he beat Hecht in four sets. The Czechs won the doubles in three quick sets.

Detailed Results

Singles: H. W. ARTENS (AUS.) beat L. Hecht (Czech.) 2–6, 6–3, 7–5, 6–1 ; lost to R. MENZEL (CZECH.) 2–6, 1–6, 7–5, 4–6. F. MATEJKA (AUS.) beat R. Menzel (Czech.) 6–3, 6–3, 3–6, 2–6, 6–4 ; beat L. Hecht (Czech.) 6–4, 6–4, 8–6.

Doubles: H. W. Artens and H. Kinzel (Aus.) lost to R. MENZEL and F. MARSALEK (CZECH.) 2–6, 1–6, 1–6.

Monaco beat Norway at Oslo on May 5, 6, and 7 by five to none. R. Gallèpe and V. Landau were Monaco's team. For Norway R. Hagen and T. Torkildsen played the singles and J. Haanes and F. T. Smith the doubles. Haanes substituted for Torkildsen on the third day in the singles. Hagen won Norway's only set—against Gallèpe.

Detailed Results

Singles: R. GALLÈPE (MON.) beat R. Hagen (Norw.) 6–3, 6–4, 6–8, 6–1 ; beat J. Haanes (Norw.) 6–1, 6–1, 6–0. V. LANDAU (MON.) beat T. Torkildsen (Norw.) 7–5, 6–2, 6–2 ; beat R. Hagen (Norw.) 6–1, 6–4, 6–0.

Doubles: R. GALLÈPE and V. LANDAU (MON.) beat J. Haanes and F. T. Smith (Norw.) 6–1, 6–3, 6–1.

Switzerland beat Belgium at Brussels on May 3, 4, and 5 by five to none. For the winners C. F. Aeschliman and H. C. Fisher played all matches. The Belgian singles players were A. Lacroix and M. Iweins d'Eeckhoutte, and the doubles pair Lacroix and L. de Borman. G. van Zuylen substituted for Lacroix on the third day. None of the Belgians could win a set in five matches.

Detailed Results

Singles: C. F. AESCHLIMAN (SWITZ.) beat A. Lacroix (Belg.) 7–5, 6–3, 6–0 ; beat M. Iweins d'Eeckhoutte (Belg.) 6–3, 6–2, 6–2. H. C. FISHER (SWITZ.) beat M. Iweins d'Eeckhoutte (Belg.) 6–1, 6–1, 6–2 ; beat G. van Zuylen (Belg.) 8–6, 6–1, 8–6.

Doubles: C. F. Aeschliman and H. C. Fisher (Switz.) beat A. Lacroix and L. de Borman (Belg.) 6–1, 6–1, 6–4.

Italy beat Egypt at Genoa on May 10, 11, and 12 after a close match, with the contestants two–all with one to play. The Italian team was G. de Stefani and O. de Minerbi in the singles and A. del Bono and A. Sertorio in the doubles. Egypt's team was P. Grandguillot and L. Wahid in the singles, and the former with his brother, J. Grandguillot, in the doubles. Egypt won the doubles in four sets, and P. Grandguillot beat de Minerbi in five sets after losing the first and second. De Stefani, however, won both his singles in three sets, and de Minerbi beat Wahid in four sets.

Detailed Results

Singles: G. de Stefani (It.) beat P. Grandguillot (Egy.) 9–7, 6–1, 6–4 ; beat L. Wahid (Egy.) 7–5, 6–4, 6–1. O. de Minerbi (It.) beat L. Wahid (Egy.) 6–3, 8–6, 6–8, 6–3 ; lost to P. Grandguillot (Egy.) 6–1, 6–3, 1–6, 4–6, 3–6.

Doubles: A. del Bono and A. Sertorio (It.) lost to J. Grandguillot and P. Grandguillot (Egy.) 2–6, 3–6, 7–5, 4–6.

In the second round Great Britain beat Rumania at Torquay on May 14, 15, and 17 by five matches to none. Great Britain's team was F. J. Perry and H. F. David in the singles, with Perry and G. P. Hughes in the doubles. Rumania's team consisted of N. Mishu and G. Poulieff. Perry won all his three matches easily, but David required five sets to beat Mishu, though he accounted for Poulieff in three.

Detailed Results

Singles: F. J. Perry (G.B.) beat N. Mishu (Rum.) 6–0, 6–1, 6–1 ; beat G. Poulieff (Rum.) 6–1, 6–2, 6–1. H. F. David (G.B.) beat G. Poulieff (Rum.) 7–5, 7–5, 6–1 ; beat N. Mishu (Rum.) 4–6, 6–0, 8–6, 3–6, 6–4.

Doubles: F. J. Perry and G. P. Hughes (G.B.) beat N. Mishu and G. Poulieff (Rum.) 6–0, 6–1, 6–1.

Poland beat the Netherlands at Warsaw on May 15, 16, and 17 by four to one. Poland's team was I. Tloczynski and M. Stolarow in the singles, with G. Stolarow partnering the former in the doubles. The Netherlands' team was H. Timmer and T. Hughan in the singles and Hughan and O. Koopman in the doubles. Tloczynski won both his singles in three sets, and Stolarow both his in five sets, finishing against Hughan by winning the fourth and fifth sets to love. The Dutch pair won the doubles after a protracted struggle in which one set alone yielded thirty-two games, and which went the full distance of five sets.

Detailed Results

Singles: I. TLOCZYNSKI (POL.) beat H. Timmer (Neth.) 7–5, 6–3, 6–4; beat T. Hughan (Neth.) 6–3, 6–4, 6–2. M. STOLAROW (POL.) beat H. Timmer (Neth.) 6–4, 6–2, 5–7, 4–6, 6–4; beat T. Hughan (Neth.) 6–8, 6–2, 5–7, 6–0, 6–0.

Doubles: I. Tloczynski and G. Stolarow (Pol.) lost to O. KOOPMAN and T. HUGHAN (NETH.) 6–3, 15–17, 6–3, 3–6, 5–7.

Ireland beat Hungary at Dublin on May 19, 20, and 21 by four to one. The winners' team was G. L. Rogers and E. A. McGuire in singles and doubles. The Hungarian team was B. von Kehrling and E. Gabrowitz in singles and doubles. Hungary's only success was von Kehrling's win over McGuire in three sets.

Detailed Results

Singles: G. L. ROGERS (IRE.) beat E. Gabrowitz (Hun.) 7–5, 3–6, 6–4, 7–5; beat B. von Kehrling (Hun.) 6–0, 6–3, 6–3. E. A. MCGUIRE (IRE.) beat E. Gabrowitz (Hun.) 6–1, 8–6, 6–2; lost to B. VON KEHRLING (HUN.) 3–6, 2–6, 4–6.

Doubles: G. L. ROGERS and E. A. MCGUIRE (IRE.) beat B. von Kehrling and E. Gabrowitz (Hun.) 4–6, 7–5, 6–4, 6–3.

Germany beat Austria at Vienna on May 21, 22, and 23 by a very narrow three–two margin. Austria's team was H. W. Artens and F. Matejka in singles and doubles, and Germany's team was D. Prenn and G. von Cramm in the singles and von Cramm and W. Dessart in the doubles. After being two down and three to play the Austrians fought back strongly to win the doubles in three sets. On the third day Artens beat

Prenn and Matejka almost beat von Cramm in five sets, needing, at one stage, only one point to do so.

Detailed Results

Singles: D. PRENN (GER.) beat F. Matejka (Aus.) 6–2, 10–8, 6–1 ; lost to H. W. ARTENS (AUS.) 4–6, 2–6, 3–6. G. VON CRAMM (GER.) beat H. W. Artens (Aus.) 6–2, 6–0, 6–4 ; beat F. Matejka (Aus.) 6–3, 2–6, 6–3, 5–7, 8–6.

Doubles: W. Dessart and G. von Cramm (Ger.) lost to F. MATEJKA and H. W. ARTENS (AUS.) 3–6, 5–7, 4–6.

Switzerland beat Monaco at Lucerne on May 21, 22, and 23 by three to two. Both countries played a two-man team, the Swiss players being C. F. Aeschliman and H. C. Fisher and the Monaco team R. Gallèpe and V. Landau. Fisher won both his singles, and with Aeschliman he won the doubles in five sets. The latter lost both his singles—to Landau in three sets and Gallèpe in five.

Detailed Results

Singles: C. F. Aeschliman (Switz.) lost to R. GALLÈPE (MON.) 4–6, 6–4, 6–3, 2–6, 3–6 ; lost to V. LANDAU (MON.) 2–6, 7–9, 6–8. H. C. FISHER (SWITZ.) beat V. Landau (Mon.) 6–0, 6–2, 4–6, 6–4 ; beat R. Gallèpe (Mon.) 6–1, 6–1, 6–2.

Doubles: C. F. AESCHLIMAN and H. C. FISHER (SWITZ.) beat R. Gallèpe and V. Landau (Mon.) 2–6, 6–2, 2–6, 7–5, 6–1.

Italy beat Spain at Rome on May 15, 16, and 17 by four to one. Italy's team was G. de Stefani and G. Palmieri in the singles and A. del Bono and O. de Minerbi in the doubles. The Spanish team was E. Maier and A. Juanico in the singles and Maier and J. Tejada in the doubles. Italy won all the singles. Three were clear-cut wins, and the fourth, between Palmieri and Maier, was defaulted by the latter at two sets to one down and 2–5 in the fourth set. Spain won the doubles in four sets.

Detailed Results

Singles: G. DE STEFANI (IT.) beat E. Maier (Sp.) 6–1, 6–4, 6–0 ; beat A. Juanico (Sp.) 6–0, 6–1, 6–2. G. PALMIERI (IT.) beat A. Juanico (Sp.) 6–0, 6–1, 6–2 ; beat E. Maier (Sp.) 2–6, 6–0, 6–2, 5–2 (retired).

Doubles: A. del Bono and O. de Minerbi (It.) lost to E. MAIER and J. TEJADA (SP.) 7–5, 2–6, 2–6, 4–6.

Denmark beat Yugoslavia at Copenhagen on May 11, 12, and 14 by four to one. Both countries were represented by two players only. The Danes were E. Ulrich and P. Henriksen, and the Yugoslavs F. Kukuljevic and F. Schaffers. Ulrich won both his singles, but Henriksen lost to Kukuljevic in four sets, and had a long battle against Schaffers, whom he beat, from two sets down, in five sets, the fourth of which went to 13–11. The Danes took the doubles in four sets.

Detailed Results

Singles: P. HENRIKSEN (DEN.) beat F. Schaffers (Yugo.) 4–6, 0–6, 6–2, 13–11, 6–1 ; lost to F. KUKULJEVIC (YUGO.) 6–4, 6–8, 3–6, 3–6. E. ULRICH (DEN.) beat F. Kukuljevic (Yugo.) 6–3, 7–5, 6–2 ; beat F. Schaffers (Yugo.) 3–6, 7–5, 6–4, 11–9.

Doubles: E. ULRICH and P. HENRIKSEN (DEN.) beat F. Kukuljevic and F. Schaffers (Yugo.) 6–3, 5–7, 6–4, 6–4.

Japan beat Greece at Athens on May 14, 15, and 16 by five to none. The Japanese team was J. Satoh and T. Kuwabara in the singles and Satoh and R. Miki in the doubles. The Greek team was M. Balli and O. Garangiotis in the singles and Balli and K. Georgiades in the doubles. Kuwabara only beat Garangiotis at 10–8 in the fifth set, after being two sets down. G. Nicholaides substituted for Balli on the third day in the singles.

Detailed Results

Singles: J. SATOH (JAP.) beat M. Balli (Gr.) 6–0, 6–3, 6–3 ; beat O. Garangiotis (Gr.) 6–4, 12–10, 6–3. T. KUWABARA (JAP.) beat O. Garangiotis (Gr.) 4–6, 5–7, 7–5, 6–1, 10–8 ; beat G. Nicholaides (Gr.) 6–3, 6–3, 6–3.

Doubles: R. MIKI and J. SATOH (JAP.) beat M. Balli and K. Georgiades (Gr.) 6–2, 3–6, 6–4, 6–2.

In the third round Great Britain and Poland met yet again, this time at Warsaw on June 10, 11, and 12, when Great Britain won by four to one. The British team was F. J. Perry and H. G. N. Lee in the singles and Perry and G. P. Hughes in the doubles. Poland's team was I. Tloczynski and M. Stolarow in the singles and J. Hebda and P. Warminski in the doubles. Tloczynski did well to beat Lee in four sets for Poland's only win.

Detailed Results

Singles: F. J. PERRY (G.B.) beat I. Tloczynski (Pol.) 7–5, 8–6, 6–2; beat M. Stolarow (Pol.) 6–3, 7–5, 6–4. H. G. N. LEE (G.B.) beat M. Stolarow (Pol.) 6–4, 6–3, 6–3; lost to I. TLOCZYNSKI (POL.) 4–6, 4–6, 6–2, 5–7.

Doubles: F. J. PERRY and G. P. HUGHES (G.B.) beat J. Hebda and P. Warminski (Pol.) 6–0, 6–2, 6–0.

Germany beat Ireland at Berlin on June 10, 11, and 12 by four to one. Both countries relied on two men only. The Germans were D. Prenn and G. von Cramm, the Irishmen E. A. McGuire and G. L. Rogers. Ireland's only success was achieved by Rogers, who beat von Cramm in five sets. McGuire lost to von Cramm in three sets, and neither he nor Rogers could win a set from Prenn. Together they won a set against Prenn and von Cramm in the doubles.

Detailed Results

Singles: D. PRENN (GER.) beat E. A. McGuire (Ire.) 6–1, 6–1, 6–1; beat G. L. Rogers (Ire.) 6–2, 7–5, 6–2. G. VON CRAMM (GER.) beat E. A. McGuire (Ire.) 6–2, 6–4, 6–2; lost to G. L. ROGERS (IRE.) 4–6, 8–10, 6–4, 7–5, 4–6.

Doubles: D. PRENN and G. VON CRAMM (GER.) beat G. L. Rogers and E. A. McGuire (Ire.) 6–4, 6–3, 3–6, 8–6.

Italy beat Switzerland at Montreux on June 11, 12, and 14 by three to two. The Italian team was G. de Stefani and G. Palmieri in the singles and Palmieri and A. Sertorio in the doubles. The Swiss team was C. F. Aeschliman and H. C. Fisher in singles and doubles. Fisher did well to win both his singles in five sets, especially against de Stefani, who led him two sets to love, the next three sets all being won by Fisher in advantage games. Aeschliman, however, was on the losing end in all his matches, including the doubles.

Detailed Results

Singles: G. DE STEFANI (IT.) beat C. F. Aeschliman (Switz.) 6–4, 7–5, 8–6 ; lost to H. C. FISHER (SWITZ.) 6–3, 6–0, 7–9, 6–8, 6–8. G. PALMIERI (IT.) beat C. F. Aeschliman (Switz.) 6–3, 6–1, 7–5 ; lost to H. C. FISHER (SWITZ.) 8–6, 4–6, 6–1, 1–6, 3–6.

Doubles: G. PALMIERI and A. SERTORIO (IT.) beat H. C. Fisher and C. F. Aeschliman (Switz.) 3–6, 6–4, 6–4, 6–4.

Japan beat Denmark at Copenhagen on June 10, 11, and 12 by five to none. Japan's team was J. Satoh and T. Kuwabara in the singles and Satoh and R. Miki in the doubles. Denmark's team was E. Ulrich and A. Jacobsen in the singles and Ulrich and P. Henriksen in the doubles. Jacobsen won the first two sets from Kuwabara, but faded away in the next three. This was the only five-set match in the tie.

Detailed Results

Singles: J. SATOH (JAP.) beat A. Jacobsen (Den.) 6–1, 6–2, 6–4 ; beat E. Ulrich (Den.) 4–6, 6–3, 7–5, 7–5. T. KUWABARA (JAP.) beat E. Ulrich (Den.) 6–4, 6–2, 6–0 ; beat A. Jacobsen (Den.) 5–7, 2–6, 6–3, 6–0, 6–1.

Doubles: J. SATOH and R. MIKI (JAP.) beat E. Ulrich and P. Henriksen (Den.) 6–3, 4–6, 6–2, 6–2.

In the fourth and semi-final round Germany beat Great Britain at Berlin on July 8, 9, and 10 by the narrowest of margins—three to two—Great Britain being within only one point of winning. Germany's team was D. Prenn and G. von Cramm in the singles and Prenn and W. Dessart in the doubles. Great Britain's team was F. J. Perry and H. W. Austin in the singles and Perry and G. P. Hughes in the doubles. At the end of the first day's play the score was one–all, Prenn having beaten Austin, Perry having beaten von Cramm. The doubles, on the second day, was won by Great Britain in three sets. On the third day von Cramm beat Austin, to bring the tie level again, and everything depended on the Perry–Prenn encounter. When Perry had recovered from two sets down to lead 5–2 in the fifth set all seemed over

—particularly when he reached match point in the next game. Prenn, always a wily warrior, managed to save the day for Germany by winning the next five games and the match in a sensational finish.

Detailed Results

Singles: D. PRENN (GER.) beat H. W. Austin (G.B.) 6–0, 8–10, 6–2, 6–3 ; beat F. J. Perry (G.B.) 6–2, 6–4, 3–6, 0–6, 7–5. G. VON CRAMM (GER.) beat H. W. Austin (G.B.) 5–7, 6–2, 6–3, 6–2 ; lost to F. J. PERRY (G.B.) 1–6, 2–6, 3–6.

Doubles: D. Prenn and W. Dessart (Ger.) lost to G. P. HUGHES and F. J. PERRY (G.B.) 3–6, 4–6, 4–6.

In the other tie in this round Italy beat Japan at Milan on July 8, 9, and 10 by three to two. Japan again played J. Satoh and T. Kuwabara in the singles and Satoh and R. Miki in the doubles. Italy's team was G. de Stefani and G. Palmieri in the singles and Palmieri and A. Sertorio in the doubles. Satoh failed to win either of his singles, even after leading, against Palmieri, by two sets to none. Kuwabara beat Palmieri, but lost to de Stefani. Japan won the doubles.

Detailed Results

Singles: G. DE STEFANI (IT.) beat J. Satoh (Jap.) 6–3, 6–4, 6–4 ; beat T. Kuwabara (Jap.) 6–2, 6–2, 6–4. G. PALMIERI (IT.) beat J. Satoh (Jap.) 4–6, 4–6, 6–1, 6–1, 6–2 ; lost to T. KUWABARA (JAP.) 0–6, 2–6, 6–1, 3–6.

Doubles: G. Palmieri and A. Sertorio (It.) lost to J. SATOH and R. MIKI (JAP.) 4–6, 4–6, 3–6.

In the European Zone final Germany beat Italy at Milan on July 15, 16, and 17 by the wide margin of five to none. Germany's team was D. Prenn and G. von Cramm for singles and doubles. Italy's team was G. de Stefani and G. Palmieri in the singles and de Stefani and A. del Bono in the doubles. Prenn and von Cramm were too good for the Italians, and G. Jaenecke, who substituted for Prenn on the third day, also proved too good for Palmieri. On the Italian side del Bono substituted for de Stefani on the third day, and lost to von Cramm.

Detailed Results

Singles: D. PRENN (GER.) beat G. de Stefani (It.) 6–1, 6–4, 1–6, 6–2. G. VON CRAMM (GER.) beat G. Palmieri (It.) 6–3, 6–4, 6–0; beat A. del Bono (It.) 8–6, 6–3, 3–6, 6–1. G. JAENECKE (GER.) beat G. Palmieri (It.) 6–3, 0–6, 6–1, 2–6, 6–1.

Doubles: D. PRENN and G. VON CRAMM (GER.) beat G. de Stefani and A. del Bono (It.) 6–3, 6–3, 6–2.

NORTH AMERICAN ZONE

In the first round in this zone U.S.A. beat Canada at Washington on April 28, 29, and 30 by five to none. The American team was H. E. Vines and W. L. Allison in the singles and Allison and J. van Ryn in the doubles. The Canadian team was J. Wright and M. Rainville in singles and doubles. The former did well to take Vines to five sets and F. X. Shields, who substituted for Allison on the third day, to four sets.

Detailed Results

Singles: H. E. VINES (U.S.A.) beat J. Wright (Can.) 8–6, 3–6, 6–4, 4–6, 6–2; beat M. Rainville (Can.) 6–3, 6–3, 6–4. F. X. SHIELDS (U.S.A.) beat J. Wright (Can.) 8–6, 6–1, 8–10, 6–1. W. L. ALLISON (U.S.A.) beat M. Rainville (Can.) 6–2, 6–4, 6–2.

Doubles: W. L. ALLISON and J. VAN RYN (U.S.A.) beat M. Rainville and J. Wright (Can.) 6–2, 6–1, 6–2.

In the second round U.S.A. beat Mexico at New Orleans on May 13, 14, and 15 by five to none. The U.S.A. team was identical with the one which had eliminated Canada—H. E. Vines and W. L. Allison in the singles and Allison and J. van Ryn in the doubles. The Mexican team was R. Tapia and A. Unda in singles and doubles. Tapia took Vines to five sets, and fought well in the doubles with Unda. F. X. Shields, substituting for Allison, beat E. Mestre, substituting for Unda, on the third day, with the loss of only one game.

Detailed Results

Singles: H. E. VINES (U.S.A.) beat A. Unda (Mex.) 6–1, 6–2, 6–4 ; beat R. Tapia (Mex.) 6–4, 5–7, 10–12, 8–6, 6–3. W. L. ALLISON (U.S.A.) beat R. Tapia (Mex.) 6–2, 6–3, 6–4. F. X. SHIELDS (U.S.A.) beat E. Mestre (Mex.) 6–0, 6–1, 6–0.

Doubles: W. L. ALLISON and J. VAN RYN (U.S.A.) beat A. Unda and R. Tapia (Mex.) 6–1, 6–2, 3–6, 9–7.

In the second round Australia beat Cuba at Havana on May 13, 14, and 15 by five to none. The Australian team was J. H. Crawford and H. C. Hopman in singles and doubles. The Cuban team was R. Morales and G. Vollmer in singles and doubles also. The Australians were never in difficulty. On the third day C. Sproule substituted for Crawford, and beat Vollmer in three sets.

Detailed Results

Singles: J. H. CRAWFORD (AUSTRAL.) beat R. Morales (Cu.) 6–3, 6–1, 7–5. C. SPROULE (AUSTRAL.) beat G. Vollmer (Cu.) 6–1, 6–1, 6–4. H. C. HOPMAN (AUSTRAL.) beat G. Vollmer (Cu.) 6–2, 6–1, 4–6, 6–1 ; beat R. Morales (Cu.) 6–2, 6–2, 6–4.

Doubles: J. H. CRAWFORD and H. C. HOPMAN (AUSTRAL.) beat G. Vollmer and R. Morales (Cu.) 4–6, 6–4, 8–6, 6–4.

The final round of this zone, between Australia and U.S.A., took place at Philadelphia on May 27, 28, and 29, when U.S.A. won by five to none. The American team was H. E. Vines and F. X. Shields in the singles and W. L. Allison and J. van Ryn in the doubles. The Australian team was J. H. Crawford and H. C. Hopman in singles and doubles. Crawford took Shields to five sets, but lost to Vines in four. Hopman lost to Vines in four sets and to Shields in three. The Americans won the doubles in four sets.

Detailed Results

Singles: F. X. SHIELDS (U.S.A.) beat H. C. Hopman (Austral.) 6–4, 6–1, 6–2 ; beat J. H. Crawford (Austral.) 6–4, 7–5, 4–6, 3–6, 6–2. H. E. VINES (U.S.A.) beat J. H. Crawford (Austral.) 6–2, 6–4, 2–6, 6–4 ; beat H. C. Hopman (Austral.) 6–2, 9–11, 6–4, 6–4.

Doubles: W. L. Allison and J. van Ryn (U.S.A.) beat J. H. Crawford and H. C. Hopman (Austral.) 6–0, 6–4, 5–7, 7–5.

South American Zone

Brazil survived the South American Zone on defaults from Chile and Paraguay.

American Inter-zone Round

This tie, between U.S.A. and Brazil, took place at New York on June 9, 10, and 11. The American team was W. L. Allison and F. X. Shields in the singles and Allison and J. van Ryn in the doubles. The Brazilian team was R. Pernambuco and N. Cruz in the singles, and in the doubles Pernambuco and I. Simoni. Brazil won only one set in five matches, Pernambuco taking it from Shields. Van Ryn substituted for Shields on the third day in the singles, and beat Simoni with the loss of two games, both in the first set.

Detailed Results

Singles: W. L. Allison (U.S.A.) beat N. Cruz (Braz.) 6–3, 6–2, 6–3; beat R. Pernambuco (Braz.) 6–1, 6–2, 6–0. F. X. Shields (U.S.A.) beat R. Pernambuco (Braz.) 6–1, 3–6, 6–3, 8–6. J. van Ryn (U.S.A.) beat I. Simoni (Braz.) 6–2, 6–0, 6–0.

Doubles: W. L. Allison and J. van Ryn (U.S.A.) beat R. Pernambuco and I. Simoni (Braz.) 6–1, 6–1, 6–2.

Inter-zone Round

U.S.A. and Germany played off this tie at Paris on July 22, 23, and 24, when U.S.A. won by three matches to two. The American team was H. E. Vines and F. X. Shields in the singles and W. L. Allison and J. van Ryn in the doubles. Germany's team was G. von Cramm and D. Prenn in singles and doubles. The Germans fought very well against what was, on paper, a much stronger team. Both Prenn and von Cramm defeated Shields in four sets, but both were beaten by Vines, also in four sets. In the vital doubles match Allison and van Ryn were clearly superior to the Germans, and won in three sets.

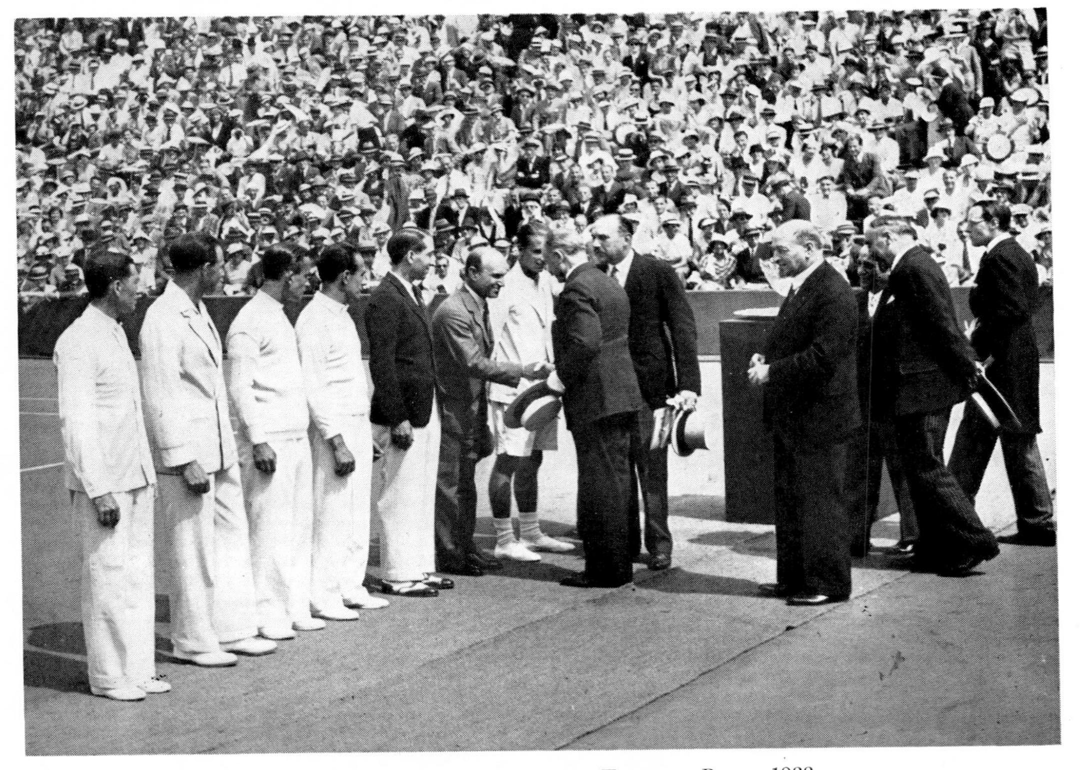

THE FRENCH PRESIDENT MEETS THE TEAMS IN PARIS, 1933

Left to right: J. Brugnon, J. Borotra, A. Merlin, H. Cochet, R. Lacoste, non-playing captain (French team); H. A. Sabelli (English L.T.A.), H. W. Austin (British team), M. Le Brun, M. P. Gillou.

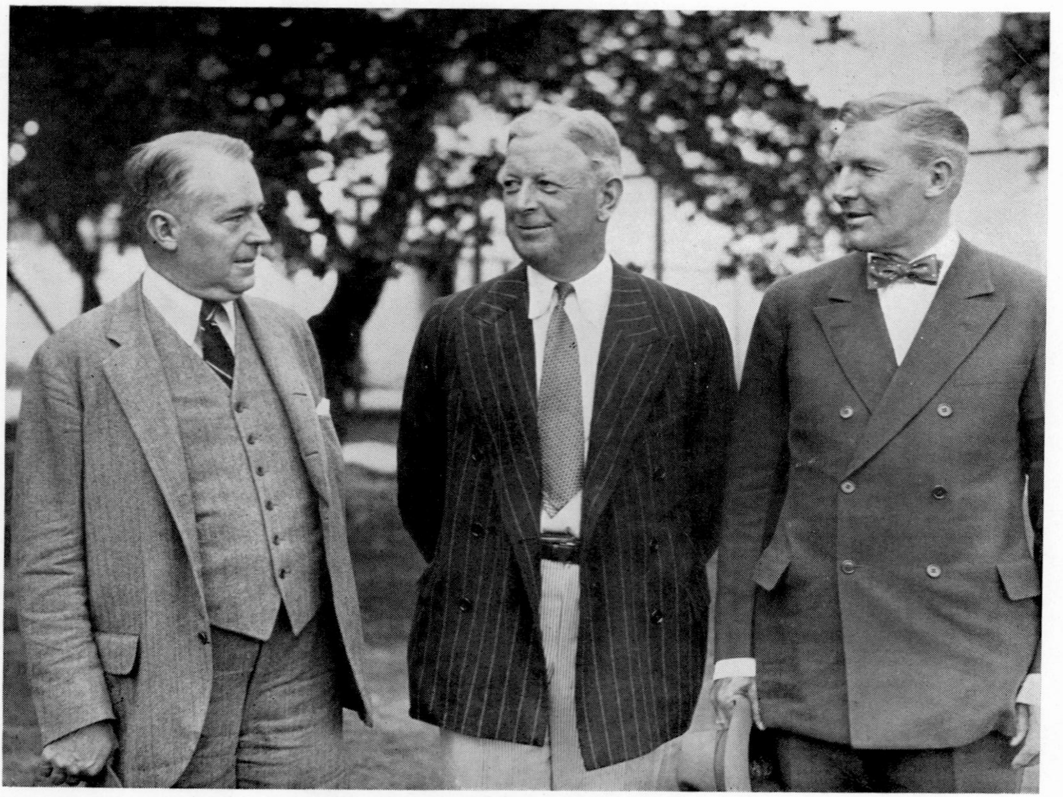

The Original U.S.A. Team in the Nineteen-thirties

Detailed Results

Singles: H. E. VINES (U.S.A.) beat D. Prenn (Ger.) 6–3, 6–3, 0–6, 6–4; beat G. von Cramm (Ger.) 3–6, 6–3, 9–7, 6–3. F. X. Shields (U.S.A.) lost to G. VON CRAMM (GER.) 5–7, 7–5, 4–6, 6–8; lost to D. PRENN (GER.) 1–6, 0–6, 8–6, 2–6.

Doubles: W. L. ALLISON and J. VAN RYN (U.S.A.) beat D. Prenn and G. von Cramm (Ger.) 6–3, 6–4, 6–1.

CHALLENGE ROUND

This final tie of the 1932 Davis Cup competition, between U.S.A., as challengers, and France, as holders, was played at Paris on July 29, 30, and 31, and was won by France by three matches to two. The defending French team was H. Cochet and J. Borotra in the singles, Cochet and J. Brugnon in the doubles. The challenging American team was H. E. Vines and W. L. Allison in the singles and Allison and J. van Ryn in the doubles. The whole tie was very close. On the opening day France won both singles, to gain a vital two–none lead. Borotra performed a near miracle in beating Vines, the Wimbledon and American champion, in four sets, a real triumph for the Frenchman, whose wonderful volleying and astute tactical ability proved too much for his young and gifted opponent. Cochet beat Allison in four sets, also being just too clever for the American, who none the less put up a good fight. On the second day Allison and van Ryn beat Cochet and Brugnon in five hectic sets, to keep America's cause alive. It was a desperately close match, U.S.A. winning the first, third, and fifth sets. On the third day Borotra performed another amazing feat by defeating Allison after the latter had led by two sets to love, and had also held several match points in the fifth set. It seems that Allison was rather unlucky to lose this match, all the rubs of the green going against him towards the end. Borotra was therefore the hero of the French team, having won both his singles—a very good effort by a man of thirty-four who relied always on his aggressive volleying to win. In the last single Cochet obtained a two-sets-to-love lead against Vines, but the young American won the next two sets in advantage games, and more or less hit Cochet off the court in the fifth, to score America's second victory. This match, of course, had no effect on the result of the tie, which had already been settled by Borotra's making France's third win against Allison, but possibly the result may not have been different had all depended on it. Who knows! It had been a very close encounter, only, apparently, one point separating the challenger from victory on four occasions. The " Three Musketeers "—Cochet, Borotra, and Brugnon—the defending team, were growing older, and the fact that their combined ages now totalled more than a hundred years was significant. This was, in fact, their last successful defence of the trophy, which they had won from U.S.A. five years earlier.

Detailed Results

Singles: H. COCHET (FR.) beat W. L. Allison (U.S.A.) 5–7, 7–5, 7–5, 6–2 ; lost to H. E. VINES (U.S.A.) 6–4, 6–0, 5–7, 6–8, 2–6. J. BOROTRA (FR.) beat H. E. Vines (U.S.A.) 6–4, 6–2, 3–6, 6–4 ; beat W. L. Allison (U.S.A.) 1–6, 3–6, 6–4, 6–2, 7–5.

Doubles: H. Cochet and J. Brugnon (Fr.) lost to W. L. ALLISON and J. VAN RYN (U.S.A.) 3–6, 13–11, 5–7, 6–4, 4–6.

1933: GREAT BRITAIN

This year there were, in all, thirty-three challengers, of whom twenty-four were entered in the European Zone, four in the North American Zone, and five in the South American Zone.

EUROPEAN ZONE

In the first round Great Britain, the ultimate winners, started their campaign by beating Spain at Barcelona on April 21, 22, and 23 by four to one. The British team was F. J. Perry and H. W. Austin in the singles, with Perry and G. P. Hughes in the doubles. The Spanish team was E. Maier and N. F. Sindreu in the singles and Maier and A. Durall in the doubles. Great Britain claimed all the singles in three sets, but lost the doubles to Maier and Durall in five.

Detailed Results

Singles: F. J. Perry (G.B.) beat E. Maier (Sp.) 7–5, 7–5, 6–2; beat N. F. Sindreu (Sp.) 6–1, 6–3, 6–0. H. W. Austin (G.B.) beat E. Maier (Sp.) 8–6, 7–5, 6–1; beat N. F. Sindreu (Sp.) 6–0, 6–3, 6–2.

Doubles: F. J. Perry and G. P. Hughes (G.B.) lost to E. Maier and A. Durall (Sp.) 3–6, 1–6, 6–1, 6–4, 3–6.

Austria beat Belgium at Brussels on May 5, 6, and 7 by three to two in a close tie. The Austrian team was H. W. Artens and F. Matejka in the singles and R. Kinzel and A. Bawarowski in the doubles. The Belgian team was A. Lacroix and L. de Borman in both singles and doubles. Artens beat de Borman and lost to Lacroix, but Matejka beat both Belgians, Lacroix in three sets and de Borman in five. Belgium took the doubles in three sets.

Detailed Results

Singles: H. W. Artens (Aus.) beat L. de Borman (Belg.) 4–6, 6–2, 6–4, 7–5; lost to A. Lacroix (Belg.) 2–6, 2–6, 4–6. F. Matejka (Aus.) beat L. de Borman (Belg.) 2–6, 6–4, 6–0, 3–6, 6–3; beat A. Lacroix (Belg.) 6–3, 6–4, 6–2.

Doubles: R. Kinzel and A. Bawarowski (Aus.) lost to A. Lacroix and L. de Borman (Belg.) 4–6, 3–6, 1–6.

Italy beat Yugoslavia at Florence on May 4, 5, and 6 by four to one. The Italian team was H. L. de Morpurgo and G. de Stefani in the singles and de Morpurgo and A. Rado in the doubles. The Yugoslav team was F. Puncec and F. Kukuljevic in the singles, with J. Pallada partnering the latter in the doubles. Pallada substituted for Puncec in the singles on the third day. The Yugoslavs won only the doubles, in five sets, the first set alone going to twenty-six games.

Detailed Results

Singles: H. L. de Morpurgo (It.) beat F. Puncec (Yugo.) 9–7, 6–3, 6–4; beat F. Kukuljevic (Yugo.) 7–5, 6–3, 6–4. G. de Stefani (It.) beat F. Kukuljevic (Yugo.) 6–4, 6–0, 3–6, 6–2; beat J. Pallada (Yugo.) 6–1, 6–2, 6–2.

Doubles: H. L. de Morpurgo and A. Rado (It.) lost to F. KUKULJEVIC and J. PALLADA (YUGO.) 14–12, 3–6, 6–1, 4–6, 3–6.

Germany eliminated Egypt at Wiesbaden on May 5, 6, and 7 by five to none. The German team was G. von Cramm and E. Nourney in the singles and von Cramm and G. Jaenecke in the doubles. The Egyptian side was L. Wahid and A. Bogdagli in the singles and Wahid and A. Shukri in the doubles. They extended two of the five matches to four sets, but did not come within real sight of winning one, though Wahid's single against Nourney was fairly close in three of the four sets played.

Detailed Results

Singles: G. VON CRAMM (GER.) beat L. Wahid (Egy.) 6–3, 6–4, 6–2 ; beat A. Bogdagli (Egy.) 6–2, 6–2, 6–2. E. NOURNEY (GER.) beat A. Bogdagli (Egy.) 8–6, 6–1, 6–1 ; beat L. Wahid (Egy.) 5–7, 8–6, 6–2, 9–7.

Doubles: G. VON CRAMM and G. JAENECKE (GER.) beat L. Wahid and A. Shukri (Egy.) 4–6, 6–4, 8–6, 6–4.

The Netherlands beat Poland at The Hague on May 5, 6, and 7 by three to two. The Dutch team was H. Timmer and T. Hughan in the singles and Timmer and A. Diemer Kool in the doubles. Poland played a two-man team, I. Tloczynski and J. Hebda. Timmer won both his singles, beating Hebda in three sets and Tloczynski in five, and with Diemer Kool won the doubles in four sets. Hughan failed to win a set in either of his singles.

Detailed Results

Singles: H. TIMMER (NETH.) beat J. Hebda (Pol.) 6–3, 6–2, 6–2 ; beat I. Tloczynski (Pol.) 6–1, 3–6, 6–4, 3–6, 6–2. T. Hughan (Neth.) lost to I. TLOCZYNSKI (POL.) 1–6, 2–6, 4–6 ; lost to J. HEBDA (POL.) 3–6, 1–6, 3–6.

Doubles: H. TIMMER and A. DIEMER KOOL (NETH.) beat I. Tloczynski and J. Hebda (Pol.) 3–6, 6–1, 6–2, 6–3.

Ireland beat Denmark at Copenhagen on May 7, 8, and 9 by three to two. Their team was G. L. Rogers and T. G. McVeagh in the singles and Rogers and E. A. McGuire in the doubles. The Danish team was E. Ulrich and A. Jacobsen in the singles and Ulrich and P. Henriksen in the doubles. The good form of Rogers won the tie for Ireland, as he won both his singles and, with McGuire, the doubles. McVeagh went down to Ulrich in three sets and to Jacobsen in five after being two sets up.

Detailed Results

Singles: G. L. ROGERS (IRE.) beat E. Ulrich (Den.) 8–6, 6–2, 6–2; beat A. Jacobsen (Den.) 6–1, 6–3, 6–4. T. G. McVeagh (Ire.) lost to A. JACOBSEN (DEN.) 6–3, 6–2, 4–6, 6–8, 3–6; lost to E. ULRICH (DEN.) 2–6, 3–6, 3–6.

Doubles: G. L. ROGERS and E. A. McGUIRE (IRE.) beat E. Ulrich and P. Henriksen (Den.) 4–6, 6–1, 8–6, 6–4.

Japan beat Hungary at Budapest on May 5, 6, and 7 by five to none. The Japanese used only two men, J. Satoh and R. Nunoi. Hungary relied on three men—E. Gabrowitz and B. von Kehrling in the singles and Gabrowitz and Count Zichy in the doubles. Satoh won his singles without dropping a set, but Nunoi was in difficulty in both his singles, being two sets down to Gabrowitz before pulling out of danger, and almost two sets down to von Kehrling.

Detailed Results

Singles: J. SATOH (JAP.) beat E. Gabrowitz (Hun.) 6–4, 6–2, 6–3; beat B. von Kehrling (Hun.) 6–4, 6–4, 9–7. R. NUNOI (JAP.) beat B. von Kehrling (Hun.) 4–6, 8–6, 6–3, 6–1; beat E. Gabrowitz (Hun.) 3–6, 1–6, 6–3, 9–7, 6–4.

Doubles: J. SATOH and R. NUNOI (JAP.) beat E. Gabrowitz and Count Zichy (Hun.) 6–0, 6–1, 6–2.

In the second round Greece beat Rumania at Athens on May 12, 13, and 14 by four to one. The Greek team was G. Nicholaides and L. Stalios in the singles, with S. Xydis partnering the latter in the doubles. The Rumanian team was T. Rety and G. Poulieff in singles and doubles, with A. Botez substituting for Rety in the singles on the third day. Greece won all the singles, but lost the doubles in four sets.

Detailed Results

Singles: G. NICHOLAIDES (GR.) beat T. Rety (Rum.) 7–5, 6–1, 6–3 ; beat G. Poulieff (Rum.) 6–2, 1–6, 6–2, 6–2. L. STALIOS (GR.) beat G. Poulieff (Rum.) 6–2, 4–6, 6–3, 7–5. S. XYDIS (GR.) beat A. Botez (Rum.) 4–6, 6–3, 6–4, 6–1.

Doubles: S. Xydis and L. Stalios (Gr.) lost to G. POULIEFF and T. RETY (RUM.) 3–6, 2–6, 6–3, 5–7.

Czechoslovakia beat Monaco at Prague on May 12, 13, and 14 by five to none. The home team was R. Menzel and J. Siba in the singles and Menzel and F. Marsalek in the doubles. Monaco relied on their two stalwarts, R. Gallèpe and V. Landau, but they could win only one set in five matches, taken by Landau in his single against Siba.

Detailed Results

Singles: R. MENZEL (CZECH.) beat V. Landau (Mon.) 6–2, 6–2, 6–4 ; beat R. Gallèpe (Mon.) 6–3, 6–2, 6–1. J. SIBA (CZECH.) beat R. Gallèpe (Mon.) 6–1, 6–2, 6–1 ; beat V. Landau (Mon.) 3–6, 9–7, 6–4, 6–1.

Doubles: R. MENZEL and F. MARSALEK (CZECH.) beat V. Landau and R. Gallèpe (Mon.) 6–1, 6–4, 8–6.

Great Britain beat Finland (who had won by default from India in the first round) in London on May 13, 15, and 16 by five to none. The home team was H. W. Austin and F. J. Perry in the singles and Perry and G. P. Hughes in the doubles. The Finns sent A. Grahn and B. Grotenfelt to play in singles and doubles, but they failed to win a set in five matches.

Detailed Results

Singles: F. J. PERRY (G.B.) beat B. Grotenfelt (Fin.) 6–0, 6–3, 6–1 ; beat A. Grahn (Fin.) 6–1, 6–2, 6–4. H. W. AUSTIN (G.B.) beat A. Grahn (Fin.) 6–0, 6–2, 6–2 ; beat B. Grotenfelt (Fin.) 6–0, 6–1, 6–4.

Doubles: F. J. PERRY and G. P. HUGHES (G.B.) beat A. Grahn and B. Grotenfelt (Fin.) 6–1, 6–1, 6–3.

Italy beat Austria at Genoa on May 19, 20, and 21 by four to one. The Italian team was H. L. de Morpurgo and G. de Stefani in the singles and A. Rado and V. Taroni in the doubles. Austria relied on H. W. Artens and F. Matejka only.

The latter scored Austria's only success when he beat de Morpurgo. The doubles went to five sets, and finally to Italy.

Detailed Results

Singles: H. L. de Morpurgo (It.) beat H. W. Artens (Aus.) 4–6, 7–5, 6–3, 6–3 ; lost to F. Matejka (Aus.) 3–6, 6–3, 6–3, 3–6, 3–6. G. de Stefani (It.) beat H. W. Artens (Aus.) 7–5, 6–2, 6–0 ; beat F. Matejka (Aus.) 6–3, 6–3, 4–6, 6–2.

Doubles: A. Rado and V. Taroni (It.) beat F. Matejka and H. W. Artens (Aus.) 6–3, 4–6, 4–6, 6–2, 7–5.

Germany beat the Netherlands on May 19, 20, and 21 by four to one. The German team was G. von Cramm and F. Kuhlmann in the singles and von Cramm and E. Nourney in the doubles. The Dutch team was H. Timmer and G. Leembruggen in the singles and Timmer and O. Koopman in the doubles. The Netherlands' only win was by Timmer over Kuhlmann in three sets.

Detailed Results

Singles: G. von Cramm (Ger.) beat H. Timmer (Neth.) 6–2, 6–3, 1–6, 6–4 ; beat G. Leembruggen (Neth.) 6–3, 6–2, 6–3. F. Kuhlmann (Ger.) beat G. Leembruggen (Neth.) 6–3, 6–3, 6–1 ; lost to H. Timmer (Neth.) 2–6, 1–6, 2–6.

Doubles: G. von Cramm and E. Nourney (Ger.) beat H. Timmer and O. Koopman (Neth.) 6–3, 6–1, 1–6, 8–6.

Japan beat Ireland at Dublin on May 18, 19, and 20 by five to none. Both countries relied on two men only. Japan's team was J. Satoh and R. Nunoi, and Ireland's G. L. Rogers and E. A. McGuire. The latter led Nunoi two sets to love in the only five-set match. Rogers did not reveal his previous-round form.

Detailed Results

Singles: J. Satoh (Jap.) beat E. A. McGuire (Ire.) 6–2, 6–2, 6–2 ; beat G. L. Rogers (Ire.) 6–1, 6–3, 6–1. R. Nunoi (Jap.) beat G. L. Rogers (Ire.) 7–5, 6–3, 7–5 ; beat E. A. McGuire (Ire.) 4–6, 3–6, 6–4, 6–3, 6–3.

Doubles: J. Satoh and R. Nunoi (Jap.) beat G. L. Rogers and E. A. McGuire (Ire.) 6–3, 8–6, 3–6, 6–2.

Australia beat Norway at Oslo on May 12, 13, and 14 by five to none. The Australian team was J. H. Crawford and V. B. McGrath in the singles and Crawford and D. P. Turnbull in the doubles. A. K. Quist took the place of Crawford in the singles on the third day, and lost the only set forfeited by his country in five matches. The Norwegian team was J. Haanes and F. T. Smith in the singles and Haanes and R. Hagen in the doubles.

Detailed Results

Singles: J. H. CRAWFORD (AUSTRAL.) beat J. Haanes (Norw.) 6–1, 6–3, 6–3. V. B. MCGRATH (AUSTRAL.) beat F. T. Smith (Norw.) 6–1, 6–1, 6–3 ; beat J. Haanes (Norw.) 7–5, 7–5, 6–2. A. K. QUIST (AUSTRAL.) beat F. T. Smith (Norw.) 7–5, 4–6, 6–1, 6–0.

Doubles: J. H. CRAWFORD and D. P. TURNBULL (AUSTRAL.) beat R. Hagen and J. Haanes (Norw.) 6–2, 6–3, 6–1.

South Africa beat Switzerland at Bâle on May 19, 20, and 21 by four to one. The winners' team was V. G. Kirby and C. J. J. Robbins in the singles and Kirby and N. G. Farquharson in the doubles. J. Condon substituted for Kirby in the singles on the third day. The Swiss team was H. C. Fisher and M. Ellmer in the singles and Fisher and W. Steiner in the doubles. Fisher led Robbins by two sets to love and Kirby by two sets to one, but failed to win either match. Ellmer gained the only Swiss victory when he beat Condon in four sets.

Detailed Results

Singles: V. G. KIRBY (S.A.) beat H. C. Fisher (Switz.) 5–7, 6–4, 0–6, 7–5, 6–3. C. J. J. ROBBINS (S.A.) beat M. Ellmer (Switz.) 6–1, 6–1, 5–7, 6–3 ; beat H. C. Fisher (Switz.) 8–10, 3–6, 6–1, 6–4, 6–4. J. Condon (S.A.) lost to M. ELLMER (SWITZ.) 4–6, 6–4, 4–6, 2–6.

Doubles: V. G. KIRBY and N. G. FARQUHARSON (S.A.) beat H. C. Fisher and W. Steiner (Switz.) 6–4, 6–3, 6–2.

In the third round Czechoslovakia beat Greece at Prague in June by five to none. The Czech team was R. Menzel and J. Siba in the singles and Menzel and F. Marsalek in the doubles. Greece's team was G. Nicholaides and L. Stalios in the singles and Nicholaides and S. Xydis in the doubles. Three of the four singles went into four sets, but Greece were unable to win a match.

Detailed Results

Singles: R. Menzel (Czech.) beat L. Stalios (Gr.) 6–2, 6–4, 9–7; beat G. Nicholaides (Gr.) 6–1, 6–2, 4–6, 6–0. J. Siba (Czech.) beat L. Stalios (Gr.) 6–3, 6–1, 3–6, 8–6; beat G. Nicholaides (Gr.) 6–3, 3–6, 6–2, 6–1.

Doubles: R. Menzel and F. Marsalek (Czech.) beat G. Nicholaides and S. Xydis (Gr.) 6–1, 6–1, 6–1.

Great Britain beat Italy at Eastbourne on June 8, 9, and 10 by four to one. Great Britain's team was again H. W. Austin and F. J. Perry in the singles and Perry and G. P. Hughes in the doubles. Italy's team was H. L. de Morpurgo and G. de Stefani in the singles and A. Rado and V. Taroni in the doubles. Austin beat both Italians in three sets, but Perry, though he beat de Morpurgo in three sets, lost to de Stefani in four. Great Britain won the doubles in three sets, the last of which went to sixteen games.

Detailed Results

Singles: F. J. Perry (G.B.) beat H. L. de Morpurgo (It.) 6–4, 7–5, 6–4; lost to G. de Stefani (It.) 7–5, 4–6, 4–6, 4–6. H. W. Austin (G.B.) beat G. de Stefani (It.) 6–2, 7–5, 7–5; beat H. L. de Morpurgo (It.) 6–4, 6–3, 6–2.

Doubles: F. J. Perry and G. P. Hughes (G.B.) beat A. Rado and V. Taroni (It.) 6–1, 6–4, 9–7.

Japan beat Germany at Berlin on June 9, 10, and 11 by four to one. Japan again relied on only two players, J. Satoh and R. Nunoi. The German team was G. von Cramm and G. Jaenecke in the singles and von Cramm and E. Nourney in the doubles. Von Gramm beat Nunoi in five sets, to score Germany's only win.

Detailed Results

Singles: J. Satoh (Jap.) beat G. von Cramm (Ger.) 6–3, 2–6, 6–3, 6–4; beat G. Jaenecke (Ger.) 6–2, 6–2, 6–2. R. Nunoi (Jap.) beat G. Jaenecke (Ger.) 6–2, 4–6, 6–3, 6–2; lost to G. von Cramm (Ger.) 6–3, 2–6, 5–7, 7–5, 3–6.

Doubles: J. SATOH and R. NUNOI (JAP.) beat G. von Cramm and E. Nourney (Ger.) 6–2, 6–3, 3–6, 6–1.

Australia beat South Africa in London on June 10, 12, and 13 by three to two. Australia's was this time a two-man team of J. H. Crawford and V. B. McGrath. South Africa's team was V. G. Kirby and C. J. J. Robbins in the singles and Kirby and N. G. Farquharson in the doubles. South Africa did well to keep the tie open to the fifth match after Australia had won both singles on the first day. Crawford won both his singles in three sets. McGrath beat Robbins on the first day in four sets, but lost to Kirby on the third day in the same number. The South African pair won the doubles in three ten-game sets.

Detailed Results

Singles: J. H. CRAWFORD (AUSTRAL.) beat V. G. Kirby (S.A.) 8–6, 6–1, 6–3 ; beat C. J. J. Robbins (S.A.) 6–4, 6–1, 6–0. V. B. MCGRATH (AUSTRAL.) beat C. J. J. Robbins (S.A.) 7–5, 6–4, 4–6, 10–8 ; lost to V. G. KIRBY (S.A.) 8–6, 0–6, 4–6, 2–6.

Doubles: J. H. Crawford and V. B. McGrath (Austral.) lost to V. G. KIRBY and N. G. FARQUHARSON (S.A.) 4–6, 4–6, 4–6.

In the fourth and semi-final round of this zone Great Britain beat Czechoslovakia at Eastbourne on June 17, 19, and 20 by five to none. Great Britain played her usual team—H. W. Austin and F. J. Perry in the singles and Perry and G. P. Hughes in the doubles. The Czech team was R. Menzel and L. Hecht in the singles and Menzel and F. Marsalek in the doubles. Perry had no difficulty in either of his singles, but Austin had trouble with Menzel before he won in four sets. The doubles went to Great Britain in three fairly close sets.

Detailed Results

Singles: F. J. PERRY (G.B.) beat R. Menzel (Czech.) 6–1, 6–4, 6–3 ; beat L. Hecht (Czech.) 6–2, 6–2, 6–2. H. W. AUSTIN (G.B.) beat L. Hecht (Czech.) 6–1, 11–9, 6–4 ; beat R. Menzel (Czech.) 3–6, 9–7, 6–0, 6–1.

Doubles: F. J. PERRY and G. P. HUGHES (G.B.) beat R. Menzel and F. Marsalek (Czech.) 6–3, 6–4, 6–4.

In the other semi-final tie Australia beat Japan at Paris on June 17, 18, and 19 by three to two. Australia's team was J. H. Crawford and V. B. McGrath in the singles and Crawford and A. K. Quist in the doubles. Japan still relied on J. Satoh and R. Nunoi in singles and doubles. It was a very close encounter. Australia took both singles on the first day, when Crawford beat Nunoi at 7–5 in the fifth set, and McGrath beat Satoh also at 7–5 in the fifth set. On the second day Crawford and Quist won the doubles in five sets and the tie for Australia. On the third day Satoh beat Crawford in five sets, and Nunoi beat McGrath in four sets. This, however, may not have happened had the tie been alive, though such speculation can only be vain.

Detailed Results

Singles: J. H. CRAWFORD (AUSTRAL.) beat R. Nunoi (Jap.) 6–2, 4–6, 6–3, 4–6, 7–5; lost to J. SATOH (JAP.) 6–3, 3–6, 1–6, 6–1, 2–6. V. B. MCGRATH (AUSTRAL.) beat J. Satoh (Jap.) 9–7, 1–6, 4–6, 6–4, 7–5; lost to R. NUNOI (JAP.) 4–6, 4–6, 8–6, 5–7.

Doubles: J. H. CRAWFORD and A. K. QUIST (AUSTRAL.) beat J. Satoh and R. Nunoi (Jap.) 7–5, 7–9, 6–3, 3–6, 6–3.

The final round of the European Zone, between Great Britain and Australia, took place at Wimbledon on July 13, 14, and 15, and was won by Great Britain by three matches to two. They relied on their usual team of H. W. Austin and F. J. Perry in the singles and Perry and G. P. Hughes in the doubles. Australia played J. H. Crawford and V. B. McGrath in the singles and A. K. Quist and D. P. Turnbull in the doubles. On the first day Crawford outplayed Austin in four sets, and McGrath, only seventeen years old, went down to Perry in three sets, to leave the countries one–all. The doubles, on the second day, on which so much depended, went to Great Britain in four sets. On the third day Austin settled the tie in Great Britain's favour by defeating young McGrath in three sets. In the last match Crawford beat H. G. N. Lee, playing in place of Perry, in three sets, all close ones. The better-balanced, more experienced team had won. Except Crawford, all the Australians were making their first Davis Cup tour.

Detailed Results

Singles: H. W. AUSTIN (G.B.) beat V. B. McGrath (Austral.) 6–4, 7–5, 6–3; lost to J. H. CRAWFORD (AUSTRAL.) 6–4, 2–6, 2–6, 3–6. F. J. PERRY (G.B.) beat V. B. McGrath (Austral.) 6–2, 6–4, 6–2. H. G. N. Lee (G.B.) lost to J. H. CRAWFORD (AUSTRAL.) 6–8, 5–7, 4–6.

Doubles: G. P. HUGHES and F. J. PERRY (G.B.) beat D. P. Turnbull and A. K. Quist (Austral.) 7–5, 6–4, 3–6, 6–3.

NORTH AMERICAN ZONE

In the first round of this zone Canada beat Cuba at Hot Springs, Virginia, on May 11, 12, and 13 by four to one. The Canadian team was J. Wright and G. Nunns in the singles and Wright and M. Rainville in the doubles. The Cuban side was R. Morales and L. Nodarse in the singles and Morales and A. Randin in the doubles. Canada won all the singles, but lost the doubles in five sets from two sets up.

Detailed Results

Singles: J. WRIGHT (CAN.) beat R. Morales (Cu.) 8–6, 2–6, 6–1, 6–2; beat L. Nodarse (Cu.) 6–1, 6–2, 6–1. G. NUNNS (CAN.) beat R. Morales (Cu.) 8–6, 6–2, 6–4; beat L. Nodarse (Cu.) 6–1, 6–2, 6–0.

Doubles: J. Wright and M. Rainville (Can.) lost to R. MORALES and A. RANDIN (CU.) 6–4, 6–0, 4–6, 8–10, 4–6.

In the other first-round tie U.S.A. beat Mexico at Mexico City on May 5, 6, and 7 by five to none. The American team was W. L. Allison and C. S. Sutter in the singles and G. M. Lott and J. van Ryn in the doubles. The Mexican team was R. Tapia and E. Reyes in the singles and E. Mestre and A. Unda in the doubles. Tapia played well, winning one set from Allison and two sets from Sutter. Mestre substituted for Reyes against Allison on the third day, but could not win a set. U.S.A. won the doubles without any trouble.

Detailed Results

Singles: W. L. ALLISON (U.S.A.) beat R. Tapia (Mex.) 4–6, 6–3, 6–4, 6–4; beat E. Mestre (Mex.) 6–0, 9–7, 6–2. C. S. SUTTER (U.S.A.) beat R. Tapia (Mex.) 6–1, 3–6, 7–5, 2–6, 6–1; beat E. Reyes (Mex.) 6–1, 6–0, 6–1.

Doubles: G. M. Lott and J. van Ryn (U.S.A.) beat E. Mestre and A. Unda (Mex.) 6–0, 6–1, 7–5.

The final round of this zone, between U.S.A. and Canada, took place at Montreal on May 18, 19, and 20, when U.S.A. won by five to none. Their team was W. L. Allison and H. E. Vines in the singles and G. M. Lott and J. van Ryn in the doubles. The Canadian team was again J. Wright and G. Nunns in the singles and Wright and M. Rainville in the doubles. The Canadians failed to win a set in any of the five matches, though they came within measurable distance of doing so more than once.

Detailed Results

Singles: W. L. Allison (U.S.A.) beat J. Wright (Can.) 6–2, 7–5, 6–2 ; beat G. Nunns (Can.) 6–4, 8–6, 6–4. H. E. Vines (U.S.A.) beat G. Nunns (Can.) 6–3, 6–1, 6–3 ; beat J. Wright (Can.) 7–5, 6–3, 7–5.

Doubles: G. M. Lott and J. van Ryn (U.S.A.) beat M. Rainville and J. Wright (Can.) 6–1, 6–3, 6–3.

South American Zone

This zone was reduced to two ties only by the withdrawal of Brazil and Peru. In the second round, but first tie, Chile beat Uruguay at Montevideo on March 31 and April 1 and 2 by five to none. The Chilean team was E. Deik and S. Deik in the singles, and the latter partnering E. Schronherr in the doubles. Uruguay's team was E. Hernandez and E. Stanham in the singles and Stanham and J. C. da Silva in the doubles. On the third day Schronherr substituted for S. Deik against J. Galceran, who took the place of Hernandez. Stanham won Uruguay's only set—from S. Deik.

Detailed Results

Singles: E. Deik (Chil.) beat E. Hernandez (Uru.) 6–2, 6–1, 6–0 ; beat E. Stanham (Uru.) 6-2, 6–2, 6–2. S. Deik (Chil.) beat E. Stanham (Uru.) 5–7, 6–0, 6–3, 6–3. E. Schronherr (Chil.) beat J. Galceran (Uru.) 6–2, 6–2, 6–3.

Doubles: E. Schronherr and S. Deik (Chil.) beat E. Stanham and J. C. da Silva (Uru.) 6–4, 8–6, 6–3,

The final round of this zone, between Chile and Argentina, was played at Buenos Aires on April 8, 9, and 10, and won by Argentina by four matches to none, one match being unfinished. The Argentina team was A. H. Cattaruzza and W. Robson in the singles and A. Zappa and L. del Castillo in the doubles. Chile's team was again E. and S. Deik in the singles and S. Deik and E. Schronherr in the doubles. E. Deik took Cattaruzza to five sets and Robson to four, but the Argentine team was too experienced to lose a match.

Detailed Results

Singles: A. H. Cattaruzza (Argent.) beat E. Deik (Chil.) 6–2, 6–8, 6–3, 3–6, 6–2; drew with S. Deik (Chil.) 6–1, 2–6, 6–6. W. Robson (Argent.) beat S. Deik (Chil.) 6–1, 6–3, 6–1; beat E. Deik (Chil.) 6–1, 6–1, 7–9, 6–2.

Doubles: A. Zappa and L. del Castillo (Argent.) beat E. Schronherr and S. Deik (Chil.) 6–4, 6–2, 6–3.

American Inter-zone Round

In this tie U.S.A. beat Argentina at Washington on May 25, 26, and 27 by four to none, again one match being unfinished. The American team was W. L. Allison and H. E. Vines in the singles and G. M. Lott and J. van Ryn in the doubles. The Argentina team was A. Zappa and A. H. Cattaruzza in the singles and Zappa and G. Echeverria in the doubles. U.S.A. dropped one set only, by Vines to Cattaruzza. The Allison–Zappa match was unfinished.

Detailed Results

Singles: H. E. Vines (U.S.A.) beat A. Zappa (Argent.) 6–2, 6–3, 6–4; beat A. H. Cattaruzza (Argent.) 7–5, 6–1, 5–7, 6–1. W. L. Allison (U.S.A.) beat A. H. Cattaruzza (Argent.) 6–2, 6–4, 6–3; led A. Zappa (Argent.) 6–2, 6–1, 2–2 (unfinished).

Doubles: G. M. Lott and J. van Ryn (U.S.A.) beat A. Zappa and G. Echeverria (Argent.) 6–1, 6–4, 6–1.

Inter-zone Round

In this round Great Britain earned the right to challenge France by defeating the U.S.A. at Paris on July 21, 22, and

23 by four matches to one, one being unfinished and won by Great Britain owing to Vines's retirement. The British team was once again H. W. Austin and F. J. Perry in the singles and Perry and G. P. Hughes in the doubles. The American team was H. E. Vines and W. L. Allison in the singles and G. M. Lott and J. van Ryn in the doubles. Great Britain made a sensational start by winning both singles on the first day in straight sets, Austin beating Vines and Perry beating Allison. On the second day Lott and van Ryn beat Perry and Hughes in three sets, to make the score two to one. On the third day Austin settled the tie by beating Allison in four sets. In the last match Perry was at match point in the final set against Vines when the latter collapsed and had to be assisted from the court. A bad fall in the fourth set was apparently the cause of the trouble, and Vines must have been playing in great pain thereafter. An unlucky incident which fortunately had no actual bearing on the result of the tie.

Detailed Results

Singles: H. W. AUSTIN (G.B.) beat H. E. Vines (U.S.A.) 6–1, 6–1, 6–4; beat W. L. Allison (U.S.A.) 6–2, 7–9, 6–3, 6–4. F. J. PERRY (G.B.) beat W. L. Allison (U.S.A.) 6–1, 7–5, 6–4; beat H. E. Vines (U.S.A.) 1–6, 6–0, 4–6, 7–5, 7–6 (retired).

Doubles: F. J. Perry and G. P. Hughes (G.B.) lost to G. M. LOTT and J. VAN RYN (U.S.A.) 6–8, 4–6, 1–6.

CHALLENGE ROUND

The challengers, Great Britain, beat France, the holders, at Paris on July 28, 29, and 30 by three matches to two in a most exciting encounter. The defending team was H. Cochet and A. Merlin in the singles and J. Borotra and J. Brugnon in the doubles. The challenging team was H. W. Austin and F. J. Perry in the singles and H. G. N. Lee and G. P. Hughes in the doubles. On the first day Austin put Great Britain one up by beating Merlin in three sets, winning the third to love, and Perry increased the lead to two up by beating Cochet in a long five-set match. Borotra and Brugnon won the doubles for France on the second day in three sets. When play commenced on the third day France were one down with two to play. Cochet fought a fine match to beat Austin on the post in the fifth set after being down two sets to one, and behind in both the fourth and fifth sets. Each of the five sets was won by the minimum two-game margin. This brought the countries level at two–all. In the final and all-important match Perry beat Merlin by three sets to one in a close fight, Merlin being twice within a point of a two-sets-to-love lead. This gave Great Britain the tie three to two and possession of the Davis Cup again after a lapse of twenty-one years, and also marked the end of France's only reign as champion country.

Detailed Results

Singles: H. W. AUSTIN (G.B.) beat A. Merlin (Fr.) 6–3, 6–4, 6–0 ; lost to H. COCHET (FR.) 7–5, 4–6, 6–4, 4–6, 4–6. F. J. PERRY (G.B.) beat H. Cochet (Fr.) 8–10, 6–4, 8–6, 3–6, 6–1 ; beat A. Merlin (Fr.) 4–6, 8–6, 6–2, 7–5.

Doubles: H. G. N. Lee and G. P. Hughes (G.B.) lost to J. BOROTRA and J. BRUGNON (FR.) 3–6, 6–8, 2–6.

1934: GREAT BRITAIN

In 1933 an idea had been introduced whereby certain preliminary rounds of the European Zone section of the competition were played in the late summer of the year previous to which their results applied. This was an attempt to relieve congestion in the current year, because of the size to which the European section was growing. After two years, however, the competition reverted to its original form, all matches being played in the current year, despite the heavy programme involved.

EUROPEAN ZONE: PRELIMINARY ROUNDS

In the only first-round tie of this innovation Belgium beat Hungary at Brussels by three to two. The Belgian team was a two-man one of A. Lacroix and L. de Borman. The Hungarian team was also a two-man one, of B. von Kehrling and E. Gabrowitz. Lacroix won both his singles in three sets, and with de Borman won the doubles in five sets. De Borman went down in three sets in both his singles.

Great Britain, Successful Defenders, 1936

Left to right : F. J. Perry, H. W. Austin, H. Roper Barrett (non-playing captain), G. P. Hughes, C. R. D. Tuckey.

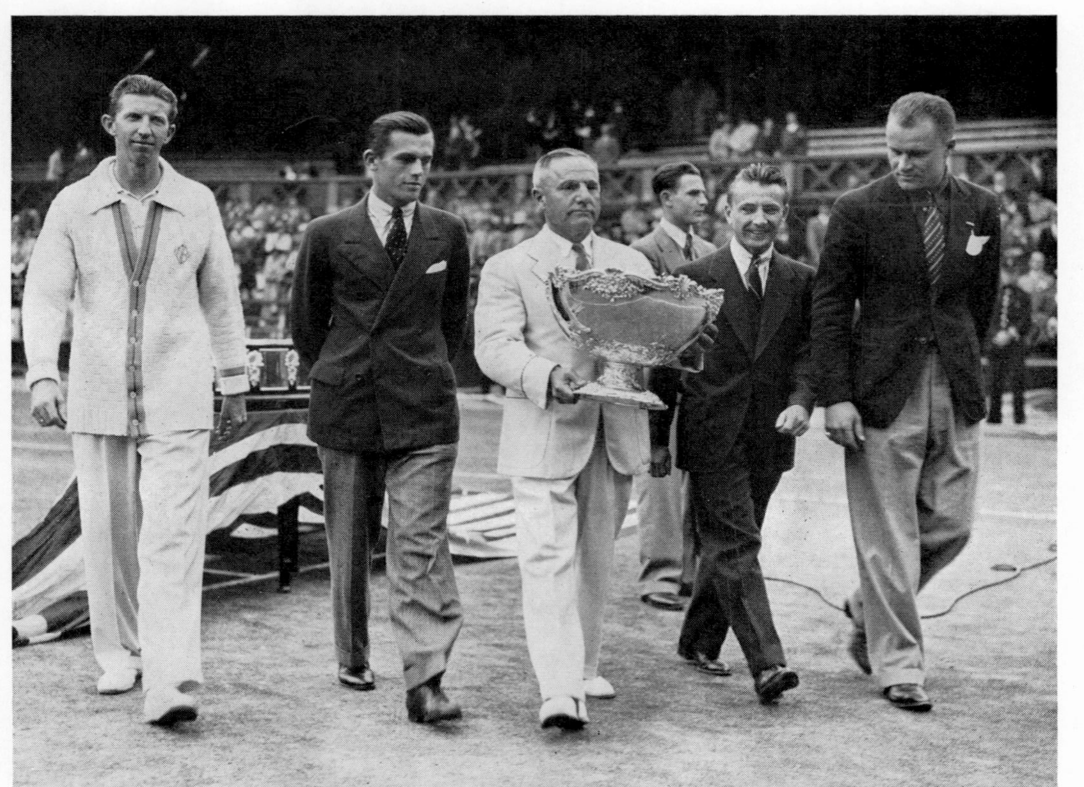

The U.S.A. Team with the Cup at Wimbledon, 1937, after beating the holders, Great Britain

Detailed Results

Singles: A. LACROIX (BELG.) beat B. von Kehrling (Hun.) 6–1, 7–5, 6–2 ; beat E. Gabrowitz (Hun.) 6–4, 6–4, 6–2. L. de Borman (Belg.) lost to E. GABROWITZ (HUN.) 0–6, 5–7, 2–6 ; lost to B. VON KEHRLING (HUN.) 5–7, 3–6, 4–6.

Doubles: A. LACROIX and L. DE BORMAN (BELG.) beat B. von Kehrling and E. Gabrowitz (Hun.) 2–6, 6–1, 7–5, 3–6, 6–4.

In the second round the Netherlands beat Rumania at Amsterdam by four to one. The Dutch team was H. Timmer and W. Karsten in the singles and Timmer and G. W. Scheurleer in the doubles. The Rumanian team was G. Poulieff and A. Cantacuzene in singles and doubles. Their only success was Poulieff's win over Karsten in five sets.

Detailed Results

Singles: H. TIMMER (NETH.) beat G. Poulieff (Rum.) 6–0, 6–0, 6–3 ; beat A. Cantacuzene (Rum.) 6–1, 6–1, 6–1. W. KARSTEN (NETH.) beat A. Cantacuzene (Rum.) 6–2, 10–8, 0–6, 8–6 ; lost to G. POULIEFF (RUM.) 3–6, 6–2, 8–6, 6–8, 4–6.

Doubles: H. TIMMER and G. W. SCHEURLEER (NETH.) beat G. Poulieff and A. Cantacuzene (Rum.) 6–3, 6–3, 6–0.

Italy beat Poland at Warsaw by three to two. Italy's team was G. de Stefani and E. Sertorio in the singles and Sertorio and V. Taroni in the doubles. The Polish team was I. Tloczynski and J. Hebda in the singles and Hebda and E. Wittmann in the doubles. Both Poles beat Sertorio, but neither could beat de Stefani, though Hebda took him to five sets. Italy took the doubles in five sets. They gained a very narrow victory in the whole tie, as Poland's total of sets was one more than theirs.

Detailed Results

Singles: G. DE STEFANI (IT.) beat I. Tloczynski (Pol.) 6–3, 2–6, 6–2, 7–5 ; beat J. Hebda (Pol.) 6–2, 6–3, 0–6, 4–6, 6–2. E. Sertorio (It.) lost to I. TLOCZYNSKI (POL.) 2–6, 6–4, 3–6, 4–6 ; lost to J. HEBDA (POL.) 5–7, 0–6, 0–6.

Doubles: E. SERTORIO and V. TARONI (IT.) beat J. Hebda and E. Wittmann (Pol.) 6–2, 6–2, 3–6, 2–6, 6–4.

Switzerland beat Monaco at Monte Carlo by four to one. The Swiss team was H. C. Fisher and M. Ellmer in the singles and C. F. Aeschliman and W. Steiner in the doubles. The Monaco team was R. Gallèpe and V. Landau in singles and doubles, with G. Medecin substituting for Gallèpe in the singles on the third day. Monaco could win only the doubles.

Detailed Results

Singles: H. C. FISHER (SWITZ.) beat R. Gallèpe (Mon.) 6–3, 6–3, 6–1 ; beat V. Landau (Mon.) 6–2, 6–1, 6–3. M. ELLMER (SWITZ.) beat V. Landau (Mon.) 6–2, 6–3, 6–2 ; beat G. Medecin (Mon.) 6–1, 6–2, 6–1.

Doubles: C. F. Aeschliman and W. Steiner (Switz.) lost to R. Gallèpe and V. Landau (Mon.) 4–6, 6–3, 3–6, 4–6.

Belgium beat Sweden at Stockholm by three to two in a close tie with sets even. Belgium's team was A. Lacroix and G. van Zuylen in the singles and Lacroix and L. de Borman in the doubles. The Swedish team was C. Ostberg and C. Ramberg in singles and doubles. Lacroix had a very close match with Ostberg, only just winning at 8–6 in the final set. He beat Ramberg in three sets, and with de Borman won the doubles in four sets. Van Zuylen was unable to win a set against either Swede.

Detailed Results

Singles: A. LACROIX (BELG.) beat C. Ostberg (Sw.) 7–5, 6–3, 2–6, 5–7, 8–6 ; beat C. Ramberg (Sw.) 6–3, 6–4, 6–3. G. van Zuylen (Belg.) lost to C. OSTBERG (Sw.) 3–6, 4–6, 8–10 ; lost to C. RAMBERG (Sw.) 2–6, 4–6, 3–6.

Doubles: A. LACROIX and L. DE BORMAN (BELG.) beat C. Ostberg and C. Ramberg (Sw.) 5–7, 7–5, 7–5, 6–2.

Yugoslavia beat Norway at Oslo by three to none. Yugoslavia used two players only, F. Puncec and F. Kukuljevic. Norway's team was J. Haanes and F. T. Smith in the singles and Haanes and R. Hagen in the doubles. The Yugoslavs were not extended.

Detailed Results

Singles: F. PUNCEC (YUGO.) beat J. Haanes (Norw.) 6–1, 6–0, 3–6, 6–4. F. KUKULJEVIC (YUGO.) beat F. T. Smith (Norw.) 6–1, 6–1, 6–1.

Doubles: F. KUKULJEVIC and F. PUNCEC (YUGO.) beat J. Haanes and R. Hagen (Norw.) 6–3, 6–4, 6–2.

Austria beat Spain at Vienna by five to none. Austria's team was H. W. Artens and F. Matejka in the singles and W. Brosch and G. von Metaxa in the doubles. The Spanish team was E. Maier and A. Suque in the singles and Maier and A. Durall in the doubles. Durall took Maier's place in the singles on the third day. Artens won both his singles in five sets, and Austria only claimed the doubles after the same number. Matejka beat Suque in three sets and Durall in four.

Detailed Results

Singles: H. W. ARTENS (AUS.) beat E. Maier (Sp.) 7–9, 6–3, 2–6, 7–5, 6–2 ; beat A. Suque (Sp.) 6–3, 4–6, 6–4, 4–6, 6–4. F. MATEJKA (AUS.) beat A. Suque (Sp.) 6–0, 6–3, 9–7 ; beat A. Durall (Sp.) 6–3, 6–1, 8–10, 6–3.

Doubles: W. BROSCH and G. VON METAXA (AUS.) beat E. Maier and A. Durall (Sp.) 6–8, 6–4, 6–4, 2–6, 6–3.

Denmark beat Greece at Copenhagen by four to one. Denmark's team was A. Jacobsen and E. Ulrich in singles and doubles. Greece's team was also a two-man one, L. Stalios and S. Xydis, the latter scoring his country's only success when he beat Ulrich in five sets.

Detailed Results

Singles: A. JACOBSEN (DEN.) beat L. Stalios (Gr.) 4–6, 6–3, 3–6, 6–2, 6–4 ; beat S. Xydis (Gr.) 6–1, 6–3, 6–3. E. ULRICH (DEN.) beat L. Stalios (Gr.) 6–4, 6–1, 6–3 ; lost to S. XYDIS (GR.) 6–4, 4–6, 12–10, 4–6, 1–6.

Doubles: A. JACOBSEN and E. ULRICH (DEN.) beat L. Stalios and S. Xydis (Gr.) 7–5, 4–6, 6–3, 7–5.

Germany beat Ireland at Dublin by four to one. Germany's team was G. von Cramm and E. Nourney in singles and doubles. The Irish team was G. L. Rogers and E. A. McGuire in the singles and McGuire and T. G. McVeagh in the doubles.

On the third day McVeagh, playing in place of Rogers, scored Ireland's only win when he beat F. Frenz, substituting for Nourney, in three sets.

Detailed Results

Singles: G. VON CRAMM (GER.) beat G. L. Rogers (Ire.) 6–1, 6–4, 6–4 ; beat E. A. McGuire (Ire.) 6–4, 6–4, 6–2. E. NOURNEY (GER.) beat E. A. McGuire (Ire.) 6–1, 1–6, 6–4, 6–3. F. Frenz (Ger.) lost to T. G. MCVEAGH (IRE.) 4–6, 3–6, 4–6.

Doubles: G. VON CRAMM and E. NOURNEY (GER.) beat E. A. McGuire and T. G. McVeagh (Ire.) 5–7, 6–2, 6–3, 6–4.

In the third round, the winners of which qualified for the competition proper in 1934, Italy eliminated the Netherlands at Rotterdam by three to two. Italy's team was G. de Stefani and A. Rado in the singles and V. Taroni and F. Quintavalle in the doubles. The Netherlands' team was H. Timmer and W. Karsten in the singles and O. Koopman and G. Scheurleer in the doubles. Timmer put up a good fight against de Stefani, but finally went down in five sets. He defeated Rado in four sets, and the Dutch took the doubles in four sets. Karsten went down easily to both Italians in his singles.

Detailed Results

Singles: G. DE STEFANI (IT.) beat H. Timmer (Neth.) 11–9, 5–7, 4–6, 6–2, 6–2 ; beat W. Karsten (Neth.) 6–3, 6–2, 6–1. A. RADO (IT.) beat W. Karsten (Neth.) 6–1, 6–3, 6–1 ; lost to H. TIMMER (NETH.) 7–5, 1–6, 1–6, 1–6.

Doubles: V. Taroni and F. Quintavalle (It.) lost to O. KOOPMAN and G. SCHEURLEER (NETH.) 4–6, 1–6, 6–2, 3–6.

Switzerland beat Belgium at Montreux by three to two. The Swiss team was H. C. Fisher and M. Ellmer in the singles and C. F. Aeschliman and Fisher in the doubles. The Belgian team was A. Lacroix and C. Naeyaert in the singles and Lacroix and L. de Borman in the doubles. Lacroix beat Ellmer in five sets from two sets down, and with de Borman won the doubles in three sets. He could win only one set against Fisher.

Detailed Results

Singles: H. C. FISHER (SWITZ.) beat A. Lacroix (Belg.) 6–2, 3–6, 6–2, 6–2 ; beat C. Naeyaert (Belg.) 6–2, 6–2, 6–3. M. ELLMER (SWITZ.) beat C. Naeyaert (Belg.) 6–2, 3–6, 7–5, 7–5 ; lost to A. LACROIX (BELG.) 6–3, 6–0, 0–6, 3–6, 2–6.

Doubles: H. C. Fisher and C. F. Aeschliman (Switz.) lost to A. LACROIX and L. DE BORMAN (BELG.) 4–6, 3–6, 4–6.

Austria beat Yugoslavia at Zagreb by four to one. The Austrian team was H. W. Artens and F. Matejka in the singles and Artens and G. von Metaxa in the doubles. The Yugoslav team was F. Puncec and F. Kukuljevic in singles and doubles. They could win only the doubles, though Kukuljevic pushed Artens to five sets after losing the first two.

Detailed Results

Singles: H. W. ARTENS (AUS.) beat F. Puncec (Yugo.) 7–5, 8–6, 6–1 ; beat F. Kukuljevic (Yugo.) 6–3, 6–2, 4–6, 3–6, 6–0. F. MATEJKA (AUS.) beat F. Puncec (Yugo.) 6–4, 6–1, 6–4 ; beat F. Kukuljevic (Yugo.) 8–6, 7–5, 6–4.

Doubles: H. W. Artens and G. von Metaxa (Aus.) lost to F. PUNCEC and F. KUKULJEVIC (YUGO.) 2–6, 6–0, 4–6, 5–7.

Germany beat Denmark at Leipzig by five to none. The German team was G. von Cramm and F. Prenz in the singles and von Cramm and E. Nourney in the doubles. The Danish team was A. Jacobsen and E. Ulrich in the singles and Ulrich and P. Henriksen in the doubles. Jacobsen should have beaten Frenz when he led two sets to love with the loss of only three games.

Detailed Results

Singles: F. FRENZ (GER.) beat E. Ulrich (Den.) 6–4, 7–5, 0–6, 6–3 ; beat A. Jacobsen (Den.) 0–6, 3–6, 7–5, 6–3, 6–3. G. von CRAMM (GER.) beat A. Jacobsen (Den.) 2–6, 6–3, 6–3, 12–10 ; beat E. Ulrich (Den.) 6–3, 6–4, 6–3.

Doubles: G. VON CRAMM and E. NOURNEY (GER.) beat E. Ulrich and P. Henriksen (Den.) 6–3, 8–6, 7–5.

Thus four countries survived to compete in the European Zone proper of 1934, and they were Italy, Germany, Switzerland, and Austria.

European Zone

In the first round Switzerland beat India at Lucerne on May 18, 19, and 20 by five to none. The Swiss team was H. C. Fisher and M. Ellmer in the singles and Fisher and W. Steiner in the doubles. The Indian team was M. Bhandari and M. Sleem in the singles and Bhandari and A. E. Browne in the doubles. Sleem took the first set in his singles with Ellmer, and it proved to be the only set India could win.

Detailed Results

Singles: H. C. Fisher (Switz.) beat M. Bhandari (Ind.) 6–1, 6–2, 7–5 ; beat M. Sleem (Ind.) 6–4, 6–2, 6–4. M. Ellmer (Switz.) beat M. Sleem (Ind.) 1–6, 6–2, 6–3, 6–0 ; beat M. Bhandari (Ind.) 6–0, 6–2, 6–2.

Doubles: H. C. Fisher and W. Steiner (Switz.) beat M. Bhandari and A. E. Browne (Ind.) 6–3, 6–0, 6–1.

France, no longer privileged to await the winning country to challenge her, beat Austria at Paris on May 18, 19, and 20 by five to none. The French team was C. Boussus and A. Merlin in the singles and J. Borotra and J. Brugnon in the doubles. The Austrian team was F. Matejka and G. von Metaxa in the singles and H. W. Artens and von Metaxa in the doubles. The Frenchmen were too good for their opponents and won decisively.

Detailed Results

Singles: C. Boussus (Fr.) beat F. Matejka (Aus.) 6–1, 6–1, 6–4 ; beat G. von Metaxa (Aus.) 7–5, 6–3, 6–3. A. Merlin (Fr.) beat G. von Metaxa (Aus.) 4–6, 8–6, 6–2, 6–2 ; beat F. Matejka (Aus.) 6–3, 3–6, 6–2, 6–2.

Doubles: J. Borotra and J. Brugnon (Fr.) beat H. W. Artens and G. von Metaxa (Aus.) 4–6, 6–3, 6–3, 6–4.

In the second round Czechoslovakia beat New Zealand at Prague on June 7, 8, and 9 by four to one. The Czech team was R. Menzel and L. Hecht in both singles and doubles. The New Zealand team was E. D. Andrews and C. E. Malfroy in the singles and Malfroy and A. C. Stedman in the doubles. Malfroy took a set from Hecht in the singles—the only one gained by New Zealand in the singles—but Malfroy and Stedman pulled off a good effort in taking the doubles from Menzel and Hecht in three sets.

Detailed Results

Singles: R. MENZEL (CZECH.) beat C. E. Malfroy (N.Z.) 6–2, 6–0, 6–1 ; beat E. D. Andrews (N.Z.) 6–1, 6–3, 6–3. L. HECHT (CZECH.) beat E. D. Andrews (N.Z.) 6–1, 6–1, 6–0 ; beat C. E. Malfroy (N.Z.) 6–4, 6–1, 4–6, 6–1.

Doubles: R. Menzel and L. Hecht (Czech.) lost to C. E. MALFROY and A. C. STEDMAN (N.Z.) 5–7, 4–6, 5–7.

Italy beat Switzerland at Rome on June 8, 9, and 10 by five to none. The Italian team was G. de Stefani and A. Rado in the singles and V. Taroni and F. Quintavalle in the doubles. The Swiss team was H. C. Fisher and M. Ellmer in the singles and C. F. Aeschliman and W. Steiner in the doubles. Italy took all the singles in straight sets, and the doubles in five after being down two love sets—a curious performance, this last one.

Detailed Results

Singles: G. DE STEFANI (IT.) beat H. C. Fisher (Switz.) 6–3, 6–2, 6–3 ; beat M. Ellmer (Switz.) 6–3, 6–3, 6–3. A. RADO (IT.) beat M. Ellmer (Switz.) 6–4, 6–2, 6–4 ; beat H. C. Fisher (Switz.) 6–1, 6–0, 11–9.

Doubles: V. TARONI and F. QUINTAVALLE (IT.) beat C. F. Aeschliman and W. Steiner (Switz.) 0–6, 0–6, 6–3, 6–3, 6–4.

France eliminated Germany at Paris on June 8, 9, and 10 by three to two. The French team was again C. Boussus and A. Merlin in the singles and J. Borotra and J. Brugnon in the doubles. The German team was G. von Cramm and E. Nourney in the singles and von Cramm and H. Denker in the doubles. Von Cramm beat both Frenchmen in four sets, but Nourney was unable to win a set from either. Hence the doubles, as so often before and since, was the key to the tie. This match the French pair won in four sets after dropping the first.

Detailed Results

Singles: C. Boussus (Fr.) beat E. Nourney (Ger.) 6–1, 6–2, 6–2 ; lost to G. von Cramm (Ger.) 1–6, 0–6, 6–0, 4–6. A. Merlin (Fr.) beat E. Nourney (Ger.) 6–4, 7–5, 6–2 ; lost to G. von Cramm (Ger.) 1–6, 9–7, 2–6, 5–7.

Doubles: J. Borotra and J. Brugnon (Fr.) beat G. von Cramm and H. Denker (Ger.) 5–7, 6–2, 6–4, 10–8.

Australia beat Japan at Eastbourne on June 7, 8, and 9 by four to one. The Australian team was J. H. Crawford and V. B. McGrath in the singles and Crawford and A. K. Quist in the doubles. D. P. Turnbull played a single on the third day in place of Crawford. The Japanese team was J. Fujikura and J. Yamagishi in the singles and Yamagishi and H. Nishimura in the doubles. Japan's only success was Fujikura's win over McGrath in four sets on the third day—after the tie had been decided.

Detailed Results

Singles: J. H. Crawford (Austral.) beat J. Fujikura (Jap.) 6–3, 6–3, 11–9. V. B. McGrath (Austral.) beat J. Yamagishi (Jap.) 2–6, 7–5, 6–2, 6–4 ; lost to J. Fujikura (Jap.) 4–6, 7–5, 2–6, 6–8. D. P. Turnbull (Austral.) beat J. Yamagishi (Jap.) 6–4, 7–5, 9–7.

Doubles: J. H. Crawford and A. K. Quist (Austral.) beat J. Yamagishi and H. Nishimura (Jap.) 6–1, 6–0, 4–6, 9–7.

In the third and semi-final round of this zone Czechoslovakia beat Italy at Milan on June 15, 16, and 17 by three matches to two. The Czech team was R. Menzel and L. Hecht in the singles and Menzel and F. Marsalek in the doubles. The Italian team was G. de Stefani and A. Rado in the singles and Rado and F. Quintavalle in the doubles. De Stefani did very well to win two singles, Italy's only points. He beat Menzel in five sets and Hecht in four. Rado went down to both Czechs in three sets, and the doubles went to Czechoslovakia in four sets.

Detailed Results

Singles: R. Menzel (Czech.) beat A. Rado (It.) 6–1, 6-2, 10–8 ; lost to G. de Stefani (It.) 6–0, 5–7, 2–6, 7–5, 3–6. L. Hecht (Czech.) beat A. Rado (It.) 6–2, 8–6, 6–2 ; lost to G. de Stefani (It.) 3–6, 5–7, 6–1, 2–6.

Doubles: R. MENZEL and F. MARSALEK (CZECH.) beat F. Quintavalle and A. Rado (It.) 6–8, 6–3, 6–0, 6–4.

Australia beat France in the other semi-final round at Paris on June 15, 16, and 17 by three matches to two in a close tussle. The Australian team was J. H. Crawford and V. B. McGrath in the singles and Crawford and A. K. Quist in the doubles. The French team was C. Boussus and A. Merlin in the singles and J. Borotra and J. Brugnon in the doubles. Merlin played extremely well for France, and won both his singles in four sets, losing the first only in each case. Boussus led by two sets to one against both Crawford and McGrath, but failed to beat either. Borotra and Brugnon went down to the Australians in the doubles in five sets.

Detailed Results

Singles: J. H. CRAWFORD (AUSTRAL.) beat C. Boussus (Fr.) 2–6, 6–2, 4–6, 6–4, 6–0 ; lost to A. MERLIN (FR.) 6-4, 4–6, 4–6, 2–6. V. B. MCGRATH (AUSTRAL.) beat C. Boussus (Fr.) 6–3, 0–6, 6–8, 6–2, 6–2 ; lost to A. MERLIN (FR.) 6–4, 2–6, 3–6, 0–6.

Doubles: J. H. CRAWFORD and A. K. QUIST (AUSTRAL.) beat J. Borotra and J. Brugnon (Fr.) 6–3, 6–4, 5–7, 4–6, 6–3.

The final round of the European Zone, between Australia and Czechoslovakia, was played at Prague on July 13, 14, and 15, when Australia won by three matches to two. The Czech team was R. Menzel and L. Hecht in both singles and doubles, while the Australian team was J. H. Crawford and V. B. McGrath in the singles and Crawford and A. K. Quist in the doubles. Menzel beat Crawford in four sets and McGrath in three, but both Australians beat Hecht, and Australia also won the doubles on the second day comfortably in three sets, and thus became the European Zone winners.

Detailed Results

Singles: J. H. CRAWFORD (AUSTRAL.) beat L. Hecht (Czech.) 6–4, 6–2, 6–2 ; lost to R. MENZEL (CZECH.) 4–6, 4–6, 6–2, 6–8. V. B. MCGRATH (AUSTRAL.) beat L. Hecht (Czech.) 3–6, 6–2, 6–1, 7–5 ; lost to R. MENZEL (CZECH.) 8–10, 2–6, 6–8.

Doubles: J. H. CRAWFORD and A. K. QUIST (AUSTRAL.) beat R. Menzel and L. Hecht (Czech.) 6–4, 6–3, 6–4.

North American Zone

In this zone there were three challengers—U.S.A., Canada, and Mexico. U.S.A. and Canada met in the opening round at Wilmington, Delaware, on May 24, 26, and 27, when U.S.A. won a sweeping five-to-none victory without losing a set. The American team was L. R. Stoeffen and F. X. Shields in the singles and G. M. Lott and J. van Ryn in the doubles. The Canadian team was W. Martin and M. Rainville in singles and doubles, but on the third day both gave way in the singles to G. Nunns and M. Laird Watt.

Detailed Results

Singles: L. R. Stoeffen (U.S.A.) beat M. Rainville (Can.) 6–1, 7–5, 6–1 ; beat G. Nunns (Can.) 6–4, 6–2, 6–3. F. X. Shields (U.S.A.) beat W. Martin (Can.) 6–2, 6–3, 9–7 ; beat M. Laird Watt (Can.) 6–1, 6–3, 6–4.

Doubles: G. M. Lott and J. van Ryn (U.S.A.) beat W. Martin and M. Rainville (Can.) 6–0, 6–4, 6–0.

In the final round of this zone U.S.A. played Mexico at Baltimore on May 30 and 31 and June 2, and again won a sweeping five-to-none victory without loss of a set. The American team was S. B. Wood and L. R. Stoeffen in the singles and Stoeffen and G. M. Lott in the doubles. F. X. Shields took Stoeffen's place in the singles on the third day. The Mexican team was R. Tapia and E. M. Reyes in the singles and Tapia and E. Mestre in the doubles. On the third day A. Roldan played the singles in place of Reyes.

Detailed Results

Singles: S. B. Wood (U.S.A.) beat E. M. Reyes (Mex.) 6–3, 6–2, 6–2 ; beat R. Tapia (Mex.) 6–4, 9–7, 6–0. F. X. Shields (U.S.A.) beat A. Roldan (Mex.) 6–2, 6–1, 6–2. L. R. Stoeffen (U.S.A.) beat R. Tapia (Mex.) 6–2, 6–3, 6–1.

Doubles: G. M. Lott and L. R. Stoeffen (U.S.A.) beat R. Tapia and E. Mestre (Mex.) 6–4, 6–4, 6–4.

South American Zone

The South American Zone did not function ; no matches were played in it. Only two countries entered, Brazil and Peru, the latter retiring, leaving Brazil as winners. Brazil then retired to the U.S.A. in the American Inter-zone Round.

Inter-zone Round

This tie, between Australia, winners of the European Zone, and U.S.A., winners of the American Zones, took place at Wimbledon on July 21–25, bad weather lengthening the usual dates. U.S.A. won a very close match by three to two. The American team was F. X. Shields and S. B. Wood in the singles and L. R. Stoeffen and G. M. Lott in the doubles. The Australian team was J. H. Crawford and V. B. McGrath in the singles and Crawford and A. K. Quist in the doubles. The Australians commenced very well by winning both singles on the first day, Crawford beating Shields in three sets and McGrath beating Wood in four. This appeared a commanding lead, but the Americans fought back very well to win the last three matches. On the second day the doubles was won by Lott and Stoeffen in four sets. Wet weather did not permit Crawford and Wood to play out their match in one day. Actually it was played in several pieces, which seemed to be more unfortunate for Crawford than Wood, as he was the slower starter. Wood ultimately won in five sets after leading by two sets to love, thus squaring the tie. In the final and deciding match Shields defeated McGrath in three sets, to put U.S.A. into the challenging round against Great Britain.

Detailed Results

Singles: F. X. Shields (U.S.A.) beat V. B. McGrath (Austral.) 6–4, 6–2, 6–4; lost to J. H. Crawford (Austral.) 1–6, 2–6, 10–12. S. B. Wood (U.S.A.) beat J. H. Crawford (Austral.) 6–3, 9–7, 4–6, 4–6, 6–2; lost to V. B. McGrath (Austral.) 5–7, 4–6, 6–1, 7–9.

Doubles: G. M. Lott and L. R. Stoeffen (U.S.A.) beat J. H. Crawford and A. K. Quist (Austral.) 6–4, 6–4, 2–6, 6–4.

Challenge Round

This final tie, between U.S.A., challengers, and Great Britain, holders, took place at Wimbledon on July 28, 30, and 31. The American challenging team was the one that had just defeated Australia—F. X. Shields and S. B. Wood in the singles and G. M. Lott and L. R. Stoeffen in the doubles. The British defending team was the same one which had won the trophy from France in Paris the previous year—to wit, F. J. Perry and H. W. Austin in the singles and H. G. N. Lee and G. P. Hughes in the doubles. Austin, in his best form, beat Shields in straight sets in the opening match, to put the holders one up, but Wood gained a two-sets-to-one lead against Perry before the Englishman recovered to win in five sets and put Great Britain two up. Lott and Stoeffen beat Lee and Hughes in the doubles on the second day in four sets, to keep U.S.A.'s chances alive. On the third day Shields put up a grand fight against Perry in the first match, hanging on grimly in the fourth set when two sets to one down, and only capitulating after a twenty-eight-game struggle in this set, almost a match in itself. In the last match, with the tie already decided, Austin beat Wood in four sets, to increase Great Britain's lead into a four-to-one victory. The holders thus showed how firm their grip was on the trophy they were defending, by dropping only one match, the doubles, and that was close enough in three of its four sets to be speculative.

Detailed Results

Singles: F. J. PERRY (G.B.) beat S. B. Wood (U.S.A.) 6–1, 4–6, 5–7, 6–0, 6–3 ; beat F. X. Shields (U.S.A.) 6–4, 4–6, 6–2, 15–13. H. W. AUSTIN (G.B.) beat F. X. Shields (U.S.A.) 6–4, 6–4, 6–1 ; beat S. B. Wood (U.S.A.) 6–4, 6–0, 6–8, 6–3.

Doubles: G. P. Hughes and H. G. N. Lee (G.B.) lost to G. M. LOTT and L. R. STOEFFEN (U.S.A.) 5–7, 0–6, 6–4, 7–9.

1935: GREAT BRITAIN

The qualifying competition for the European Zone was again in operation, the matches being played in the late summer of 1934. Twelve European countries took part.

EUROPEAN ZONE: PRELIMINARY ROUNDS

In the only first-round match Poland beat Belgium at Warsaw by four to one. The Polish team was I. Tloczynski and J. Hebda in the singles, the former also playing in the doubles with M. Stolarow. The Belgian team was A. Lacroix and C. Naeyaert in the singles and Lacroix and L. de Borman in the doubles. The Poles took all the singles comfortably, but lost the doubles in four sets.

Detailed Results

Singles: J. Hebda (Pol.) beat C. Naeyaert (Belg.) 0–6, 6–3, 6–2, 8–6; beat A. Lacroix (Belg.) 6–0, 6–4, 6–4. I. Tloczynski (Pol.) beat A. Lacroix (Belg.) 6–3, 6–3, 10–8; beat C. Naeyaert (Belg.) 6–4, 10–8, 8–6.

Doubles: I. Tloczynski and M. Stolarow (Pol.) lost to A. Lacroix and L. de Borman (Belg.) 2–6, 4–6, 6–4, 2–6.

In the second round Sweden beat Ireland at Stockholm by three to two. The Swedish team was C. Ostberg and K. Schröder in singles and doubles. The Irish team was G. L. Rogers and T. G. McVeagh in the singles and Rogers and E. A. McGuire in the doubles. Rogers beat both Swedes in the singles, but Ireland could not claim any other match.

Detailed Results

Singles: C. Ostberg (Sw.) beat T. G. McVeagh (Ire.) 6–3, 6–3, 4–6, 6–3; lost to G. L. Rogers (Ire.) 4–6, 6–1, 3–6, 5–7. K. Schröder (Sw.) beat T. G. McVeagh (Ire.) 6–3, 6–2, 6–2; lost to G. L. Rogers (Ire.) 1–6, 4–6, 4–6.

Doubles: C. Ostberg and K. Schröder (Sw.) beat G. L. Rogers and E. A. McGuire (Ire.) 5–7, 6–2, 6–2, 6–3.

The Netherlands beat Monaco at Amsterdam by four to one. The Dutch team was H. Timmer and J. H. Knottenbelt in the singles and Timmer and O. Koopman in the doubles. Monaco were represented by V. Landau and R. Gallèpe, who won the doubles, and both took Knottenbelt to five sets in their singles, Landau in particular nearly defeating him. Timmer was too good for them both.

Detailed Results

Singles: H. Timmer (Neth.) beat V. Landau (Mon.) 6–4, 6–1, 6–4; beat R. Gallèpe (Mon.) 5–7, 6–2, 6–3, 6–4. J. H. Knottenbelt (Neth.) beat R. Gallèpe (Mon.) 6–3, 4–6, 6–1, 2–6, 6–4; beat V. Landau (Mon.) 2–6, 6–2, 5–7, 8–6, 7–5.

Doubles: H. Timmer and O. Koopman (Neth.) lost to V. LANDAU and R. GALLÈPE (MON.) 4–6, 3–6, 5–7.

Poland beat Estonia at Warsaw by five to none. The Polish team was I. Tloczynski and K. Tarlowski in the singles, and in the doubles the former was partnered by E. Wittmann. Estonia, making her only appearance in the Davis Cup competition, was represented by H. Pukk and R. Lassen in singles and doubles. The doubles went to five sets before Estonia lost it.

Detailed Results

Singles: I. TLOCZYNSKI (POL.) beat H. Pukk (Eston.) 6–4, 6–4, 6–3; beat R. Lassen (Eston.) 6–3, 6–2, 6–2. K. TARLOWSKI (POL.) beat R. Lassen (Eston.) 6–2, 6–4, 2–6, 6–4; beat H. Pukk (Eston.) 6–3, 6–4, 6–1.

Doubles: I. TLOCZYNSKI and E. WITTMANN (POL.) beat R. Lassen and H. Pukk (Eston.) 6–3, 6–8, 6–4, 1–6, 6–4.

Hungary beat Norway at Budapest by three to two. The home team was E. Gabrowitz and F. Straub in the singles and Count Zichy and E. Ferenczy in the doubles. The Norwegian team was J. Haanes and F. T. Smith in singles and doubles. Straub beat Smith after being two sets down, and lost to Haanes in three sets. Gabrowitz won both his singles. Norway took the doubles in five sets.

Detailed Results

Singles: E. GABROWITZ (HUN.) beat J. Haanes (Norw.) 6–2, 6–4, 9–11, 6–3; beat F. T. Smith (Norw.) 6–3, 7–5, 6–4. F. STRAUB (HUN.) beat F. T. Smith (Norw.) 5–7, 5–7, 6–1, 6–4, 6–2; lost to J. HAANES (NORW.) 2–6, 3–6, 3–6.

Doubles: Count Zichy and E. Ferenczy (Hun.) lost to J. HAANES and F. T. SMITH (NORW.) 6–3, 4–6, 6–4, 4–6, 3–6.

Germany beat Rumania at Berlin by five to none. The German team was G. von Cramm and H. Henkel in singles and doubles. Rumania played A. Hamburger and O. Schmidt in singles and doubles. They were not able to win a set in five matches.

Detailed Results

Singles: G. VON CRAMM (GER.) beat A. Hamburger (Rum.) 6–1, 6–2, 6–3 ; beat O. Schmidt (Rum.) 7–5, 6–4, 6–1. H. HENKEL (GER.) beat O. Schmidt (Rum.) 6–1, 6–1, 6–0 ; beat A. Hamburger (Rum.) 6–2, 6–3, 6–3.

Doubles: G. VON CRAMM and H. HENKEL (GER.) beat A. Hamburger and O. Schmidt (Rum.) 6–1, 6–2, 6–2.

In the third round the Netherlands beat Sweden at Stockholm by three to two. The Dutch team was again H. Timmer and J. H. Knottenbelt in the singles and Timmer and O. Koopman in the doubles. Sweden relied once more on C. Ostberg and K. Schröder in singles and doubles. Both Swedes beat Knottenbelt in three sets, but neither could win a set against Timmer or in partnership in the doubles against Timmer and Koopman.

Detailed Results

Singles: H. TIMMER (NETH.) beat C. Ostberg (Sw.) 6–1, 6–3, 6–1 ; beat K. Schröder (Sw.) 6–0, 6–4, 6–3. J. H. Knottenbelt (Neth.) lost to K. SCHRÖDER (Sw.) 1–6, 5–7, 0–6 ; lost to C. OSTBERG (Sw.) 1–6, 1–6, 4–6.

Doubles: H. TIMMER and O. KOOPMAN (NETH.) beat C. Ostberg and K. Schröder (Sw.) 6–4, 6–1, 6–1.

Poland beat Greece at Warsaw by three to none. The Polish team was I. Tloczynski and J. Hebda in the singles and K. Tarlowski and W. Bratek in the doubles. The Greek team was L. Stalios and K. Zachos in singles and doubles, and they failed to win a set in any match.

Detailed Results

Singles: I. TLOCZYNSKI (POL.) beat K. Zachos (Gr.) 6–1, 6–0, 6–2. J. HEBDA (POL.) beat L. Stalios (Gr.) 6–3, 6–0, 7–5.

Doubles: K. TARLOWSKI and W. BRATEK (POL.) beat L. Stalios and K. Zachos (Gr.) 7–5, 6–1, 6–1.

Yugoslavia beat Hungary at Budapest three to two. The Yugoslav team was F. Puncec and J. Pallada in the singles and Puncec and F. Schaffers in the doubles. The Hungarian team was E. Gabrowitz and F. Straub in the singles and Gabrowitz and Count Zichy in the doubles. Puncec won both his singles, and the doubles with Schaffers. Pallada lost to Straub, and Schaffers, playing in place of Pallada against Gabrowitz, retired when in a losing position and rain caused play to stop, the tie not being in jeopardy.

Detailed Results

Singles: F. PUNCEC (YUGO.) beat E. Gabrowitz (Hun.) 3–6, 6–1, 7–5, 6–3 ; beat F. Straub (Hun.) 6–3, 6–4, 7–5. J. Pallada (Yugo.) lost to F. STRAUB (HUN.) 0–6, 1–6, 4–6 ; F. Schaffers (Yugo.) lost to E. GABROWITZ (HUN.) 4–6, 4–6, 2–5 (retired).

Doubles: F. PUNCEC and F. SCHAFFERS (YUGO.) beat E. Gabrowitz and Count Zichy (Hun.) 6–4, 6–4, 6–3.

Germany beat Denmark at Copenhagen by five to none. The German team was G. von Cramm and H. Henkel in the singles and von Cramm and H. Denker in the doubles. The Danish team was A. Jacobsen and E. Ulrich in both singles and doubles. Germany did not lose a set in five matches, though some sets were protracted.

Detailed Results

Singles: G. VON CRAMM (GER.) beat E. Ulrich (Den.) 6–3, 6–1, 6–2 ; beat A. Jacobsen (Den.) 6–2, 6–2, 6–0. H. HENKEL (GER.) beat A. Jacobsen (Den.) 13–11, 6–3, 6–2 ; beat E. Ulrich (Den.) 6–2, 6–4, 6–1.

Doubles: G. VON CRAMM and H. DENKER (GER.) beat A. Jacobsen and E. Ulrich (Den.) 8–6, 6–3, 7–5.

Thus Germany, Poland, the Netherlands, and Yugoslavia qualified for the European Zone competition proper in 1935.

EUROPEAN ZONE

In addition to the four qualifiers there were seven other entrants. In the first round Czechoslovakia beat Yugoslavia at Prague on May 10, 11, and 12 by four to one. The Czech team was R. Menzel and J. Caska in the singles and Menzel and L. Hecht in the doubles. The Yugoslav team was F. Puncec and J. Pallada in the singles and Puncec and F. Kukuljevic in the doubles. Menzel won both his singles easily, but Caska dropped a set to Puncec, and lost to Pallada in three sets. The Czechs won the doubles from two sets down.

Detailed Results

Singles: R. MENZEL (CZECH.) beat F. Puncec (Yugo.) 6–3, 6–1, 6–1; beat J. Pallada (Yugo.) 6–0, 6–1, 6–1. J. CASKA (CZECH.) beat F. Puncec (Yugo.) 6–4, 6–1, 4–6, 6–0; lost to J. PALLADA (YUGO.) 2–6, 3–6, 3–6.

Doubles: R. MENZEL and L. HECHT (CZECH.) beat F. Kukuljevic and F. Puncec (Yugo.) 4–6, 4–6, 6–2, 8–6, 6–2.

Japan beat the Netherlands on May 10, 11, and 12 by five to none. Japan's team was J. Yamagishi and H. Nishimura in singles and doubles. The Dutch team was H. Timmer and T. Hughan in the singles and Hughan and O. Koopman in the doubles. D. Teshmacher substituted for Timmer in the singles on the third day. Yamagishi won both his singles in three sets, but Nishimura lost a set to Timmer and two to Hughan. Japan took the doubles in three sets without any difficulty.

Detailed Results

Singles: J. YAMAGISHI (JAP.) beat T. Hughan (Neth.) 6–4, 6–3, 6–1; beat D. Teshmacher (Neth.) 6–1, 6–4, 6–3. H. NISHIMURA (JAP.) beat H. Timmer (Neth.) 7–5, 2–6, 7–5, 6–4; beat T. Hughan (Neth.) 6–3, 4–6, 6–3, 9–11, 6–2.

Doubles: J. YAMAGISHI and H. NISHIMURA (JAP.) beat T. Hughan and O. Koopman (Neth.) 6–4, 6–0, 6–3.

Australia beat New Zealand at Eastbourne on May 12, 13, and 14 by three to none. Australia's team was J. H. Crawford and V. B. McGrath in the singles and A. K. Quist and Crawford in the doubles. New Zealand's team was E. D. Andrews and A. C. Stedman in the singles and Stedman and C. E. Malfroy in the doubles. The tie was chiefly noteworthy for the performance of Stedman against Crawford, a match which was abandoned owing to rain on the third day. Play was stopped half-way through the third set with Crawford two sets up, and leading in the third, but no fewer than sixty-five games had already been played in 150 minutes. The first set had yielded twenty-six games, and the second thirty-two. A record.

Detailed Results

Singles: J. H. CRAWFORD (AUSTRAL.) beat E. D. Andrews (N.Z.) 6–4, 6–4, 7–5 ; drew with A. C. Stedman (N.Z.) 14–12, 17–15, 4–3 (abandoned). V. B. MCGRATH (AUSTRAL.) beat A. C. Stedman (N.Z.) 6–3, 6–2, 8–6.

Doubles: J. H. CRAWFORD and A. K. QUIST (AUSTRAL.) beat A. C. Stedman and C. E. Malfroy (N.Z.) 6–3, 4–6, 6–1, 6–4.

In the second round South Africa beat Poland at Warsaw on May 17, 18, and 19 by three to two. South Africa's team was N. G. Farquharson and V. G. Kirby in singles and doubles. Poland's team was J. Hebda and K. Tarlowski in the singles and Hebda and I. Tloczynski in the doubles. Kirby was in poor form, and lost to both Poles in five sets—to Tarlowski after leading two sets to love, and to Hebda after leading two sets to one. Hebda also had a match ball against Farquharson in the fifth set, but the South African finally got home. He also beat Tarlowski in four sets, and won the doubles with Kirby in three sets.

Detailed Results

Singles: N. G. FARQUHARSON (S.A.) beat J. Hebda (Pol.) 6–4, 7–5, 4–6, 0–6, 8–6 ; beat K. Tarlowski (Pol.) 3–6, 6–1, 7–5, 6–3. V. G. Kirby (S.A.) lost to K. TARLOWSKI (POL.) 9–7, 9–7, 6–8, 4–6, 2–6 ; lost to J. HEBDA (POL.) 6–4, 4–6, 6–4, 1–6, 2–6.

Doubles: N. G. FARQUHARSON and V. G. KIRBY (S.A.) beat I. Tloczynski and J. Hebda (Pol.) 6–3, 6–2, 6–2.

Czechoslovakia beat Japan at Prague on June 7, 8, and 9 by four to one. The Czech team was R. Menzel and J. Caska in the singles and Menzel and F. Malacek in the doubles. Japan relied on J. Yamagishi and H. Nishimura in singles and doubles. Japan's only success was gained on the third day, when Yamagishi beat L. Hecht, who was substituting for Menzel, in three sets.

Detailed Results

Singles: R. MENZEL (CZECH.) beat H. Nishimura (Jap.) 6–2, 6–3, 8–6. J. CASKA (CZECH.) beat J. Yamagishi (Jap.) 6–1, 8–6, 6–3 ; beat H. Nishimura (Jap.) 6–2, 6–3, 6–8, 6–4. L. Hecht (Czech.) lost to J. YAMAGISHI (JAP.) 1–6, 4–6, 4–6.

Doubles: R. Menzel and F. Malacek (Czech.) beat J. Yamagishi and H. Nishimura (Jap.) 2–6, 6–2, 6–2, 6–1.

Australia beat France at Paris on June 8, 9, and 10 by three to two, the same margin as in the previous year when the two countries met. The Australian team was the same as in 1934—J. H. Crawford and V. B. McGrath in the singles and Crawford and A. K. Quist in the doubles. The French singles players were, as in 1934, C. Boussus and A. Merlin, but the doubles pair was this time J. Borotra and M. Bernard. In 1934 Merlin had been the undefeated singles player; this time it was Crawford who had that honour. He beat Merlin in four sets and Boussus in five. McGrath went down to both Frenchmen in four sets. Australia won the doubles in the same number.

Detailed Results

Singles: J. H. Crawford (Austral.) beat A. Merlin (Fr.) 6–4, 4–6, 6–3, 6–3; beat C. Boussus (Fr.) 2–6, 6–4, 6–4, 3–6, 9–7. V. B. McGrath (Austral.) lost to C. Boussus (Fr.) 4–6, 6–4, 6–8, 1–6; lost to A. Merlin (Fr.) 4–6, 7–5, 3–6, 4–6.

Doubles: J. H. Crawford and A. K. Quist (Austral.) beat J. Borotra and M. Bernard (Fr.) 6–3, 4–6, 10–8, 6–4.

Germany beat Italy at Berlin on June 8, 9, and 10 by four to one. The German team was G. von Cramm and H. Henkel in the singles and von Cramm and H. Denker in the doubles. Italy's team was G. de Stefani and S. Mangold in the singles and F. Quintavalle and V. Taroni in the doubles. De Stefani beat Henkel in three sets, but could win only one set against von Cramm. Italy led two sets to one in the doubles, but finally lost in five sets.

Detailed Results

Singles: G. von Cramm (Ger.) beat S. Mangold (It.) 6–0, 6–4, 6–4; beat G. de Stefani (It.) 6–3, 6–4, 5–7, 6–1. H. Henkel (Ger.) beat S. Mangold (It.) 6–1, 6–8, 6–4, 6–4; lost to G. de Stefani (It.) 1–6, 3–6, 4–6.

Doubles: G. von Cramm and H. Denker (Ger.) beat F. Quintavalle and V. Taroni (It.) 4–6, 6–3, 2–6, 6–3, 6–1.

In the third, or semi-final, round Czechoslovakia beat South Africa at Prague on June 15, 16, and 17 by five to none. The Czech team was R. Menzel and J. Caska in the singles and Menzel and F. Malacek in the doubles. The South African team was N. G. Farquharson and M. Bertram in the singles, the former partnering V. G. Kirby in the doubles. The only full five-set match was between Bertram and Malacek, who took Menzel's place in the singles on the third day. As so often before, the Czechs proved too difficult to beat in Prague.

Detailed Results

Singles: R. MENZEL (CZECH.) beat N. G. Farquharson (S.A.) 6–2, 5–7, 6–3, 6–2. J. CASKA (CZECH.) beat M. Bertram (S.A.) 6–2, 6–4, 6–1 ; beat N. G. Farquharson (S.A.) 6–4, 6–2, 6–0. F. MALACEK (CZECH.) beat M. Bertram (S.A.) 6–1, 2–6, 6–3, 3–6, 6–2.

Doubles: R. MENZEL and F. MALACEK (CZECH.) beat N. G. Farquharson and V. G. Kirby (S.A.) 9–11, 6–4, 6–2, 6–1.

Germany beat Australia in the other semi-final tie at Berlin on June 14, 15, and 16 by four to one. The German team was G. von Cramm and H. Henkel in the singles and K. Lund and H. Denker in the doubles. The Australian team was J. H. Crawford and V. B. McGrath in the singles and Crawford and A. K. Quist in the doubles. Both Australians failed to reproduce their best form, and Germany won all the singles, to show how uncertain the game of tennis can be. Germany got away to a two-love lead on the first day, when von Cramm beat Crawford in three sets and Henkel beat McGrath in four. As von Cramm was rested in the doubles on the second day, Quist and Crawford had not much difficulty in winning in three sets, to make their score one–two. McGrath fought stubbornly to keep Australia alive, and took von Cramm to five sets before losing. Henkel beat Crawford in five sets in the last match, after the tie had been decided.

Detailed Results

Singles: G. VON CRAMM (GER.) beat J. H. Crawford (Austral.) 6–3, 7–5, 6–2 ; beat V. B. McGrath (Austral.) 6–3, 4–6, 6–3, 4–6, 6–2. H. HENKEL (GER.) beat V. B. McGrath (Austral.) 4–6, 6–2, 6–0, 6–2 ; beat J. H. Crawford (Austral.) 2–6, 6–3, 9–7, 4–6, 6–4.

Doubles: K. Lund and H. Denker (Ger.) lost to J. H. Crawford and A. K. Quist (Austral.) 1–6, 9–11, 3–6.

In the final round of this zone Germany beat Czechoslovakia at Prague on July 12, 13, and 14 by four to one. The German team was G. von Cramm and H. Henkel in the singles and von Cramm and K. Lund in the doubles. The Czech team was R. Menzel and J. Caska in the singles and Menzel and F. Malacek in the doubles. Menzel beat Henkel in five sets, and forced von Cramm to the same number before losing. Caska could not extend either German, though he won a set from Henkel. Germany took the doubles in three sets, and so were the winners of the European Zone for 1935, very largely thanks to G. von Cramm, who had not lost a single or a doubles for his country.

Detailed Results

Singles: G. von Cramm (Ger.) beat R. Menzel (Czech.) 6–2, 6–4, 3–6, 5–7, 6–1 ; beat J. Caska (Czech.) 6–2, 6–4, 6–2. H. Henkel (Ger.) beat J. Caska (Czech.) 2–6, 7–5, 6–4, 6–0 ; lost to R. Menzel (Czech.) 5–7, 1–6, 6–4, 6–2, 4–6.

Doubles: G. von Cramm and K. Lund (Ger.) beat R. Menzel and F. Malacek (Czech.) 6–3, 9–7, 6–4.

North American Zone

In the first round U.S.A. beat China at Mexico City on May 10, 11, and 12. The American team was B. M. Grant and J. D. Budge in the singles and Budge and C. G. Mako in the doubles. The Chinese team was G. Cheng and Kho Sin Kie in singles and doubles. Cheng took a set from Grant, and Kho Sin Kie one from Budge.

Detailed Results

Singles: B. M. Grant (U.S.A.) beat G. Cheng (Chin.) 4–6, 6–3, 6–2, 6–2 ; beat Kho Sin Kie (Chin.) 6–1, 6–4, 6–3. J. D. Budge (U.S.A.) beat Kho Sin Kie (Chin.) 6–2, 6–1, 6–8, 6–2 ; beat G. Cheng (Chin.) 6–4, 6–2, 6–1.

Doubles: J. D. Budge and C. G. Mako (U.S.A.) beat G. Cheng and Kho Sin Kie (Chin.) 7–5, 6–2, 6–1.

In the other first-round tie Mexico beat Cuba at Mexico City on May 3, 4, and 5 by five to none. The Mexican team was E. Reyes and D. Hernandez in the singles and A. Unda and J. Llano in the doubles. The Cuban team was L. Nodarse and A. Randin in the singles, the latter playing also in the doubles with J. Aguero. On the third day J. Etcheverry and Aguero played the singles for Cuba in place of Nodarse and Randin. Hernandez did well to save several match points against Nodarse in the fourth set of their match and go on to win the fifth set.

Detailed Results

Singles: E. REYES (MEX.) beat A. Randin (Cu.) 6–2, 6–0, 6–3; beat J. Etcheverry (Cu.) 8–6, 6–1, 6–3. D. HERNANDEZ (MEX.) beat L. Nodarse (Cu.) 5–7, 6–3, 4–6, 8–6, 6–2; beat J. Aguero (Cu.) 6–3, 7–5, 3–6, 7–5.

Doubles: A. UNDA and J. LLANO (MEX.) beat A. Randin and J. Aguero (Cu.) 6–4, 6–1, 6–3.

In the final round of this zone U.S.A. beat Mexico at Mexico City on May 17, 18, and 19 by four to one. The American team was B. M. Grant and J. D. Budge in the singles and Budge and C. G. Mako in the doubles. The Mexican team was D. Hernandez and E. Reyes in the singles andA. Unda and J. Llano in the doubles. Mako, substituting for Budge on the last day, retired to Reyes in the fifth set, to give Mexico her only win.

Detailed Results

Singles: B. M. GRANT (U.S.A.) beat E. Reyes (Mex.) 6–2, 6–3, 6–3; beat D. Hernandez (Mex.) 6–1, 6–3, 6–0. J. D. BUDGE (U.S.A.) beat D. Hernandez (Mex.) 6–4, 6–3, 6–4. C. G. Mako (U.S.A.) lost to E. REYES (MEX.) 6–1, 3–6, 6–8, 6–4, 2–0 (retired).

Doubles: J. D. BUDGE and C. G. MAKO (U.S.A.) beat A. Unda and J. Llano (Mex.) 6–0, 6–2, 6–3.

SOUTH AMERICAN ZONE

There was only one tie in this zone, between Brazil and Uruguay, played at Montevideo on April 26, 27, and 28 and won by Brazil by three matches to two. The Brazilian team was S. L. Campos and I. Simone in the singles and Simone and T. de Freitas in the doubles. Uruguay's team was P. de Leon and M. Harreguy in the singles and M. Cat and E. Stanham in the doubles. De Leon won both his singles comfortably, but Uruguay could not win any other match, the nearest to success being Harreguy's effort against Campos, in which Harreguy led by two sets to one, but lost in five sets ultimately.

Detailed Results

Singles: S. L. Campos (Braz.) beat M. Harreguy (Uru.) 4–6, 7–5, 3–6, 6–4, 6–1 ; lost to P. de Leon (Uru.) 4–6, 0–6, 4–6. I. Simone (Braz.) beat M. Harreguy (Uru.) 7–5, 6–4, 6–4 ; lost to P. de Leon (Uru.) 2–6, 2–6, 8–6, 1–6.

Doubles: I. Simone and T. de Freitas (Braz.) beat M. Cat and E. Stanham (Uru.) 7–5, 4–6, 6–1, 8–6.

American Inter-zone Round

Brazil defaulted to U.S.A. in the American inter-zone final round.

Inter-zone Round

This tie, between Germany, the European Zone winners, and U.S.A., the American Zone winners, took place at Wimbledon on July 20–24. The American team was W. L. Allison and J. D. Budge in the singles and Allison and J. van Ryn in the doubles. The German team was G. von Cramm and H. Henkel in the singles and von Cramm and K. Lund in the doubles. On the first round of the singles honours were divided. Budge beat Henkel in the first match in four sets, and von Cramm evened the tie by beating Allison in three sets. The doubles match could not really have been closer: Allison and van Ryn came from behind to snatch the match from von Cramm and Lund, who held match points in both the fourth and fifth sets. This put U.S.A. ahead two–one, and on the last day the Americans increased the margin to four–one when Allison beat Henkel in three sets and Budge accounted for von Cramm in four.

Detailed Results

Singles: W. L. ALLISON (U.S.A.) beat H. Henkel (Ger.) 6–1, 7–5, 11–9; lost to G. VON CRAMM (GER.) 6–8, 3–6, 4–6. J. D. BUDGE (U.S.A.) beat H. Henkel (Ger.) 7–5, 11–9, 6–8, 6–1; beat G. von Cramm (Ger.) 0–6, 9–7, 8–6, 6–3.

Doubles: W. L. ALLISON and J. VAN RYN (U.S.A.) beat G. von Cramm and K. Lund (Ger.) 3–6, 6–3, 5–7, 9–7, 8–6.

CHALLENGE ROUND

This final tie, between Great Britain, the holders, and U.S.A., once again challengers, as in 1934, took place at Wimbledon on July 27, 29, and 30, and resulted in a decisive victory of five–love for the holders, an unusually wide margin, marking the peak of Great Britain's supremacy as champion country. The defending team was F. J. Perry and H. W. Austin in the singles and G. P. Hughes and C. R. D. Tuckey in the doubles, the latter being a new man playing his first Davis Cup match. The challenging American team was W. L. Allison and J. D. Budge in the singles and Allison and J. van Ryn in the doubles. Austin led off by beating Allison in a close five-set tussle, and then Perry beat Budge in four sets, to put the holders two up. Hughes and Tuckey clinched the tie by a fine win over Allison and van Ryn in the doubles in five sets, from two sets to one down. On the third day Great Britain made a clean sweep, when Perry beat Allison in four sets and Austin beat Budge in the same number. This was Great Britain's most dominant year.

Detailed Results

Singles: F. J. PERRY (G.B.) beat J. D. Budge (U.S.A.) 6–0, 6–8, 6–3, 6–4; beat W. L. Allison (U.S.A.) 4–6, 6–4, 7–5, 6–3. H. W. AUSTIN (G.B.) beat W. L. Allison (U.S.A.) 6–2, 2–6, 4–6, 6–3, 7–5; beat J. D. Budge (U.S.A.) 6–2, 6–4, 6–8, 7–5.

Doubles: G. P. HUGHES and C. R. D. TUCKEY (G.B.) beat W. L. Allison and J. van Ryn (U.S.A.) 6–2, 1–6, 6–8, 6–3, 6–3.

1936: GREAT BRITAIN

This year the qualifying system in the European Zone was abolished, the competition reverting to its old form. There were twenty-three challengers altogether—nineteen in the European Zone and four in the North American Zone.

European Zone

In the first round the Netherlands beat Monaco at Monte Carlo on May 1, 2, and 3 by three to two. The Dutch team was H. Timmer and T. Hughan in the singles and Hughan and W. Karsten in the doubles. Monaco had their faithful two-man team of V. Landau and R. Gallèpe. Timmer won both his singles in three sets, and Hughan beat Landau in four sets. He lost to Gallèpe in three, and Monaco won the doubles in four sets.

Detailed Results

Singles: H. Timmer (Neth.) beat R. Gallèpe (Mon.) 6–3, 6–2, 6–1; beat V. Landau (Mon.) 6–2, 6–3, 8–6. T. Hughan (Neth.) beat V. Landau (Mon.) 6–3, 5–7, 6–2, 6–1; lost to R. Gallèpe (Mon.) 2–6, 4–6, 3–6.

Doubles: T. Hughan and W. Karsten (Neth.) lost to V. Landau and R. Gallèpe (Mon.) 4–6, 5–7, 6–3, 5–7.

France beat China at Paris on May 1, 2, and 3 by five to none. The French team was C. Boussus and B. Destremau in the singles and J. Borotra and M. Bernard in the doubles. China's team was Kho Sin Kie and G. Cheng in the singles with Kho Sin Kie and G. Lum as the doubles pair. Boussus won both his singles with the loss of only three games—one to Kho Sin Kie and two to Cheng. Destremau dropped a set in each of his, and so did Borotra and Bernard in the doubles.

Detailed Results

Singles: C. Boussus (Fr.) beat Kho Sin Kie (Chin.) 6–0, 6–0, 6–1; beat G. Cheng (Chin.) 6–0, 6–0, 6–2. B. Destremau (Fr.) beat G. Cheng (Chin.) 6–1, 6–3, 6–8, 6–3; beat Kho Sin Kie (Chin.) 6–3, 6–2, 4–6, 6–2.

Doubles: J. Borotra and M. Bernard (Fr.) beat Kho Sin Kie and G. Lum (Chin.) 6–1, 6–3, 4–6, 6–2.

Germany beat Spain at Barcelona on April 24, 25, and 26 by four to one. The German team was G. von Cramm and H. Henkel in the singles and von Cramm and K. Lund in the doubles. The Spanish team was E. Maier and M. Alonso in the singles and Maier and J. M. Blanc in the doubles.

Maier beat von Cramm on the third day in three sets, after the tie had been decided. Germany won all the other matches without loss of a set.

Detailed Results

Singles: G. VON CRAMM (GER.) beat M. Alonso (Sp.) 6–3, 6–4, 6–3 ; lost to E. MAIER (SP.) 3–6, 2–6, 1–6. H. HENKEL (GER.) beat E. Maier (Sp.) 6–4, 7–5, 8–6 ; beat M. Alonso (Sp.) 6–2, 6–3, 6–4.

Doubles: G. VON CRAMM and K. LUND (GER.) beat E. Maier and J. M. Blanc (Sp.) 6–3, 6–3, 9–7.

In the second round Belgium beat Norway at Oslo on May 14, 15, and 16 by three matches to two. Belgium's team was A. Lacroix and P. Geelhand in the singles and Lacroix and L. de Borman in the doubles. Norway relied on J. Haanes and F. Jenssen in singles and doubles. Lacroix gained Belgium's three successes. Geelhand lost to Jenssen, and J. van den Eynde, substituting for Geelhand on the third day, lost to Haanes.

Detailed Results

Singles: A. LACROIX (BELG.) beat F. Jenssen (Norw.) 7–5, 6–2, 6–4 ; beat J. Haanes (Norw.) 4–6, 6–3, 6–0, 6–2. P. Geelhand (Belg.) lost to F. JENSSEN (NORW.) 6–8, 6–4, 2–6, 4–6. J. van den Eynde (Belg.) lost to J. HAANES (NORW.) 4–6, 6–2, 6–8, 2–6.

Doubles: A. LACROIX and L. DE BORMAN (BELG.) beat J. Haanes and F. Jenssen (Norw.) 6–4, 6–2, 7–9, 6–3.

Austria beat Poland at Vienna on May 15, 16, and 17 in a close tie by three to two. The Austrian team was A. Bawarowski and G. von Metaxa in singles and doubles. The Polish team was J. Hebda and I. Tloczynski in the singles and Hebda and K. Tarlowski in the doubles. Hebda won both his singles, but Tloczynski lost both his, and Poland also lost the doubles.

Detailed Results

Singles: A. BAWAROWSKI (AUS.) beat I. Tloczynski (Pol.) 6–4, 6–3, 6–3 ; lost to J. HEBDA (POL.) 0–6, 6–2, 6–4, 1–6, 5–7. G. VON METAXA (AUS.) beat I. Tloczynski (Pol.) 6–4, 6–8, 3–6, 7–5, 6–3 ; lost to J. HEBDA (POL.) 4–6, 5–7, 4–6.

Doubles: A. BAWAROWSKI and G. VON METAXA (AUS.) beat J. Hebda and K. Tarlowski (Pol.) 6–1, 6–2, 6–4.

Yugoslavia beat Czechoslovakia at Zagreb on May 15, 16, and 17 by three to two. The Yugoslav team was F. Puncec and J. Pallada in the singles and Puncec and F. Kukuljevic in the doubles. The Czech team was L. Hecht and J. Siba in the singles and Hecht and F. Malacek in the doubles. Puncec beat both Hecht and Siba in the singles, the former in five sets and the latter in four, and Pallada, though losing to Hecht, beat Siba in three sets in the fifth and deciding match of the tie. The Czechs won the doubles on the second day in five sets.

Detailed Results

Singles: F. PUNCEC (YUGO.) beat J. Siba (Czech.) 6–1, 6–2, 2–6, 6–0 ; beat L. Hecht (Czech.) 6–3, 4–6, 1–6, 6–4, 6–2. J. PALLADA (YUGO.) beat J. Siba (Czech.) 6–3, 6–2, 6–4 ; lost to L. HECHT (CZECH.) 6–8, 1–6, 6–2, 2–6.

Doubles: F. Puncec and F. Kukuljevic (Yugo.) lost to L. HECHT and F. MALACEK (CZECH.) 6–4, 7–9, 6–2, 3–6, 4–6.

France beat the Netherlands at The Hague on May 9, 10, and 11 by four to one. The French team was again C. Boussus and B. Destremau in the singles and J. Borotra and M. Bernard in the doubles. The Dutch team was H. Timmer and T. Hughan in the singles and Timmer and W. Karsten in the doubles. Timmer played well to beat Boussus in three sets, but he lost to Destremau in four. Hughan led Destremau two sets to one, but lost in five sets, and he also went down to Boussus in four sets after winning the first. France lost a set in the doubles, but the French pair was never really threatened.

Detailed Results

Singles: C. BOUSSUS (FR.) beat T. Hughan (Neth.) 3–6, 10–8, 6–2, 6–0 ; lost to H. TIMMER (NETH.) 3–6, 3–6, 1–6. B. DESTREMAU (FR.) beat T. Hughan (Neth.) 6–4, 3–6, 3–6, 6–4, 6–1 ; beat H. Timmer (Neth.) 0–6, 6–1, 6–3, 6–2.

Doubles: J. BOROTRA and M. BERNARD (FR.) beat H. Timmer and W. Karsten (Neth.) 6–1, 6–3, 6–8, 6–2.

Germany beat Hungary at Düsseldorf on May 15, 16, and 17 by five to none. The German team was G. von Cramm and H. Henkel in the singles and von Cramm and K. Lund in the doubles. Hungary's team was G. Dallos and E. Gabrowitz in the singles and E. Ferenczy and E. Gabory in the doubles. Germany did not drop a set in all five matches.

Detailed Results

Singles: G. VON CRAMM (GER.) beat E. Gabrowitz (Hun.) 6–3, 6–2, 6–3; beat G. Dallos (Hun.) 6–1, 7–5, 6–3. H. HENKEL (GER.) beat G. Dallos (Hun.) 6–1, 6–1, 6–2; beat E. Gabrowitz (Hun.) 8–6, 6–3, 7–5.

Doubles: G. VON CRAMM and K. LUND (GER.) beat E. Ferenczy and E. Gabory (Hun.) 6–3, 7–5, 6–0.

Argentina beat Greece at Athens on May 8, 9, and 10 by four to one. The Argentine team was A. Zappa and L. del Castillo in singles and doubles. The Greek team was L. Stalios and G. Nicholaides in singles and doubles. Stalios beat Zappa in three sets in the first match, but in the remaining four matches the Argentinians were comfortable winners.

Detailed Results

Singles: L. DEL CASTILLO (ARGENT.) beat G. Nicholaides (Gr.) 6–4, 6–0, 6–1; beat L. Stalios (Gr.) 6–2, 6–4, 9–7. A. ZAPPA (ARGENT.) beat G. Nicholaides (Gr.) 6–3, 6–1, 5–7, 6–1; lost to L. STALIOS (GR.) 4–6, 3–6, 4–6.

Doubles: A. ZAPPA and L. DEL CASTILLO (ARGENT.) beat L. Stalios and G. Nicholaides (Gr.) 4–6, 6–1, 6–1, 6–2.

Ireland beat Sweden at Dublin on May 14, 15, and 16 by four to one. The Irish team was G. L. Rogers and T. G. McVeagh in singles and doubles. The Swedish team was K. Schröder and C. Ostberg in singles and doubles. Ireland won all four singles, McVeagh being in especially good form, and losing only one set—to Schröder. The Swedes won the doubles in four sets.

Detailed Results

Singles: G. L. ROGERS (IRE.) beat K. Schröder (Sw.) 9–7, 2–6, 1–6, 6–3, 6–4 ; beat C. Ostberg (Sw.) 0–6, 6–2, 6–4, 6–3. T. G. MCVEAGH (IRE.) beat C. Ostberg (Sw.) 6–4, 6–4, 6–4 ; beat K. Schröder (Sw.) 2–6, 7–5, 6–3, 6–3.

Doubles: G. L. Rogers and T. G. McVeagh (Ire.) lost to K. SCHRÖDER and C. OSTBERG (Sw.) 6–3, 2–6, 7–9, 5–7.

Switzerland beat Denmark at Montreux on May 15, 16, and 17 by five to none. The Swiss team was H. C. Fisher and M. Ellmer in the singles and H. Steiner and B. Maneff in the doubles. The Danish team was N. K. Koerner and H. Plougmann in the singles and Plougmann and E. Ulrich in the doubles. In the closest match Plougmann forced Fisher to five sets from two sets down.

Detailed Results

Singles: H. C. FISHER (SWITZ.) beat N. K. Koerner (Den.) 6–2, 6–1, 6–0 ; beat H. Plougmann (Den.) 6–0, 7–5, 4–6, 6–8, 6–1. M. ELLMER (SWITZ.) beat H. Plougmann (Den.) 6–1, 6–4, 6–1 ; beat N. K. Koerner (Den.) 6–3, 6–0, 3–6, 6–0.

Doubles: H. STEINER and B. MANEFF (SWITZ.) beat E. Ulrich and H. Plougmann (Den.) 6–1, 6–3, 11–9.

In the third round Austria beat Belgium at Vienna on June 5, 6, and 7 by four to one. Austria relied on A. Bawarowski and G. von Metaxa in both singles and doubles. Belgium's team was A. Lacroix and J. van den Eynde in the singles and Lacroix and L. de Borman in the doubles. Austria won all the singles and lost the doubles. Bawarowski beat van den Eynde in five sets and Lacroix in three. Von Metaxa beat Lacroix in five sets and van den Eynde in four. Belgium took the doubles in four sets.

Detailed Results

Singles: A. BAWAROWSKI (AUS.) beat J. van den Eynde (Belg.) 6–3, 3–6, 4–6, 6–3, 6–2 ; beat A. Lacroix (Belg.) 6–4, 6–3, 11–9. G. VON METAXA (AUS.) beat A. Lacroix (Belg.) 3–6, 6–3, 6–4, 2–6, 6–3 ; beat J. van den Eynde (Belg.) 6–3, 4–6, 6–3, 6–2.

Doubles: A. Bawarowski and G. von Metaxa (Aus.) lost to A. LACROIX and L. DE BORMAN (BELG.) 6–2, 6–8, 5–7, 3–6.

Yugoslavia beat France at Paris on June 5, 6, and 7 by three to two. The Yugoslav team was F. Puncec and J. Pallada in the singles and D. Mitic and F. Kukuljevic in the doubles. The French team was unchanged from earlier rounds, being C. Boussus and B. Destremau in the singles and J. Borotra and M. Bernard in the doubles. Pallada was in good form, and beat both Frenchmen in four sets. Puncec lost a very close five-setter to Destremau, and won an equally close one from Boussus. The Yugoslav doubles pair carried Borotra and Bernard to five sets from two sets down, but they could not hold the French pair in the fifth set.

Detailed Results

Singles: F. PUNCEC (YUGO.) beat C. Boussus (Fr.) 3–6, 6–1, 4–6, 7–5, 6–1 ; lost to B. DESTREMAU (FR.) 6–3, 2–6, 5–7, 6–0, 7–9. J. PALLADA (YUGO.) beat C. Boussus (Fr.) 6–2, 2–6, 6–3, 6–2 ; beat B. Destremau (Fr.) 6–1, 1–6, 8–6, 6–4.

Doubles: D. Mitic and F. Kukuljevic (Yugo.) lost to J. BOROTRA and M. BERNARD (FR.) 6–8, 5–7, 6–4, 6–3, 2–6.

Germany beat Argentina at Berlin on June 5, 6, and 7 by four to one. The German team was G. von Cramm and H. Henkel in singles and doubles. The Argentine team was A. Zappa and L. del Castillo in singles and doubles. Germany were not pressed. On the third day, when the tie was decided, H. Denker took the place of von Cramm in the singles, and lost to Zappa in five sets.

Detailed Results

Singles: G. VON CRAMM (GER.) beat L. del Castillo (Argent.) 6–0, 4–6, 6–4, 6–1. H. HENKEL (GER.) beat A. Zappa (Argent.) 6–1, 6–1, 6–3 ; beat L. del Castillo (Argent.) 6–0, 6–1, 6–1. H. Denker (Ger.) lost to A. ZAPPA (ARGENT.) 6–3, 0–6, 6–2, 1–6, 1–6.

Doubles: G. VON CRAMM and H. HENKEL (GER.) beat L. del Castillo and A. Zappa (Argent.) 6–1, 6–2, 6–3.

Ireland beat Switzerland at Dublin on June 4, 5, and 6 by three to two. The Irish team was again G. L. Rogers and T. G. McVeagh in singles and doubles. The Swiss team was

H. C. Fisher and B. Maneff in the singles and Fisher and H. Steiner in the doubles. Fisher did well to beat Rogers in four sets and McVeagh in five. Ireland took the doubles in four sets. Unfortunately for Switzerland, Maneff strained a muscle when playing against Rogers, to whom he lost in five sets, on the first day, and could not play again in the tie. McVeagh beat M. Ellmer, who took Maneff's place in the singles on the third day, in four sets, to gain Ireland's third victory and the tie.

Detailed Results

Singles: G. L. ROGERS (IRE.) beat B. Maneff (Switz.) 6–2, 6–3, 3–6, 3–6, 6–0 ; lost to H. C. FISHER (SWITZ.) 6–3, 2–6, 3–6, 2–6. T. G. MCVEAGH (IRE.) beat M. Ellmer (Switz.) 6–3, 4–6, 6–4, 11–9 ; lost to H. C. FISHER (SWITZ.) 1–6, 6–3, 8–6, 0–6, 2–6.

Doubles: G. L. ROGERS and T. G. MCVEAGH (IRE.) beat H. C. Fisher and H. Steiner (Switz.) 5–7, 6–4, 6–1, 6–4.

In the fourth and semi-final round Yugoslavia beat Austria at Vienna on June 13, 14, and 15 by four to one. The Yugoslav team was F. Puncec and J. Pallada in the singles and D. Mitic and F. Kukuljevic in the doubles. For Austria A. Bawarowski and G. von Metaxa played both singles and doubles. Pallada won both his singles, but he had to go to five sets to do so in each. Puncec beat von Metaxa in three sets, and Kukuljevic, who took Puncec's place on the third day, beat Bawarowski in five sets. Austria won the doubles in five sets.

Detailed Results

Singles: F. PUNCEC (YUGO.) beat G. von Metaxa (Aus.) 6–4, 6–3, 6–1. J. PALLADA (YUGO.) beat A. Bawarowski (Aus.) 3–6, 6–4, 6–3, 3–6, 7–5 ; beat G. von Metaxa (Aus.) 8–6, 6–3, 2–6, 3–6, 6–4. F. KUKULJEVIC (YUGO.) beat A. Bawarowski (Aus.) 5–7, 6–4, 1–6, 6–2, 6–3.

Doubles: F. Kukuljevic and D. Mitic (Yugo.) lost to A. BAWAROWSKI and G. VON METAXA (AUS.) 6–4, 3–6, 4–6, 6–4, 2–6.

Germany beat Ireland at Berlin on June 12, 13, and 14 by five to none. Both countries played only two men. For

Germany G. von Cramm and H. Henkel played singles and doubles, and for Ireland G. L. Rogers and T. G. McVeagh did the same. The Irish team had apparently shot its bolt in reaching this round, as it was unable to win a set from the German team in five matches.

Detailed Results

Singles: G. von Cramm (Ger.) beat G. L. Rogers (Ire.) 6–1, 6–2, 6–3 ; beat T. G. McVeagh (Ire.) 6–2, 6–3, 6–1. H. Henkel (Ger.) beat T. G. McVeagh (Ire.) 6–1, 8–6, 6–2 ; beat G. L. Rogers (Ire.) 6–2, 6–0, 6–0.

Doubles: G. von Cramm and H. Henkel (Ger.) beat G. L. Rogers and T. G. McVeagh (Ire.) 6–0, 6–1, 6–4.

In the final round of the European Zone Germany beat Yugoslavia at Zagreb on July 10, 11, and 12 by three matches to two—officially. Actually Germany won the only three matches completed, and defaulted both singles on the last day, one being part played. The German team was G. von Cramm and H. Henkel in singles and doubles. The Yugoslav team was F. Puncec and J. Pallada in the singles and F. Kukuljevic and D. Mitic in the doubles. Pallada won a set from von Cramm, but Henkel easily beat Puncec in three sets. The doubles was a long, well-fought encounter, the Yugoslav pair doing their utmost to keep the tie alive, but failing after holding an initial lead in the fifth set. Germany, with three wins to their credit, did not play the tie out, and it ended after rain had interfered with the first match on the third day. They were definitely the stronger team.

Detailed Results

Singles: G. von Cramm (Ger.) beat J. Pallada (Yugo.) 6–4, 6–2, 6–8, 6–2. H. Henkel (Ger.) beat F. Puncec (Yugo.) 6–1, 6–2, 6–4.

Doubles: G. von Cramm and H. Henkel (Ger.) beat D. Mitic and F. Kukuljevic (Yugo.) 8–6, 4–6, 6–3, 4–6, 6–3.

North American Zone

In the first round U.S.A. beat Mexico at Houston, Texas, on April 10, 11, and 12 by five to none. The American team was J. D. Budge and B. M. Grant in the singles and W. L.

Allison and J. van Ryn in the doubles. The Mexican team was E. Reyes and D. Hernandez in the singles and M. A. Mestre and F. Martinez in the doubles. The Mexicans won only one set in five matches, taken from Grant by Hernandez.

Detailed Results

Singles: J. D. Budge (U.S.A.) beat E. Reyes (Mex.) 6–3, 6–1, 6–1 ; beat D. Hernandez (Mex.) 6–1, 6–1, 6–3. B. M. Grant (U.S.A.) beat D. Hernandez (Mex.) 3–6, 6–2, 6–3, 6–3 ; beat E. Reyes (Mex.) 6–4, 13–11, 6–2

Doubles: W. L. Allison and J. van Ryn (U.S.A.) beat M. A. Mestre and F. Martinez (Mex.) 6–0, 6–1, 6–2.

In the final round of this zone Australia, having received a walk-over from Cuba in the first round, beat U.S.A. at Philadelphia on May 30 and 31 and June 1 by three matches to two. The Australian team was J. H. Crawford and A. K. Quist in both singles and doubles. The American team was J. D. Budge and W. L. Allison in the singles and Budge and C. G. Mako in the doubles. Quist beat Allison in four sets and Crawford beat him in five. Budge beat both Australians —Crawford in five sets, with a twenty-four-game final set, and Quist, after the tie had been decided, in three sets. The doubles was the key to the contest, and this was won by Australia from two sets down. America almost won it in four sets, and also held a four–one lead in the final set, only to lose the next five games and the match.

Detailed Results

Singles: A. K. Quist (Austral.) beat W. L. Allison (U.S.A.) 6–3, 5–7, 6–4, 6–1 ; lost to J. D. Budge (U.S.A.) 2–6, 2–6, 4–6. J. H. Crawford (Austral.) beat W. L. Allison (U.S.A.) 4–6, 6–3, 4–6, 6–2, 6–2 ; lost to J. D. Budge (U.S.A.) 2–6, 3–6, 6–4, 6–1, 11–13.

Doubles: J. H. Crawford and A. K. Quist (Austral.) beat J. D. Budge and C. G. Mako (U.S.A.) 4–6, 2–6, 6–4, 7–5, 6–4.

Inter-zone Round

This tie, between Australia, winners of the American Zone, and Germany, winners of the European Zone, took place at Wimbledon on July 18, 20, and 21, and was won by Australia by four matches to one. The Australian team was J. H. Crawford and A. K. Quist in singles and doubles, but, owing to Quist's spraining an ankle in his first match, V. B. McGrath took his place in the doubles and the single on the third day. The German team was G. von Cramm and H. Henkel in singles and doubles. On the opening day Henkel, suffering from a chill, retired to Crawford after the Australian had reached two sets to love. Quist and von Cramm played a most dramatic match, which was finally won by von Cramm in the twentieth game of the fifth set, after Quist, who sprained his ankle in the third set, had held three match balls, and saved nine match balls before going down. On the second day Crawford and McGrath put Australia ahead by beating von Cramm and Henkel in four sets. On the third day McGrath gained Australia's third point when he beat Henkel in four sets, and thus put Australia into the challenge round for the first time in twelve years. In the last match of this tie Crawford beat H. Denker, substituting for von Cramm, in three sets, increasing Australia's margin to four to one. McGrath had proved a valuable reserve, and had discounted most adequately Quist's misfortune on the first day.

Detailed Results

Singles: A. K. Quist (Austral.) lost to G. VON CRAMM (GER.) 6–4, 4–6, 6–4, 4–6, 9–11. J. H. CRAWFORD (AUSTRAL.) beat H. Henkel (Ger.) 6–2, 6–2, retired; beat H. Denker (Ger.) 6–3, 6–1, 6–4. V. B. MCGRATH (AUSTRAL.) beat H. Henkel (Ger.) 6–3, 5–7, 6–4, 6–4.

Doubles: J. H. CRAWFORD and V. B. MCGRATH (AUSTRAL.) beat G. von Cramm and H. Henkel (Ger.) 6–4, 4–6, 6–4, 6–4.

CHALLENGE ROUND

Australia, challengers, and Great Britain, holders, met at Wimbledon on July 25, 27, and 28. The holders won by three to two. The defending team was the same as a year earlier—H. W. Austin and F. J. Perry in the singles and G. P. Hughes and C. R. D. Tuckey in the doubles. The Australian challengers were J. H. Crawford and A. K. Quist in singles and doubles. The holders gained an invaluable lead on the first day by winning both singles. Austin led off by beating Crawford in four sets, a somewhat unexpected result, and then Perry beat Quist in four sets also. On the second day Crawford and Quist reduced this lead by beating Hughes and Tuckey in four sets. On the third day Quist brought the countries level by defeating Austin in four sets. Everything now depended on the fifth match, between Perry and Crawford. Perry, playing his last Davis Cup match—for he was to join the professional ranks later in the year—gave a magnificent display of forceful, accurate tennis, and beat Crawford in three sets, and so Great Britain retained the Davis Cup for the fourth successive year, if only by the narrow margin of the odd match in five. Their defending team of the following year was to contain only two of this year's four men. The withdrawal of Perry and Hughes, particularly the former, was to weaken the team too much to withstand any more challenges successfully. At the height of his form Perry was nearly a team by himself.

Detailed Results

Singles: F. J. PERRY (G.B.) beat A. K. Quist (Austral.) 6–1, 4–6, 7–5, 6–2; beat J. H. Crawford (Austral.) 6–2, 6–3, 6–3. H. W. AUSTIN (G.B.) beat J. H. Crawford (Austral.) 4–6, 6–3, 6–1, 6–1; lost to A. K. QUIST (AUSTRAL.) 4–6, 6–3, 5–7, 2–6.

Doubles: G. P. Hughes and C. R. D. Tuckey (G.B.) lost to J. H. CRAWFORD and A. K. QUIST (AUSTRAL.) 4–6, 6–2, 5–7, 8–10.

1937: U.S.A.

This year twenty-four countries challenged, twenty being in the European Zone and four in the American Zone.

EUROPEAN ZONE

In the first round Belgium beat Hungary at Budapest on April 30 and May 1 and 2 by three to two in a close encounter. The Belgian team was A. Lacroix and C. Naeyaert in the singles and L. de Borman and P. Geelhand in the doubles. The Hungarian team was G. Dallos and E. Gabory in the singles and Gabory and E. Ferenczy in the doubles. Lacroix lost to Dallos in five sets after winning the first two, and he and de Borman won the doubles in five sets after being down two. Naeyaert beat Gabory in five sets, but retired in the fourth set to Dallos on the third day when two sets to one down.

Detailed Results

Singles: C. NAEYAERT (BELG.) beat E. Gabory (Hun.) 7–5, 4–6, 4–6, 6–0, 6–4 ; lost to G. DALLOS (HUN.) 5–7, 6–4, 2–6, 3–3 (retired). A. Lacroix (Belg.) lost to G. DALLOS (HUN.) 6–4, 9–7, 4–6, 3–6, 3–6 ; beat E. Gabory (Hun.) 6–1, 6–2, 6–4.

Doubles: L. DE BORMAN and P. GEELHAND (BELG.) beat E. Gabory and E. Ferenczy (Hun.) 2–6, 1–6, 6–4, 6–3, 6–1.

Switzerland beat Ireland at Montreux on April 30 and May 1 and 2 by three to two. The Swiss team was H. C. Fisher and M. Ellmer in the singles and Fisher and B. Maneff in the doubles. Ireland relied on G. L. Rogers and T. G. McVeagh in both singles and doubles. Rogers beat Ellmer in four sets, but went down to Fisher in five. With McVeagh he won the doubles in five sets. The latter lost both his singles.

Detailed Results

Singles: M. ELLMER (SWITZ.) beat T. G. McVeagh (Ire.) 5–7, 8–6, 6–4, 6–1 ; lost to G. L. ROGERS (IRE.) 6–8, 6–1, 1–6, 3–6. H. C. FISHER (SWITZ.) beat T. G. McVeagh (Ire.) 6–4, 6–2, 6–1 ; beat G. L. Rogers (Ire.) 6–3, 6–4, 4–6, 2–6, 6–2.

Doubles: B. Maneff and H. C. Fisher (Switz.) lost to G. L. ROGERS and T. G. MCVEAGH (IRE.) 0–6, 1–6, 7–5, 7–5, 4–6.

South Africa beat the Netherlands at Amsterdam on April 30 and May 1 and 2 by five to none. The South African team was N. G. Farquharson and V. G. Kirby in singles and doubles. The Dutch team was D. Teshmacher and T. Hughan in the singles and Hughan and A. C. van Swol in the doubles. E. E. Fannin took Kirby's place in singles on the third day, and beat Hughan in four sets, all the other matches having gone to South Africa in straight sets,

Detailed Results

Singles: V. G. KIRBY (S.A.) beat D. Teshmacher (Neth.) 6–2, 7–5, 8–6. N. G. FARQUHARSON (S.A.) beat T. Hughan (Neth.) 6–1, 6–1, 6–1 ; beat D. Teshmacher (Neth.) 9–7, 6–1, 6–3. E. E. FANNIN (S.A.) beat T. Hughan (Neth.) 6–2, 7–5, 3–6, 6–3.

Doubles: N. G. FARQUHARSON and V. G. KIRBY (S.A.) beat T. Hughan and A. C. van Swol (Neth.) 6–4, 6–3, 6–2.

New Zealand beat China at Brighton on April 29 and 30 and May 1 by three to two. The New Zealand team was A. C. Stedman and C. E. Malfroy in singles and doubles. The Chinese team was Kho Sin Kie and W. C. Choy in the singles and Kho Sin Kie and Tsui Wai Pui in the doubles. Kho Sin Kie was in grand form, and won both his singles in four sets, dropping the third in each case. Choy, however, could not win a set in either of his, and New Zealand also took the doubles in four sets.

Detailed Results

Singles: A. C. STEDMAN (N.Z.) beat W. C. Choy (Chin.) 6–4, 6–0, 6–2 ; lost to KHO SIN KIE (CHIN.) 4–6, 4–6, 6–1, 4–6. C. E. MALFROY (N.Z.) beat W. C. Choy (Chin.) 6–1, 6–3, 6–1 ; lost to KHO SIN KIE (CHIN.) 0–6, 3–6, 6–4, 2–6.

Doubles: A. C. STEDMAN and C. E. MALFROY (N.Z.) beat Kho Sin Kie and Tsui Wai Pui (Chin.) 6–3, 6–8, 6–3, 6–2.

In the second round Italy beat Monaco at Bologna on May 8, 9, and 10 by three to none, only three matches being played. Italy's team was G. de Stefani and V. Canapele in the singles and V. Taroni and F. Quintavalle in the doubles. Monaco's team was V. Landau and G. Medecin in singles and doubles. The Italians won all three matches easily.

Detailed Results

Singles: G. DE STEFANI (IT.) beat V. Landau (Mon.) 6–2, 6–0, 6–3. V. CANAPELE (IT.) beat G. Medecin (Mon.) 6–0, 6–1, 6–0.

Doubles: V. TARONI and F. QUINTAVALLE (IT.) beat V. Landau and G. Medecin (Mon.) 6–1, 6–3, 6–3.

Germany beat Austria at Munich on May 8, 9, and 10 by three to two. The German team was G. von Cramm and

H. Henkel in singles and doubles. The Austrian team was G. von Metaxa and A. Bawarowski in singles and doubles. The German team won the singles on the first day and the doubles on the second day without loss of a set. On the third day H. Redl, playing instead of von Metaxa, beat Dettmer, who played in place of Henkel, and von Cramm retired to Bawarowski when rain stopped play after one set, won by von Cramm.

Detailed Results

Singles: G. VON CRAMM (GER.) beat G. von Metaxa (Aus.) 6–3, 6–4, 6–3 ; retired to A. BAWAROWSKI (AUS.) after winning first set at 10–8. H. HENKEL (GER.) beat A. Bawarowski (Aus.) 6–1, 6–4, 6–1. E. Dettmer (Ger.) lost to H. REDL (AUS.) 6–8, 1–6, 6–3, 1–6.

Doubles: G. VON CRAMM and H. HENKEL (GER.) beat A. Bawarowski and G. von Metaxa (Aus.) 8–6, 11–9, 7–5.

Sweden beat Greece at Stockholm on May 15, 16, and 17 by three to two in a very close tie. The Swedish team was K. Schröder and S. Karlberg in the singles and Schröder and C. Ostberg in the doubles. The Greek team was G. Nicholaides and L. Stalios in singles and doubles. Schröder won all his matches—his singles in straight sets, but the doubles, with Ostberg, only after a long struggle at 8–6 in the fifth set. Karlberg lost both his singles.

Detailed Results

Singles: K. SCHRÖDER (SW.) beat L. Stalios (Gr.) 6–3, 6–3, 6–4 ; beat G. Nicholaides (Gr.) 6–2, 6–4, 6–4. S. Karlberg (Sw.) lost to G. NICHOLAIDES (GR.) 6–4, 2–6, 2–6, 3–6 ; lost to L. STALIOS (GR.) 2–6, 2–6, 3–6.

Doubles: K. SCHRÖDER and C. OSTBERG (SW.) beat G. Nicholaides and L. Stalios (Gr.) 6–2, 6–2, 8–10, 3–6, 8–6.

Belgium beat Switzerland at Brussels on May 15, 16, and 17 by four to one. The Belgian team was A. Lacroix and C. Naeyaert in the singles and Lacroix and L. de Borman in the doubles. The Swiss team was H. C. Fisher and M. Ellmer in the singles and B. Maneff and H. Steiner in the doubles. Fisher beat Lacroix, and carried Naeyaert into five sets. The other three matches went to Belgium in three sets each.

Detailed Results

Singles: A. LACROIX (BELG.) beat M. Ellmer (Switz.) 6–0, 6–4, 6–1 ; lost to H. C. FISHER (SWITZ.) 4–6, 2–6, 6–8. C. NAEYAERT (BELG.) beat M. Ellmer (Switz.) 13–11, 6–3, 6–3 ; beat H. C. Fisher (Switz.) 4–6, 6–0, 4–6, 6–3, 7–5.

Doubles: A. LACROIX and L. DE BORMAN (BELG.) beat H. Steiner and B. Maneff (Switz.) 6–2, 6–4, 6–1.

South Africa beat New Zealand at Brighton on May 8, 10, and 11 by four to one. South Africa's team was V. G. Kirby and N. G. Farquharson in singles and doubles. The New Zealand team was A. C. Stedman and C. E. Malfroy in singles and doubles. Stedman won the opening match against Farquharson, but, unfortunately, in so doing pulled a muscle, and was able to take no further part in the tie. His place was taken by E. D. Andrews in the doubles and in the singles on the third day. In the last match, on the third day, D. C. Coombe, playing instead of C. E. Malfroy, lost to E. E. Fannin, who took Farquharson's place.

Detailed Results

Singles: N. G. Farquharson (S.A.) lost to A. C. STEDMAN (N.Z.) 5–7, 3–6, 6–3, 2–6. V. G. KIRBY (S.A.) beat C. E. Malfroy (N.Z.) 7–5, 6–2, 6–3 ; beat E. D. Andrews (N.Z.) 6–2, 6–4, 6–3. E. E. FANNIN (S.A.) beat D. C. Coombe (N.Z.) 6–4, 6–4, 6–3.

Doubles: N. G. FARQUHARSON and V. G. KIRBY (S.A.) beat E. D. Andrews and C. E. Malfroy (N.Z.) 7–5, 6–2, 6–2.

Yugoslavia beat Rumania at Belgrade on May 8, 9, and 10 by five to none. The Yugoslav team was J. Pallada and F. Puncec in the singles and F. Kukuljevic and D. Mitic in the doubles. The Rumanian team, in singles and doubles, was C. Caralulis and O. Schmidt, who, though they fought hard, did not come within measurable distance of winning a match.

Detailed Results

Singles: J. PALLADA (YUGO.) beat C. Caralulis (Rum.) 6–3, 6–0, 2–6, 6–2 ; beat O. Schmidt (Rum.) 6–4, 6–3, 5–7, 6–0. F. PUNCEC (YUGO.) beat O. Schmidt (Rum.) 6–3, 6–3, 7–5 ; beat C. Caralulis (Rum.) 6–4, 1–6, 6–3, 6–2.

Doubles: F. KUKULJEVIC and D. MITIC (YUGO.) beat O. Schmidt and C. Caralulis (Rum.) 7–5, 6–3, 4–6, 6–2.

Czechoslovakia beat Poland at Warsaw on May 15, 16, and 17 by five to none. The Czech team was R. Menzel and L. Hecht in the singles and J. Caska and Hecht in the doubles. The Polish team was J. Hebda and K. Tarlowski in the singles and Hebda and I. Tloczynski in the doubles. J. Siba played in place of Hecht against Tarlowski on the third day. The Czechs were never really threatened in any of the five matches.

Detailed Results

Singles: R. MENZEL (CZECH.) beat K. Tarlowski (Pol.) 6–3, 6–4, 2–6, 6–3; beat J. Hebda (Pol.) 7–5, 6–3, 6–3. L. HECHT (CZECH.) beat J. Hebda (Pol.) 6–2, 6–0, 3–6, 6–1. J. SIBA (CZECH.) beat K. Tarlowski (Pol.) 6–3, 6–4, 6–3.

Doubles: J. CASKA and L. HECHT (CZECH.) beat J. Hebda and I. Tloczynski (Pol.) 6–1, 5–7, 6–1, 6–4.

France beat Norway at Paris on May 8, 9, and 10 by five to none. The French team was B. Destremau and M. Bernard in the singles and Y. Petra and Bernard in the doubles. The Norwegian team was F. Jenssen and D. Bjurstedt in the singles and Jenssen and J. Beer in the doubles. Petra took the place of Bernard in the singles on the third day. France lost only two sets in five matches.

Detailed Results

Singles: B. DESTREMAU (FR.) beat F. Jenssen (Norw.) 6–0, 6–3, 6–3; beat D. Bjurstedt (Norw.) 7–5, 6–2, 6–1. M. BERNARD (FR.) beat D. Bjurstedt (Norw.) 2–6, 6–1, 6–0, 6–0. Y. PETRA (FR.) beat F. Jenssen (Norw.) 6–1, 6–3, 4–6, 7–5.

Doubles: M. BERNARD and Y. PETRA (FR.) beat J. Beer and F. Jenssen (Norw.) 6–2, 6–2, 6–2.

In the third round Germany beat Italy at Milan on June 4, 5, and 6 by four to one. The German team was G. von Cramm and H. Henkel in singles and doubles. The Italian team was G. de Stefani and V. Canapele in the singles and V. Taroni and F. Quintavalle in the doubles. De Stefani scored Italy's only win when he beat Henkel in four sets.

Detailed Results

Singles: G. VON CRAMM (GER.) beat V. Canapele (It.) 6–1, 6–4, 1–6, 6–4 ; beat G. de Stefani (It.) 6–0, 6–1, 6–4. H. HENKEL (GER.) beat V. Canapele (It.) 3–6, 6–3, 6–1, 6–4 ; lost to G. DE STEFANI (IT.) 2–6, 3–6, 7–5, 2–6.

Doubles: G. VON CRAMM and H. HENKEL (GER.) beat V. Taroni and F. Quintavalle (It.) 6–3, 6–1, 6–1.

Belgium beat Sweden at Brussels on June 5, 6, and 7 by three to two. The Belgian team was, as previously, A. Lacroix and C. Naeyaert in the singles and Lacroix and L. de Borman in the doubles. The Swedish team was K. Schröder and S. Märtensson in the singles and Schröder and C. Ostberg in the doubles. Schröder won two singles for Sweden, beating Lacroix in five sets and Naeyaert in four. Märtensson failed to win a set in his singles, and the Belgian pair also won the doubles in three sets.

Detailed Results

Singles: A. LACROIX (BELG.) beat S. Märtensson (Sw.) 6–2, 6–0, 6–3 ; lost to K. SCHRÖDER (SW.) 3–6, 6–3, 0–6, 6–4, 2–6. C. NAEYAERT (BELG.) beat S. Märtensson (Sw.) 6–1, 6–2, 6–1 ; lost to K. SCHRÖDER (SW.) 9–7, 2–6, 0–6, 3–6.

Doubles: A. LACROIX and L. DE BORMAN (BELG.) beat K. Schröder and C. Ostberg (Sw.) 6–0, 6–4, 6–4.

Yugoslavia beat South Africa at Zagreb on June 5, 6, and 7 by four to one. The Yugoslav team was F. Puncec and J. Pallada in the singles and F. Kukuljevic and D. Mitic in the doubles. The South African team was V. G. Kirby and N. G. Farquharson in singles and doubles. On the first day both singles went to five sets and to Yugoslavia. The South Africans won the doubles on the second day in three sets, but both failed to win a set in the singles on the third day.

Detailed Results

Singles: F. PUNCEC (YUGO.) beat V. G. Kirby (S.A.) 1–6, 6–0, 6–3, 2–6, 6–4 ; beat N. G. Farquharson (S.A.) 6–1, 6–1, 6–1. J. PALLADA (YUGO.) beat V. G. Kirby (S.A.) 6–1, 6–4, 6–2 ; beat N. G. Farquharson (S.A.) 3–6, 3–6, 6–3, 6–0, 6–3.

Doubles: F. Kukuljevic and D. Mitic (Yugo.) lost to N. G. FARQUHARSON and V. G. KIRBY (S.A.) 2–6, 3–6, 2–6.

Czechoslovakia beat France at Prague on June 5, 6, and 7 by four to one. The Czech team was R. Menzel and L. Hecht in both singles and doubles. The French team was C. Boussus and B. Destremau in the singles and J. Borotra and Y. Petra in the doubles. The Czechs won all the singles; France had to be content with winning the doubles.

Detailed Results

Singles: R. MENZEL (CZECH.) beat B. Destremau (Fr.) 6–0, 6–3, 6–4; beat C. Boussus (Fr.) 6–2, 6–3, 6–4. L. HECHT (CZECH.) beat C. Boussus (Fr.) 2–6, 6–1, 7–5, 6–0; beat B. Destremau (Fr.) 6–3, 6–3, 6–1.

Doubles: R. Menzel and L. Hecht (Czech.) lost to J. BOROTRA and Y. PETRA (FR.) 3–6, 6–2, 2–6, 3–6.

In the fourth and semi-final round Germany beat Belgium at Berlin on June 12, 13, and 14 by four to one. The German team was G. von Cramm and H. Henkel in singles and doubles. Belgium played her usual team of A. Lacroix and C. Naeyaert in the singles and Lacroix and L. de Borman in the doubles. Germany did not lose a set in the four matches she won. E. Dettmer, playing in place of von Cramm on the third day, lost to Lacroix in four sets.

Detailed Results

Singles: G. VON CRAMM (GER.) beat C. Naeyaert (Belg.) 6–3, 6–0, 6–4. E. Dettmer (Ger.) lost to A. LACROIX (BELG.) 4–6, 6–3, 2–6, 6–8. H. HENKEL (GER.) beat A. Lacroix (Belg.) 6–1, 6–1, 6–1; beat C. Naeyaert (Belg.) 6–3, 6–2, 6–2.

Doubles: G. VON CRAMM and H. HENKEL (GER.) beat A. Lacroix and L. de Borman (Belg.) 6–4, 6–3, 6–4.

In the other semi-final tie Czechoslovakia beat Yugoslavia at Prague on June 12, 13, and 14 by three to two, the Czech team winning the first three matches and then defaulting the next two. The Czech team was R. Menzel and L. Hecht in singles and doubles. The Yugoslav team was J. Pallada and F. Puncec in singles and doubles. Menzel and Hecht beat Pallada and Puncec respectively in three sets each, but in the doubles against the same players they had to wage a five-set match before emerging victorious.

Detailed Results

Singles: R. MENZEL (CZECH.) beat J. Pallada (Yugo.) 6–2, 6–1, 6–0. L. HECHT (CZECH.) beat F. Puncec (Yugo.) 7–5, 6–2, 6–3.

Doubles: R. MENZEL and L. HECHT (CZECH.) beat J. Pallada and F. Puncec (Yugo.) 2–6, 6–1, 6–0, 7–9, 6–1.

In the final round Germany beat Czechoslovakia at Berlin on July 10, 11, and 12 by four to one. The Germans again relied on G. von Cramm and H. Henkel in singles and doubles. The Czech team was R. Menzel and L. Hecht in the singles and Hecht and J. Caska in the doubles. Henkel led off for Germany and beat Hecht in three sets. Menzel then made a great effort to square the account. He forged ahead against von Cramm, winning the first two sets and gaining a lead in the third. The German champion, however, fought hard, and finally won in the fifth set, to put his country two up. On the second day von Cramm and Henkel won the doubles in four sets—and the tie. On the third day von Cramm beat Hecht in three sets. F. Cejnar, playing in place of Menzel, gained Czechoslovakia's only point when he beat H. Denker, substituting for Henkel, in five sets, after losing the first two. Germany had certainly proved the outstanding country in this zone.

Detailed Results

Singles: G. VON CRAMM (GER.) beat R. Menzel (Czech.) 3–6, 4–6, 6–4, 6–3, 6–2 ; beat L. Hecht (Czech.) 6–3, 7–5, 6–2. H. HENKEL (GER.) beat L. Hecht (Czech.) 6–1, 7–5, 7–5. H. Denker (Ger.) lost to F. CEJNAR (CZECH.) 6–4, 6–3, 4–6, 4–6, 2–6.

Doubles: G. VON CRAMM and H. HENKEL (GER.) beat L. Hecht and J. Caska (Czech.) 6–1, 6–2, 10–12, 6–0.

AMERICAN ZONE

In the first round U.S.A. beat Japan at San Francisco on April 30 and May 1 and 2 by five to none. The American team was J. D. Budge and F. A. Parker in the singles, Budge and C. G. Mako in the doubles. Japan played J. Yamagishi and F. Nakano in singles and doubles. America were too strong, and lost only one set in five matches.

Detailed Results

Singles: J. D. BUDGE (U.S.A.) beat F. Nakano (Jap.) 6–1, 6–1, 6–0; beat J. Yamagishi (Jap.) 6–2, 6–2, 6–4. F. A. PARKER (U.S.A.) beat J. Yamagishi (Jap.) 6–3, 2–6, 8–6, 6–1; beat F. Nakano (Jap.) 6–0, 6–3, 6–2.

Doubles: J. D. BUDGE and C. G. MAKO (U.S.A.) beat J. Yamagishi and F. Nakano (Jap.) 6–0, 6–1, 6–4.

In the other first-round tie Australia beat Mexico at Mexico City by five to none. The Australian team was A. K. Quist and V. B. McGrath in the singles and Quist and J. H. Crawford in the doubles. The Mexican team was E. Reyes and R. Tapia in the singles and A. Unda and D. Hernandez in the doubles. Australia dropped only one set in five matches. On the third day J. E. Bromwich played in place of McGrath, and proved an effective substitute by beating Reyes in three sets.

Detailed Results

Singles: A. K. QUIST (AUSTRAL.) beat E. Reyes (Mex.) 6–3, 6–1, 6–3; beat R. Tapia (Mex.) 6–2, 6–4, 4–6, 6–3. V. B. MCGRATH (AUSTRAL.) beat R. Tapia (Mex.) 6–2, 6–4, 6–4. J. E. BROMWICH (AUSTRAL.) beat E. Reyes (Mex.) 6–2, 6–2, 7–5.

Doubles: J. H. CRAWFORD and A. K. QUIST (AUSTRAL.) beat A. Unda and D. Hernandez (Mex.) 6–2, 6–3, 6–3.

In the final round of this zone U.S.A. beat Australia at New York on May 29, 30, and 31 by five to none. The American team was J. D. Budge and B. M. Grant in the singles and Budge and C. G. Mako in the doubles. The Australian team was suffering from illness, and had to be drastically altered from the one intended, and finally took the court as follows: in the singles, J. H. Crawford and J. E. Bromwich; in the doubles, Crawford and V. B. McGrath. The result was a wide margin of victory for the American team, who dropped only one set in five matches.

Detailed Results

Singles: J. D. BUDGE (U.S.A.) beat J. H. Crawford (Austral.) 6–1, 6–3, 6–2; beat J. E. Bromwich (Austral.) 6–2, 6–3, 5–7, 6–1. B. M. GRANT (U.S.A.) beat J. E. Bromwich (Austral.) 6–2, 7–5, 6–1; beat J. H. Crawford (Austral.) 6–0, 6–2, 7–5.

Doubles: J. D. Budge and C. G. Mako (U.S.A.) beat J. H. Crawford and V. B. McGrath (Austral.) 7–5, 6–1, 8–6.

Inter-zone Round

This tie, between Germany and U.S.A., took place at Wimbledon on July 17, 18, and 20, when U.S.A. won by three to two in a very exciting contest. The American team was J. D. Budge and B. M. Grant in the singles and Budge and C. G. Mako in the doubles. The German team was G. von Cramm and H. Henkel in singles and doubles. Honours were even at the end of the first day, in which Budge beat Henkel and von Cramm beat Grant, both matches being won in straight sets. America took the doubles on the second day in a close four-set struggle, in which the Germans almost had a two-set lead. On the third day Henkel brought the countries level again by beating Grant in four sets. The fifth and deciding match, between von Cramm and Budge, provided a thrilling battle. Budge was two sets down and also behind at 1–4 in the final set, but managed to get home at last at 8–6, and so put America into the challenge round.

Detailed Results

Singles: J. D. Budge (U.S.A.) beat H. Henkel (Ger.) 6–2, 6–1, 6–3 ; beat G. von Cramm (Ger.) 6–8, 5–7, 6–4, 6–2, 8–6. B. M. Grant (U.S.A.) lost to G. von Cramm (Ger.) 3–6, 4–6, 2–6 ; lost to H. Henkel (Ger.) 5–7, 6–2, 3–6, 4–6.

Doubles: J. D. Budge and C. G. Mako (U.S.A.) beat G. von Cramm and H. Henkel (Ger.) 4–6, 7–5, 8–6, 6–4.

Challenge Round

This final tie, between Great Britain, the holders, and U.S.A., the challengers, took place at Wimbledon on July 24, 26, and 27, and was won by U.S.A. by four to one. The defenders had only two of their men of the previous two years, and were without their sheet anchor, F. J. Perry. The British team was H. W. Austin and C. E. Hare in the singles and C. R. D. Tuckey and F. H. D. Wilde in the doubles. The American team was J. D. Budge and F. A. Parker in the singles, Budge and C. G. Mako in the doubles. Austin put the holders one up by defeating Parker in the first match in three sets. Budge equalized matches by beating Hare in three sets also, but the first required twenty-eight games. Once Budge had collared this set Hare had no more to offer. U.S.A. moved into the lead by winning the doubles against Tuckey and Wilde in four sets, containing fifty-nine games. On the third day Great Britain lost the cup when Parker beat Hare in three sets, and, to wind up, Budge beat Austin in four sets. U.S.A. thus regained the cup after ten years.

Detailed Results

Singles: J. D. Budge (U.S.A.) beat C. E. Hare (G.B.) 15–13, 6–1, 6–2; beat H. W. Austin (G.B.) 8–6, 3–6, 6–4, 6–3. F. A. Parker (U.S.A.) beat C. E. Hare (G.B.) 6–2, 6–4, 6–2; lost to H. W. Austin (G.B.) 3–6, 2–6, 5–7.

Doubles: J. D. Budge and C. G. Mako (U.S.A.) beat C. R. D. Tuckey and F. H. D. Wilde (G.B.) 6–3, 7–5, 7–9, 12–10.

1938: U.S.A.

This year there were in all twenty-five challengers, twenty-one in the European Zone and four in the American Zone.

European Zone

In the first round France beat the Netherlands at Scheveningen, Holland, on May 5, 6, and 7 by three matches to two. The French team was B. Destremau and Y. Petra in the singles and Petra and H. Bolelli in the doubles. The Dutch team was A. C. van Swol and T. Hughan in singles and doubles. Petra won both his singles in straight sets, but Destremau fell to van Swol, and the Dutch pair won the doubles in five sets after being two sets down. Hughan could not win a set in either of his singles.

Detailed Results

Singles: B. Destremau (Fr.) beat T. Hughan (Neth.) 6–4, 6–2, 6–2; lost to A. C. van Swol (Neth.) 3–6, 0–6, 6–8. Y. Petra (Fr.) beat T. Hughan (Neth.) 6–3, 6–2, 6–2; beat A. C. van Swol (Neth.) 6–0, 6–3, 6–2.

Doubles: Y. Petra and H. Bolelli (Fr.) lost to T. Hughan and A. C. van Swol (Neth.) 8–6, 6–1, 1–6, 5–7, 2–6.

Poland beat Denmark at Warsaw on May 5, 6, and 7 by five to none. The Polish team was I. Tloczynski and J. Hebda in singles and doubles. The Danish team was H. Plougmann and F. Bekevold in the singles and E. Ulrich and N. K. Koerner in the doubles. The Danes could not win a set in the singles, and took only one in the doubles.

Detailed Results

Singles: J. Hebda (Pol.) beat H. Plougmann (Den.) 6–2, 6–2, 6–1 ; beat F. Bekevold (Den.) 6–4, 7–5, 6–1. I. Tloczynski (Pol.) beat H. Plougmann (Den.) 6–0, 6–2, 6–1 ; beat F. Bekevold (Den.) 6–2, 6–3, 6–2.

Doubles: J. Hebda and I. Tloczynski (Pol.) beat E. Ulrich and N. K. Koerner (Den.) 6–2, 6–3, 6–8, 6–3.

Italy beat Ireland at Dublin on May 5, 6, and 7 by four to one. The Italian team was G. de Stefani and V. Canapele in the singles and V. Taroni and F. Quintavalle in the doubles. The Irish team was G. L. Rogers and T. G. McVeagh in singles and doubles. Rogers beat de Stefani in four sets and extended Canapele to five. H. J. Ryan played in place of McVeagh on the third day, but could do little against de Stefani.

Detailed Results

Singles: G. de Stefani (It.) beat H. J. Ryan (Ire.) 6–2, 6–2, 6–2 ; lost to G. L. Rogers (Ire.) 5–7, 6–2, 3–6, 2–6. V. Canapele (It.) beat T. G. McVeagh (Ire.) 6–0, 6–2, 6–0 ; beat G. L. Rogers (Ire.) 5–7, 6–3, 1–6, 6–3, 6–1.

Doubles: V. Taroni and F. Quintavalle (It.) beat G. L. Rogers and T. G. McVeagh (Ire.) 6–3, 4–6, 6–1, 6–2.

Yugoslavia beat Czechoslovakia at Zagreb on April 29 and 30 and May 1 by three to two in a match in which feeling ran high. The Czech team was R. Menzel and L. Hecht in the singles and Menzel and F. Cejnar in the doubles. The Yugoslav team was F. Puncec and J. Pallada in the singles and Puncec and D. Mitic in the doubles. On the first day

Puncec beat Hecht and Menzel beat Pallada. The Czechs won the doubles in four sets, to go ahead, but Puncec squared matters on the third day when he beat Menzel. Mitic and Cejnar, both substitutes, played the vital fifth match, which was never completed. Cejnar appealed against the failing light in the fifth set, and when the appeal was not upheld the Czech captain withdrew Cejnar from the match—thus giving Mitic the victory and Yugoslavia the tie.

Detailed Results

Singles: F. PUNCEC (YUGO.) beat L. Hecht (Czech.) 7–5, 6–3, 6–3 ; beat R. Menzel (Czech.) 3–6, 6–1, 6–1, 6–2. J. Pallada (Yugo.) lost to R. MENZEL (CZECH.) 2–6, 2–6, 1–6. D. MITIC (YUGO.) beat F. Cejnar (Czech.) 3–6, 7–5, 4–6, 6–2, 2–1 (retired).

Doubles: F. Puncec and D. Mitic (Yugo.) lost to R. MENZEL and F. CEJNAR (CZECH.) 9–11, 6–3, 7–9, 2–6.

Great Britain beat Rumania at Harrogate on May 7, 9, and 10 by three to two. The British team was entirely new except for one man. It was C. M. Jones and R. A. Shayes in the singles and F. H. D. Wilde and D. W. Butler in the doubles. The Rumanian team was C. Caralulis and O. Schmidt in singles and doubles. Jones lost both his singles, but otherwise the Englishmen did not lose a set.

Detailed Results

Singles: C. M. Jones (G.B.) lost to C. CARALULIS (RUM.) 3–6, 6–3, 2–6, 6–8 ; lost to O. SCHMIDT (RUM.) 3–6, 1–6, 6–0, 6–2, 6–8. R. A. SHAYES (G.B.) beat O. Schmidt (Rum.) 6–3, 6–2, 6–2 ; beat C. Caralulis (Rum.) 6–3, 6–0, 6–3.

Doubles: D. W. BUTLER and F. H. D. WILDE (G.B.) beat C. Caralulis and O. Schmidt (Rum.) 8–6, 7–5, 6–2.

In the second round Germany beat Norway at Berlin on May 20, 21, and 22 by five to none. The German team was H. Henkel and G. von Metaxa and the Norwegian team J. Haanes and F. Jenssen in singles and doubles. Haanes led von Metaxa by two sets to none, but finally lost at 7–5 in the fifth set. R. Goepfert took Henkel's place on the third day, and beat Haanes in three sets.

THE VICTORIOUS AUSTRALIAN TEAM OF 1939

Left to right: J. E. Bromwich, A. K. Quist, H. E. Hopman, J. H. Crawford.

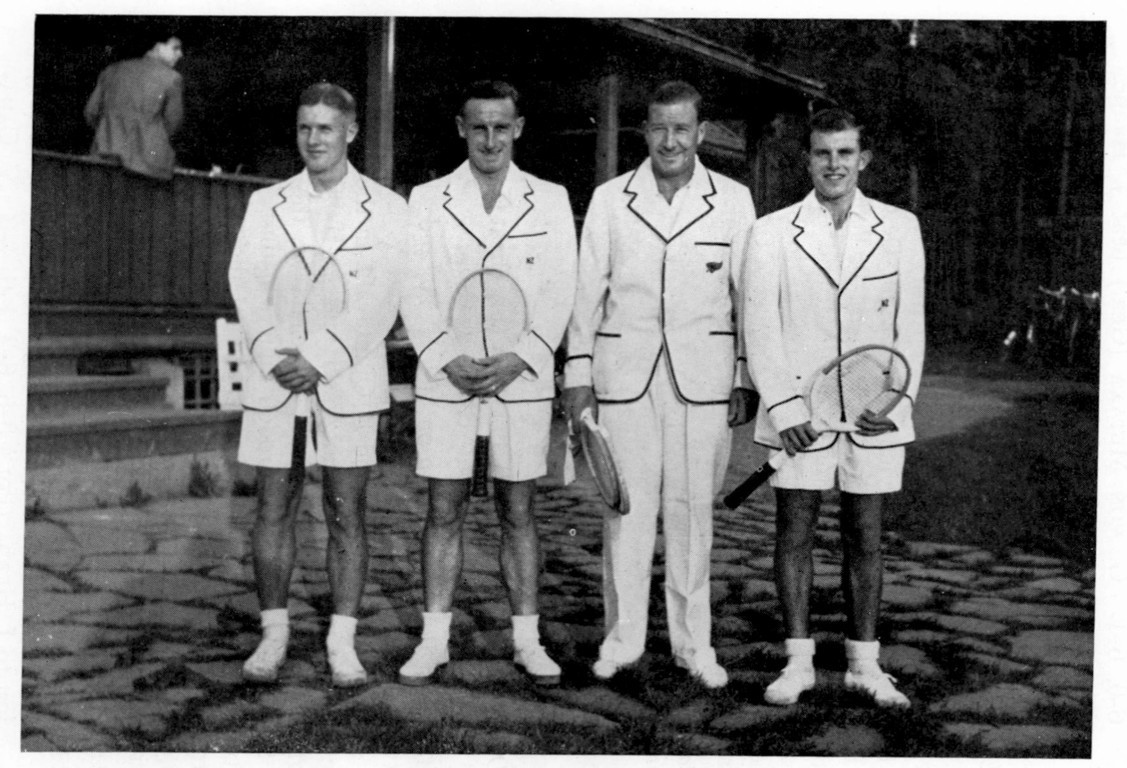

THE 1947 NEW ZEALAND TEAM IN OSLO

Left to right: J. A. Barry, R. S. McKenzie, D. C. Coombe (captain), J. E. Robson,

Detailed Results

Singles: H. HENKEL (GER.) beat F. Jenssen (Norw.) 6–0, 6–0, 6–1. G. VON METAXA (GER.) beat J. Haanes (Norw.) 2–6, 5–7, 6–2, 6–3, 7–5 ; beat F. Jenssen (Norw.) 6–1, 6–0, 6–0. R. GOEPFERT (GER.) beat J. Haanes (Norw.) 6–3, 8–6, 6–2.

Doubles: H. HENKEL and G. VON METAXA (GER.) beat J. Haanes and F. Jenssen (Norw.) 6–1, 6–2, 6–3.

France beat Monaco at Versailles on May 21, 22, and 23 by five to none. The French team was B. Destremau and Y. Petra in the singles and H. Bolelli and P. Pellizza in the doubles. Monaco's team was G. Medecin and A. Noghes in the singles and Medecin and V. Landau in the doubles. On the third day Bolelli and Pellizza took the places of Destremau and Petra in the singles. France lost only one set in five matches.

Detailed Results

Singles: B. DESTREMAU (FR.) beat G. Medecin (Mon.) 6–3, 6–0, 6–1. Y. PETRA (FR.) beat A. Noghes (Mon.) 6–1, 6–1, 6–0. P. PELLIZZA (FR.) beat G. Medecin (Mon.) 6–2, 6–1, 3–6, 6–4. H. BOLELLI (FR.) beat A. Noghes (Mon.) 6–1, 6–1, 6–2.

Doubles: H. BOLELLI and P. PELLIZZA (FR.) beat G. Medecin and V. Landau (Mon.) 6–2, 6–1, 6–3.

Italy beat Poland at Milan on May 19, 20, and 21 by three to two. Italy's team was G. de Stefani and V. Canapele in the singles and V. Taroni and F. Quintavalle in the doubles. The Polish team was I. Tloczynski and J. Hebda in the singles and Tloczynski and C. Spychala in the doubles. De Stefani had to retire, through injury, against Tloczynski at two sets all. His place was taken on the third day by Taroni, who lost to Hebda. The latter took Canapele to five sets, and the doubles only went to Italy in the same number after a long fight. Canapele beat Tloczynski in four sets.

Detailed Results

Singles: G. de Stefani (It.) lost to I. TLOCZYNSKI (POL.) 8–6, 6–4, 2–6, 2–6 (retired, injured). V. Taroni (It.) lost to J. HEBDA (POL.) 3–6, 6–3, 1–6, 4–6. V. CANAPELE (IT.) beat J. Hebda (Pol.) 6–1, 7–9, 6–2, 7–9, 6–2 ; beat I. Tloczynski (Pol.) 6–2, 6–1, 2–6, 6–2.

Doubles: V. TARONI and F. QUINTAVALLE (IT.) beat I. Tloczynski and C. Spychala (Pol.) 11–9, 2–6, 6–4, 3–6, 7–5.

Sweden beat Switzerland at Stockholm on May 19, 20, and 21 by four to one. The Swedish team was K. Schröder and N. Rohlsson in singles and doubles. The Swiss team was H. C. Fisher and B. Maneff in singles and doubles also. The latter won Switzerland's only match when he beat Rohlsson on the first day in four sets. Rohlsson beat Fisher from two sets down, as Schröder did Maneff. The Swedes won the doubles in four sets.

Detailed Results

Singles: K. SCHRÖDER (Sw.) beat H. C. Fisher (Switz.) 8–6, 6–2, 6–0; beat B. Maneff (Switz.) 3–6, 1–6, 6–2, 6–4, 6–2. N. ROHLSSON (Sw.) beat H. C. Fisher (Switz.) 3–6, 4–6, 6–4, 6–3, 6–1; lost to B. MANEFF (SWITZ.) 1–6, 4–6, 6–2, 1–6.

Doubles: K. SCHRÖDER and N. ROHLSSON (Sw.) beat H. C. Fisher and B. Maneff (Switz.) 6–2, 5–7, 6–4, 7–5.

Belgium beat Greece at Athens on May 5, 6, and 7 by five to none. The Belgian team was A. Lacroix and C. Naeyaert in the singles and Lacroix and L. de Borman in the doubles. The Greek team was L. Stalios and J. Michailides in singles and doubles, and they failed to win a single set in five matches. P. Geelhand substituted for Lacroix on the third day.

Detailed Results

Singles: A. LACROIX (BELG.) beat L. Stalios (Gr.) 6–1, 6–2, 6–1. C. NAEYAERT (BELG.) beat J. Michailides (Gr.) 6–1, 6–4, 9–7; beat L. Stalios (Gr.) 6–4, 6–3, 6–2. P. GEELHAND (BELG.) beat J. Michailides (Gr.) 6–4, 6–3, 6–3.

Doubles: A. LACROIX and L. DE BORMAN (BELG.) beat L. Stalios and J. Michailides (Gr.) 6–2, 6–1, 6–1.

Yugoslavia beat Great Britain at Zagreb on May 20, 21, and 22 by five to none. The Yugoslav team was F. Puncec and D. Mitic in singles and doubles. The British team was R. A. Shayes and D. W. Butler in the singles and Butler and F. H. D. Wilde in the doubles. Puncec lost a set in each of his singles, but Mitic was able to win in three sets in both of his. The British pair carried the doubles to five sets after being down two. A sad end to the holders of the cup a year earlier.

Detailed Results

Singles: F. Puncec (Yugo.) beat R. A. Shayes (G.B.) 6–4, 4–6, 6–2, 6–4; beat D. W. Butler (G.B.) 6–3, 6–2, 3–6, 6–3. D. Mitic (Yugo.) beat D. W. Butler (G.B.) 6–3, 6–1, 6–4; beat R. A. Shayes (G.B.) 6–2, 6–3, 11–9.

Doubles: D. Mitic and F. Puncec (Yugo.) beat D. W. Butler and F. H. D. Wilde (G.B.) 7–5, 6–3, 3–6, 5–7, 6–3.

In the third round Germany beat Hungary at Budapest on May 26, 27, and 28 by three to one. The German team was H. Henkel and G. von Metaxa in singles and doubles. The Hungarian team was G. Dallos and E. Gabory in the singles and Dallos and J. Asboth in the doubles. Von Metaxa lost to Gabory in five sets, of which he lost the first two, and, of course, the fifth, but he beat Dallos in four sets. Henkel beat Dallos in three sets, and with von Metaxa won the doubles in four. The Henkel–Gabory match was never completed owing to rain's intervening.

Detailed Results

Singles: H. Henkel (Ger.) beat G. Dallos (Hun.) 6–4, 11–9, 6–0; v. E. Gabory (Hun.) 6–1 (unfinished). G. von Metaxa (Ger.) beat G. Dallos (Hun.) 6–2, 3–6, 6–3, 6–2; lost to E. Gabory (Hun.) 5–7, 4–6, 6–4, 6–2, 5–7.

Doubles: H. Henkel and G. von Metaxa (Ger.) beat G. Dallos and J. Asboth (Hun.) 5–7, 6–1, 8–6, 6–3.

France beat Italy at Paris on May 27, 28, and 29 by four to one. The French team was B. Destremau and Y. Petra in the singles and H. Bolelli and P. Pellizza in the doubles. The Italian team was V. Taroni and V. Canapele in the singles and Taroni and F. Quintavalle in the doubles. Taroni beat Destremau in four sets, to win Italy's only match. On the third day Pellizza took the place of Petra in the singles, and beat L. Bossi, playing instead of Canapele, in five sets.

Detailed Results

Singles: Y. Petra (Fr.) beat V. Taroni (It.) 6–0, 6–2, 6–3. B. Destremau (Fr.) beat V. Canapele (It.) 3–6, 6–0, 6–2, 7–5 ; lost to V. Taroni (It.) 6–8, 7–5, 4–6, 2–6. P. Pellizza (Fr.) beat L. Bossi (It.) 4–6, 6–4, 5–7, 6–3, 7–5.

Doubles: H. Bolelli and P. Pellizza (Fr.) beat V. Taroni and F. Quintavalle (It.) 9–7, 6–3, 6–4.

Yugoslavia beat Sweden at Zagreb on May 26, 27, and 28 by four to one, only four matches actually being played. The Yugoslav team was F. Puncec and J. Pallada in the singles and Puncec and F. Kukuljevic in the doubles. Sweden relied on only two men, K. Schröder and N. Rohlsson, in singles and doubles, and were forced to give one match to Yugoslavia when Schröder could not play on the third day owing to an injured foot. Schröder beat Pallada in five sets on the first day. Rohlsson could not win a set in either of his singles.

Detailed Results

Singles: J. Pallada (Yugo.) beat N. Rohlsson (Sw.) 7–5, 7–5, 6–1 ; lost to K. Schröder (Sw.) 5–7, 6–1, 2–6, 8–6, 3–6. F. Puncec (Yugo.) beat N. Rohlsson (Sw.) 6–2, 6–3, 6–3 ; w.o., K. Schröder (Sw.) retired.

Doubles: F. Puncec and F. Kukuljevic (Yugo.) beat K. Schröder and N. Rohlsson (Sw.) 6–3, 9–7, 6–3.

Belgium beat India at Brussels on May 26, 27, and 28 by four to one. The Belgian team was A. Lacroix and C. Naeyaert in the singles and Lacroix and L. de Borman in the doubles. The Indian team was Ghaus Mohammed Khan and S. L. R. Sawhney in singles and doubles. The former took part in three five-set matches. He beat Naeyaert after being two sets down, and almost beat Lacroix in four sets, actually having match point. He lost finally in five sets. India held a two-set lead in the doubles, and held some match points in the fourth set, but had no luck, and went down in five sets. Sawhney, who lost to Lacroix in four sets, retired in his second singles, thus widening Belgium's margin.

Detailed Results

Singles: A. LACROIX (BELG.) beat S. L. R. Sawhney (Ind.) 6–4, 6–3, 4–6, 6–3; beat Ghaus Mohammed Khan (Ind.) 7–5, 0–6, 2–6, 7–5, 6–3. C. Naeyaert (Belg.) lost to GHAUS MOHAMMED KHAN (IND.) 7–5, 6–2, 3–6, 1–6, 7–9. P. GEELHAND (BELG.) w.o., S. L. R. Sawhney (Ind.) retired.

Doubles: A. LACROIX and L. DE BORMAN (BELG.) beat S. L. R. Sawhney and Ghaus Mohammed Khan (Ind.) 4–6, 3–6, 6–3, 7–5, 6–4.

In the fourth and semi-final round Germany beat France at Berlin on July 21, 22, and 23 by three to two. The German team was again H. Henkel and G. von Metaxa in singles and doubles. France's team was Y. Petra and B. Destremau in the singles and Petra and J. Lesueur in the doubles. Germany won the first three matches. Henkel beat Petra and von Metaxa beat Destremau on the first day, the latter match going to five sets. France held match points in the fourth set of the doubles, but Germany finally got home in the fifth set, to claim the tie. On the third day von Metaxa went down to Petra, and H. Redl, substituting for Henkel, lost to Destremau.

Detailed Results

Singles: H. HENKEL (GER.) beat Y. Petra (Fr.) 4–6, 6–1, 11–9, 6–2. G. VON METAXA (GER.) beat B. Destremau (Fr.) 6–4, 7–5, 5–7, 5–7, 6–3; lost to Y. PETRA (FR.) 7–9, 6–8, 4–6. H. Redl (Ger.) lost to B. DESTREMAU (FR.) 8–6, 4–6, 4–6, 2–6.

Doubles: H. HENKEL and G. VON METAXA (GER.) beat Y. Petra and J. Lesueur (Fr.) 4–6, 6–4, 2–6, 10–8, 6–4.

In the other semi-final tie Yugoslavia beat Belgium at Brussels on July 21, 22, and 23 by five to none. The Yugoslav team was F. Puncec and J. Pallada in the singles and D. Mitic and F. Kukuljevic in the doubles. The Belgian team was A. Lacroix and J. van den Eynde in the singles and L. de Borman and P. Geelhand in the doubles. The Yugoslavs were too strong, and were not extended to the full distance in any match.

Detailed Results

Singles: F. PUNCEC (YUGO.) beat J. van den Eynde (Belg.) 2–6, 6–0, 6–1, 6–2; beat A. Lacroix (Belg.) 6–4, 6–1, 6–2. J. PALLADA (YUGO.) beat A. Lacroix (Belg.) 6–4, 6–1, 6–2; beat J. van den Eynde (Belg.) 6–3, 6–3, 6–1.

Doubles: F. KUKULJEVIC and D. MITIC (YUGO.) beat L. de Borman and P. Geelhand (Belg.) 6–3, 6–3, 3–6, 10–8.

In the final round of this zone Germany beat Yugoslavia at Berlin on July 29, 30, and 31 by three to two. The German team was the usual one of H. Henkel and G. von Metaxa in singles and doubles. The Yugoslav team was F. Puncec and J. Pallada in the singles and Puncec and F. Kukuljevic in the doubles. Puncec beat Henkel in three sets in the first match, but von Metaxa evened the tie when he beat Pallada in five sets at 12–10 in the fifth. Germany won the doubles from a losing position, the Yugoslav pair being two sets up and 4–0 in the third. On the third day Henkel beat Pallada in three sets, to clinch the tie and win the European Zone for his country. In the last match H. Redl played in place of von Metaxa against Kukuljevic, who took Puncec's place, and the Yugoslav won in three sets.

Detailed Results

Singles: H. HENKEL (GER.) beat J. Pallada (Yugo.) 6–3, 7–5, 6–1; lost to F. PUNCEC (YUGO.) 1–6, 5–7, 3–6. G. VON METAXA (GER.) beat J. Pallada (Yugo.) 1–6, 6–4, 6–1, 3–6, 12–10. H. Redl (Ger.) lost to F. KUKULJEVIC (YUGO.) 4–6, 3–6, 2–6.

Doubles: H. HENKEL and G. VON METAXA (GER.) beat F. Puncec and F. Kukuljevic (Yugo.) 1–6, 7–9, 7–5, 6–4, 6–4.

AMERICAN ZONE

In the first round Japan beat Canada at Montreal on July 28, 29, and 30 by five to none. Japan's team was J. Yamagishi and F. Nakano in singles and doubles. The Canadian team was R. Murray and Ross Wilson in the singles and Ross Wilson and M. Laird Watt in the doubles. Japan lost one set only—in the doubles. D. Cameron took Ross Wilson's place on the third day.

Detailed Results

Singles: J. YAMAGISHI (JAP.) beat R. Murray (Can.) 6–1, 6–3, 6–3; beat D. Cameron (Can.) 6–4, 6–1, 6–0. F. NAKANO (JAP.) beat Ross Wilson (Can.) 6–2, 6–3, 6–2; beat R. Murray (Can.) 6–4, 6–3, 6–0.

Doubles: J. YAMAGISHI and F. NAKANO (JAP.) beat Ross Wilson and M. Laird Watt (Can.) 6–3, 3–6, 6–3, 7–5.

In the other first-round tie Australia beat Mexico at Kansas City on July 29, 30, and 31 by five to none. The Australian team was J. E. Bromwich and A. K. Quist in singles and doubles. The Mexican team was R. Tapia and D. Hernandez in singles and doubles. They failed to win a set in any of the five matches. On the third day L. Schwartz played in the singles instead of Bromwich and beat Hernandez in three sets.

Detailed Results

Singles: J. E. BROMWICH (AUSTRAL.) beat R. Tapia (Mex.) 6–4, 6–4, 6–4. A. K. QUIST (AUSTRAL.) beat D. Hernandez (Mex.) 6–1, 7–5, 6–4; beat R. Tapia (Mex.) 6–1, 6–1, 6–4. L. SCHWARTZ (AUSTRAL.) beat D. Hernandez (Mex.) 6–4, 6–1, 6–2.

Doubles: J. E. BROMWICH and A. K. QUIST (AUSTRAL.) beat D. Hernandez and R. Tapia (Mex.) 6–1, 6–0, 6–3.

The final round of this zone, between Australia and Japan, was played at Montreal on August 12, 13, and 14, and was won by Australia by three to two. The winners' team was J. E. Bromwich and A. K. Quist in singles and doubles. Japan's team was J. Yamagishi and F. Nakano in singles and doubles. Bromwich failed to win a single, losing to Yamagishi in four sets and retiring to Nakano at 12–all in the fifth set. Quist, however, was able to put Australia into the inter-zone round. He won both his singles in four sets.

Detailed Results

Singles: J. E. Bromwich (Austral.) lost to J. YAMAGISHI (JAP.) 0–6, 6–3, 5–7, 4–6; lost to F. NAKANO (JAP.) 1–6, 6–1, 4–6, 6–3, 12–12 (retired). A. K. QUIST (AUSTRAL.) beat J. Yamagishi (Jap.) 6–4, 6–4, 2–6, 9–7; beat F. Nakano (Jap.) 6–3, 4–6, 9–7, 6–1.

Doubles: J. E. BROMWICH and A. K. QUIST (AUSTRAL.) beat F. Nakano and J. Yamagishi (Jap.) 6–2, 6–4, 6–3.

INTER-ZONE ROUND

In this round Australia beat Germany at Boston on August 18, 19, and 20 by five to none and without loss of a set. The Australian team was J. E. Bromwich and A. K. Quist in singles and doubles. The German team was H. Henkel and G. von Metaxa in singles and doubles. The Germans were quite unable to reproduce their European form, and could not cope with either of the Australians in any of the five matches. It was a hollow victory, and calls for little comment.

Detailed Results

Singles: J. E. BROMWICH (AUSTRAL.) beat H. Henkel (Ger.) 6–2, 6–3, 6–3; beat G. von Metaxa (Ger.) 6–3, 6–2, 6–1. A. K. QUIST (AUSTRAL.) beat H. Henkel (Ger.) 6–1, 6–0, 8–6; beat G. von Metaxa (Ger.) 6–3, 6–2, 6–1.

Doubles: J. E. BROMWICH and A. K. QUIST (AUSTRAL.) beat H. Henkel and G. von Metaxa (Ger.) 6–2, 6–1, 6–4.

CHALLENGE ROUND

Australia, the challengers, met U.S.A., the holders, at Philadelphia on September 3, 4, and 5, when U.S.A. successfully defended the trophy by winning three matches to two. The American team was J. D. Budge and R. L. Riggs in the singles and Budge and C. G. Mako in the doubles. Budge was making his last Davis Cup appearance, as he, like Perry two years previously, was shortly to go over to the professional ranks. The Australian team was J. E. Bromwich and A. K. Quist in singles and doubles. On the opening day U.S.A. gained a two–love lead when Riggs beat Quist and Budge beat Bromwich, both matches going to four sets, Bromwich almost carrying Budge into five. On the second day Australia won the doubles in four sets after losing the first to love. On the third day Budge, in his last Davis Cup match, beat Quist in three sets, thus retaining the cup for America. In the final match Bromwich beat Riggs in four sets, and emphasized that U.S.A. without Budge would be very hard put to it to beat Australia. Actually they failed to do so in the following year, but we shall come to that in due course. Even with Budge U.S.A.'s margin was only a narrow one.

Detailed Results

Singles: J. D. BUDGE (U.S.A.) beat J. E. Bromwich (Austral.) 6–2, 6–3, 4–6, 7–5; beat A. K. Quist (Austral.) 8–6, 6–1, 6–2. R. L. RIGGS (U.S.A.) beat A. K. Quist (Austral.) 4–6, 6–0, 8–6, 6–1; lost to J. E. BROMWICH (AUSTRAL.) 4–6, 6–4, 0–6, 2–6.

Doubles: J. D. Budge and C. G. Mako (U.S.A.) lost to J. E. BROMWICH and A. K. QUIST (AUSTRAL.) 6–0, 3–6, 4–6, 2–6.

1939: AUSTRALIA

This year there were twenty-six challengers, of whom twenty were in the European Zone and six in the American Zone.

EUROPEAN ZONE

In the first round Yugoslavia beat Ireland at Zagreb on May 7, 8, and 9 by five to none. The Yugoslav team was F. Puncec and D. Mitic in singles and doubles. The Irish team was G. L. Rogers and R. F. Egan in singles and doubles. Rogers extended Mitic to five sets in the only match to go beyond three sets.

Detailed Results

Singles: F. PUNCEC (YUGO.) beat R. F. Egan (Ire.) 6–2, 6–0, 6–4; beat G. L. Rogers (Ire.) 6–4, 6–2, 6–4. D. MITIC (YUGO.) beat R. F. Egan (Ire.) 7–5, 6–3, 6–2; beat G. L. Rogers (Ire.) 7–5, 6–2, 3–6, 3–6, 6–3.

Doubles: F. PUNCEC and D. MITIC (YUGO.) beat G. L. Rogers and R. F. Egan (Ire.) 6–1, 6–4, 6–2.

Hungary beat Rumania at Bucharest on May 6, 7, and 8 by three to two. The Hungarian team was E. Gabory and J. Asboth in the singles and G. Dallos and M. Csikos in the doubles. The Rumanian team was C. Caralulis and O. Schmidt in singles and doubles. Asboth won both his singles in five sets. Caralulis beat Gabory, but Schmidt retired to Gabory in the fifth set. The Rumanian pair won the doubles from two sets down. A good effort.

Detailed Results

Singles: E. Gabory (Hun.) beat O. Schmidt (Rum.) 4–6, 4–6, 6–4, 6–2, 1–0 (retired); lost to C. Caralulis (Rum.) 6–3, 2–6, 3–6, 5–7. J. Asboth (Hun.) beat C. Caralulis (Rum.) 1–6, 6–3, 7–9, 10–8, 6–4 ; beat O. Schmidt (Rum.) 1–6, 6–2, 6–3, 6–8, 6–3.

Doubles: G. Dallos and M. Csikos (Hun.) lost to C. Caralulis and O. Schmidt (Rum.) 8–6, 6–4, 2–6, 2–6, 4–6.

Poland beat the Netherlands at Warsaw on May 7, 8, and 9 by four to one. The Polish team was I. Tloczynski and A. Bawarowski in the singles and Tloczynski and J. Hebda in the doubles. The Dutch team was A. C. van Swol and T. Hughan in singles and doubles. The Dutchmen won only the doubles.

Detailed Results

Singles: A. Bawarowski (Pol.) beat A. C. van Swol (Neth.) 9–7, 6–3, 6–0 ; beat T. Hughan (Neth.) 0–6, 6–3, 6–4, 6–2. I. Tloczynski (Pol.) beat T. Hughan (Neth.) 6–0, 6–2, 6–1 ; beat A. C. van Swol (Neth.) 13–11, 4–6, 6–3, 6–2.

Doubles: I. Tloczynski and J. Hebda (Pol.) lost to A. C. van Swol and T. Hughan (Neth.) 4–6, 4–6, 10–12.

Germany beat Switzerland at Vienna on May 7, 8, and 9 by five to none. The German team was H. Henkel and R. Menzel in the singles and Henkel and G. von Metaxa in the doubles. The Swiss team was H. C. Fisher and B. Maneff in singles and doubles. Maneff played well against Menzel, whom he extended to five sets. H. Redl took Henkel's place in the singles on the third day.

Detailed Results

Singles: H. Henkel (Ger.) beat H. C. Fisher (Switz.) 6–2, 2–6, 6–1, 6–3 ; R. Menzel (Ger.) beat B. Maneff (Switz.) 6–8, 6–3, 5–7, 6–2, 6–3 ; beat H. C. Fisher (Switz.) 8–6, 6–4, 6–2. H. Redl (Ger.) beat B. Maneff (Switz.) 6–1, 6–2, 6–2.

Doubles: H. Henkel and G. von Metaxa (Ger.) beat B. Maneff and H. C. Fisher (Switz.) 6–2, 6–2, 6–4.

In the second round Belgium beat India at Brussels on May 18, 19, and 20 by three to two. The Belgian team was A. Lacroix and C. Naeyaert in the singles and P. Geelhand and J. van den Eynde in the doubles. The Indian team was Ghaus Mohammed Khan and Y. Savoor in singles and doubles. Ghaus Mohammed Khan beat Naeyaert in three sets, and the Indians took the doubles in four sets. Lacroix was too good for both the visitors, and Naeyaert beat Savoor in four sets.

Detailed Results

Singles: A. LACROIX (BELG.) beat Ghaus Mohammed Khan (Ind.) 6–1, 6–3, 5–7, 6–0 ; beat Y. Savoor (Ind.) 6–2, 6–2, 6–4. C. NAEYAERT (BELG.) beat Y. Savoor (Ind.) 6–0, 10–8, 1–6, 6–3 ; lost to GHAUS MOHAMMED KHAN (IND.) 8–10, 2–6, 1–6.

Doubles: P. Geelhand and J. van den Eynde (Belg.) lost to GHAUS MOHAMMED KHAN and Y. SAVOOR (IND.) 4–6, 4–6, 7–5, 4–6.

Italy beat Monaco on May 18, 19, and 20 by three to none. Italy's team was G. de Stefani and V. Canapele in the singles and G. Vido and G. Cucelli in the doubles. Monaco's team was G. Medecin and A. Noghes in the singles and Noghes and V. Landau in the doubles. The Italians were far superior, and lost only a handful of games in the three matches played.

Detailed Results

Singles: G. DE STEFANI (IT.) beat G. Medecin (Mon.) 6–1, 6–2, 6–2. V. CANAPELE (IT.) beat A. Noghes (Mon.) 6–0, 6–3, 6–1.

Doubles: G. VIDO and G. CUCELLI (IT.) beat V. Landau and A. Noghes (Mon.) 6–3, 6–1, 6–0.

Yugoslavia beat Hungary at Budapest on May 19, 20, and 21 by four to one. The Yugoslav team was F. Puncec and D. Mitic in singles and doubles. The Hungarian team was E. Gabory and J. Asboth in singles and doubles. The latter did well to defeat Puncec in four sets, and also to give Mitic a hard fight for four sets. Gabory went down to Puncec in three sets and to Mitic in five. The Yugoslavs won the doubles in four sets.

Detailed Results

Singles: F. PUNCEC (YUGO.) beat E. Gabory (Hun.) 6–1, 6–1, 6–4 ; lost to J. ASBOTH (HUN.) 5–7, 6–4, 5–7, 9–11. D. MITIC (YUGO.) beat E. Gabory (Hun.) 6–3, 0–6, 2–6, 6–1, 6–1 ; beat J. Asboth (Hun.) 9–7, 2–6, 10–8, 6–3.

Doubles: F. PUNCEC and D. MITIC (YUGO.) beat J. Asboth and E. Gabory (Hun.) 6–1, 4–6, 6–2, 7–5.

Germany beat Poland at Warsaw on May 19, 20, and 21 by three to two. The German team was H. Henkel and R. Menzel in the singles and Henkel and G. von Metaxa in the doubles. The Polish team was I. Tloczynski and A. Bawarowski in the singles and the latter and J. Hebda in the doubles. Tloczynski produced his best to defeat both Henkel and Menzel in five sets. Bawarowski also forced Menzel to go to five sets to beat him after leading two sets to love. He lost to Henkel in three sets, and the Germans took the doubles in four.

Detailed Results

Singles: H. HENKEL (GER.) beat A. Bawarowski (Pol.) 6–4, 6–2, 6–3 ; lost to I. TLOCZYNSKI (POL.) 4–6, 8–6, 4–6, 6–3, 3–6. R. MENZEL (GER.) beat A. Bawarowski (Pol.) 7–5, 6–3, 2–6, 2–6, 6–4 ; lost to I. TLOCZYNSKI (POL.) 6–2, 1–6, 7–5, 2–6, 7–9.

Doubles: H. HENKEL and G. VON METAXA (GER.) beat J. Hebda and A. Bawarowski (Pol.) 5–7, 6–4, 6–2, 6–2.

Sweden beat Denmark at Djursholm on May 19, 20, and 21 by four to one. The Swedish team was K. Schröder and M. Hultman in the singles and Schröder and N. Rohlsson in the doubles. The Danish team was H. Plougmann and N. Holst in the singles and Plougmann and A. Wium in the doubles. Their only success was Plougmann's defeat of Hultman in three sets.

Detailed Results

Singles: K. SCHRÖDER (SW.) beat N. Holst (Den.) 6–4, 6–2, 6–3 ; beat H. Plougmann (Den.) 6–1, 6–1, 6–1. M. HULTMAN (SW.) beat N. Holst (Den.) 6–1, 6–3, 6–1 ; lost to H. PLOUGMANN (DEN.) 1–6, 0–6, 3–6.

Doubles: K. SCHRÖDER and N. ROHLSSON (SW.) beat H. Plougmann and A. Wium (Den.) 6–1, 8–6, 6–0.

Great Britain beat New Zealand at Brighton on May 11, 12, and 13 by three to two. The British team was C. E. Hare and R. A. Shayes in the singles and Hare and F. H. D. Wilde in the doubles. The New Zealand team was C. E. Malfroy and A. D. Brown in the singles and Malfroy and D. C. Coombe in the doubles. Malfroy beat Shayes in five sets, and with Coombe beat Hare and Wilde in four. He lost to Hare in three sets in the fifth and deciding match of the tie. Brown was unable to win a set in either of his singles.

Detailed Results

Singles: C. E. Hare (G.B.) beat A. D. Brown (N.Z.) 6–3, 6–4, 6–3 ; beat C. E. Malfroy (N.Z.) 7–5, 6–4, 6–4. R. A. Shayes (G.B.) beat A. D. Brown (N.Z.) 6–3, 6–4, 7–5 ; lost to C. E. Malfroy (N.Z.) 6–4, 2–6, 2–6, 7–5, 3–6.

Doubles: C. E. Hare and F. H. D. Wilde (G.B.) lost to C. E. Malfroy and D. C. Coombe (N.Z.) 3–6, 6–2, 3–6, 2–6.

France beat China at Paris on May 17, 18, and 19 by four to one. The French team was B. Destremau and C. Boussus in the singles and Y. Petra and P. Pellizza in the doubles. The Chinese team was Kho Sin Kie and W. C. Choy in the singles and doubles. On the third day Petra took the place of Boussus in the singles and lost to Kho Sin Kie. Pellizza took the place of Destremau and beat J. H. Ho, playing instead of Choy. Kho Sin Kie extended Destremau to five sets on the first day.

Detailed Results

Singles: B. Destremau (Fr.) beat Kho Sin Kie (Chin.) 5–7, 6–3, 1–6, 7–5, 6–0. C. Boussus (Fr.) beat W. C. Choy (Chin.) 1–6, 6–4, 6–4, 6–1. Y. Petra (Fr.) lost to Kho Sin Kie (Chin.) 6–2, 7–9, 3–6, 4–6. P. Pellizza (Fr.) beat J. H. Ho (Chin.) 7–5, 4–6, 6–2, 6–4.

Doubles: Y. Petra and P. Pellizza (Fr.) beat Kho Sin Kie and W. C. Choy (Chin.) 6–2, 6–0, 6–3.

In the third round Belgium beat Norway at Brussels on May 27, 28, and 29 by three to none. The Belgian team was A. Lacroix and C. Naeyaert in the singles and P. Geelhand and L. de Borman in the doubles. The Norwegian team was J. Haanes and S. Rinde in the singles and Haanes and

L. Anderson in the doubles. The Belgians won the three matches played quite comfortably.

Detailed Results

Singles: A. Lacroix (Belg.) beat J. Haanes (Norw.) 6–1, 6–4, 6–2. C. Naeyaert (Belg.) beat S. Rinde (Norw.) 6–1, 6–0, 6–0.

Doubles: P. Geelhand and L. de Borman (Belg.) beat L. Anderson and J. Haanes (Norw.) 6–0, 6–1, 5–7, 6–2.

Yugoslavia beat Italy at Rome on May 27, 28, and 29 by three to two. The Yugoslav team was F. Puncec and D. Mitic in singles and doubles. The Italian team was G. de Stefani and V. Canapele in the singles and V. Taroni and G. Cucelli in the doubles. Mitic lost both his singles, but Puncec's solid strength pulled his country through the other three matches of the tie. He beat de Stefani in three sets and Canapele in four ; with Mitic he won the doubles in three.

Detailed Results

Singles: F. Puncec (Yugo.) beat G. de Stefani (It.) 6–4, 6–1, 7–5 ; beat V. Canapele (It.) 13–11, 6–1, 6–8, 6–3. D. Mitic (Yugo.) lost to V. Canapele (It.) 3–6, 3–6, 5–7 ; lost to G. de Stefani (It.) 1–6, 4–6, 6–4, 3–6.

Doubles: F. Puncec and D. Mitic (Yugo.) beat V. Taroni and G. Cucelli (It.) 6–2, 6–2, 6–0.

Germany beat Sweden at Berlin on May 25, 26, and 27 by four to one. The German team was H. Henkel and R. Menzel in the singles and Henkel and G. von Metaxa in the doubles. The Swedish team was K. Schröder and M. Hultman in the singles and Schröder and N. Rohlsson in the doubles. Schröder did well to take Henkel to five sets and Menzel to four sets, and win the doubles in four. Hultman was not able to win a set against either of his opponents. R. Goepfert substituted for Henkel on the third day.

Detailed Results

Singles: H. Henkel (Ger.) beat K. Schröder (Sw.) 5–7, 3–6, 6–2, 8–6, 6–3. R. Menzel (Ger.) beat M. Hultman (Sw.) 6–0, 6–2, 6–1 ; beat K. Schröder (Sw.) 2–6, 6–3, 6–3, 6–3. R. Goepfert (Ger.) beat M. Hultman (Sw.) 6–2, 6–3, 6–3.

Doubles: H. Henkel and G. von Metaxa (Ger.) lost to K. SCHRÖDER and N. ROHLSSON (Sw.) 2–6, 6–1, 3–6, 3–6.

Great Britain beat France at Wimbledon on May 25, 26, and 28 by three to two. The British team was C. E. Hare and R. A. Shayes in the singles and Hare and F. H. D. Wilde in the doubles. The French team was C. Boussus and B. Destremau in the singles and Y. Petra and P. Pellizza in the doubles. Both Hare and Shayes beat Destremau in four sets, and Hare and Wilde won the doubles in five sets, to secure three British points. Boussus beat Shayes on the first day in three sets, and on the third day he beat L. Shaffi, who played in place of Hare, in three sets.

Detailed Results

Singles: C. E. HARE (G.B.) beat B. Destremau (Fr.) 6–2, 6–3, 3–6, 14–12. R. A. SHAYES (G.B.) beat B. Destremau (Fr.) 6–3, 4–6, 6–4, 7–5; lost to C. BOUSSUS (FR.) 2–6, 4–6, 0–6. L. Shaffi (G.B.) lost to C. BOUSSUS (FR.) 0–6, 2–6, 5–7.

Doubles: C. E. HARE and F. H. D. WILDE (G.B.) beat Y. Petra and P. Pellizza (Fr.) 6–3, 6–3, 3–6, 4–6, 6–3.

In the fourth and semi-final round Yugoslavia beat Belgium at Zagreb on June 4, 5, and 6 by three to two. The Yugoslav team was again F. Puncec and D. Mitic in singles and doubles. The Belgian team was A. Lacroix and P. Geelhand in the singles and Lacroix and L. de Borman in the doubles. Lacroix beat Mitic in four sets, and with de Borman won the doubles in three sets.

Detailed Results

Singles: F. PUNCEC (YUGO.) beat A. Lacroix (Belg.) 1–6, 6–3, 6–3, 7–5; beat P. Geelhand (Belg.) 6–3, 8–6, 6–3. D. MITIC (YUGO.) beat P. Geelhand (Belg.) 6–1, 6–4, 6–1; lost to A. LACROIX (BELG.) 3–6, 2–6, 8–6, 2–6.

Doubles: F. Puncec and D. Mitic (Yugo.) lost to A. LACROIX and L. DE BORMAN (BELG.) 2–6, 2–6, 3–6.

Germany beat Great Britain at Berlin on June 4, 5, and 6 by five to none. The German team was H. Henkel and R. Menzel in the singles and Henkel and G. von Metaxa in the doubles. The British team was R. A. Shayes and C. E.

Hare in the singles and L. Shaffi and F. H. D. Wilde in the doubles. Hare strained his back and retired to Menzel when two sets down on the first day. Wilde took his place in the singles on the third day, and played against von Metaxa, who took Henkel's place. The British team was routed, winning only one set in five matches.

Detailed Results

Singles: H. HENKEL (GER.) beat R. A. Shayes (G.B.) 6–2, 6–3, 6–1. R. MENZEL (GER.) beat C. E. Hare (G.B.) 6–0, 6–1 (retired) ; beat R. A. Shayes (G.B.) 6–1, 6–1, 6–0. G. VON METAXA (GER.) beat F. H. D. Wilde (G.B.) 3–6, 6–0, 6–2, 6–3.

Doubles: H. HENKEL and G. VON METAXA (GER.) beat F. H. D. Wilde and L. Shaffi (G.B.) 6–4, 6–2, 6–2.

In the final round of this zone Yugoslavia beat Germany at Zagreb on July 28, 29, and 30 by three to two. The Yugoslav team was F. Puncec and D. Mitic in the singles and Puncec and F. Kukuljevic in the doubles. The German team was H. Henkel and R. Goepfert in the singles and Henkel and R. Menzel in the doubles. Puncec beat both Henkel and Goepfert in three sets, finishing with a love set each time. Mitic beat Goepfert in three sets, but lost to Henkel in four. Germany won the doubles in five sets. None the less a new country had won the European Zone after a steady advance over the recent years.

Detailed Results

Singles: F. PUNCEC (YUGO.) beat R. Goepfert (Ger.) 6–3, 6–1, 6–0 ; beat H. Henkel (Ger.) 10–8, 6–3, 6–0. D. MITIC (YUGO.) beat R. Goepfert (Ger.) 6–1, 6–2, 6–3 ; lost to H. HENKEL (GER.) 0–6, 1–6, 6–4, 4–6.

Doubles: F. Puncec and F. Kukuljevic (Yugo.) lost to H. HENKEL and R. MENZEL (GER.) 7–9, 6–4, 4–6, 6–3, 1–6.

AMERICAN ZONE

In the first round Australia beat Mexico at Mexico City by five to none. The Australian team was J. E. Bromwich and A. K. Quist, the Mexican team R. Tapia and D. Hernandez, in singles and doubles. The Australians did not lose a set in

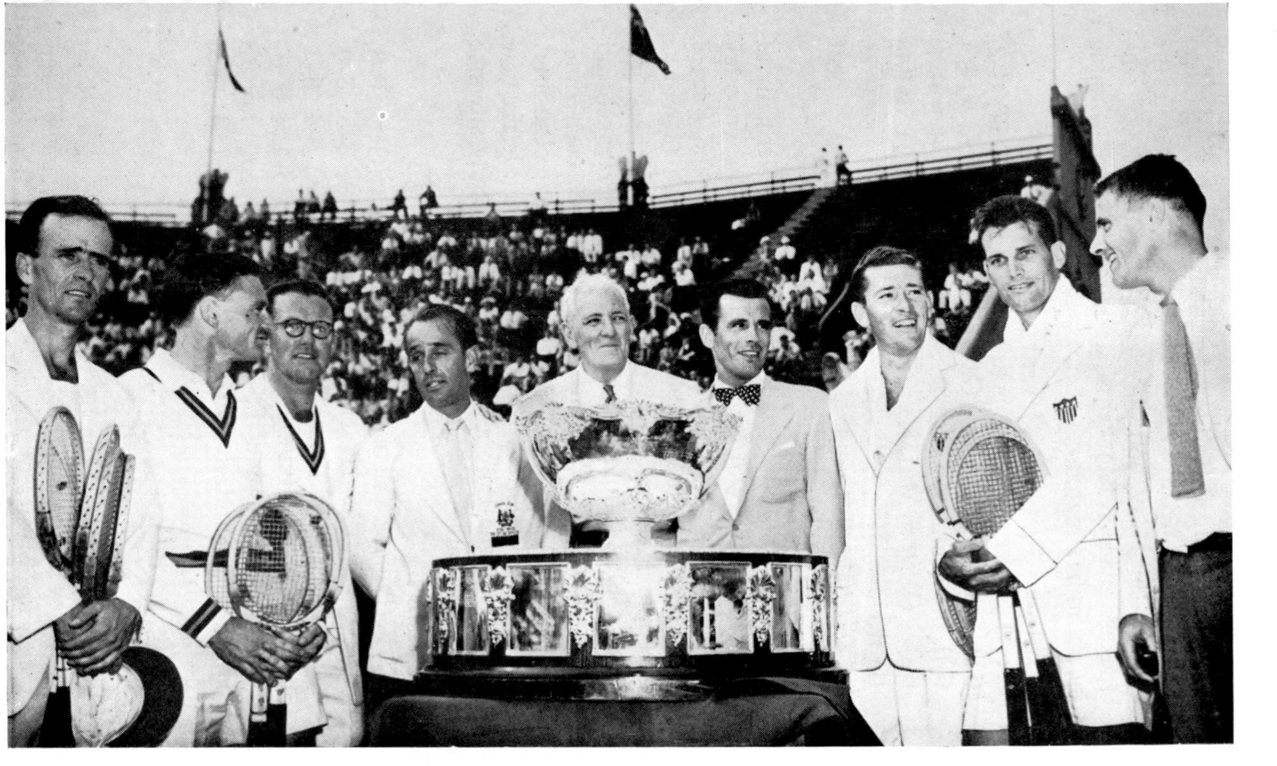

The Challenge-round Teams of 1948

Left to right: O. W. Sidwell, G. E. Brown, C. F. Long, A. K. Quist (Australia) ; Alrick H. Mann (non-playing captain, U.S.A.), F. A. Parker, W. F. Talbert, G. Mulloy, F. R. Schroeder (U.S.A.), the winners.

MR TRYGVE LIE MAKES THE DRAW FOR THE 1949 COMPETITION

Left to right: Mr W. M. Hall, Chairman of the Davis Cup Committee of Management; Mr Trygve Lie, U.N. Secretary General; Mr L. A. Baker, President of the American Lawn Tennis Association.

five matches. Bromwich accomplished the feat, performed twice before, of winning his singles against Hernandez in eighteen games.

Detailed Results

Singles: J. E. Bromwich (Austral.) beat D. Hernandez (Mex.) 6–0, 6–0, 6–0 ; beat R. Tapia (Mex.) 6–1, 6–3, 6–1. A. K. Quist (Austral.) beat R. Tapia (Mex.) 6–1, 6–4, 6–2 ; beat D. Hernandez (Mex.) 11–9, 6–3, 6–2.

Doubles: J. E. Bromwich and A. K. Quist (Austral.) beat D. Hernandez and R. Tapia (Mex.) 8–6, 6–0, 6–1.

In the other first-round tie Cuba beat Canada at Havana by three to one. The Cuban team was R. Morales and J. Aguero in the singles and Morales and L. Nodarse in the doubles. The Canadian team was B. Hall and E. Tarshis in the singles and P. Pearson and W. Pedlar in the doubles. Tarshis took Morales to five sets and beat Aguero in four sets. The doubles went to Cuba in five sets.

Detailed Results

Singles: R. Morales (Cu.) beat B. Hall (Can.) 6–1, 6–2, 6–2 ; beat E. Tarshis (Can.) 6–2, 6–4, 3–6, 0–6, 6–4. J. Aguero (Cu.) lost to E. Tarshis (Can.) 5–7, 7–5, 3–6, 4–6.

Doubles: R. Morales and L. Nodarse (Cu.) beat W. Pedlar and P. Pearson (Can.) 9–7, 4–6, 6–4, 4–6, 6–1.

In the second round Australia beat the Philippines at Long Beach by five to none. The Australian team was again J. E. Bromwich and A. K. Quist in singles and doubles. The Philippine team was A. Sanchez and F. Ampon in singles and doubles. Australia again did not lose a set in five matches, though some were close.

Detailed Results

Singles: A. K. Quist (Austral.) beat A. Sanchez (Phil.) 6–1, 6–2, 6–2 ; beat F. Ampon (Phil.) 7–5, 6–4, 6–3. J. E. Bromwich (Austral.) beat F. Ampon (Phil.) 8–6, 9–7, 6–3 ; beat A. Sanchez (Phil.) 6–1, 6–1, 6–3.

Doubles: A. K. Quist and J. E. Bromwich (Austral.) beat F. Ampon and A. Sanchez (Phil.) 7–5, 6–4, 6–2.

Cuba received a walk-over from Japan in the other tie of this round.

In the final round of this zone Australia beat Cuba at Havana by five to none. The Australian team was the usual one of J. E. Bromwich and A. K. Quist in singles and doubles. The Cuban team was R. Morales and J. Aguero in the singles and Morales and L. Nodarse in the doubles. Again Australia did not lose a set in five matches.

Detailed Results

Singles: J. E. Bromwich (Austral.) beat J. Aguero (Cu.) 8–6, 6–0, 6–2 ; beat R. Morales (Cu.) 8–6, 8–6, 6–1. A. K. Quist (Austral.) beat R. Morales (Cu.) 6–0, 6–2, 6–2 ; beat J. Aguero (Cu.) 6–1, 6–0, 6–0.

Doubles: A. K. Quist and J. E. Bromwich (Austral.) beat R. Morales and L. Nodarse (Cu.) 6–1, 6–0, 6–3.

Inter-zone Round

This tie, between Australia, the American Zone winners, and Yugoslavia, who won the European Zone, was played on August 24, 25, and 26, and won by Australia by four to one. Australia relied on J. E. Bromwich and A. K. Quist in singles and doubles. The Yugoslav team was F. Puncec and D. Mitic in the singles and Puncec and F. Kukuljevic in the doubles. Mitic lost to both Australians in three sets, but Puncec beat Bromwich in four sets—a good effort. Bromwich and Quist won the doubles in three sets, and Kukuljevic, playing in place of Puncec on the third day, lost to Quist in three sets. And so Australia reached the challenge round once again.

Detailed Results

Singles: J. E. Bromwich (Austral.) beat D. Mitic (Yugo.) 6–1, 6–3, 6–2 ; lost to F. Puncec (Yugo.) 2–6, 6–8, 6–0, 2–6. A. K. Quist (Austral.) beat D. Mitic (Yugo.) 6–0, 6–4, 6–3 ; beat F. Kukuljevic (Yugo.) 6–2, 6–3, 6–4.

Doubles: A. K. Quist and J. E. Bromwich (Austral.) beat F. Puncec and F. Kukuljevic (Yugo.) 6–2, 6–3, 6–3.

Challenge Round

This final tie, between Australia, the challengers, and U.S.A., the holders, was played at Philadelphia on September 2, 4, and 5, and was won by Australia by three matches to two. The defending team was R. L. Riggs and F. A. Parker in the singles and J. A. Kramer and J. Hunt in the doubles. Australia stuck to her two-man team of A. K. Quist and J. E. Bromwich. On the first day U.S.A. got a flying start by winning both singles, Riggs beating Bromwich in three sets and Parker beating Quist in five. Australia's cause looked very black, but Quist and Bromwich won the doubles in four sets on the second day, to keep the tie alive. On the third day Quist made the tie all square when he beat Riggs in five sets in the first match. And then Bromwich beat Parker in three sets, with the loss of only four games, to win the tie and the cup for Australia. A very fine performance by the two Australians to come from two down to three–two, as in the history of the cup two–love has almost without fail spelt victory.

The curtain of war now came down for the second time on the competition, this time for seven years—until 1946. As mentioned earlier, the Australians, by a strange coincidence, were the custodians of the Davis Cup for each of the World Wars, and each time they snatched it from U.S.A. in the challenge round as war commenced, and, odder still, each time to the score of three matches to two. As in 1914, so in 1939.

Detailed Results

Singles: J. E. Bromwich (Austral.) beat F. A. Parker (U.S.A.) 6–0, 6–3, 6–1 ; lost to R. L. Riggs (U.S.A.) 4–6, 0–6, 5–7. A. K. Quist (Austral.) beat R. L. Riggs (U.S.A.) 6–1, 6–3, 3–6, 3–6, 6–4 ; lost to F. A. Parker (U.S.A.) 3–6, 6–2, 4–6, 6–1, 5–7.

Doubles: J. E. Bromwich and A. K. Quist (Austral.) beat J. A. Kramer and J. Hunt (U.S.A.) 5–7, 6–2, 7–5, 6–2.

THE RESUMPTION AND AFTER

1946–48

1946: U.S.A.

THE competition was resumed once again in this year, when twenty nations challenged, fifteen in the European Zone, four in the American Zone, and one (New Zealand) in the Pacific section of the American Zone—an innovation. New Zealand defaulted to America without playing the Inter-zone Round.

EUROPEAN ZONE

In the first round Switzerland beat Spain at Barcelona on May 3, 4, and 5 by three to two. The Swiss team was J. Spitzer and H. Huonder in the singles and Spitzer and R. Buser in the doubles. The Spanish team was H. Castella and L. Carles in the singles and J. Bartroli and Carles in the doubles. Carles won both his singles, beating Spitzer in five sets and Huonder in three. Castella, however, went down to Huonder in five sets and to Spitzer in three. The Swiss pair won the doubles match in four sets, all of which went to advantage games.

Detailed Results

Singles: J. SPITZER (SWITZ.) beat H. Castella (Sp.) 6–0, 6–1, 6–4; lost to L. CARLES (SP.) 9–7, 5–7, 5–7, 6–3, 2–6.
H. HUONDER (SWITZ.) beat H. Castella (Sp.) 3–6, 6–3, 6–1, 4–6, 6–4; lost to L. CARLES (SP.) 3–6, 4–6, 3–6.

Doubles: R. BUSER and J. SPITZER (SWITZ.) beat J. Bartroli and L. Carles (Sp.) 5–7, 8–6, 11–9, 9–7.

France beat Great Britain at Paris on May 10, 11, and 12 by five to none. The French team was Y. Petra and P. Pellizza in the singles and B. Destremau and M. Bernard in the doubles. The British team was D. W. Barton and D. MacPhail in the singles and J. S. Olliff and H. Billington in the doubles. France took all the singles in straight sets and the doubles in four.

Detailed Results

Singles: Y. PETRA (FR.) beat D. W. Barton (G.B.) 6–4, 6–4, 6–3; beat D. MacPhail (G.B.) 6–0, 6–2, 6–1. P. PELLIZZA (FR.) beat D. MacPhail (G.B.) 6–1, 6–2, 6–2; beat D. W. Barton (G.B.) 6–2, 6–3, 6–1.

Doubles: B. DESTREMAU and M. BERNARD (FR.) beat J. S. Olliff and H. Billington (G.B.) 13–11, 4–6, 7–5, 6–1.

Yugoslavia beat Egypt at Zagreb on May 10, 11, and 12 by five to none. The Yugoslav team was F. Puncec and D. Mitic in the singles and Mitic and J. Pallada in the doubles. The Egyptian team was A. Najar and A. Shafie in the singles and M. Talaat and J. Grandguillot in the doubles. Pallada took the place of Puncec in the singles on the third day. Yugoslavia were not menaced in any match, though the doubles went to four sets.

Detailed Results

Singles: F. PUNCEC (YUGO.) beat A. Shafie (Egy.) 6–0, 6–1, 6–3. D. MITIC (YUGO.) beat A. Najar (Egy.) 7–5, 6–1, 6–3; beat A. Shafie (Egy.) 6–0, 6–1, 6–3. J. PALLADA (YUGO.) beat A. Najar (Egy.) 6–0, 6–1, 6–2.

Doubles: D. MITIC and J. PALLADA (YUGO.) beat M. Talaat and J. Grandguillot (Egy.) 6–2, 6–4, 3–6, 10–8.

China beat Denmark at Copenhagen on May 10, 11, and 12 by four to one. The Chinese team was Kho Sin Kie and W. C. Choy in singles and doubles. The Danish team was J. Ipsen and W. Rasmussen in the singles and Ipsen and P. Thielsen in the doubles. K. Lo took Choy's place in the singles on the third day, and lost to E. Bjerre, who took Rasmussen's place, in four sets. This was Denmark's only win.

Detailed Results

Singles: KHO SIN KIE (CHIN.) beat W. Rasmussen (Den.) 6–0, 6–1, 6–0; beat J. Ipsen (Den.) 6–0, 6–1, 6–4. W. C. CHOY (CHIN.) beat J. Ipsen (Den.) 6–2, 6–3, 6–2. K. Lo (Chin.) lost to E. BJERRE (DEN.) 6–3, 4–6, 1–6, 3–6.

Doubles: KHO SIN KIE and W. C. CHOY (CHIN.) beat J. Ipsen and P. Thielsen (Den.) 5–7, 6–2, 6–4, 7–5.

Belgium beat Monaco at Brussels on May 10, 11, and 12 by five to none. The Belgian team was J. van den Eynde and P. Washer in the singles and Washer and P. Geelhand in the doubles. Monaco had their veteran two-man team of V. Landau and R. Gallèpe in singles and doubles. They could win only eighteen games in fifteen sets.

Detailed Results

Singles: J. VAN DEN EYNDE (BELG.) beat R. Gallèpe (Mon.) 6–0, 6–0, 6–2 ; beat V. Landau (Mon.) 6–2, 6–3, 6–1. P. WASHER (BELG.) beat V. Landau (Mon.) 6–1, 6–1, 6–1 ; beat R. Gallèpe (Mon.) 6–1, 6–0, 6–2.

Doubles: P. WASHER and P. GEELHAND (BELG.) beat R. Gallèpe and V. Landau (Mon.) 6–1, 6–2, 6–1.

Sweden beat the Netherlands at Stockholm on May 10, 11, and 12 by five to none. The Swedish team was L. Bergelin and T. Johansson in singles and doubles, and the Dutch team A. C. van Swol and I. Rinkel. The Swedes won the singles easily enough, but had to fight hard to capture the doubles in five sets.

Detailed Results

Singles: L. BERGELIN (Sw.) beat I. Rinkel (Neth.) 5–7, 6–0, 6–4, 6–2 ; beat A. C. van Swol (Neth.) 7–5, 6–3, 6–1. T. JOHANSSON (Sw.) beat A. C. van Swol (Neth.) 8–6, 6–4, 7–5 ; beat I. Rinkel (Neth.) 9–7, 6–1, 6–1.

Doubles: L. BERGELIN and T. JOHANSSON (Sw.) beat I. Rinkel and A. C. van Swol (Neth.) 6–4, 5–7, 4–6, 7–5, 6–2.

In the second round France beat Switzerland at Montreux on May 10, 11, and 12 by three to two. The French team was Y. Petra and P. Pellizza in the singles and Petra and M. Bernard in the doubles. The Swiss team was J. Spitzer and H. Huonder in the singles and Spitzer and R. Buser in the doubles. Spitzer did well to beat Pellizza on the first day, as did Huonder on the third day, but France were too strong.

Detailed Results

Singles: Y. PETRA (FR.) beat H. Huonder (Switz.) 10–8, 6–0, 6–1 ; beat J. Spitzer (Switz.) 6–3, 6–3, 6–4. P. Pellizza (Fr.) lost to J. SPITZER (SWITZ.) 2–6, 3–6, 2–6 ; lost to H. HUONDER (SWITZ.) 5–7, 4–6, 5–7.

Doubles: Y. PETRA and M. BERNARD (FR.) beat J. Spitzer and R. Buser (Switz.) 6–0, 6–1, 6–2.

Yugoslavia beat Czechoslovakia at Prague on May 17, 18, and 19 by three to two. The Yugoslav team was F. Puncec and D. Mitic in the singles and Mitic and J. Pallada in the doubles. The Czech team was J. Drobny and J. Vodicka in the singles and Drobny and J. Caska in the doubles. Drobny beat Puncec in three sets, but went down to Mitic in five sets on the opening day. Vodicka could not win a set in either of his singles. The Czechs won the doubles in three sets.

Detailed Results

Singles: F. PUNCEC (YUGO.) beat J. Vodicka (Czech.) 6–3, 7–5, 7–5 ; lost to J. DROBNY (CZECH.) 3–6, 2–6, 4–6. D. MITIC (YUGO.) beat J. Drobny (Czech.) 3–6, 6–4, 0–6, 6–1, 6–3 ; beat J. Vodicka (Czech.) 6–2, 6–0, 6–0.

Doubles: D. Mitic and J. Pallada (Yugo.) lost to J. DROBNY and J. CASKA (CZECH.) 8–10, 2–6, 4–6.

Belgium beat China at Brussels on May 17, 18, and 19 by three to two. The Belgian team was P. Washer and J. van den Eynde in the singles and Washer and P. Geelhand in the doubles. The Chinese team was Kho Sin Kie and W. C. Choy in the singles and the same pair in the doubles. Kho Sin Kie won both his singles, and with Choy carried the doubles to five sets. Unfortunately, his partner, Choy, was not in such good form. He won one set against van den Eynde, but none against Washer.

Detailed Results

Singles: J. VAN DEN EYNDE (BELG.) beat W. C. Choy (Chin.) 4–6, 6–1, 6–3, 6–4 ; lost to KHO SIN KIE (CHIN.) 3–6, 5–7, 3–6. P. WASHER (BELG.) beat W. C. Choy (Chin.) 7–5, 6–4, 6–2 ; lost to KHO SIN KIE (CHIN.) 6–1, 7–5, 3–6, 4–6, 1–6.

Doubles: P. WASHER and P. GEELHAND (BELG.) beat Kho Sin Kie and W. C. Choy (Chin.) 5–7, 6–3, 6–0, 3–6, 6–2.

Sweden beat Ireland at Stockholm on May 17, 18, and 19 by five to none. The Swedish team was L. Bergelin and T. Johansson in singles and doubles. The Irish team was

C. A. Kemp and R. F. Egan in singles and doubles. The Irishmen put up a good fight, but could not win a match. Both extended Johansson to five sets, but both fared less well against Bergelin, who beat Kemp in four sets and Egan in three. The doubles went to five sets and to Sweden also.

Detailed Results

Singles: L. BERGELIN (Sw.) beat C. A. Kemp (Ire.) 2–6, 6–2, 6–2, 6–4 ; beat R. F. Egan (Ire.) 6–4, 6–2, 6–0. T. JOHANSSON (Sw.) beat R. F. Egan (Ire.) 6–2, 7–5, 1–6, 3–6, 6–3 ; beat C. A. Kemp (Ire.) 3–6, 6–1, 6–3, 2–6, 6–3.

Doubles: L. BERGELIN and T. JOHANSSON (Sw.) beat C. A. Kemp and R. F. Egan (Ire.) 3–6, 6–1, 6–3, 2–6, 6–3.

In the third and semi-final round Yugoslavia beat France at Paris at the beginning of June by three to two in perhaps the closest tie on record. Every match went to five sets, France winning the first two matches and Yugoslavia the remainder. The Yugoslav team was F. Puncec and D. Mitic in singles and doubles. The French team was Y. Petra and M. Bernard in the singles and B. Destremau and P. Pellizza in the doubles. On the first day Petra beat Mitic and Bernard beat Puncec, and France looked to be out of trouble, but Puncec and Mitic kept the tie alive by winning the doubles in the eighteenth game of the fifth set on the second day. On the third day Mitic levelled the score by beating Bernard after being two to one down, and Puncec won the tie for his country when he beat Petra 6–0 in the fifth set of the fifth match. It was a fine recovery for the winners and a sad disappointment for the losers.

Detailed Results

Singles: D. MITIC (YUGO.) beat M. Bernard (Fr.) 6–3, 4–6, 3–6, 6–0, 6–3; lost to Y. PETRA (FR.) 6–2, 6–8, 4–6, 6–3, 6–8. F. PUNCEC (YUGO.) beat Y. Petra (Fr.) 6–3, 3–6, 6–4, 7–9, 6–0 ; lost to M. BERNARD (FR.) 6–2, 1–6, 6–0, 5–7, 3–6.

Doubles: D. MITIC and F. PUNCEC (YUGO.) beat B. Destremau and P. Pellizza (Fr.) 8–10, 8–6, 6–3, 5–7, 10–8.

In the other semi-final tie Sweden beat Belgium at Stockholm at the beginning of June by four to one. The Swedes played their usual team of two, L. Bergelin and T. Johansson, in singles and doubles. The Belgian team was P. Washer and J. Peten in the singles and Washer and P. Geelhand in the doubles. Bergelin won both his singles in four sets, but Johansson, though beating Peten in three sets, lost to Washer in the same number. The Swedes took the doubles in four sets.

Detailed Results

Singles: L. Bergelin (Sw.) beat J. Peten (Belg.) 3–6, 6–3, 6–1, 6–1 ; beat P. Washer (Belg.) 7–5, 3–6, 6–3, 9–7. T. Johansson (Sw.) beat J. Peten (Belg.) 6–3, 6–3, 6–0 ; lost to P. Washer (Belg.) 2–6, 1–6, 4–6.

Doubles: L. Bergelin and T. Johansson (Sw.) beat P. Washer and P. Geelhand (Belg.) 4–6, 6–2, 6–4, 6–4.

In the final round of the European Zone Sweden beat Yugoslavia at Varberg on July 14, 16, and 17 by three to two in another very close tie, the ultimate winners again being two down after the first day's play. The Swedish team was L. Bergelin and T. Johansson in singles and doubles. The Yugoslav team was J. Pallada and D. Mitic in singles and doubles. On the first day Pallada beat Bergelin in three sets and Mitic beat Johansson in five after being two sets down. On the second day Sweden won the doubles in five sets after coming near to defeat in the fourth set. On the third day Johansson beat Pallada in three sets, to even the tie. Bergelin then defeated Mitic in the all-important fifth set. It was a most exciting match, lasting just on three hours. The Swede lost the first two sets, but recovered, to squeeze home at 10–8 in the fifth set and make Sweden European Zone winners for the first time.

Detailed Results

Singles: L. Bergelin (Sw.) beat D. Mitic (Yugo.) 5–7, 3–6, 6–3, 6–2, 10–8 ; lost to J. Pallada (Yugo.) 2–6, 2–6, 3–6. T. Johansson (Sw.) beat J. Pallada (Yugo.) 6–3, 6–4, 6–4 ; lost to D. Mitic (Yugo.) 6–4, 6–1, 1–6, 2–6, 0–6.

Doubles: L. Bergelin and T. Johansson (Sw.) beat J. Pallada and D. Mitic (Yugo.) 6–1, 3–6, 3–6, 8–6, 6–2.

American Zone

In the first round Mexico beat Canada at Mexico City by five to none. The Mexican team was R. Vega and A. Vega in singles and doubles. The Canadian team was B. Macken and H. Rochon in the singles and Macken and M. Laird Watt in the doubles. D. McDiarmed took Macken's place in the singles on the third day. The Canadians failed to win a set in five matches.

Detailed Results

Singles: R. Vega (Mex.) beat B. Macken (Can.) 6–4, 6–2, 7–5 ; beat H. Rochon (Can.) 6–3, 8–6, 6–4. A. Vega (Mex.) beat H. Rochon (Can.) 7–5, 6–2, 6–4 ; beat D. McDiarmed (Can.) 6–0, 6–0, 6–3.

Doubles: A. Vega and R. Vega (Mex.) beat M. Laird Watt and B. Macken (Can.) 6–3, 6–4, 6–3.

In the other first-round tie U.S.A. beat the Philippines at St Louis by five to none. The American team was F. A. Parker and W. F. Talbert in the singles and Talbert and G. Mulloy in the doubles. The Philippine team was F. H. Ampon and A. J. Sanchez in the singles and Ampon and C. L. Carmona in the doubles. They were no match for the Americans. Parker beat Ampon without loss of a game. F. R. Schroeder took Talbert's place on the third day in the singles against Ampon.

Detailed Results

Singles: F. A. Parker (U.S.A.) beat F. H. Ampon (Phil.) 6–0, 6–0, 6–0 ; beat A. J. Sanchez (Phil.) 6–1, 6–4, 6–0. W. F. Talbert (U.S.A.) beat A. J. Sanchez (Phil.) 6–1, 6–3, 6–0. F. R. Schroeder (U.S.A.) beat F. H. Ampon (Phil.) 6–2, 6–2, 6–4.

Doubles: W. F. Talbert and G. Mulloy (U.S.A.) beat F. H. Ampon and C. L. Carmona (Phil.) 6–1, 6–3, 6–1.

In the American Zone final round U.S.A. beat Mexico at Orange L.T.C., New Jersey, by five to none. The American team was F. A. Parker and W. F. Talbert in the singles and Talbert and G. Mulloy in the doubles. The Mexican team was A. Vega and R. Vega in singles and doubles. On the third day Mulloy took Talbert's place in the singles and beat F. Guerrero, who played instead of R. Vega. The Americans won all matches in three sets.

Detailed Results

Singles: F. A. PARKER (U.S.A.) beat R. Vega (Mex.) 6–0, 6–0, 6–2 ; beat A. Vega (Mex.) 6–3, 6–3, 6–2. W. F. TALBERT (U.S.A.) beat A. Vega (Mex.) 6–1, 6–2, 6–1. G. MULLOY (U.S.A.) beat F. Guerrero (Mex.) 6–3, 6–4, 6–4.

Doubles: W. F. TALBERT and G. MULLOY (U.S.A.) beat R. Vega and A. Vega (Mex.) 6–0, 9–7, 6–2.

INTER-ZONE ROUND

In this tie U.S.A. beat Sweden at New York on September 13, 14, and 15 by five to none. The American team was J. A. Kramer and F. A. Parker in the singles and W. F. Talbert and G. Mulloy in the doubles. The Swedish team was L. Bergelin and T. Johansson in singles and doubles. Kramer won both his singles comfortably in three sets. Parker beat Johansson in three sets and Bergelin in four. The Swedes put up a good fight in the doubles, but finally lost in the fourteenth game of the fifth set after leading two sets to one. They had, however, done very well to win the European Zone, since they relied on only two men, both new to international competition.

Detailed Results

Singles: J. A. KRAMER (U.S.A.) beat T. Johansson (Sw.) 6–2, 6–2, 6–2 ; beat L. Bergelin (Sw.) 6–2, 6–2, 8–6. F. A. Parker (U.S.A.) beat L. Bergelin (Sw.) 6–0, 3–6, 6–1, 6–1 ; beat T. Johansson (Sw.) 9–7, 6–2, 6–1.

Doubles: W. F. TALBERT and G. MULLOY (U.S.A.) beat L. Bergelin and T. Johansson (Sw.) 3–6, 9–7, 3–6, 6–0, 8–6.

CHALLENGE ROUND

In this final round, commencing on December 26, U.S.A., the challengers, beat Australia, the holders, at Melbourne by five to none. America relied on J. A. Kramer and F. R. Schroeder in singles and doubles. The defending Australian team was J. E. Bromwich and D. Pails in the singles and

Bromwich and A. K. Quist in the doubles. On the first day Schroeder beat Bromwich in five sets in the first match, giving a magnificent display of volleying and smashing, and generally playing most spectacular tennis. Kramer followed up this win for the U.S.A. by beating Pails in three sets, to place the challengers two up. On the second day Kramer and Schroeder beat Quist and Bromwich in three sets, to settle the tie and give America back the cup. In the remaining two matches Kramer beat Bromwich in three sets, and G. Mulloy, playing in place of Schroeder, beat Pails in three sets also. The holders had managed to win only two sets out of five matches. This tie stands out as the biggest defeat a defending team has ever suffered in a challenge round.

Detailed Results

Singles: F. R. Schroeder (U.S.A.) beat J. E. Bromwich (Austral.) 3–6, 6–1, 6–2, 0–6, 6–3. J. A. Kramer (U.S.A.) beat D. Pails (Austral.) 8–6, 6–2, 9–7; beat J. E. Bromwich (Austral.) 8–6, 6–4, 6–4. G. Mulloy (U.S.A.) beat D. Pails (Austral.) 6–3, 6–3, 6–4.

Doubles: J. A. Kramer and F. R. Schroeder (U.S.A.) beat J. E. Bromwich and A. K. Quist (Austral.) 6–2, 7–5, 6–4.

1947: U.S.A.

This year there were twenty-two challengers, twenty in the European Zone and two in the American Zone.

European Zone

In the first round Belgium beat Luxembourg at Brussels by five to none. The Belgian team was P. Washer and J. Peten in the singles and Washer and P. Geelhand in the doubles. The Luxembourg team was G. Wampach and G. Wertheim in singles and doubles, but they could not hold their opponents.

Detailed Results

Singles: P. Washer (Belg.) beat G. Wertheim (Lux.) 6–2, 6–2, 6–1; beat G. Wampach (Lux.) 7–5, 1–6, 6–2, 6–2. J. Peten (Belg.) beat G. Wertheim (Lux.) 6–2, 6–0, 6–0; beat G. Wampach (Lux.) 4–6, 6–2, 9–7, 3–6, 6–3.

Doubles: P. WASHER and P. GEELHAND (BELG.) beat G. Wampach and G. Wertheim (Lux.) 6–4, 6–3, 6–2.

Egypt beat Spain at Barcelona by three to two. The Egyptian team was A. Najar and A. Shafie in the singles and M. Talaat and M. Coen in the doubles. The Spanish team was M. Szawoszt and L. Carles in the singles and J. Bartroli and Carles in the doubles. Bartroli took Carles's place in the singles on the third day. Najar beat Szawoszt in five sets, but lost to Bartroli in three. Shafie beat Carles in four sets and lost to Szawoszt in five. The Egyptian pair won the doubles in five seesaw sets.

Detailed Results

Singles: A. NAJAR (EGY.) beat M. Szawoszt (Sp.) 6–3, 6–3, 7–9, 3–6, 6–3; lost to J. BARTROLI (SP.) 3–6, 1–6, 3–6. A. SHAFIE (EGY.) beat L. Carles (Sp.) 3–6, 6–3, 6–4, 7–5; lost to M. SZAWOSZT (SP.) 2–6, 6–3, 4–6, 6–3, 4–6.

Doubles: M. TALAAT and M. COEN (EGY.) beat J. Bartroli and L. Carles (Sp.) 6–4, 3–6, 6–3, 3–6, 6–4.

Czechoslovakia beat Sweden at Malmö by three to two in a very close tie hinging on the last match. The Czechs relied on two men only, J. Drobny and V. Cernik, and the Swedes also used only two men, L. Bergelin and T. Johansson. Both these men beat Cernik in four sets, but both failed against Drobny, Bergelin going down in four sets and Johansson in five, after holding a winning lead of four to one in the final set. The Czechs took the doubles in four sets.

Detailed Results

Singles: V. Cernik (Czech.) lost to T. JOHANSSON (SW.) 5–7, 4–6, 8–6, 2–6; lost to L. BERGELIN (SW.) 4–6, 8–6, 1–6, 1–6. J. DROBNY (CZECH.) beat L. Bergelin (Sw.) 4–6, 6–1, 6–4, 6–4; beat T. Johansson (Sw.) 6–1, 2–6, 6–3, 4–6, 6–4.

Doubles: J. DROBNY and V. CERNIK (CZECH.) beat L. Bergelin and T. Johansson (Sw.) 6–1, 7–9, 7–5, 6–2.

In the remaining first-round tie Switzerland beat Greece by four to one. The Swiss team was J. Spitzer and H. Huonder in singles and doubles. The Greek team was Manouilidis and L. Stalios in the singles and Stalios and G. Nicholaides in the doubles. Stalios beat Huonder, and with Nicholaides almost won the doubles, as they led the Swiss pair by two sets to none, and only lost the fourth set 9–7.

Detailed Results

Singles: J. Spitzer (Switz.) beat Manouilidis (Gr.) 6–2, 7–5, 6–1 ; beat L. Stalios (Gr.) 1–6, 8–6, 6–0, 6–1. H. Huonder (Switz.) beat Manouilidis (Gr.) 6–0, 6–1, 6–1 ; lost to L. Stalios (Gr.) 6–2, 8–10, 3–6, 3–6.

Doubles: J. Spitzer and H. Huonder (Switz.) beat L. Stalios and G. Nicholaides (Gr.) 5–7, 6–8, 6–0, 9–7, 6–1.

In the second round Great Britain beat Poland at Warsaw on May 15, 16, and 17 by three matches to two. Britain's team was A. J. Mottram and D. W. Barton in the singles and G. L. Paish and D. W. Butler in the doubles. The Polish team was J. Hebda and W. Sconecki in singles and doubles. The tie was made close by Barton's inability to win either of his singles. Mottram, however, redressed the balance, and Butler and Paish won the critical doubles match in three sets.

Detailed Results

Singles: A. J. Mottram (G.B.) beat J. Hebda (Pol.) 2–6, 6–1, 6–1, 6–3 ; beat W. Sconecki (Pol.) 6–4, 6–2, 7–5. D. W. Barton (G.B.) lost to W. Sconecki (Pol.) 3–6, 5–7, 11–13 ; lost to J. Hebda (Pol.) 6–2, 3–6, 4–6, 6–4, 4–6.

Doubles: G. L. Paish and D. W. Butler (G.B.) beat J. Hebda and W. Sconecki (Pol.) 6–2, 6–4, 6–3.

South Africa beat the Netherlands at Amsterdam by four to one. The South African team was E. W. Sturgess and E. E. Fannin in singles and doubles. The Dutch team was A. C. van Swol and H. Wilton in the singles and van Swol and I. Rinkel in the doubles. All the singles went to four sets and to South Africa. The Netherlands took the doubles in three sets.

Detailed Results

Singles: E. W. STURGESS (S.A.) beat H. Wilton (Neth.) 4–6, 6–1, 6–3, 6–2; beat A. C. van Swol (Neth.) 6–2, 7–5, 2–6, 6–3. E. E. FANNIN (S.A.) beat A. C. van Swol (Neth.) 3–6, 6–3, 7–5, 6–2; beat H. Wilton (Neth.) 7–9, 6–3, 6–1, 6–3.

Doubles: E. W. Sturgess and E. E. Fannin (S.A.) lost to A. C. VAN SWOL and I. RINKEL (NETH.) 3–6, 1–6, 0–6.

Yugoslavia beat Ireland at Dublin by three to two. The Yugoslav team was D. Mitic and J. Pallada in singles and doubles. The Irish team was C. A. Kemp and J. R. McHale in the singles and Kemp and R. F. Egan in the doubles. The Yugoslavs won the first three matches, but on the third day Kemp beat Pallada and McHale beat J. Solc, who substituted for Mitic.

Detailed Results

Singles: D. MITIC (YUGO.) beat C. A. Kemp (Ire.) 8–10, 7–9, 6–3, 6–4, 6–1. J. PALLADA (YUGO.) beat J. R. McHale (Ire.) 6–3, 6–3, 6–3; lost to C. A. KEMP (IRE.) 6–4, 1–6, 0–6, 3–6. J. Solc (Yugo.) lost to J. R. MCHALE (IRE.) 7–9, 1–6, 5–7.

Doubles: D. MITIC and J. PALLADA (YUGO.) beat C. A. Kemp and R. F. Egan (Ire.) 6–2, 6–4, 6–2.

Belgium beat Egypt at Brussels by four to one. The Belgian team was P. Washer and P. Geelhand in the singles and Washer and A. Lacroix in the doubles. The Egyptian team was A. Najar and A. Shafie in the singles and M. Talaat and M. Coen in the doubles. Washer beat Shafie in four sets, but Geelhand required five to defeat Najar. The Belgians won the doubles in three sets.

Detailed Results

Singles: P. WASHER (BELG.) beat A. Shafie (Egy.) 6–2, 2–6, 6–0, 8–6; beat A. Najar (Egy.) 6–2, 6–4, 6–2. P. GEELHAND (BELG.) beat A. Najar (Egy.) 4–6, 6–3, 0–6, 6–3, 6–2; lost to A. SHAFIE (EGY.) 4–6, 4–6, 5–7.

Doubles: A. LACROIX and P. WASHER (BELG.) beat M. Talaat and M. Coen (Egy.) 6–4, 6–1, 6–3.

Czechoslovakia beat Switzerland at Prague by four to one. The Czech team was J. Drobny and V. Cernik in singles and doubles. The Swiss team was J. Spitzer and H. Huonder in the singles and Spitzer and H. Pfaff in the doubles. Spitzer scored the only Swiss point when he beat Cernik on the first day after five sets, having almost lost in four. The Czechs won all the other matches in three sets.

Detailed Results

Singles: J. DROBNY (CZECH.) beat H. Huonder (Switz.) 6–1, 6–1, 6–1 ; beat J. Spitzer (Switz.) 6–2, 6–1, 6–2. V. CERNIK (CZECH.) beat H. Huonder (Switz.) 6–3, 6–3, 6–4 ; lost to J. SPITZER (SWITZ.) 2–6, 6–4, 6–0, 5–7, 1–6.

Doubles: J. DROBNY and V. CERNIK (CZECH.) beat J. Spitzer and H. Pfaff (Switz.) 6–1, 6–2, 6–3.

New Zealand beat Norway at Oslo on May 15, 16, and 17 by three to two. The New Zealand team was R. S. McKenzie and J. A. Barry in the singles and McKenzie and J. E. Robson in the doubles. The Norwegian team was J. Haanes and J. Staubo in the singles and Haanes and D. Brem in the doubles. The Norwegians started well, and won both singles on the opening day. New Zealand rallied to win the doubles in four sets. In the opening match on the third day nineteen-year-old John Barry beat Staubo, to square the tie after being two sets to one down and 2–5 in the fourth set. In the final match, on which all depended, McKenzie beat Haanes in four sets. A fine recovery by a young team all playing in their first Davis Cup match.

Detailed Results

Singles: R. S. MCKENZIE (N.Z.) beat J. Haanes (Norw.) 6–4, 0–6, 6–3, 9–7 ; lost to J. STAUBO (NORW.) 2–6, 3–6, 6–3, 2–6. J. A. BARRY (N.Z.) beat J. Staubo (Norw.) 4–6, 7–5, 3–6, 7–5, 6–2 ; lost to J. HAANES (NORW.) 0–6, 5–7, 4–6.

Doubles: R. S. MCKENZIE and J. E. ROBSON (N.Z.) beat J. Haanes and D. Brem (Norw.) 4–6, 6–4, 6–4, 6–2.

France beat India at Paris by five to none. The French team was B. Destremau and M. Bernard in the singles and Bernard and P. Pellizza in the doubles. The Indian team was S. C. Misra and Ghaus Mohammed Khan in the singles and

Misra and J. M. Mehta in the doubles. D. K. Bose substituted for Ghaus Mohammed Khan on the third day against Destremau. The Indians failed to win a set in any of the five matches.

Detailed Results

Singles: B. DESTREMAU (FR.) beat S. C. Misra (Ind.) 6–0, 6–3, 6–3; beat D. K. Bose (Ind.) 6–0, 6–1, 6–2. M. BERNARD (FR.) beat Ghaus Mohammed Khan (Ind.) 6–3, 6–2, 6–0; beat S. C. Misra (Ind.) 6–4, 6–3, 6–1.

Doubles: M. BERNARD and P. PELLIZZA (FR.) beat S. C. Misra and J. M. Mehta (Ind.) 6–3, 6–2, 6–3.

Monaco had a walk-over from Denmark.

In the third round South Africa beat Great Britain at Scarborough on May 29, 30, and 31 by four matches to one. South Africa were again represented by E. W. Sturgess and E. E. Fannin in singles and doubles. The British team was A. J. Mottram and D. W. Butler in the singles and Mottram and G. L. Paish in the doubles. Mottram beat Fannin, but could not hold Sturgess. Butler could win only two games from Sturgess, but did much better against Fannin, till forced to retire in the fourth set with cramp when two sets to one down. The doubles was a five-setter, in which the South Africans finally prevailed.

Detailed Results

Singles: E. W. STURGESS (S.A.) beat A. J. Mottram (G.B.) 5–7, 6–2, 6–1, 6–3; beat D. W. Butler (G.B.) 6–1, 6–1, 6–0. E. E. FANNIN (S.A.) beat D. W. Butler (G.B.) 6–4, 4–6, 9–7, 3–3 (retired); lost to A. J. MOTTRAM (G.B.) 4–6, 7–5, 2–6, 5–7.

Doubles: E. W. STURGESS and E. E. FANNIN (S.A.) beat A. J. Mottram and G. L. Paish (G.B.) 6–1, 4–6, 2–6, 6–3, 6–4.

Yugoslavia beat Belgium at Brussels by four to one. The Yugoslav team was D. Mitic and J. Pallada in singles and doubles. The Belgian team was P. Washer and P. Geelhand in the singles and A. Lacroix and Washer in the doubles. Washer beat Mitic on the opening day in four sets, but the home team could not score any further successes, though they won the first two sets of the doubles.

Detailed Results

Singles: D. MITIC (YUGO.) beat P. Geelhand (Belg.) 6–0, 6–3, 6–4; lost to P. WASHER (BELG.) 4–6, 3–6, 6–1, 3–6. J. PALLADA (YUGO.) beat P. Washer (Belg.) 6–3, 6–2, 6–0; beat P. Geelhand (Belg.) 6–1, 4–6, 6–3, 6–3.

Doubles: D. MITIC and J. PALLADA (YUGO.) beat P. Washer and A. Lacroix (Belg.) 2–6, 1–6, 6–2, 6–1, 6–2.

Czechoslovakia beat New Zealand at Prague by five to none. The Czech team was J. Drobny and V. Cernik in singles and doubles. The New Zealand team was R. S. McKenzie and J. E. Robson in singles and doubles. The Czechs, at home, were too strong for the young New Zealanders, though the latter almost snatched the doubles on the second day, only losing this match at 10–8 in the fifth set. On the third day J. A. Barry took McKenzie's place in the singles and opposed V. Vbra, who substituted for Drobny.

Detailed Results

Singles: J. DROBNY (CZECH.) beat J. E. Robson (N.Z.) 6–2, 6–2, 8–6. V. CERNIK (CZECH.) beat R. S. McKenzie (N.Z.) 6–3, 6–4, 7–5; beat J. E. Robson (N.Z.) 6–3, 6–0, 6–0. V. VBRA (CZECH.) beat J. A. Barry (N.Z.) 6–4, 6–2, 6–2.

Doubles: J. DROBNY and V. CERNIK (CZECH.) beat R. S. McKenzie and J. E. Robson (N.Z.) 6–2, 4–6, 9–7, 3–6, 10–8.

France beat Monaco at Paris by five to none. The French team was M. Bernard and B. Destremau in the singles and P. Pellizza and R. Abdesselam in the doubles. The Monaco team was A. Noghes and V. Landau in the singles and Landau and G. Medecin in the doubles. On the third day Abdesselam took Bernard's place in the singles. France did not lose a set in any match.

Detailed Results

Singles: M. BERNARD (FR.) beat A. Noghes (Mon.) 6–1, 6–2, 6–0. B. DESTREMAU (FR.) beat V. Landau (Mon.) 6–3, 6–2, 6–1; beat A. Noghes (Mon.) 7–5, 6–2, 6–1. R. ABDESSELAM (FR.) beat V. Landau (Mon.) 6–2, 6–1, 6–0.

Doubles: P. Pellizza and R. Abdesselam (Fr.) beat V. Landau and G. Medecin (Mon.) 6–2, 6–1, 6–0.

In the semi-final round Yugoslavia beat South Africa at Zagreb by three to two. Both countries relied on two players only, the Yugoslavs being D. Mitic and J. Pallada and the South Africans E. W. Sturgess and E. E. Fannin. Yugoslavia won both singles on the first day, when Mitic beat Sturgess in five sets and Pallada beat Fannin in three. South Africa took the doubles on the second day in three sets, but went down on the third day when Mitic defeated Fannin in straight sets. In the last match of the tie Sturgess beat Pallada in five sets.

Detailed Results

Singles: D. Mitic (Yugo.) beat E. W. Sturgess (S.A.) 3–6, 7–5, 6–2, 3–6, 6–3; beat E. E. Fannin (S.A.) 6–2, 6–3, 6–4. J. Pallada (Yugo.) beat E. E. Fannin (S.A.) 6–1, 6–4, 7–5; lost to E. W. Sturgess (S.A.) 6–3, 3–6, 0–6, 7–5, 3–6.

Doubles: D. Mitic and J. Pallada (Yugo.) lost to E. W. Sturgess and E. E. Fannin (S.A.) 3–6, 5–7, 5–7.

In the other semi-final tie Czechoslovakia beat France by four to one, though only four matches were played. Czechoslovakia conceded Cernik's second single when rain interfered with play. The Czech team was J. Drobny and V. Cernik in singles and doubles. The French team was M. Bernard and B. Destremau in the singles and J. Borotra and Y. Petra in the doubles. Both Czechs overcame Bernard in five sets, and Drobny beat Destremau in three easy sets. Drobny and Cernik took the doubles in three sets, the first two of which were very long ones.

Detailed Results

Singles: J. Drobny (Czech.) beat B. Destremau (Fr.) 6–2, 6–0, 6–1; beat M. Bernard (Fr.) 6–3, 2–6, 6–4, 4–6, 6–4. V. Cernik (Czech.) beat M. Bernard (Fr.) 2–6, 9–7, 6–4, 4–6, 6–4. (One match conceded.)

Doubles: J. Drobny and V. Cernik (Czech.) beat J. Borotra and Y. Petra (Fr.) 10–8, 14–12, 6–3.

In the final round of this zone Czechoslovakia beat Yugoslavia at Zagreb by four to none. The Czech team was again J. Drobny and V. Cernik in singles and doubles. The Yugoslav team was D. Mitic and J. Pallada. Drobny beat Pallada in four sets, and Cernik beat Mitic in five. The Czechs took the doubles in three sets on the second day, to win the European Zone for the first time in their country's history.

Detailed Results

Singles: J. DROBNY (CZECH.) beat J. Pallada (Yugo.) 6–3, 8–6, 2–6, 6–3. V. CERNIK (CZECH.) beat D. Mitic (Yugo.) 3–6, 6–0, 2–6, 6–1, 6–2. J. DROBNY (CZECH.) beat D. Mitic (Yugo.) 1–6, 6–3, 6–4, 4–6, 6–1.

Doubles: J. DROBNY and V. CERNIK (CZECH.) beat D. Mitic and J. Pallada (Yugo.) 6–3, 6–1, 6–3.

AMERICAN ZONE

There was only one tie in this zone, and it took place at Montreal between Canada and Australia, and was won by the latter by five to none. The Australian team was D. Pails and G. E. Brown in the singles and J. E. Bromwich and C. F. Long in the doubles. The Canadian team was H. Rochon and B. Macken in the singles and G. McNiel and E. Lanthier in the doubles. They failed to win a set in any of the five matches.

Detailed Results

Singles: D. PAILS (AUSTRAL.) beat H. Rochon (Can.) 6–1, 6–4, 6–2; beat B. Macken (Can.) 6–4, 6–2, 6–2. G. E. BROWN (AUSTRAL.) beat B. Macken (Can.) 6–4, 6–4, 6–1; beat H. Rochon (Can.) 6–3, 9–7, 6–2.

Doubles: J. E. BROMWICH and C. F. LONG (AUSTRAL.) beat G. McNiel and E. Lanthier (Can.) 6–2, 6–1, 6–0.

INTER-ZONE ROUND

This tie, between Australia, American Zone winners, and Czechoslovakia, winners of the European Zone, was played at Montreal on August 15, 16, and 17, and was won by Australia by four to one. The Australian team was J. E. Bromwich and D. Pails in the singles and Bromwich and C. F. Long in the doubles. The Czech team was, as before, J. Drobny and V. Cernik in singles and doubles. On the first day Bromwich beat Cernik in three sets, with the loss of three games only. Drobny beat Pails in four sets. Australia took the doubles on the second day, and on the third day the remaining singles, when Bromwich beat Drobny in three sets and Pails beat Cernik in five. The Czech two-man team had at last found its master.

Detailed Results

Singles: J. E. Bromwich (Austral.) beat V. Cernik (Czech.) 6–1, 6–1, 6–1 ; beat J. Drobny (Czech.) 6–2, 7–5, 6–4. D. Pails (Austral.) beat V. Cernik (Czech.) 6–3, 4–6, 3–6, 6–2, 6–3 ; lost to J. Drobny (Czech.) 3–6, 4–6, 6–4, 4–6.

Doubles: J. E. Bromwich and C. F. Long (Austral.) beat J. Drobny and V. Cernik (Czech.) 6–2, 6–2, 6–2.

Challenge Round

Australia, the challengers, met U.S.A., the holders, at Forest Hills, New York, where the home team successfully defended the trophy by four matches to one. The defending team was identical with the one which regained the trophy from Australia in 1946—that is, J. A. Kramer and F. R. Schroeder in singles and doubles. The challenging Australian team was J. E. Bromwich and D. Pails in the singles and Bromwich and C. F. Long in the doubles. In the opening match Kramer beat Pails in three sets in well under an hour's play, Pails never being in the hunt. In the second match Schroeder beat Bromwich in a well-played four-set match, to put U.S.A. two up and three to play. On the second day Bromwich and Long played very well to beat Kramer and Schroeder in four sets in the doubles. On the third day Pails almost levelled the scores when he pulled up from two sets down and reached match point in the fifth set against Schroeder. He failed to clinch it, however, and the defenders were home. This match set up a new long-distance Davis Cup singles record of seventy-one games. The last match, between Kramer and Bromwich, on which nothing now depended, was won by the former in three sets.

Detailed Results

Singles: J. A. KRAMER (U.S.A.) beat D. Pails (Austral.) 6–2, 6–1, 6–2 ; beat J. E. Bromwich (Austral.) 6–3, 6–2, 6–2. F. R. SCHROEDER (U.S.A.) beat J. E. Bromwich (Austral.) 6–4, 5–7, 6–3, 6–3 ; beat D. Pails (Austral.) 6–3, 8–6, 4–6, 9–11, 10–8.

Doubles: J. A. Kramer and F. R. Schroeder (U.S.A.) lost to J. E. BROMWICH and C. F. LONG (AUSTRAL.) 4–6, 6–2, 2–6, 4–6.

1948: U.S.A.

In the third year after the Second World War twenty-nine nations challenged—twenty-five in the European Zone and the remaining four in the American Zone.

EUROPEAN ZONE

In the first round Great Britain beat India at Harrogate on April 22, 23, and 24 by three matches to two. The British team consisted of A. J. Mottram and H. F. Walton in the singles and Mottram and G. L. Paish in the doubles. The Indian team was S. C. Misra and D. K. Bose in the singles, with Misra and S. L. R. Sawhney in the doubles. Walton, a newcomer to the British team, failed to beat either Misra or Bose, though he had beaten both in tournament play shortly before the match. Mottram, however, was in such form that he won both singles and the doubles with Paish, with the loss of one set, to Misra, thus giving his team the odd-match lead.

Detailed Results

Singles: A. J. MOTTRAM (G.B.) beat S. C. Misra (Ind.) 6–0, 6–3, 7–9, 7–5 ; beat D. K. Bose (Ind.) 6–3, 6–4, 6–4. H. F. Walton (G.B.) lost to D. K. BOSE (IND.) 3–6, 3–6, 2–6 ; lost to S. C. MISRA (IND.) 6–2, 6–8, 7–9, 2–6.

Doubles: A. J. MOTTRAM and G. L. PAISH (G.B.) beat S. C. Misra and S. L. R. Sawhney (Ind.) 6–3, 7–5, 6–2.

Rumania gave France a close match at Bucharest when the visiting side got home by three to two. The French team was M. Bernard and B. Destremau in the singles and Bernard and H. Bolelli in the doubles. The Rumanian team, in both singles and doubles, was C. Caralulis and G. Viziru, who made a great start for their country when Caralulis beat Bernard on the first day and Viziru beat Destremau. They were, however, unable to hold the Frenchmen in the remaining three matches, in which they failed to win a single set.

Detailed Results

Singles: M. BERNARD (FR.) beat G. Viziru (Rum.) 6–2, 6–1, 6–4 ; lost to C. CARALULIS (RUM.) 6–3, 4–6, 3–6, 2–6. B. DESTREMAU (FR.) beat C. Caralulis (Rum.) 6–2, 6–4, 7–5 ; lost to G. VIZIRU (RUM.) 3–6, 2–6, 5–7.

Doubles: M. BERNARD and H. BOLELLI (FR.) beat C. Caralulis and G. Viziru (Rum.) 6–3, 8–6, 8–6.

Hungary beat Austria at Budapest by five to none. The Hungarian team was J. Asboth and J. Adam in the singles and Asboth and A. Feher in the doubles. Austria were represented by H. Redl and A. Specht. Adam had to go to five sets in both his singles before winning, but in the three matches in which Asboth took part Hungary was unthreatened.

Detailed Results

Singles: J. ASBOTH (HUN.) beat A. Specht (Aus.) 6–2, 6–2, 6–0 ; beat H. Redl (Aus.) 6–4, 6–2, 6–2. J. ADAM (HUN.) beat A. Specht (Aus.) 4–6, 6–0, 6–1, 4–6, 6–3 ; beat H. Redl (Aus.) 6–3, 4–6, 6–4, 4–6, 6–3.

Doubles: J. ASBOTH and A. FEHER (HUN.) beat H. Redl and A. Specht (Aus.) 6–2, 6–3, 8–6.

Sweden beat Spain at Barcelona by five to none. The Swedish team was L. Bergelin and T. Johansson in singles and doubles. The Spanish team was M. Szawoszt and L. Castella in the singles and J. Bartroli and Szawoszt in the doubles. The Swedes were unthreatened in the four matches played, Castella giving Bergelin a win by default in the fifth match.

Detailed Results

Singles: L. BERGELIN (SW.) beat M. Szawoszt (Sp.) 6–4, 6–2, 4–6, 6–3 ; w.o. L. Castella. T. JOHANSSON (SW.) beat L. Castella (Sp.) 6–3, 6–2, 6–1 ; beat M. Szawoszt (Sp.) 6–3, 11–9, 6–3.

Doubles: L. BERGELIN and T. JOHANSSON (SW.) beat J. Bartroli and M. Szawoszt (Sp.) 7–5, 6–4, 6–4.

Switzerland beat the newly constituted Pakistan at Montreux by three to two. The Swiss team was H. Huonder and M. Albrecht in singles and doubles. Pakistan were represented by I. Ahmed and S. Alam, both of whom had played for India in pre-Pakistan days. Ahmed won both his singles, but Alam could not offer enough support for Pakistan to score the necessary third match.

Detailed Results

Singles: H. HUONDER (SWITZ.) beat S. Alam (Pak.) 6–1, 6–1, 6–2 ; lost to I. AHMED (PAK.) 2–6, 4–6, 3–6. M. ALBRECHT (SWITZ.) beat S. Alam (Pak.) 6–1, 6–1, 6–2 ; lost to I. AHMED (PAK.) 1–6, 5–7, 6–1, 6–4, 4–6.

Doubles: M. ALBRECHT and H. HUONDER (SWITZ.) beat I. Ahmed and S. Alam (Pak.) 7–5, 6–4, 6–4.

Yugoslavia beat Turkey at Zagreb by five to none. The Yugoslav team was D. Mitic and J. Pallada in singles and doubles. The Turkish team was Gurel and Kizil in the singles and Kizil and Eihat in the doubles. On the third day by arrangement the two remaining singles were reduced to the best of three sets only ; also each side played a substitute in the last match—Laslo for Yugoslavia and Belig for Turkey.

Detailed Results

Singles: D. MITIC (YUGO.) beat Gurel (Turk.) 6–1, 6–1, 6–0. J. PALLADA (YUGO.) beat Kizil (Turk.) 6–1, 1–6, 8–6, 6–3 ; beat Gurel (Turk.) 6–4, 6–2. LASLO (YUGO.) beat Belig (Turk.) 6–2, 6–4.

Doubles: D. MITIC and J. PALLADA (YUGO.) beat Kizil and Eihat (Turk.) 6–2, 6–3, 6–3.

Ireland beat Luxembourg at Dublin by five to none. Ireland's team was C. A. Kemp and G. P. Jackson in the singles and Kemp and T. G. McVeagh in the doubles. The Luxembourg players were G. Wampach and G. Wertheim in singles and doubles. They failed to extend their hosts.

Detailed Results

Singles: C. A. KEMP (IRE.) beat G. Wampach (Lux.) 7–5, 6–3, 6–8, 6–4 ; beat G. Wertheim (Lux.) 6–0, 6–2, 6–4. G. P. JACKSON (IRE.) beat G. Wertheim (Lux.) 7–5, 6–1, 6–1 ; beat G. Wampach (Lux.) 7–5, 4–6, 6–2, 6–0.

Doubles: C. A. KEMP and T. G. MCVEAGH (IRE.) beat G. Wertheim and G. Wampach (Lux.) 10–8, 6–4, 6–3.

Denmark beat Egypt at Copenhagen by three to two. The Danish team must surely be the youngest on record in the competition, comprising two youngsters, T. Ulrich and K. Nielsen, whose combined years totalled only thirty-six. They played singles and doubles. The Egyptian team was A. Najar and A. Shafei in the singles and Shafei and M. Coen in the doubles. On the first day Ulrich beat Shafei in a long five-setter, after leading two sets to love, and Nielsen put Denmark two up by beating Najar in four sets after losing the first. The Egyptian pair took the doubles in five sets after trailing two sets to one down. On the third day Nielsen beat Shafei in three sets, and settled the tie. In the last match Coen took Najar's place and beat Ulrich in five sets, giving Egypt her second win.

Detailed Results

Singles: T. ULRICH (DEN.) beat A. Shafei (Egy.) 6–1, 7–5, 5–7, 5–7, 8–6 ; lost to M. COEN (EGY.) 6–2, 1–6, 10–8, 10–12, 0–6. K. NIELSEN (DEN.) beat A. Najar (Egy.) 3–6, 6–2, 6–2, 6–3 ; beat A. Shafei (Egy.) 6–3, 6–1, 8–6.

Doubles: K. Nielsen and T. Ulrich (Den.) lost to A. SHAFEI and M. COEN (EGY.) 5–7, 8–6, 8–6, 4–6, 3–6.

In the remaining tie of this round Italy received a win by default from Poland.

In the second round the Netherlands beat Portugal at Scheveningen, Holland, by five to none. The Dutch team was A. C. van Swol and R. van Meegeren in the singles and van Swol and I. Rinkel in the doubles. For Portugal Roquette and Ricciardi played the singles and Ricciardi and da Silva the doubles. The Dutch were much too strong for the Portuguese, and did not lose a set in the five matches.

Detailed Results

Singles: A. C. VAN SWOL (NETH.) beat Roquette (Port.) 6–0, 6–3, 6–2 ; beat Ricciardi (Port.) 6–4, 6–2, 6–4. R. VAN MEEGEREN (NETH.) beat Ricciardi (Port.) 6–2, 6–1, 6–1 ; beat Roquette (Port.) 6–1, 6–1, 6–3.

Doubles: A. C. van Swol and I. Rinkel (Neth.) beat Ricciardi and da Silva (Port.) 6–1, 6–0, 6–3.

Great Britain beat Norway at Oslo on May 11, 12, and 13 by four matches to one. The British team was A. J. Mottram and G. L. Paish in the singles and Mottram and H. Billington in the doubles. The Norwegian team was J. Haanes and J. Staubo in singles and doubles. Haanes gained Norway's only success when he beat Paish in four sets in the opening match.

Detailed Results

Singles: G. L. Paish (G.B.) beat J. Staubo (Norw.) 4–6, 6–4, 6–1, 6–2 ; lost to J. Haanes (Norw.) 2–6, 6–4, 3–6, 2–6. A. J. Mottram (G.B.) beat J. Staubo (Norw.) 6–2, 6–1, 6–1 ; beat J. Haanes (Norw.) 6–1, 6–0, 5–7, 6–1.

Doubles: A. J. Mottram and H. Billington (G.B.) beat J. Haanes and J. Staubo (Norw.) 6–1, 7–5, 6–3.

Hungary beat France at Paris by four to one. The Hungarian team was J. Asboth and A. Stolpa in singles and doubles. France relied on M. Bernard and R. Abdesselam in the singles and Bernard and B. Destremau in the doubles. Honours were even at the end of the first day's play, Asboth having lost to Bernard and Stolpa having beaten Abdesselam, both matches going to four sets. The Hungarians took the doubles in five sets, and on the third day Stolpa beat Bernard from two sets down, and Asboth beat Abdesselam.

Detailed Results

Singles: J. Asboth (Hun.) beat R. Abdesselam (Fr.) 7–5, 6–1, 6–2 ; lost to M. Bernard (Fr.) 1–6, 4–6, 6–4, 2–6. A. Stolpa (Hun.) beat R. Abdesselam (Fr.) 2–6, 6–4, 6–3, 8–6 ; beat M. Bernard (Fr.) 1–6, 3–6, 6–0, 6–3, 6–4.

Doubles: J. Asboth and A. Stolpa (Hun.) beat M. Bernard and B. Destremau (Fr.) 6–3, 6–3, 6–8, 2–6, 6–2.

Sweden beat Switzerland at Stockholm by five to none. The Swedish team was again L. Bergelin and T. Johansson in singles and doubles. The Swiss team was H. Huonder and M. Albrecht in singles and doubles. The Swedes held a clear margin of superiority in all matches.

Detailed Results

Singles: L. BERGELIN (Sw.) beat H. Huonder (Switz.) 6–2, 6–4, 6–1 ; beat M. Albrecht (Switz.) 7–5, 6–3, 6–3. T. JOHANSSON (Sw.) beat H. Huonder (Switz.) 6–2, 6–4, 6–3 ; beat M. Albrecht (Switz.) 11–9, 0–6, 6–2, 6–4.

Doubles: L. BERGELIN and T. JOHANSSON (Sw.) beat M. Albrecht and H. Huonder (Switz.) 6–1, 6–1, 6–3.

Italy beat Yugoslavia at Zagreb by three matches to two. Each country used only two men for singles and doubles: for Italy G. Cucelli and M. del Bello, and for Yugoslavia D. Mitic and J. Pallada. Cucelli lost both his singles, but del Bello responded by winning both his, and in partnership with Cucelli won the doubles in four sets. Yet again the doubles proved the key to the contest.

Detailed Results

Singles: G. Cucelli (It.) lost to D. MITIC (YUGO.) 7–5, 6–8, 1–6, 2–6 ; lost to J. PALLADA (YUGO.) 7–5, 4–6, 1–6, 4–6. M. DEL BELLO (IT.) beat J. Pallada (Yugo.) 6–2, 6–3, 6–8, 9–7 ; beat D. Mitic (Yugo.) 7–5, 6–4, 8–6.

Doubles: G. CUCELLI and M. DEL BELLO (IT.) beat D. Mitic and J. Pallada (Yugo.) 6–0, 6–3, 1–6, 7–5.

Denmark beat Ireland at Dublin by three matches to two. The Danish team was T. Ulrich and K. Nielsen in singles and doubles, and the Irish team was C. A. Kemp and G. P. Jackson in singles and doubles too. The young Danes both beat Kemp in three sets, and Nielsen also beat Jackson in five sets. Both the other matches went to Ireland in five sets.

Detailed Results

Singles: T. ULRICH (DEN.) beat C. A. Kemp (Ire.) 8–6, 6–3, 6–4 ; lost to G. P. JACKSON (IRE.) 4–6, 8–6, 6–2, 2–6, 3–6. K. NIELSEN (DEN.) beat G. P. Jackson (Ire.) 6–4, 2–6, 6–4, 5–7, 6–4 ; beat C. A. Kemp (Ire.) 6–4, 8–6, 6–3.

Doubles: K. Nielsen and T. Ulrich (Den.) lost to C. A. KEMP and G. P. JACKSON (IRE.) 0–6, 3–6, 8–6, 6–3, 2–6.

Czechoslovakia beat Brazil at Prague by four to one. The Czech team was J. Drobny and V. Vbra in the singles and Drobny and V. Zabrodsky in the doubles. The Brazilian team was E. Petersen and M. Fernandez in singles and doubles. The latter beat Vbra on the first day, to notch Brazil's only win in the tie.

Detailed Results

Singles: J. DROBNY (CZECH.) beat E. Petersen (Braz.) 6–2, 6–2, 6–2 ; beat M. Fernandez (Braz.) 6–0, 4–1 (retired). V. VBRA (CZECH.) beat E. Petersen (Braz.) 7–9, 6–3, 6–4, 6–3 ; lost to M. FERNANDEZ (BRAZ.) 2–6, 4–6, 3–6.

Doubles: J. DROBNY and V. ZABRODSKY (CZECH.) beat E. Petersen and M. Fernandez (Braz.) 6–3, 6–4, 6–0.

Belgium beat Argentina at Brussels by three to two. The Belgian team was J. Peten and P. Washer in singles and doubles. The Argentine team was E. Morea and H. Weiss in the singles and Morea and A. Russell in the doubles. Washer won both his singles, and Peten beat Weiss, and almost beat Morea too, holding a lead of two sets to love, and only losing in the eighteenth game of the fifth set. Morea and Russell won the doubles for Argentina in four sets, after losing the first.

Detailed Results

Singles: J. PETEN (BELG.) beat H. Weiss (Argent.) 6–1, 1–6, 6–2, 6–3 ; lost to E. MOREA (ARGENT.) 6–1, 6–3, 6–8, 4–6, 8–10. P. WASHER (BELG.) beat E. Morea (Argent.) 6–1, 7–5, 6–2 ; beat H. Weiss (Argent.) 8–6, 4–6, 6–4, 6–4.

Doubles: J. Peten and P. Washer (Belg.) lost to E. MOREA and A. RUSSELL (ARGENT.) 10–8, 3–6, 2–6, 6–8.

In the third round of this zone Great Britain beat the Netherlands on June 10, 11, and 12 at Birmingham by four matches to one. The British team was A. J. Mottram and G. L. Paish in singles and doubles also. The Dutch team was A. C. van Swol and R. van Meegeren in the singles and van Swol and I. Rinkel in the doubles. Mottram beat both Dutchmen with the loss of one set, to van Swol, but Paish had to wage five sets in each of his singles. In partnership Mottram and Paish were beaten in five sets.

Detailed Results

Singles: A. J. MOTTRAM (G.B.) beat A. C. van Swol (Neth.) 6–3, 6–4, 9–11, 6–3; beat R. van Meegeren (Neth.) 6–3, 6–4, 6–3. G. L. PAISH (G.B.) beat R. van Meegeren (Neth.) 6–3, 6–2, 3–6, 7–9, 6–1; beat A. C. van Swol (Neth.) 6–1, 2–6, 7–5, 1–6, 6–4.

Doubles: A. J. Mottram and G. L. Paish (G.B.) lost to A. C. VAN SWOL and I. RINKEL (NETH.) 3–6, 7–5, 2–6, 6–1, 4–6.

Sweden beat Hungary at Budapest by three to two. The Swedish team was the usual one of L. Bergelin and T. Johansson in singles and doubles, while J. Asboth and J. Adam represented Hungary. Asboth proved too good for both the Swedes, but Adam was not the equal of either. In partnership the Swedes took the vital doubles match in four sets.

Detailed Results

Singles: L. BERGELIN (Sw.) beat J. Adam (Hun.) 5–7, 6–4, 6–2, 6–1; lost to J. ASBOTH (HUN.) 4–6, 3–6, 4–6. T. JOHANSSON (Sw.) beat J. Adam (Hun.) 7–5, 6–1, 6–4; lost to J. ASBOTH (HUN.) 6–3, 7–9, 4–6, 0–6.

Doubles: L. BERGELIN and T. JOHANSSON (Sw.) beat J. Asboth and J. Adam (Hun.) 5–7, 6–3, 7–5, 7–5.

Italy beat Denmark at Turin by five to none. The Italian team was G. Cucelli and M. del Bello in singles and doubles. The Danish team was T. Ulrich and K. Nielsen in singles and doubles. They were too young and inexperienced to extend the Italians, especially on the latter's own courts.

Detailed Results

Singles: G. CUCELLI (IT.) beat K. Nielsen (Den.) 6–4, 4–6, 6–1, 6–1; beat T. Ulrich (Den.) 6–3, 6–3, 6–1. M. DEL BELLO (IT.) beat T. Ulrich (Den.) 6–3, 6–3, 6–3; beat K. Nielsen (Den.) 6–2, 7–5, 6–3.

Doubles: G. CUCELLI and M. DEL BELLO (IT.) beat K. Nielsen and T. Ulrich (Den.) 6–3, 6–3, 8–6.

Czechoslovakia beat Belgium at Prague by three to two. The Czech team was J. Drobny and V. Cernik in singles and doubles. The Belgian team was P. Washer and J. Peten in the singles and Washer and P. Geelhand in the doubles.

Drobny won both his singles in straight sets, but Cernik offset this by losing both of his in four sets. The all-important doubles was taken by the Czechs in four sets.

Detailed Results

Singles: J. Drobny (Czech.) beat P. Washer (Belg.) 6–2, 6–4, 6–2 ; beat J. Peten (Belg.) 6–4, 6–3, 6–1. V. Cernik (Czech.) lost to J. Peten (Belg.) 4–6, 6–2, 1–6, 4–6 ; lost to P. Washer (Belg.) 4–6, 6–2, 4–6, 3–6.

Doubles: J. Drobny and V. Cernik (Czech.) beat P. Washer and P. Geelhand (Belg.) 7–5, 4–6, 6–1, 6–3.

In the fourth and semi-final round Sweden beat Great Britain at Stockholm on July 9, 10, and 11 by four to one. Both countries relied on a two-man team. For Sweden L. Bergelin and T. Johansson played all matches, and for Great Britain A. J. Mottram and G. L. Paish. The only British success was when Mottram beat Johansson on the third day, when the result was already known, the Swedes having won the first three matches. They clearly demonstrated their superiority, though the British team fought hard all the time.

Detailed Results

Singles: L. Bergelin (Sw.) beat A. J. Mottram (G.B.) 6–3, 6–2, 6–3 ; beat G. L. Paish (G.B.) 4–6, 6–4, 6–1, 6–2. T. Johansson (Sw.) beat G. L. Paish (G.B.) 6–2, 2–6, 8–6, 6–1 ; lost to A. J. Mottram (G.B.) 3–6, 6–2, 2–6, 2–6.

Doubles: L. Bergelin and T. Johansson (Sw.) beat A. J. Mottram and G. L. Paish (G.B.) 2–6, 7–5, 6–4, 6–3.

In the other semi-final Czechoslovakia beat Italy at Milan on July 9, 10, and 11 by three to two. The Czech team was J. Drobny and V. Cernik in singles and doubles. The Italian team was G. Cucelli and M. del Bello in singles and doubles. The Czechs made a good start by capturing both singles on the first day, Drobny beating Cucelli and Cernik beating del Bello, both matches going to four sets. The Italians revived to take the doubles on the second day in three sets, but Drobny beat del Bello in three sets in the first match on the third day, to clinch the tie for his country. In the last match Cucelli beat Cernik in four sets.

Detailed Results

Singles: J. DROBNY (CZECH.) beat G. Cucelli (It.) 6–3, 3–6, 6–2, 6–3; beat M. del Bello (It.) 11–9, 6–3, 6–2. V. CERNIK (CZECH.) beat M. del Bello (It.) 6–2, 6–4, 7–9, 6–3; lost to G. CUCELLI (IT.) 2–6, 6–2, 3–6, 3–6.

Doubles: J. Drobny and V. Cernik (Czech.) lost to G. CUCELLI and M. DEL BELLO (IT.) 1–6, 6–8, 2–6.

In the European Zone final round Czechoslovakia beat Sweden at Prague on July 26, 27, and 28 by four to one. The Czech team was J. Drobny and V. Cernik in singles and doubles, and for Sweden L. Bergelin and T. Johansson played singles and doubles, as usual. The Czechs quickly settled the tie by winning the first three matches without any difficulty. Drobny crushed Bergelin in three sets, and Cernik beat Johansson in four sets, on the first day. On the second day Drobny and Cernik lost only five games in three sets to Bergelin and Johansson in the doubles match. With the tie decided, substitutes appeared in force on the third day. V. Zabrodsky played in place of Drobny, and went down to Johansson in four sets. V. Vbra took Cernik's place, and beat B. Fornstedt, Bergelin's substitute, in three sets.

Detailed Results

Singles: J. DROBNY (CZECH.) beat L. Bergelin (Sw.) 6–0, 6–3, 7–5. V. CERNIK (CZECH.) beat T. Johansson (Sw.) 6–4, 4–6, 6–3, 6–3. V. Zabrodsky (Czech.) lost to T. JOHANSSON (SW.) 3–6, 6–3, 2–6, 3–6. V. VBRA (CZECH.) beat B. Fornstedt (Sw.) 6–3, 6–1, 6–3.

Doubles: J. DROBNY and V. CERNIK (CZECH.) beat L. Bergelin and T. Johansson (Sw.) 6–2, 6–1, 6–2.

NORTH AMERICAN ZONE

Australia beat Cuba at Havana in the first round by three to none. The Australian team was O. W. Sidwell and A. K. Quist in the singles and Sidwell and C. F. Long in the doubles. The Cuban team was J. Etcheverry and J. Aguero in the singles and Aguero and R. Morales in the doubles. They were unable to win a set against their stronger opponents.

Detailed Results

Singles: A. K. QUIST (AUSTRAL.) beat J. Etcheverry (Cu.) 6–1, 6-0, 6–0. O. W. SIDWELL (AUSTRAL.) beat J. Aguero (Cu.) 6–3, 6–1, 6–4.

Doubles: O. W. SIDWELL and C. F. LONG (AUSTRAL.) beat J. Aguero and R. Morales (Cu.) 7–5, 6–2, 6–3.

Mexico beat Canada at Montreal by four to one. The Mexican team was A. Vega and F. Guerrero in the singles and Vega and G. Palafox in the doubles. The Canadian team was H. Rochon and B. Macken in the singles and B. Macken and J. Macken in the doubles. Rochon beat Guerrero in the first match, but that was Canada's only success. On the third day W. Stohlberg took B. Macken's place in the singles against Guerrero.

Detailed Results

Singles: A. VEGA (MEX.) beat B. Macken (Can.) 6–4, 6–1, 6–3; beat H. Rochon (Can.) 6–2, 6–1, 6–3. F. GUERRERO (MEX.) beat W. Stohlberg (Can.) 12–10, 6–1, 6–2; lost to H. ROCHON (CAN.) 2–6, 5–7, 4–6.

Doubles: A. VEGA and G. PALAFOX (MEX.) beat B. Macken and J. Macken (Can.) 6–2, 6–3, 6–4.

In the zone final Australia beat Mexico at Mexico City on August 6, 7, and 8 by four to one. The Australian team was A. K. Quist and O. W. Sidwell in the singles and C. F. Long and G. E. Brown in the doubles. The Mexican team was G. Palafox and A. Vega in singles and doubles. Vega played very well, extending Sidwell to five sets and beating Quist in three. The Australian pair dominated the doubles, losing only four games in three sets. On the third day F. Guerrero played in place of Palafox against Sidwell, but could not win a set.

Detailed Results

Singles: A. K. QUIST (AUSTRAL.) beat G. Palafox (Mex.) 6–4, 6–1, 6–4; lost to A. VEGA (MEX.) 7–9, 4–6, 2–6. O. W. SIDWELL (AUSTRAL.) beat A. Vega (Mex.) 2–6, 8–6, 3–6, 6–4, 7–5; beat F. Guerrero (Mex.) 6–1, 6–4, 6–2.

Doubles: C. F. LONG and G. E. BROWN (AUSTRAL.) beat A. Vega and G. Palafox (Mex.) 6–0, 6–2, 6–2.

Inter-zone Round

The tie between the winners of the European Zone, Czechoslovakia, and the winners of the American Zone, Australia, was played at Boston commencing on August 19. Australia won by the odd-match margin at three to two.

The Czechs played their usual two-man team—J. Drobny and V. Cernik in singles and doubles. The Australians played four men, A. K. Quist and O. W. Sidwell in the singles and C. F. Long and G. E. Brown in the doubles. On the first day Australia got a flying start when Quist beat Cernik in three sets and Sidwell beat Drobny in four, the last two of which were divided and required the playing of forty-six games. On the second day Drobny and Cernik beat Long and Brown in four sets, to keep the tie alive. On the third day Drobny beat Quist to even the tie, in the longest single yet recorded in Davis Cup annals. Quist won the first two sets, but Drobny hung on to take the third set in its thirty-fourth game, and finally to win the match at 7–5 in the fifth set, after seventy-eight games had been played. With the tie all square Sidwell beat Cernik in straight sets, to put his country once again into the challenge round against the holders, U.S.A.

Detailed Results

Singles: A. K. Quist (Austral.) beat V. Cernik (Czech.) 6–2, 13–11, 6–0 ; lost to J. Drobny (Czech.) 8–6, 6–3, 16–18, 3–6, 5–7. O. W. Sidwell (Austral.) beat J. Drobny (Czech.) 6–3, 6–2, 9–11, 14–12 ; beat V. Cernik (Czech.) 7–5, 6–4, 6–2.

Doubles: C. F. Long and G. E. Brown (Austral.) lost to J. Drobny and V. Cernik (Czech.) 8–10, 6–4, 3–6, 4–6.

Challenge Round

Australia, the challengers, met U.S.A., the holders, in this final tie for 1948 at Forest Hills, New York, on September 4, 5, and 6. U.S.A. won easily by five to none. The defending American team was F. A. Parker and F. R. Schroeder in the singles and G. Mulloy and W. F. Talbert in the doubles. The Australian challenging team was O. W. Sidwell and A. K.

Quist in the singles and Sidwell and C. F. Long in the doubles. On the first day Parker beat Sidwell in three ten-game sets, and Schroeder beat Quist in four sets, winning twelve straight games after Quist had evened the match at one set all. On the second day Sidwell and Long put up a good fight before going down in four sets to Mulloy and Talbert. On the last day neither Quist nor Sidwell could get anything like a set against Parker and Schroeder respectively.

And so U.S.A. were champions again for the sixteenth time in thirty-seven years of competition.

Detailed Results

Singles: F. A. PARKER (U.S.A.) beat O. W. Sidwell (Austral.) 6–4, 6–4, 6–4 ; beat A. K. Quist (Austral.) 6–2, 6–2, 6–3. F. R. SCHROEDER (U.S.A.) beat A. K. Quist (Austral.) 6–3, 4–6, 6–0, 6–0 ; beat O. W. Sidwell (Austral.) 6–2, 6–1, 6–1.

Doubles: W. F. TALBERT and G. MULLOY (U.S.A.) beat O. W. Sidwell and C. F. Long (Austral.) 8–6, 9–7, 2–6, 7–5.

THE PLAYERS AND THE TEAMS, 1900–48

This list does not include those players who, though members of their countries' Davis Cup teams, did not take part in any tie.

ARGENTINA

1926 W. Robson
E. M. Obarrio
1928 W. Robson
R. Boyd
1931 L. del Castillo
A. Zappa
W. Robson
A. R. Sissener
R. Boyd
1933 A. H. Cattaruzza
W. Robson
A. Zappa
L. del Castillo
G. Echeverria
1936 L. del Castillo
A. Zappa
1948 E. Morea
H. Weiss
A. Russell

AUSTRALASIA

1905 N. E. Brookes
A. F. Wilding
A. W. Dunlop
1906 A. F. Wilding
L. O. S. Poidevin
1907 N. E. Brookes
A. F. Wilding
1908 N. E. Brookes
A. F. Wilding
1909 N. E. Brookes
A. F. Wilding
1911 N. E. Brookes
R. W. Heath
A. W. Dunlop
1912 N. E. Brookes
R. W. Heath
A. W. Dunlop
1913 H. Rice
S. N. Doust
A. B. Jones
1914 N. E. Brookes
A. F. Wilding
1919 G. L. Patterson
J. O. Anderson
N. E. Brookes
1920 N. E. Brookes
G. L. Patterson
1921 J. O. Anderson
J. B. Hawkes
C. V. Todd
N. Peach
1922 J. O. Anderson
G. L. Patterson
P. O'Hara Wood
R. C. Wertheim

After 1922 *Australia and New Zealand challenged separately, and the name Australasia thus passed from the competition.*

AUSTRALIA

1923 J. O. Anderson
J.B. Hawkes
1923 R. E. Schlesinger
I. McInnes
1924 G. L. Patterson
P. O'Hara Wood
1925 J. O. Anderson
G. L. Patterson
J. B. Hawkes
1928 G. L. Patterson
J. H. Crawford
H. C. Hopman
1930 J. H. Crawford
H. C. Hopman
E. F. Moon
J. Willard
1932 J. H. Crawford
H. C. Hopman
C. Sproule
1933 J. H. Crawford
V. B. McGrath
A. K. Quist
D. P. Turnbull
1934 J. H. Crawford
V. B. McGrath
A. K. Quist
D. P. Turnbull
1935 J. H. Crawford
V. B. McGrath
A. K. Quist
1936 J. H. Crawford
V. B. McGrath
A. K. Quist
1937 J. H. Crawford
V. B. McGrath
A. K. Quist
J. E. Bromwich
1938 A. K. Quist
J. E. Bromwich
L. Schwartz
1939 A. K. Quist
J. E. Bromwich
1946 J. E. Bromwich
D. Pails
A. K. Quist
1947 J. E. Bromwich
D. Pails
C. F. Long
G. E. Brown
1948 A. K. Quist
O. W. Sidwell
C. F. Long
G. E. Brown

AUSTRIA

1905 R. Kinzl
C. von Wessely
1924 Count L. Salm
P. Brick
Count O. Salm
1925 Count L. Salm
P. Brick
M. Relly
1927 F. Matejka
H. W. Artens
Count L. Salm
1928 F. Matejka
H. W. Artens
Count L. Salm
1929 F. Matejka
H. W. Artens
1930 F. Matejka
H. W. Artens
1931 F. Matejka
H. W. Artens
M. Haberl
1932 F. Matejka
H. W. Artens
R. Kinzel
1933 H. W. Artens
F. Matejka
R. Kinzel
A. Bawarowski
1934 F. Matejka
G. von Metaxa
H. W. Artens
W. Brosch
1936 A. Bawarowski
G. von Metaxa
1937 A. Bawarowski
G. von Metaxa
H. Redl

In 1938 *Austria was incorporated in the German Reich, and ceased to compete as a separate nation. She returned to the competition in* 1948.

1948 H. Redl
A. Specht

BELGIUM

1904 P. de Borman
W. Lemaire
1913 P. de Borman
A. G. Watson
W. H. Duvivier
1914 A. G. Watson
P. de Borman
W. H. Duvivier
1919 P. de Borman
M. Lammens
1921 J. Washer
M. Lammens
1922 J. Washer
A. G. Watson
1923 J. Washer
A. G. Watson
1924 J. Washer
A. G. Watson
1925 J. Washer
A. G. Watson
1926 J. Washer
A. Laloux
G. François
1927 J. Washer
H. W. Botsford
1928 M. Iweins d'Eeckhoutte
A. Ewbank
A. Lacroix
1929 A. Lacroix
A. Ewbank

1930 A. Lacroix
A. Ewbank
L. de Borman
1931 L. de Borman
A. Lacroix
1932 A. Lacroix
M. Iweins d'Eeckhoutte
G. van Zuylen
L. de Borman
1933 L. de Borman
A. Lacroix
1934 L. de Borman
A. Lacroix
G. van Zuylen
C. Naeyaert
1935 C. Naeyaert
A. Lacroix
L. de Borman
1936 A. Lacroix
P. Geelhand
J. van den Eynde
L. de Borman
1937 C. Naeyaert
A. Lacroix
L. de Borman
P. Geelhand
1938 C. Naeyaert
A. Lacroix
L. de Borman
P. Geelhand
J. van den Eynde
1939 A. Lacroix
C. Naeyaert
P. Geelhand
J. van den Eynde
L. de Borman
1946 J. van den Eynde
P. Washer
P. Geelhand
J. Peten
1947 P. Washer
J. Peten
P. Geelhand
A. Lacroix
1948 J. Peten
P. Washer
P. Geelhand

BRAZIL

1932 N. Cruz
R. Pernambuco
I. Simone
1935 S. L. Campos
I. Simone
T. de Freitas
1948 E. Petersen
M. Fernandez

BRITISH ISLES

1900 A. W. Gore
E. D. Black
H. Roper Barrett
1902 J. Pim
R. F. Doherty
H. L. Doherty
1903 R. F. Doherty
H. L. Doherty
1904 H. L. Doherty
F. L. Riseley
R. F. Doherty
1905 H. L. Doherty
S. H. Smith
R. F. Doherty
1906 H. L. Doherty
S. H. Smith
R. F. Doherty
1907 A. W. Gore
H. Roper Barrett
1908 M. J. G. Ritchie
J. C. Parke
1909 C. P. Dixon
J. C. Parke
W. C. Crawley
1911 C. P. Dixon
A. H. Lowe
A. E. Beamish
1912 C. P. Dixon
A. W. Gore
H. Roper Barrett
J. C. Parke
A. E. Beamish
1913 J. C. Parke
C. P. Dixon
H. Roper Barrett
1914 J. C. Parke
T. M. Mavrogordato
H. Roper Barrett
A. H. Lowe
1919 A. R. F. Kingscote
T. M. Mavrogordato
H. Roper Barrett
P. M. Davson
O. G. N. Turnbull
A. H. Lowe
A. E. Beamish
1920 J. C. Parke
A. R. F. Kingscote
1921 F. G. Lowe
R. Lycett
M. Woosnam
O. G. N. Turnbull
1922 A. R. F. Kingscote
F. G. Lowe
F. L. Riseley

After 1922 *Great Britain and Ireland challenged separately. The name British Isles, therefore, no longer appeared in the competition.*

CANADA

1913 R. B. Powell
B. P. Schwengers
1914 R. B. Powell
B. P. Schwengers
1921 E. H. Laframbois
P. Bennett
G. D. Holmes
1923 W. Crocker
W. Le Roy Rennie
J. Wright
1924 J. Wright
W. Crocker
1925 J. Wright
W. Crocker
1926 J. Wright
W. Crocker
1927 J. Wright
W. Crocker
G. Nunns
1928 J. Wright
W. Crocker
A. Ham
1929 J. Wright
W. Crocker
A. Ham
1930 J. Wright
M. Rainville
W. Crocker
1931 J. Wright
M. Rainville
1932 J. Wright
M. Rainville
1933 J. Wright
M. Rainville
G. Nunns
1934 M. Rainville
G. Nunns
W. Martin
M. Laird Watt
1938 R. Murray
D. Cameron
Ross Wilson
M. Laird Watt
1939 B. Hall
E. Tarshis
W. Pedlar
P. Pearson
1946 B. Macken
H. Rochon
D. McDiarmed
M. Laird Watt
1947 B. Macken
H. Rochon
G. McNiel
E. Lanthier
1948 H. Rochon
B. Macken
J. Macken
W. Stohlberg

CHILE

1928 D. I. Tarralva
L. Tarralva
1929 D. I. Tarralva
L. Tarralva
1931 E. Schronherr
L. Page
R. Conrads
H. Müller
1933 E. Deik
S. Deik
E. Schronherr

CHINA

1924 W. Lock Wei
P. Kong
C. K. Huang
1928 P. Kong
G. Lum
1935 G. Cheng
Kho Sin Kie
1936 Kho Sin Kie
G. Cheng
G. Lum
1937 Kho Sin Kie
W. C. Choy
Tsui Wai Pui
1939 Kho Sin Kie
W. C. Choy
J. H. Ho
1946 Kho Sin Kie
W. C. Choy
K. Lo

CUBA

1924 R. Paris
V. Banet
I. Zagas
Vellaba
1925 V. Banet
R. Paris
R. Chacon
1926 V. Banet
R. Paris
R. Chacon
1927 V. Banet
R. Paris
R. Chacon
1928 R. Paris
V. Banet
1929 V. Banet
G. Vollmer
R. Morales
G. Upmann
1932 G. Vollmer

1932 R. Morales
1933 R. Morales
L. Nodarse
A. Randin
1935 A. Randin
J. Etcheverry
L. Nodarse
J. Aguero
1939 R. Morales
J. Aguero
L. Nodarse
1948 J. Etcheverry
J. Aguero
R. Morales

CZECHOSLOVAKIA

1921 K. Ardelt
M. Zemla
Just
1922 F. von Röhrer
K. Ardelt
1923 M. Zemla
F. von Röhrer
1924 F. von Röhrer
M. Zemla
J. Kozeluh
P. Macenauer
1925 M. Zemla
P. Macenauer
J. Kozeluh
1926 M. Zemla
P. Macenauer
J. Kozeluh
1927 J. Kozeluh
M. Gottlieb
F. Soyka
M. Zemla
F. von Röhrer
1928 J. Kozeluh
P. Macenauer
R. Menzel
1929 J. Kozeluh
P. Macenauer
R. Menzel
J. Malecek
1930 J. Kozeluh
R. Menzel
F. von Röhrer
1931 R. Menzel
L. Hecht
F. von Röhrer
F. Marsalek
1932 R. Menzel
L. Hecht
F. von Röhrer
F. Marsalek
1933 R. Menzel
F. Marsalek
J. Siba
L. Hecht
1934 R. Menzel
L. Hecht
F. Marsalek
1935 R. Menzel
J. Caska
L. Hecht
J. Malecek
1936 L. Hecht
J. Malecek
J. Siba
1937 R. Menzel
L. Hecht
J. Siba
J. Caska
F. Cejnar
1938 R. Menzel
L. Hecht
F. Cejnar
1946 J. Drobny
1946 J. Vodicka
J. Caska
1947 J. Drobny
V. Cernik
V. Vbra
1948 J. Drobny
V. Vbra
V. Zabrodsky
V. Cernik

DENMARK

1921 V. Ingersley
E. Tegner
P. Henriksen
1922 E. Tegner
V. Ingersley
E. Worm
1923 E. Tegner
E. Worm
H. Larsen
1924 A. Petersen
E. Ulrich
Thalbitzer
E. Worm
E. Tegner
1925 E. Worm
E. Ulrich
P. Henriksen
A. Petersen
1926 A. Petersen
E. Ulrich
P. Henriksen
1927 A. Petersen
E. Ulrich
P. Henriksen
E. Worm
1928 E. Ulrich
A. Petersen
P. Henriksen
1929 P. Henriksen
E. Ulrich
1930 E. Ulrich
E. Worm
1931 E. Ulrich
P. Henriksen
E. Worm
1932 P. Henriksen
E. Ulrich
A. Jacobsen
1933 E. Ulrich
A. Jacobsen
P. Henriksen
1934 A. Jacobsen
E. Ulrich
P. Henriksen
1935 E. Ulrich
A. Jacobsen
1936 N. K. Koerner
H. Plougmann
E. Ulrich
1938 H. Plougmann
F. Bekevold
E. Ulrich
N. K. Koerner
1939 N. Holst
H. Plougmann
A. Wium
1946 W. Rasmussen
J. Ipsen
E. Bjerre
P. Thielsen
1948 T. Ulrich
K. Nielsen

EGYPT

1929 J. Grandguillot
L. Wahid
N. Zahar
R. Danon
1930 J. Grandguillot
L. Wahid
N. Zahar
Riches
1931 J. Grandguillot
L. Wahid
A. Shukri
P. Grandguillot
1932 J. Grandguillot
P. Grandguillot
L. Wahid
1933 L. Wahid
A. Shukri
A. Bogdagli
1946 A. Shafie
A. Najar
M. Talaat
J. Grandguillot
1947 A. Najar
A. Shafie
M. Talaat
M. Coen
1948 A. Najar
A. Shafie
M. Coen

ESTONIA

1935 R. Lassen
H. Pukk

FINLAND

1928 A. Grahn
R. Granholm
B. Grotenfelt
1929 A. Grahn
R. Granholm
B. Grotenfelt
1930 A. Grahn
R. Granholm
B. Grotenfelt
1931 A. Grahn
B. Grotenfelt
1932 B. Grotenfelt
A. Biaudet
1933 B. Grotenfelt
A. Grahn

FRANCE

1904 M. Decugis
P. Ayme
1905 M. Decugis
M. Germot
1912 M. Decugis
A. H. Gobert
W. H. Laurentz
1913 A. H. Gobert
M. Decugis
M. Germot
1914 M. Decugis
M. Germot
1919 M. Decugis
W. H. Laurentz
A. H. Gobert
1920 A. H. Gobert
W. H. Laurentz
1921 W. H. Laurentz
J. Samazeuilh
J. Brugnon
1922 J. Borotra
H. Cochet
J. Couitéas
A. H. Gobert
1923 H. Cochet
R. Lacoste
J. Brugnon
P. Hirsch
J. Samazeuilh
P. Blanchy
1924 J. Couitéas

1924 R. Lacoste
J. Brugnon
H. Cochet
J. Borotra
1925 J. Borotra
R. Lacoste
P. Feret
J. Brugnon
1926 R. Lacoste
J. Brugnon
H. Cochet
J. Borotra
1927 R. Lacoste
J. Borotra
J. Brugnon
H. Cochet
1928 R. Lacoste
H. Cochet
J. Borotra
1929 H. Cochet
J. Borotra
1930 J. Borotra
H. Cochet
J. Brugnon
1931 J. Borotra
H. Cochet
J. Brugnon
1932 J. Borotra
H. Cochet
J. Brugnon
1933 H. Cochet
A. Merlin
J. Borotra
J. Brugnon
1934 C. Boussus
A. Merlin
J. Brugnon
J. Borotra
1935 C. Boussus
A. Merlin
J. Borotra
M. Bernard
1936 C. Boussus
B. Destremau
J. Borotra
M. Bernard
1937 B. Destremau
M. Bernard
Y. Petra
J. Borotra
C. Boussus
1938 B. Destremau
Y. Petra
H. Bolelli
P. Pellizza
J. Lesueur
1939 B. Destremau
C. Boussus
Y. Petra
P. Pellizza
1946 Y. Petra
P. Pellizza
B. Destremau
M. Bernard
1947 B. Destremau
M. Bernard
P. Pellizza
R. Abdesselam
J. Borotra
Y. Petra
1948 M. Bernard
B. Destremau
H. Bolelli
R. Abdesselam

GERMANY

1913 O. Kreuzer
F. W. Rahe
H. Kleinschroth
O. Froitzheim
1914 O. Froitzheim
O. Kreuzer
1927 G. Demasius
F. W. Rahe
H. Moldenhauer
O. Froitzheim
H. Landmann
H. Kleinschroth
1928 O. Froitzheim
Dr Buss
H. Kleinschroth
K. Bergmann
H. Moldenhauer
D. Prenn
1929 H. Moldenhauer
D. Prenn
H. Landmann
H. Kleinschroth
1930 H. Landmann
D. Prenn
H. Kleinschroth
W. Dessart
1931 Dr Buss
E. Nourney
W. Dessart
1932 D. Prenn
G. von Cramm
E. Nourney
W. Dessart
G. Jaenecke
1933 G. von Cramm
E. Nourney
G. Jaenecke
F. Kuhlmann
1934 G. von Cramm
E. Nourney
F. Frenz
H. Denker
1935 G. von Cramm
H. Henkel
H. Denker
K. Lund
1936 G. von Cramm
H. Henkel
H. Denker
K. Lund
1937 G. von Cramm
H. Henkel
H. Denker
E. Dettmer
1938 H. Henkel
G. von Metaxa
R. Goepfert
H. Redl
1939 H. Henkel
G. von Metaxa
H. Redl
R. Menzel
R. Goepfert

GREAT BRITAIN

1923 R. Lycett
J. B. Gilbert
L. A. Godfree
J. D. P. Wheatley
1924 A. R. F. Kingscote
J. B. Gilbert
L. A. Godfree
M. Woosnam
J. D. P. Wheatley
1925 F. G. Lowe
J. D. P. Wheatley
L. A. Godfree
C. H. Kingsley
J. B. Gilbert
O. G. N. Turnbull
G. R. O. Crole-Rees
1926 O. G. N. Turnbull
J. D. P. Wheatley
G. R. O. Crole-Rees
1926 C. H. Kingsley
J. C. Gregory
H. K. Lester
1927 C. H. Kingsley
E. Higgs
J. C. Gregory
L. A. Godfree
1928 J. C. Gregory
E. Higgs
G. R. O. Crole-Rees
C. G. Eames
1929 H. W. Austin
G. P. Hughes
G. R. O. Crole-Rees
C. G. Eames
J. C. Gregory
I. G. Collins
1930 H. W. Austin
H. G. N. Lee
J. C. Gregory
I. G. Collins
N. Sharpe
1931 H. W. Austin
F. J. Perry
C. H. Kingsley
G. P. Hughes
1932 F. J. Perry
G. P. Hughes
H. F. David
H. G. N. Lee
H. W. Austin
1933 F. J. Perry
H. W. Austin
G. P. Hughes
H. G. N. Lee
1934 F. J. Perry
H. W. Austin
G. P. Hughes
H. G. N. Lee
1935 F. J. Perry
H. W. Austin
G. P. Hughes
C. R. D. Tuckey
1936 F. J. Perry
H. W. Austin
G. P. Hughes
C. R. D. Tuckey
1937 H. W. Austin
C. E. Hare
C. R. D. Tuckey
F. H. D. Wilde
1938 R. A. Shayes
C. M. Jones
F. H. D. Wilde
D. W. Butler
1939 R. A. Shayes
C. E. Hare
F. H. D. Wilde
L. Shaffi
1946 D. W. Barton
D. MacPhail
J. S. Olliff
H. Billington
1947 D. W. Barton
A. J. Mottram
G. L. Paish
D. W. Butler
1948 A. J. Mottram
G. L. Paish
H. Billington
H. F. Walton

GREECE

1927 A. J. Zerlendi
M. Zachos
1928 A. J. Zerlendi
M. Balli
1929 A. J. Zerlendi
C. Efstratiades
K. Georgiades

1929 G. Zafiropoulo
1930 A. J. Zerlendi
O. Garangiotis
M. Balli
1931 A. J. Zerlendi
O. Garangiotis
M. Balli
K. Georgiades
G. Nicholaides
1932 M. Balli
O. Garangiotis
K. Georgiades
G. Nicholaides
1933 G. Nicholaides
S. Xydis
L. Stalios
1934 L. Stalios
S. Xydis
1935 L. Stalios
K. Zachos
1936 L. Stalios
G. Nicholaides
1937 L. Stalios
G. Nicholaides
1938 L. Stalios
J. Michailides
1947 L. Stalios
Manouilidis
G. Nicholaides

HAWAII

1923 B. Detrick
W. N. Ecklund

HUNGARY

1924 I. de Takacs
B. von Kehrling
Dr Peteri
1925 I. de Takacs
B. von Kehrling
Kelemen
1926 B. von Kehrling
I. de Takacs
1927 I. de Takacs
B. von Kehrling
Dr Peteri
1928 I. de Takacs
B. von Kehrling
Dr Peteri
1929 B. von Kehrling
I. de Takacs
Dr Peteri
K. Aschner
1930 B. von Kehrling
I. de Takacs
K. Aschner
1931 B. von Kehrling
I. de Takacs
E. Gabrowitz
1932 B. von Kehrling
E. Gabrowitz
1933 E. Gabrowitz
B. von Kehrling
Count Zichy
1934 B. von Kehrling
E. Gabrowitz
1935 E. Gabrowitz
F. Straub
Count Zichy
E. Ferenczy
1936 E. Gabrowitz
G. Dallos
E. Ferenczy
E. Gabory
1937 E. Gabory
G. Dallos
E. Ferenczy
1938 E. Gabory
G. Dallos
J. Asboth
1939 E. Gabory
J. Asboth
G. Dallos
M. Csikos
1948 J. Asboth
J. Adam
A. Feher
A. Stolpa

INDIA

1921 M. Sleem
S. M. Jacob
L. S. Deane
A. A. Fyzee
A. H. Fyzee
1922 A. A. Fyzee
A. H. Fyzee
C. Ramaswami
1923 S. M. Jacob
A. H. Fyzee
L. S. Deane
1924 S. M. Jacob
M. Sleem
S. M. Hadi
A. H. Fyzee
1925 S. M. Jacob
E. B. Andreae
S. M. Hadi
Jagat Mohan Lal
A. H. Fyzee
1926 A. A. Fyzee
A. H. Fyzee
S. W. Bobb
1927 K. Prasada
A. H. Fyzee
1928 M. Sleem
E. V. Bobb
A. M. D. Pitt
H. L. Soni
1930 J. Charanjiva
H. L. Soni
A. Madan Mohan
1932 A. Madan Mohan
J. Charanjiva
K. Prasada
1934 M. Bhandari
M. Sleem
A. E. Browne
1938 S. L. R. Sawhney
Ghaus Mohammed
1939 Ghaus Mohammed
Y. Savoor
1947 Ghaus Mohammed
D. K. Bose
S. C. Misra
J. M. Mehta
1948 S. C. Misra
D. K. Bose
S. L. R. Sawhney

IRELAND

1923 Hon. C. Campbell
E. D. McCrea
S. F. Scroope
L. A. Meldon
1924 E. D. McCrea
H. V. S. Dillon
L. A. Meldon
1925 C. F. Scroope
L. A. Meldon
S. F. Scroope
1926 E. A. McGuire
L. A. Meldon
B. Haughton
1927 Hon. C. Campbell
A. St J. Mahony
L. A. Meldon
1928 C. F. Scroope
C. H. D. O'Callaghan
1929 G. L. Rogers
E. A. McGuire
N. G. Holmes
1930 E. A. McGuire
G. L. Rogers
V. Allman Smith
1931 G. L. Rogers
E. A. McGuire
C. F. Scroope
1932 G. L. Rogers
E. A. McGuire
1933 G. L. Rogers
T. G. McVeagh
E. A. McGuire
1934 G. L. Rogers
E. A. McGuire
T. G. McVeagh
1935 G. L. Rogers
E. A. McGuire
T. G. McVeagh
1936 G. L. Rogers
T. G. McVeagh
1937 G. L. Rogers
T. G. McVeagh
1938 G. L. Rogers
T. G. McVeagh
H. J. Ryan
1939 G. L. Rogers
R. F. Egan
1946 R. F. Egan
C. A. Kemp
1947 C. A. Kemp
R. F. Egan
J. R. McHale
1948 C. A. Kemp
T. G. McVeagh
G. P. Jackson

ITALY

1922 C. Colombo
Count Balbi
di Robecco
1923 H. L. de Morpurgo
C. Colombo
1924 H. L. de Morpurgo
C. Colombo
1925 H. L. de Morpurgo
C. Serventi
P. Gaslini
C. Colombo
1926 H. L. de Morpurgo
C. Serventi
1927 H. L. de Morpurgo
G. de Stefani
1928 H. L. de Morpurgo
G. de Stefani
P. Gaslini
1929 H. L. de Morpurgo
G. de Stefani
A. del Bono
1930 H. L. de Morpurgo
G. de Stefani
P. Gaslini
1931 H. L. de Morpurgo
G. de Stefani
A. del Bono
1932 G. de Stefani
O. de Minerbi
A. del Bono
A. Sertorio
G. Palmieri
1933 H. L. de Morpurgo
G. de Stefani
A. Rado
V. Taroni
1934 G. de Stefani
A. Sertorio
V. Taroni

1934 F. Quintavalle
A. Rado
1935 G. de Stefani
S. Mangold
F. Quintavalle
V. Taroni
1937 G. de Stefani
V. Canapele
F. Quintavalle
V. Taroni
1938 G. de Stefani
V. Canapele
F. Quintavalle
V. Taroni
L. Bossi
1939 G. de Stefani
V. Canapele
G. Vido
G. Cucelli
V. Taroni
1948 G. Cucelli
M. del Bello

JAPAN

1921 Z. Shimizu
I. Kumagae
1923 Z. Shimizu
M. Fukuda
S. Kashio
1924 Z. Shimizu
S. Okamoto
T. Harada
1925 T. Harada
Z. Shimizu
M. Fukuda
1926 T. Harada
T. Toba
T. Tawara
1927 Y. Ohta
T. Harada
Z. Shimizu
T. Toba
1928 Y. Ohta
T. Toba
T. Abe
1929 T. Abe
Y. Ohta
1930 Y. Ohta
T. Harada
H. Satoh
T. Abe
1931 J. Satoh
H. Satoh
M. Kawachi
1932 J. Satoh
T. Kuwabara
R. Miki
1933 J. Satoh
R. Nunoi
1934 J. Fujikura
J. Yamagishi
H. Nishimura
1935 J. Yamagishi
H. Nishimura
1937 J. Yamagishi
F. Nakano
1938 J. Yamagishi
F. Nakano

LUXEMBOURG

1947 G. Wampach
G. Wertheim
1948 G. Wampach
G. Wertheim

MEXICO

1924 M. Llano
I. de la Borbolla
F. Gerdes
1925 I. de la Borbolla
C. Butlin
1926 M. Llano
A. Unda
Lozano
C. Butlin
1927 R. Kinsey
A. Unda
C. Butlin
1928 R. Kinsey
A. Unda
R. Tapia
1929 I. de la Borbolla
R. Tapia
R. Kinsey
A. Unda
1930 I. de la Borbolla
R. Tapia
M. Llano
F. Sendel
A. Unda
1931 A. Unda
R. Tapia
M. Llano
J. Acosta
1932 A. Unda
R. Tapia
E. Mestre
1933 R. Tapia
E. Mestre
A. Unda
E. Reyes
1934 E. Reyes
R. Tapia
E. Mestre
A. Roldan
1935 E. Reyes
D. Hernandez
A. Unda
M. Llano
1936 E. Reyes
D. Hernandez
E. Mestre
F. Martinez
1937 E. Reyes
R. Tapia
A. Unda
D. Hernandez
1938 R. Tapia
D. Hernandez
1939 R. Tapia
D. Hernandez
1946 A. Vega
R. Vega
F. Guerrero
1948 A. Vega
F. Guerrero
G. Palafox

MONACO

1929 R. Gallèpe
V. Landau
1930 R. Gallèpe
V. Landau
1931 V. Landau
R. Gallèpe
1932 V. Landau
R. Gallèpe
1933 V. Landau
R. Gallèpe
1934 V. Landau
R. Gallèpe
G. Medecin
1935 V. Landau
R. Gallèpe
1936 V. Landau
R. Gallèpe
1937 V. Landau
G. Medecin
1938 G. Medecin
A. Noghes
V. Landau
1939 G. Medecin
A. Noghes
V. Landau
1946 V. Landau
R. Gallèpe
1947 A. Noghes
G. Medecin
V. Landau

THE NETHERLANDS

1920 C. J. van Lennep
A. Diemer Kool
1923 C. J. van Lennep
A. Diemer Kool
Van der Feen
H. Timmer
C. A. Bryan
1924 C. J. van Lennep
H. Timmer
1925 A. Diemer Kool
H. Timmer
C. J. van Lennep
1926 C. J. van Lennep
H. Timmer
A. Diemer Kool
C. A. Bryan
1927 H. Timmer
C. A. Bryan
C. J. van Lennep
1928 H. Timmer
A. Diemer Kool
O. Koopman
C. J. van Lennep
1929 A. Diemer Kool
H. Timmer
1930 A. Diemer Kool
H. Timmer
1931 Knappert
I. van der Heide
1932 H. Timmer
T. Hughan
O. Koopman
1933 H. Timmer
T. Hughan
O. Koopman
A. Diemer Kool
G. Leembruggen
1934 H. Timmer
W. Karsten
G. W. Scheurleer
O. Koopman
1935 H. Timmer
J. H. Knottenbelt
O. Koopman
T. Hughan
D. Teshmacher
1936 H. Timmer
T. Hughan
W. Karsten
1937 D. Teshmacher
T. Hughan
A. C. van Swol
1938 T. Hughan
A. C. van Swol
1939 T. Hughan
A. C. van Swol
1946 A. C. van Swol
I. Rinkel
1947 A. C. van Swol
I. Rinkel
H. Wilton
1948 A. C. van Swol
I. Rinkel
R. van Meegeren

NEW ZEALAND

1924 F. M. B. Fisher

1924 J. C. Peacock
1928 E. D. Andrews
R. R. T. Young
1934 E. D. Andrews
C. E. Malfroy
A. C. Stedman
1935 E. D. Andrews
C. E. Malfroy
A. C. Stedman
1937 E. D. Andrews
C. E. Malfroy
A. C. Stedman
D. C. Coombe
1939 C. E. Malfroy
D. C. Coombe
A. D. Brown
1947 R. S. McKenzie
J. E. Robson
J. A. Barry

NORWAY

1928 T. Torkildsen
R. Christoffersen
1929 T. Torkildsen
J. Neilsen
1930 T. Torkildsen
J. Neilsen
R. Christoffersen
1931 T. Torkildsen
J. Neilsen
R. Christoffersen
O. Fagerstroem
1932 T. Torkildsen
J. Haanes
R. Hagen
F. T. Smith
1933 J. Haanes
F. T. Smith
R. Hagen
1934 J. Haanes
F. T. Smith
R. Hagen
1935 J. Haanes
F. T. Smith
1936 J. Haanes
F. Jenssen
1937 F. Jenssen
A. Bjurstedt
J. Beer
1938 J. Haanes
F. Jenssen
1939 J. Haanes
S. Rinde
L. Anderson
1947 J. Haanes
J. Staubo
D. Brem
1948 J. Haanes
J. Staubo

PAKISTAN

1948 I. Ahmed
S. Alam

PARAGUAY

1931 A. Cusmanich
A. Portaluppi
I. Ubaldi
L. Sosa
H. R. Walters

PHILIPPINES

1926 F. Aragon
G. Aragon
1928 Aragon
Ingayo
1939 F. Ampon
A. Sanchez
1946 F. Ampon
A. Sanchez
C. L. Carmona

POLAND

1925 M. Sjwede
M. Soerster
M. Kuchar
J. Steinart
1926 R. Kleinadel
S. Czetwertynski
J. Steinart
1927 S. Czetwertynski
R. Kleinadel
M. Stolarow
1928 M. Stolarow
G. Stolarow
P. Warminski
1929 M. Stolarow
A. Tarnowski
J. Loth
1930 I. Tloczynski
M. Stolarow
G. Stolarow
P. Warminski
1931 J. Hebda
I. Tloczynski
M. Stolarow
1932 I. Tloczynski
M. Stolarow
G. Stolarow
J. Hebda
P. Warminski
1933 I. Tloczynski
J. Hebda
1934 I. Tloczynski
J. Hebda
E. Wittmann
1935 I. Tloczynski
K. Tarlowski
E. Wittmann
J. Hebda
M. Stolarow
W. Bratek
1936 J. Hebda
I. Tloczynski
K. Tarlowski
1937 J. Hebda
I. Tloczynski
K. Tarlowski
1938 J. Hebda
I. Tloczynski
C. Spychala
1939 J. Hebda
I. Tloczynski
A. Bawarowski
1947 J. Hebda
W. Sconecki

PORTUGAL

1925 J. de Verda
A. Casanovas
F. de Vasconcelos
1926 J. de Verda
A. Casanovas
F. de Vasconcelos
1927 J. de Verda
A. Casanovas
1928 A. Pinto Coelho
J. de Verda
F. de Vasconcelos
1948 Roquette
Ricciardi
da Silva

RUMANIA

1922 N. Mishu
M. Steen
1925 N. Mishu
1925 Dr Luppu
1926 N. Mishu
A. San Galli
1927 N. Mishu
G. Poulieff
1928 N. Mishu
Dr Luppu
L. Dorner
1929 N. Mishu
Dr Luppu
L. Dorner
1930 N. Mishu
G. Poulieff
1931 N. Mishu
C. Bunea
1932 N. Mishu
G. Poulieff
1933 T. Rety
G. Poulieff
A. Botez
1934 G. Poulieff
A. Cantacuzene
1935 A. Hamburger
O. Schmidt
1937 C. Caralulis
O. Schmidt
1938 C. Caralulis
O. Schmidt
1939 C. Caralulis
O. Schmidt
1948 C. Caralulis
G. Viziru

SOUTH AFRICA

1913 R. F. Le Sueur
V. R. Gauntlett
1919 G. H. Dodd
L. Raymond
H. Aitken
1920 L. Raymond
C. L. Winslow
1924 P. D. B. Spence
I. Richardson
L. Raymond
1926 P. D. B. Spence
J. Lezard
G. R. Sherwell
1927 J. Condon
P. D. B. Spence
L. Raymond
1929 L. Raymond
C. J. J. Robbins
N. G. Farquharson
1931 V. G. Kirby
P. D. B. Spence
L. Raymond
N. G. Farquharson
1933 V. G. Kirby
C. J. J. Robbins
N. G. Farquharson
J. Condon
1935 N. G. Farquharson
V. G. Kirby
M. Bertram
1937 N. G. Farquharson
V. G. Kirby
E. E. Fannin
1947 E. E. Fannin
E. W. Sturgess

SPAIN

1921 Count de Gomar
M. Alonso
1922 Count de Gomar
M. Alonso
E. Flaquer
1923 Count de Gomar
E. Flaquer
1924 M. Alonso

1924 J. M. Alonso
E. Flaquer
1925 M. Alonso
J. M. Alonso
E. Flaquer
1926 N. F. Sindreu
A. Juanico
E. Flaquer
J. Morales
1927 E. Flaquer
A. Juanico
J. Morales
1928 E. Flaquer
J. Morales
A. Juanico
N. F. Sindreu
1929 E. Maier
J. Tejada
N. F. Sindreu
1930 E. Maier
A. Juanico
Saprissa
N. F. Sindreu
1931 E. Maier
M. Alonso
1932 E. Maier
A. Juanico
J. Tejada
1933 E. Maier
N. F. Sindreu
A. Durall
1934 E. Maier
A. Suque
A. Durall
1936 M. Alonso
E. Maier
J. M. Blanc
1946 L. Castella
L. Carles
J. Bartroli
1947 M. Szawoszt
L. Carles
J. Bartroli
1948 M. Szawoszt
L. Castella
J. Bartroli

SWEDEN

1925 S. Malmstrom
M. Wallenberg
C. E. von Braun
1926 M. Wallenberg
S. Malmstrom
O. Garell
1927 S. Malmstrom
O. Garell
H. Müller
1928 S. Malmstrom
O. Garell
Wennergren
1929 S. Malmstrom
H. Müller
C. Ostberg
1930 H. Ramberg
J. Soederstrom
1934 C. Ostberg
H. Ramberg
1935 C. Ostberg
K. Schröder
1936 C. Ostberg
K. Schröder
1937 K. Schröder
S. Karlberg
C. Ostberg
S. Märtensson
1938 K. Schröder
N. Rohlsson
1939 K. Schröder
M. Hultman
1939 N. Rohlsson
1946 L. Bergelin
T. Johansson
1947 L. Bergelin
T. Johansson
1948 L. Bergelin
T. Johansson
B. Fornstedt

SWITZERLAND

1923 C. F. Aeschliman
C. Martin
G. A. Sautter
M. Ferrier
1924 C. F. Aeschliman
C. Martin
G. A. Sautter
1925 C. F. Aeschliman
C. Martin
1926 C. F. Aeschliman
J. Wuarin
1927 C. F. Aeschliman
J. Wuarin
M. Ferrier
1928 C. F. Aeschliman
J. Wuarin
M. Ferrier
1929 C. F. Aeschliman
J. Wuarin
1930 C. F. Aeschliman
H. Chiesa
J. Wuarin
1931 C. F. Aeschliman
H. C. Fisher
1932 C. F. Aeschliman
H. C. Fisher
1933 H. C. Fisher
M. Ellmer
W. Steiner
1934 H. C. Fisher
M. Ellmer
C. F. Aeschliman
W. Steiner
1936 H. C. Fisher
M. Ellmer
W. Steiner
B. Maneff
1937 M. Ellmer
H. C. Fisher
B. Maneff
W. Steiner
1938 H. C. Fisher
B. Maneff
1939 H. C. Fisher
B. Maneff
1946 J. Spitzer
H. Huonder
R. Buser
1947 J. Spitzer
H. Huonder
H. Pfaff
1948 H. Huonder
M. Albrecht

TURKEY

1948 Gurel
Kizil
Eihat
Belig

URUGUAY

1931 J. C. da Silva
C. E. Gainza
E. Stanham
E. Hernandez
1933 E. Hernandez
E. Stanham
J. C. da Silva
J. Galceran
1935 M. Harreguy
P. de Leon
M. Cat
E. Stanham

U.S.A.

1900 M. D. Whitman
D. F. Davis
H. Ward
1902 M. D. Whitman
W. A. Larned
D. F. Davis
H. Ward
1903 W. A. Larned
R. D. Wrenn
G. L. Wrenn
1905 H. Ward
W. J. Clothier
B. C. Wright
W. A. Larned
1906 H. Ward
R. D. Little
1907 B. C. Wright
K. Behr
1908 W. A. Larned
B. C. Wright
F. B. Alexander
H. H. Hackett
1909 W. A. Larned
W. J. Clothier
H. H. Hackett
R. D. Little
M. E. McLoughlin
M. H. Long
1911 W. A. Larned
M. E. McLoughlin
R. D. Little
T. C. Bundy
B. C. Wright
1913 M. E. McLoughlin
R. N. Williams
W. F. Johnson
H. H. Hackett
1914 M. E. McLoughlin
R. N. Williams
T. C. Bundy
1920 W. T. Tilden
W. M. Johnston
1921 W. T. Tilden
W. M. Johnston
R. N. Williams
W. M. Washburn
1922 W. T. Tilden
W. M. Johnston
V. Richards
1923 W. T. Tilden
W. M. Johnston
R. N. Williams
1924 W. T. Tilden
W. M. Johnston
V. Richards
1925 W. T. Tilden
W. M. Johnston
V. Richards
R. N. Williams
1926 W. T. Tilden
W. M. Johnston
V. Richards
R. N. Williams
1927 W. T. Tilden
W. M. Johnston
F. T. Hunter
1928 W. T. Tilden
J. F. Hennessey
A. Jones
G. M. Lott
W. F. Coen
F. T. Hunter
1929 J. van Ryn

1929 J. F. Hennessey
W. L. Allison
G. M. Lott
W. T. Tilden
F. T. Hunter
1930 J. van Ryn
G. M. Lott
J. H. Doeg
W. L. Allison
W. T. Tilden
1931 W. L. Allison
F. X. Shields
S. B. Wood
C. S. Sutter
J. van Ryn
G. M. Lott
1932 H. E. Vines
W. L. Allison
J. van Ryn
F. X. Shields
1933 W. L. Allison
C. S. Sutter
G. M. Lott
J. van Ryn
H. E. Vines
1934 L. R. Stoeffen
F. X. Shields
G. M. Lott
J. van Ryn
S. B. Wood
1935 B. M. Grant
J. D. Budge
C. G. Mako
W. L. Allison
J. van Ryn
1936 J. D. Budge
B. M. Grant
1936 W. L. Allison
J. van Ryn
C. G. Mako
1937 J. D. Budge
C. G. Mako
F. A. Parker
B. M. Grant
1938 J. D. Budge
C. G. Mako
R. L. Riggs
1939 R. L. Riggs
F. A. Parker
J. A. Kramer
J. Hunt
1946 F. A. Parker
W. F. Talbert
G. Mulloy
F. R. Schroeder
J. A. Kramer
1947 F. R. Schroeder
J. A. Kramer
1948 F. A. Parker
F. R. Schroeder
W. F. Talbert
G. Mulloy

YUGOSLAVIA

1927 G. Dungyersky
D. Balas
1928 A. Popovic
F. Schaffers
1929 K. Friedrich
Sefer
1930 K. Friedrich
F. Schaffers
I. Radovic
1931 F. Kukuljevic
F. Schaffers
1932 F. Kukuljevic
F. Schaffers
1933 F. Puncec
J. Pallada
F. Kukuljevic
1934 F. Kukuljevic
F. Puncec
1935 F. Puncec
J. Pallada
F. Schaffers
F. Kukuljevic
1936 F. Puncec
J. Pallada
F. Kukuljevic
D. Mitic
1937 F. Puncec
J. Pallada
F. Kukuljevic
D. Mitic
1938 F. Puncec
J. Pallada
F. Kukuljevic
D. Mitic
1939 F. Puncec
D. Mitic
F. Kukuljevic
1946 F. Puncec
D. Mitic
J. Pallada
1947 D. Mitic
J. Pallada
J. Solc
1948 D. Mitic
J. Pallada
Laslo

THE NATIONS WHO HAVE CHALLENGED 1900–48

U.S.A. . . were the original holders of the Davis Cup when it was put into competition in 1900. Since then U.S.A. have won 15 challenge rounds, 7 in succession (from 1920 to 1926 inclusive) and lost in 15 challenge rounds. Challenge-round appearances, 30.

France . . has won 6 successive challenge rounds (from 1927 to 1932), and lost in 3 challenge rounds. Challenge-round appearances, 9.

Australasia won 6 challenge rounds, 4 in succession, a break, and then 2 in succession, and lost in 3 challenge rounds. Challenge-round appearances, 9.

Australia . has won 1 challenge round and lost in 7. Challenge-round appearances, 8.

British Isles won 5 challenge rounds and lost in 5. Challenge-round appearances, 10.

Great Britain . . has won 4 challenge rounds and lost in 2. Challenge-round appearances, 6.

Japan . . has reached the challenge round once, and lost the tie.

Belgium . . has reached the challenge round once, and lost the tie.

There was no play in the following years: 1901 and 1910, in which there were no challengers; 1915, 1916, 1917, and 1918, because of the First World War; and 1940, 1941, 1942, 1943, 1944, and 1945, because of the Second World War.

WHEN THE NATIONS PLAYED, 1900–48

Argentina	1923, 1926, 1928, 1931, 1933, 1936, 1948.
Australasia	1905, 1906, 1907, 1908, 1909, 1911, 1912, 1913, 1914, 1919, 1920, 1921, 1922.
Australia	1923, 1924, 1925, 1928, 1930, 1932, 1933, 1934, 1935, 1936, 1937, 1938, 1939, 1946, 1947, 1948.
Austria	1905, 1924, 1925, 1927, 1928, 1929, 1930, 1931, 1932, 1933, 1934, 1936, 1937, 1948.
Belgium	1904, 1913, 1914, 1919, 1921, 1922, 1923, 1924, 1925, 1926, 1927, 1928, 1929, 1930, 1931, 1932, 1933, 1934, 1935, 1936, 1937, 1938, 1939, 1946, 1947, 1948.
Brazil	1935, 1948.
British Isles	1900, 1902, 1903, 1904, 1905, 1906, 1907, 1908, 1909, 1911, 1912, 1913, 1914, 1919, 1920, 1921, 1922.
Canada	1913, 1914, 1923, 1924, 1925, 1926, 1927, 1928, 1929, 1930, 1931, 1932, 1933, 1934, 1938, 1939, 1946, 1947, 1948.
Chile	1928, 1929, 1931, 1933.
China	1924, 1928, 1935, 1936, 1937, 1939, 1946.
Cuba	1924, 1925, 1927, 1928, 1929, 1932, 1933, 1939, 1948.
Czecho-slovakia	1921, 1922, 1923, 1924, 1925, 1926, 1927, 1928, 1929, 1930, 1931, 1932, 1933, 1934, 1935, 1936, 1937, 1938, 1946, 1947, 1948.
Denmark	1921, 1922, 1923, 1924, 1925, 1926, 1927, 1928, 1929, 1930, 1931, 1932, 1933, 1934, 1935, 1936, 1938, 1939, 1946, 1948.
Egypt	1929, 1930, 1931, 1932, 1933, 1946, 1947, 1948.
Estonia	1935.
Finland	1928, 1929, 1930, 1931, 1932, 1933.
France	1904, 1905, 1912, 1913, 1914, 1919, 1920, 1921, 1922, 1923, 1924, 1925, 1926, 1927, 1928, 1929, 1930, 1931, 1932, 1933, 1934, 1935, 1936, 1937, 1938, 1939, 1946, 1947, 1948.
Germany	1913, 1914, 1927, 1928, 1929, 1930, 1931, 1932, 1933, 1934, 1935, 1936, 1937, 1938, 1939.
Great Britain	1923, 1924, 1925, 1926, 1927, 1928, 1929, 1930, 1931, 1932, 1933, 1934, 1935, 1936, 1937, 1938, 1939, 1946, 1947, 1948.
Greece	1927, 1928, 1929, 1930, 1931, 1932, 1933, 1934, 1935, 1936, 1937, 1938, 1947.
Hawaii	1923.
Hungary	1924, 1925, 1926, 1927, 1928, 1929, 1930, 1931, 1932, 1933, 1934, 1935, 1936, 1937, 1938, 1939, 1948.
India	1921, 1922, 1923, 1924, 1925, 1926, 1927, 1928, 1930, 1932, 1934, 1938, 1939, 1947, 1948.
Ireland	1923, 1924, 1925, 1926, 1927, 1928, 1929, 1930, 1931, 1932, 1933, 1934, 1935, 1936, 1937, 1938, 1939, 1946, 1947, 1948.
Italy	1922, 1923, 1924, 1925, 1926, 1927, 1928, 1929, 1930, 1931, 1932, 1933, 1934, 1935, 1937, 1938, 1939, 1948.
Japan	1921, 1923, 1924, 1925, 1926, 1927, 1928, 1929, 1930, 1931, 1932, 1933, 1934, 1935, 1937, 1938.
Luxembourg	1947, 1948.
Mexico	1924, 1925, 1926, 1927, 1928, 1929, 1930, 1931, 1932, 1933, 1934, 1935, 1936, 1937, 1938, 1939, 1946, 1948.
Monaco	1931, 1932, 1933, 1934, 1935, 1936, 1937, 1938, 1939, 1946, 1947.
Netherlands	1920, 1923, 1924, 1925, 1926, 1927, 1928, 1929, 1930, 1931, 1932, 1933, 1934, 1935, 1936, 1937, 1938, 1939, 1946, 1947, 1948.

New Zealand	1924, 1928, 1934, 1935, 1937, 1939, 1947.
Norway . .	1928, 1929, 1930, 1931, 1932, 1933, 1934, 1935, 1936, 1937, 1938, 1939, 1947, 1948.
Pakistan . .	1948.
Paraguay .	1931.
Philippines .	1926, 1939, 1946.
Poland . .	1925, 1926, 1927, 1928, 1929, 1930, 1931, 1932, 1933, 1934, 1935, 1936, 1937, 1938, 1939, 1947.
Portugal . .	1925, 1926, 1927, 1928, 1948.
Rumania .	1922, 1925, 1926, 1927, 1928, 1929, 1930, 1931, 1932, 1933, 1934, 1935, 1937, 1938, 1939, 1948.
South Africa	1913, 1919, 1920, 1924, 1926, 1927, 1929, 1931, 1933, 1935, 1937, 1947.
Spain . . .	1921, 1922, 1923, 1924, 1925, 1926, 1927, 1928, 1929, 1930, 1931, 1932, 1933, 1934, 1936, 1946, 1947, 1948.
Sweden . .	1925, 1926, 1927, 1928, 1929, 1930, 1934, 1935, 1936, 1937, 1938, 1939, 1946, 1947, 1948.
Switzerland .	1923, 1924, 1925, 1926, 1927, 1928, 1929, 1930, 1931, 1932, 1933, 1934, 1936, 1937, 1938, 1939, 1946, 1947, 1948.
Turkey . .	1948.
Uruguay .	1931, 1933, 1935.
U.S.A. . .	1900, 1902, 1903, 1905, 1906, 1907, 1908, 1909, 1911, 1913, 1914, 1920, 1921, 1922, 1923, 1924, 1925, 1926, 1927, 1928, 1929, 1930, 1931, 1932, 1933, 1934, 1935, 1936, 1937, 1938, 1939, 1946, 1947, 1948.
Yugoslavia .	1927, 1928, 1929, 1930, 1931, 1932, 1933, 1934, 1935, 1936, 1937, 1938, 1939, 1946, 1947, 1948.